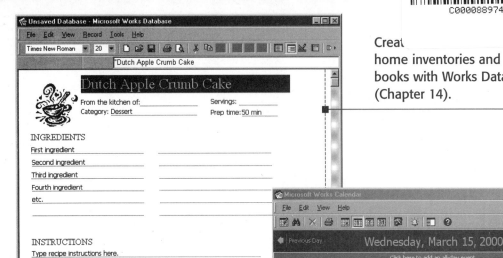

Creat[...]
home inventories and recipe
books with Works Database
(Chapter 14).

Organize your appointments,
events, and holidays with
Works Calendar (Chapter 15).

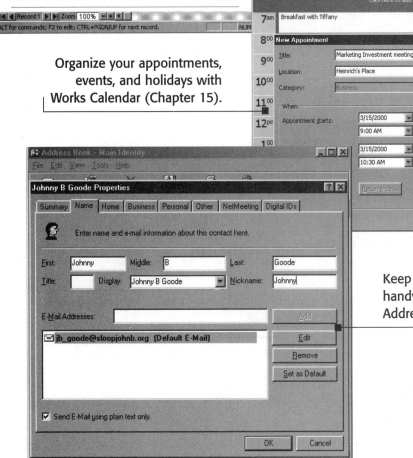

Keep all your contact information
handy and up to date with
Address Book (Chapter 15).

SYBEX

MASTERING™
MICROSOFT®
WORKS SUITE 2000

Guy Hart-Davis

SYBEX®

San Francisco • Paris • Düsseldorf • Soest • London

Associate Publisher: Cheryl Applewood

Contracts and Licensing Manager: Kristine O'Callaghan

Acquisitions Editor: Sherry Bonelli

Developmental Editor: Benjamin Tomkins

Editor: Liz Welch

Production Editor: Bronwyn Shone Erickson

Technical Editor: Maryann Brown

Book Designer: Patrick Dintino, Catalin Dulfu, Franz Baumhackl

Graphic Illustrator: Tony Jonick

Electronic Publishing Specialists: Bill Gibson, Cyndy Johnsen, Grey Magauran, and Adrian Woolhouse

Proofreaders: Carrie Bradley, Nelson Kim, Laurie O'Connell, and Suzanne Stein

Indexer: Matthew Spence

Cover Designer: Design Site

Cover Illustrator/Photographer: Sergie Loobkoff, Design Site

This book is dedicated to
my sister, Alice.

ACKNOWLEDGMENTS

I'd like to thank the following people for their help and support with this book:

- Rima Regas, for writing Chapters 16, 17, 18, and 19.
- Sherry Bonelli, acquisitions and developmental editor, for thinking of me for this project.
- Celeste Robinson, for help in drawing up the outline for the book.
- Cheryl Applewood, associate publisher, for publishing the book.
- Ben Tomkins, associate developmental editor, for developing the book.
- Liz Welch, Editor, for thorough, patient, and tactful editing.
- Maryann Brown, technical editor, for reviewing the manuscript for technical accuracy.
- Cyndy Johnsen, Grey Magauran, Bill Gibson, and Adrian Woolhouse, Electronic publishing specialists, for typesetting the book.
- Bronwyn Shone Erickson, production editor, for coordinating the production of the book.
- Carrie Bradley, Nelson Kim, Laurie O'Connell, and Suzanne Stein, proofreaders, for proofing the galleys.
- Matthew Spence, indexer, for creating the index for the book.

CONTENTS AT A GLANCE

TABLE OF CONTENTS

6   Using Styles and Advanced Formatting   109

7   Using Graphical Elements and Text Boxes   133

INTRODUCTION

Microsoft Works Suite 2000 claims to be "everything you need for your home PC"—and although there's plenty of marketing hype in that statement, there's also a lot of truth.

Works Suite 2000 is a massive suite of programs with wide-ranging capabilities:

- Microsoft Word 2000 is the world's leading word processor. With it, you can create anything from a one-page memo, to a fully typeset work, to a Web site.

- The Works Word Processor is a modest word processor that you can use for creating modest documents.

- Works Spreadsheet is a straightforward spreadsheet program.

- Works Database is an easy-to-use database that you can use to store information for home and home-business purposes.

- Works Calendar is an effective calendaring program with which you can organize your home and work schedules.

- The Address Book provides easy management of your personal and professional contacts, and integrates with the Calendar and Outlook Express.

- Encarta Encyclopedia is a comprehensive online encyclopedia with information on and pictures of most things under the sun.

- Money is a powerful tool for managing your finances.

- Home Publishing is a suite of, uh, home-publishing tools that you can use to design items such as flyers, brochures, announcements, and graphical Web sites.

- Picture It! Express is a graphics-manipulation program that you can use for everything from creating a postcard to removing red-eye from a digital photograph.

- Expedia Streets & Trips is a sophisticated mapping and route-planning program that you can use for finding places and planning trips.

- Internet Explorer is one of the most powerful and sleek Web browsers available.

- Outlook Express is a capable e-mail and newsreader application.

If you've used any of the Microsoft Office 2000 applications (such as Word, Excel, Access, or Outlook) at work, you'll find the Works applications particularly easy to use: Works includes essentially the same version of Word 2000 as comes with Office 2000 (Works has a Word add-in, but the difference is minor); Works Spreadsheet has many similarities to Excel; Works Database is far simpler than Access, but you use many of the same techniques for it; and Outlook Express is closely related to Outlook.

But even if you're not familiar with the Microsoft Office 2000 applications, you should have no difficulty getting up to speed with the Works applications—especially with the help of this book.

What Will You Learn from This Book?

This book aims to teach you everything you need to know to use Works effectively for your home or home-business projects. Here's what you'll learn:

How to get started with Works You'll learn what Works can do, how to start Works and its applications, and how to navigate the Task Launcher and the applications.

How to use Word to create documents Create anything from grocery lists and recipes to mail-merge letters to clients or relatives you wish belonged to someone else.

How to use Works' spreadsheet and database capabilities Store and crunch the numbers you need. You'll learn to create spreadsheets to present and process information, and to create databases for items such as home inventories.

How to use Works' tools Learn to use tools such as the Calendar and Address Book, the Encarta Encyclopedia, the road atlas Expedia Streets & Trips, and Microsoft Money.

How to use Works' features that relate to the Web Surf the Web with Internet Explorer, send e-mail and read news with Outlook Express, and create Web pages of your own with Word and Home Publishing.

Conventions Used in the Book

This book uses a number of conventions to convey information succinctly:

- The ➤ arrow designates choosing a command from a menu. For example, "choose File ➤ Open" means that you should pull down the File menu and choose the Open command from it.

- The + sign indicates key combinations. For example, "press Ctrl+Shift+F9" means that you should hold down the Ctrl and Shift keys, then press the F9 key. Some of these key combinations are confusing (for example, "Ctrl++" means that you hold down Ctrl and press the + key—in other words, hold down Ctrl and Shift together and press the = key), so you may need to read them carefully.

- Likewise, "Shift+click" means that you should hold down the Shift key as you click with the mouse, and "Ctrl+click" means you should hold down the Ctrl key as you click. "Ctrl+Shift+click" means..., okay, I see you've got it already.

- ← , → , ↑ , and ↓ represent the arrow keys that should appear in some form on your keyboard. The important thing to note is that ← is not the Backspace key (which on many keyboards bears a similar arrow). The Backspace key is represented by "Backspace" or "the Backspace key."

- **Boldface** indicates items that you may want to type in letter for letter.

CHAPTER 1

The Works Suite Applications

I n this chapter, I'll introduce you briefly to the applications contained in Microsoft Works Suite 2000. I'll show you what each application looks like, and I'll give you some examples of what you can do with each application.

Works Suite Applications

As you'll see in this chapter, Works contains an impressive variety of apparently disparate applications that give you the means to complete many home or home-office tasks. But as you'll see in the next chapter, the Task Launcher interface that Works provides draws together the applications and gives you an easy way of launching the applications, using the many and varied templates that they come with, and accessing documents that you've created or worked on.

Word 2000

Microsoft Word 2000 is the world's most widely used word-processing application for Windows. With Word, you can create any kind of word-processing document, from a short brochure or menu, to a newsletter, to mail-merged letters.

Word comes with many templates for creating documents for the home and home office. Figure 1.1 shows Word with a document containing notes for a babysitter.

FIGURE 1.1
Word 2000 is a powerful word processor that you can use to create anything from a letter to a book.

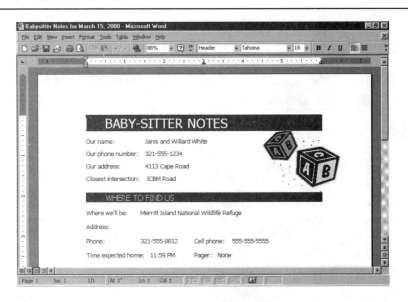

Chapters 3 through 10 discuss how to use Word.

Works Word Processor

The Works Word Processor is a bare-bones word-processing application that you can use to create simple documents. Because Works includes Word 2000, by default Works hides the Works Word Processor from you, though even the automated Typical installation of Works installs the Works Word Processor on your computer. But if you want a word processor that's less complex than Word, give the Works Word Processor a try.

Figure 1.2 shows the Works Word Processor with a document under way. As you can see, the Works Word Processor is closely related to Word, sharing Word's overall look, a number of toolbar buttons, and its ruler.

FIGURE 1.2
The Works Word Processor is a bare-bones word processor that you can use if you don't want all of Word 2000's bells and whistles.

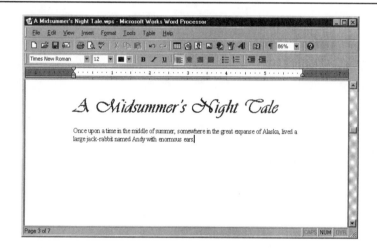

Chapter 11 discusses where to find the Works Word Processor and how to use it.

Works Spreadsheet

Works Spreadsheet is a spreadsheet application with which you can create anything from a financial worksheet to a workout log. If you've used Microsoft Excel, or another spreadsheet program such as Lotus 1-2-3 or Quattro Pro, you'll have little or no difficulty getting the hang of Works Spreadsheet.

Works Spreadsheet comes with a number of templates for creating home and home-office spreadsheets. Figure 1.3 shows Works Spreadsheet with an emergency-preparation spreadsheet under way.

FIGURE 1.3
Works Spreadsheet is an effective spreadsheet program that you can use to create spreadsheets from the abstruse to the mundane and practical.

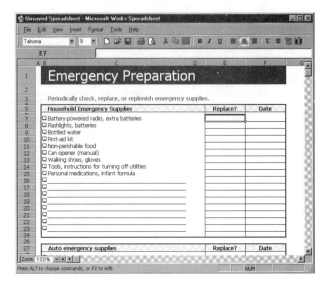

Chapters 12 and 13 discuss how to create spreadsheets with Works Spreadsheet.

Works Database

Works Database is an easy-to-use database program that lets you create simple databases such as home inventories. Compared to a "business" database program such as Microsoft Access, Corel Paradox, or Oracle, Works Database is very limited in its capabilities, but it's great for creating straightforward databases for home use.

Figure 1.4 shows Works Database with the beginning of a recipe database.

FIGURE 1.4
Works Database provides simple database capabilities.

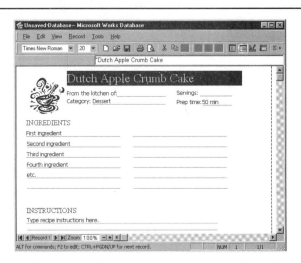

Chapter 14 discusses how to create and use databases with Works Database.

Works Calendar

Works Calendar is a full-fledged electronic calendar that you can use to track your appointments, events, and holidays. You can create repeating appointments and events, which are great for tracking recurring items such as biweekly meetings or birthdays and anniversaries. For any item, you can place a reminder to warn you when you should be paying attention.

Figure 1.5 shows an appointment being added to the calendar.

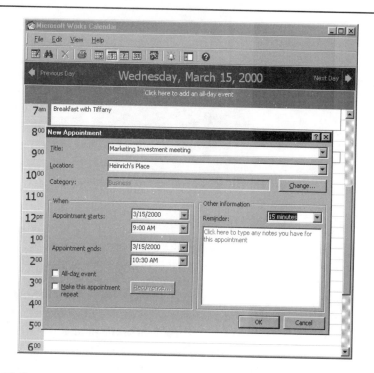

FIGURE 1.5
Works Calendar gives you an easy way to keep track of your schedule.

Chapter 15 discusses how to use Works Calendar to manage your schedule and appointments.

Address Book

The Address Book is an electronic address book in which you can keep the names, addresses, and so on of your family, friends, and personal or business contacts. The Address Book integrates with the Works Calendar to help you keep track of date-related contact information such as birthdays and anniversaries.

Figure 1.6 shows an example of adding a contact to the Address Book.

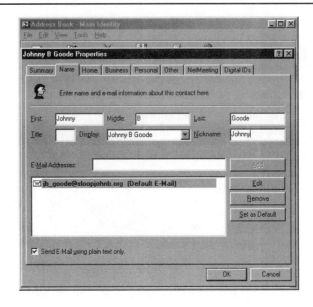

FIGURE 1.6
The Address Book provides storage for everything you need to know about your contacts.

Chapter 15 discusses how to use the Address Book to manage your contacts.

Encarta Encyclopedia

Encarta Encyclopedia is a multimedia encyclopedia with Web links to supplement the large amount of information it contains. You can access information in Encarta in a variety of ways, including searching for keywords, searching alphabetically, examining its yearbook directory by date or by category, and browsing with its Explorer. Once you've found information you're interested in, you can create a Favorite (a bookmark) so that you can access it with a click of the mouse.

Figure 1.7 shows part of Encarta's entry on the Hanging Gardens of Babylon.

Chapter 16 discusses how to use Encarta.

FIGURE 1.7

Encarta is a full-featured multimedia encyclopedia.

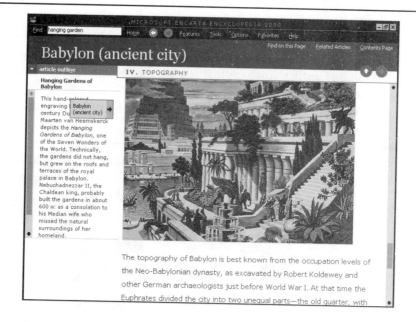

Money

Money is a personal-finance application that offers a full set of features for managing your money. With Money, you can do anything from tracking your expenditures and balancing your assorted accounts (checking, savings, credit cards) to planning your taxes and your investments. Money even includes features for paying your bills online, which can save you time, effort, and stamps.

Figure 1.8 shows Money preparing to do battle with some fictitious finances. Chapter 18 shows you how to use Money to work on your fiscal health.

FIGURE 1.8

Money provides sophisticated tools for helping you manage your money (or lack of it).

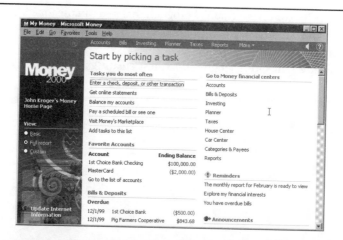

Home Publishing

Home Publishing is a design application with which you can create publications, from a flyer or lost-cat poster, to a report, to a Web project. For these publications, and for others, Home Publishing provides a wide variety of templates and a large number of designs, together with tools that you can use to customize the resulting publications so that they meet your needs.

Figure 1.9 shows the beginning of a Web project announcing a new arrival to a family.

Chapter 19 teaches you how to use Home Publishing.

Picture It! Express

Picture It! Express is a graphics program that you can use for editing pictures (for example, cropping out parts you don't want or adjusting their color balance) and creating graphical items (such as cards or collages).

Figure 1.10 shows Picture It! Express creating a one-month calendar.

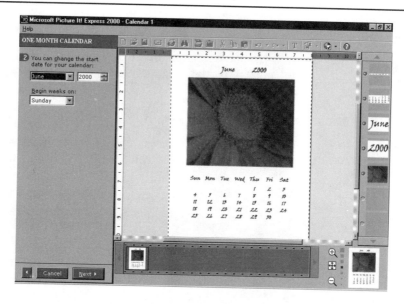

FIGURE 1.10
Picture It! Express is a graphics program with wide-ranging capabilities.

Chapter 20 gets you started working with Picture It! Express.

Expedia Streets & Trips

Expedia Streets & Trips is a street-map and trip-planning program. With Expedia Streets & Trips, you can do everything from locating a place or an address, to finding all known Thai restaurants within the general vicinity of Albuquerque, to getting driving directions from one point to another. Expedia Streets & Trips even downloads new construction data from the Web to keep up to date its knowledge of what's threatening your tires, your temper, and your timeliness.

Figure 1.11 shows Expedia Streets & Trips zoning in the Jack London Village area in scenic downtown Oakland, California.

Chapter 17 discusses how to make the most of Expedia Streets & Trips.

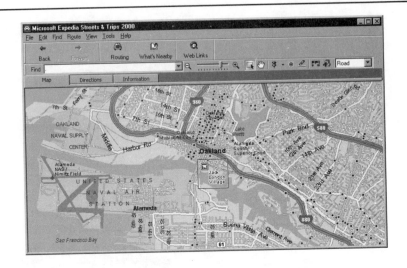

Internet Explorer

Internet Explorer is a capable Web browser that you can use to surf the Internet. Internet Explorer provides a full suite of browsing features, including the ability to create Favorites to bookmark sites you want to be able to access easily, and the ability to schedule the download of pages that you want to be able to browse when your computer is offline.

Figure 1.12 shows Internet Explorer in action at the MSN (Microsoft Network) Web site.

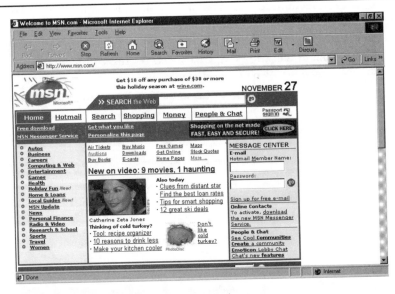

Chapter 21 discusses how to use Internet Explorer.

Outlook Express

Outlook Express is an e-mail and newsreader application that comes as part of Internet Explorer 5. With Outlook Express, you can create, read, and send e-mail, and read and participate in online newsgroups.

Figure 1.13 shows the Outlook Express Inbox with a message displayed.

FIGURE 1.13
Outlook Express is a capable e-mail and newsreader application. This figure shows the Outlook Express Inbox with a message displayed.

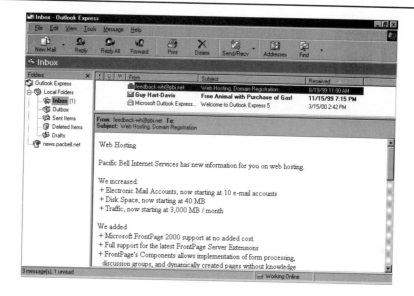

Chapter 22 discusses how to create, send, and receive e-mail with Outlook Express. Chapter 23 shows you how to read news with Outlook Express.

CHAPTER **2**

Using the Task Launcher

n this chapter, I'll show you how to get started with Works. You'll learn how to start Works; how to navigate the Task Launcher, Works' central application; how to find files in Works; and how to get Help in Works.

I'll assume that Works is already installed on your computer—that it either came preinstalled on your computer, or that you've installed it yourself. If you don't yet have Works installed, or if you need to install additional components, turn to the Appendix for instructions.

Starting Works

Microsoft
Works

Start Works by double-clicking the Microsoft Works icon on your desktop or by choosing Start ➤ Programs ➤ Microsoft Works. You'll see the Microsoft Works Task Launcher, as shown in Figure 2.1.

FIGURE 2.1

When you start Works, it displays the Task Launcher to give you quick access to its features.

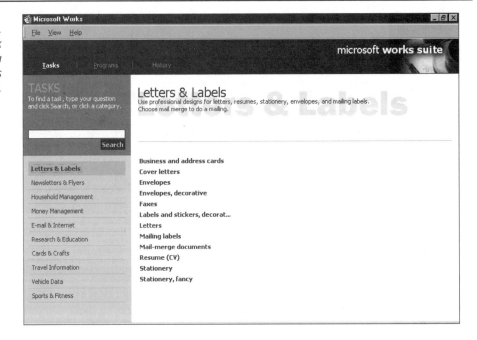

NOTE The first time you start Works, it will display the Microsoft Product Registration dialog box. If you want to register, click the Online Registration button and follow the steps in the Registration Wizard. Otherwise, click the OK button to continue launching Works.

 TIP The quickest way to get Works started when you need it is to add an icon for it to your Quick Launch toolbar, the toolbar that Windows 98 displays by default on the Taskbar. (If you don't have the Quick Launch toolbar displayed, right-click in open space on the Taskbar and choose Toolbars ➤ Quick Launch to display it.) To move the Works icon from the Desktop (where the Works installation places it by default) to the Quick Launch bar, right-click it and drag it to the Quick Launch bar, then choose Move Here from the context menu that Windows displays.

Using the Task Launcher

The Task Launcher gives you quick access to all areas of Works:

- The Tasks page provides access to Works' various capabilities by task. You can browse the tasks by category or search for a particular task by using keywords.

- The Programs page provides access to the Works applications. For example, if you want to launch Works Spreadsheet without using one of the wizards that Works provides, you can launch it from here.

- The History page provides access to documents you've recently created or worked on with Word, Works Spreadsheet, Works Database, Home Publishing, and Picture It! Express.

As you can see in Figure 2.1, the Task Launcher has three pages, each identified by a tab in the upper-left corner: Tasks, Programs, and History. To change from one page of the Task Launcher to another, use any of these three techniques:

- Click the tab for the page you want to display. For example, to display the History page, click the History tab.

- From the menu bar, choose View ➤ Tasks, View ➤ Programs, or View ➤ History.

- Press Ctrl+Tab to move forward through the pages (Tasks, then Programs, then History, then Tasks again), or Ctrl+Shift+Tab to move backward through the pages (Tasks, then History, then Programs, then Tasks again).

Using the Tasks Page

The Tasks page (see Figure 2.2) provides access to Works' capabilities by grouped lists of tasks.

FIGURE 2.2

Use the Tasks page of the Task Launcher to access any of the tasks for which Works provides a solution.

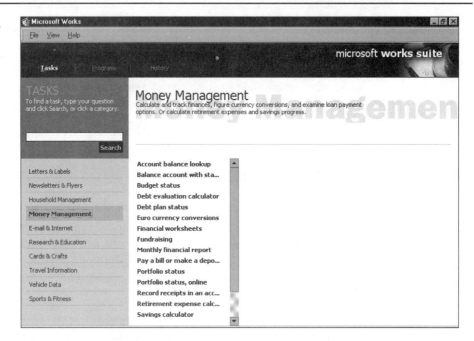

To start performing a task, follow these steps:

1. If the Tasks page of the Task Launcher isn't already displayed, click the Tasks tab to display it.

2. Select the category of task in the left-hand column of the page. The Task Launcher will display the list of tasks in the category. Figure 2.3 shows the Household Management category.

3. In the list of tasks, select the task you want to perform. Works will display a small illustration of the end result, an icon indicating the application needed for the task, and a Start button. Figure 2.4 shows the Grocery Lists task, which uses Word (as you can see from the icon).

FIGURE 2.3
Choose the category of task you want to perform; this screen shows the Household Management category.

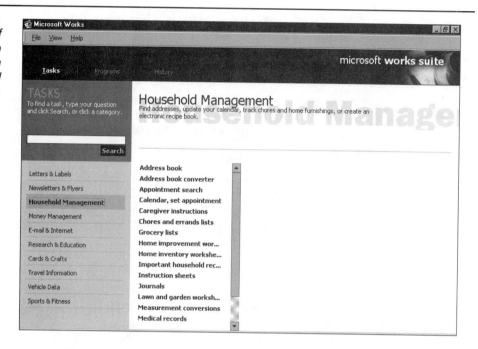

FIGURE 2.4
Select the task you want to perform.

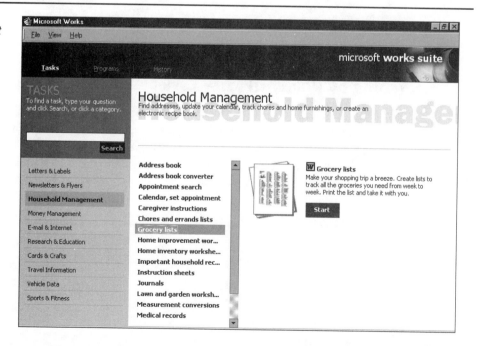

4. Click the Start button to start performing the task. Works will start the application (if it's not currently running) or will switch to it (if it is running), and will start any wizard involved. Figure 2.5 shows the Works Grocery List Wizard, which creates the grocery list for you in Word.

FIGURE 2.5
*Works will start
(or activate) the
application needed for
the task and will fire up
any wizard involved.*

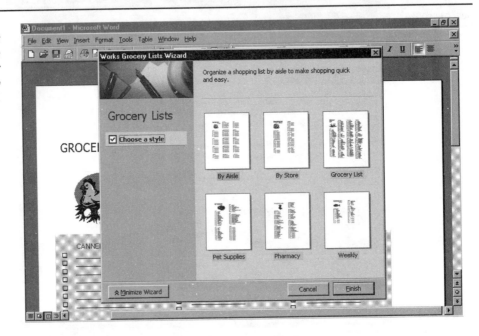

5. Follow the steps in the wizard to perform the task.

Searching by Keyword for a Task

If you can't immediately find the task you're looking for, you can search for it by using one or more keywords. Click in the Search text box and enter the word or words you're looking for, then click the Search button. Works will display a list of the results it finds; if you see a task that meets your need, click it to display that task. Figure 2.6 shows the result of searching for the word *resume*.

FIGURE 2.6
*To find a task quickly,
you can search by one
or more keywords; this
screen shows the result
of searching for the
word* resume.

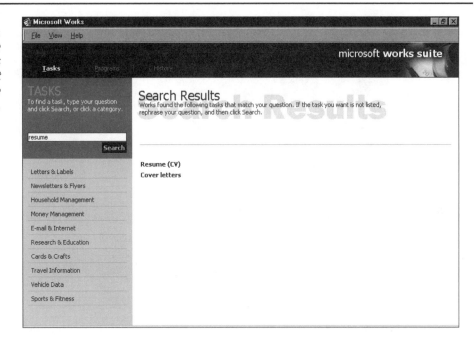

Using the Programs Page

The Programs page of the Task Launcher gives you quick access to the programs in Works and the tasks that each of them offers. Figure 2.7 shows the Programs page with Word selected.

From the Programs page, you can either launch the program by clicking the link above the list of tasks (for example, the Start A Blank Word Document link in Figure 2.7), or start one of the tasks by selecting it and then clicking the Start button that appears.

FIGURE 2.7
Use the Programs page of the Task Launcher to launch a particular program.

Using the History Page

The History page of the Task Launcher gives you quick access to the documents you've used most recently, listing documents created in Word, Works Spreadsheet, Works Database, Home Publishing, and Picture It! Express. Figure 2.8 shows the History page with a modest number of documents and tasks listed.

To open a document, click its name (or anywhere in its listing). Works will launch the appropriate application (if it's not currently running) or activate it (if it is running) and will open the document in it.

FIGURE 2.8
The History page of the Task Launcher gives you quick access to recently used documents.

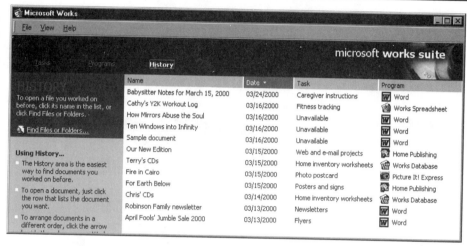

Sorting the Documents Listed on the History Page

To help find the document you need, you can sort the documents on the History page of the Task Launcher by name, date, task, or program by clicking the column headings. Click the column heading once to sort in ascending order (from A to Z, from low numbers to high); click the column heading again to sort in descending order. Figure 2.9 demonstrates sorting the documents alphabetically by clicking the Name column.

FIGURE 2.9
You can sort the documents on the History page of the Task Launcher by clicking one of the column headings.

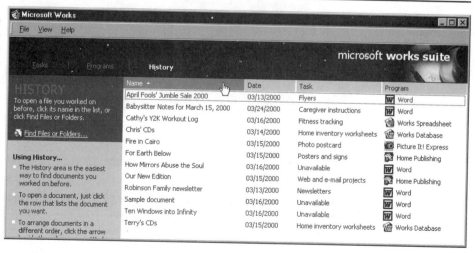

Turning Off History Tracking

If you prefer not to have Works track your history of work—for example, if having the list of recent files could be an embarrassment (for whatever reason) or a security threat—you can turn off the history tracking:

1. Choose View ➢ Options to display the Options dialog box (see Figure 2.10).

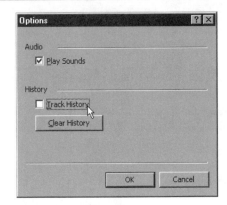

2. Clear the Track History check box.

3. To get rid of any history that Works has tracked so far, click the Clear History button. Works will display the Microsoft Works dialog box shown in Figure 2.11.

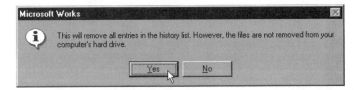

4. Click the Yes button to clear your history.

5. Click the OK button to close the Options dialog box.

 TIP You can delete a file's listing from the History page by right-clicking it and choosing Delete from the context menu. Removing the listing like this does not delete the file itself.

Finding Files and Folders

If you can't find the item easily on the History page, try using the Find feature instead by following these steps:

1. Click the Find Files Or Folders link to display the Find dialog box (shown in Figure 2.12 with some information already entered).

FIGURE 2.12
Use the Find dialog box to find files or folders.

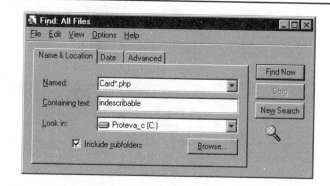

2. In the Named text box on the Name & Location page of the Find dialog box, enter the closest approximation of the name of the file you want to find. For example, enter ***.doc** if you're looking for Word documents with any name, or **Card*.php** for all paper projects in Home Publishing with names that begin with *Card*.

3. In the Containing Text text box, you can enter some text that appears in the document you're looking for. Choose text that's as unusual as possible rather than a common word or phrase. (If you don't remember any distinctive text in the document, skip this step—it's not essential.)

4. In the Look In drop-down list, choose the drive or location (for example, the My Documents folder or your Desktop) you want to search. To specify a folder on the drive, click the Browse button to display the Browse For Folder dialog box (see Figure 2.13), navigate to the folder you want, and click the OK button.

FIGURE 2.13
*Use the Browse For
Folder dialog box to
select the folder you
want to search.*

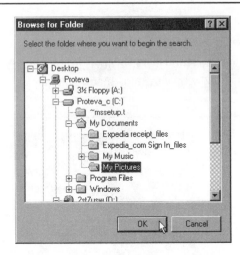

5. On the Date page of the Find dialog box (see Figure 2.14), you can specify a timeframe and an action for the search to narrow down the possibilities. By default, the All Files option button is selected, but you can use the Between option button to find files between two dates you specify, the During The Previous *NN* Month(s) option button to find files affected within a given number of months, or the During The Previous *NN* Day(s) option button to find files affected within a given number of days. From the drop-down list next to the Find All Files option button, select the action you want: Modified, Created, or Last Accessed.

FIGURE 2.14
*You can limit the search
to a specified time
period by using the
options on the Date
page of the Find
dialog box.*

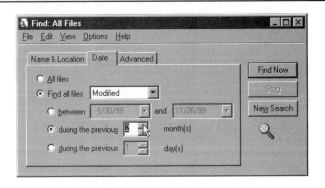

6. On the Advanced page of the Find dialog box (see Figure 2.15), choose advanced options if necessary:

- From the Of Type drop-down list, choose the type of file you're looking for, such as Microsoft Works Database.

- From the Size Is drop-down list, choose At Least or At Most as appropriate, then specify the minimum or maximum file size in kilobytes in the KB text box. For example, you could specify At Least 2048KB to find only files larger than 2MB. Size can be a useful differentiator when you have many files with similar names (for example, different versions of documents with the same name but different amounts of content), but you may not need to use it for run-of-the-mill searches.

FIGURE 2.15
You can specify advanced options on the Advanced page of the Find dialog box.

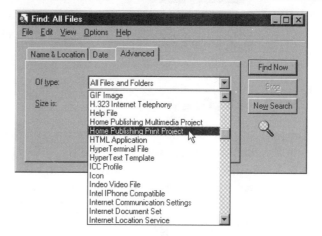

7. Click the Find Now button to find the files that match the criteria you've specified. Windows will display the found files in the Find window, as shown in Figure 2.16.

To clear the results of your current search and start a new search, click the New Search button and click the OK button in the warning message box that Find displays.

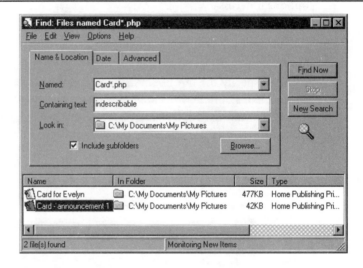

FIGURE 2.16
Windows displays the
results of your search.
You can open a file by
double-clicking it in the
Find window.

Getting Help in Works

In this section, I'll show you the several types of Help that Works provides to assist you in accomplishing your tasks. You can display Help directly in the Help pane in the Task Launcher, in Works Spreadsheet, in Works Database, and in Works Calendar. Other applications, such as Word, Internet Explorer, Address Book, and Picture It! Express, have separate Help applications that use the conventional Windows Help system.

To get Help, start by displaying the Help pane if it's not already displayed. The Task Launcher, Works Spreadsheet, Works Database, and Works Calendar display Help by default at first until you tell them not to by dismissing the Help pane. To display the Help pane, choose Help ➤ Microsoft Works Help or press the F1 key. Works will display the Help pane showing the Answer Wizard, as shown in Figure 2.17. To see more of the Help pane at the expense of the rest of the Task Launcher, you can drag the left border of the Help pane to the left.

FIGURE 2.17
To get Help, start by choosing Help ➤ Microsoft Works Help (or pressing the F1 key) to display the Help pane showing the Answer Wizard.

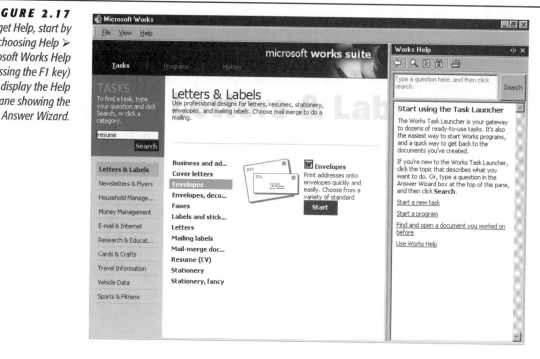

Figure 2.18 shows the five buttons on the Works Help toolbar.

FIGURE 2.18
The Works Help toolbar contains five buttons.

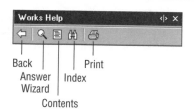

To use the Answer Wizard, enter a question, or the keywords that the question would contain, in the text box and press Enter or click the Search button. The Answer Wizard will display its suggestions for the question (see Figure 2.19). To view a topic, click the item for it.

FIGURE 2.19
Type a question in the Answer Wizard and press Enter or click the Search button to get a list of relevant Help topics.

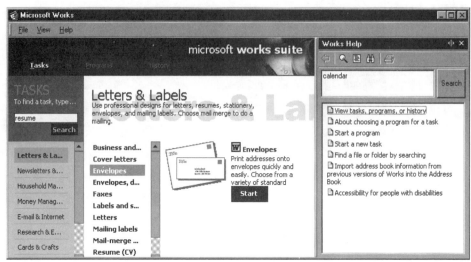

To display the Help Table of Contents, click the Contents button on the Works Help toolbar. Help initially displays the Table of Contents as a short list of topics, but you can expand this list (as shown in Figure 2.20) until you find the topic you want. Then double-click that topic to access it.

FIGURE 2.20
Use the Table of Contents in Help to access the topics you want to learn more about.

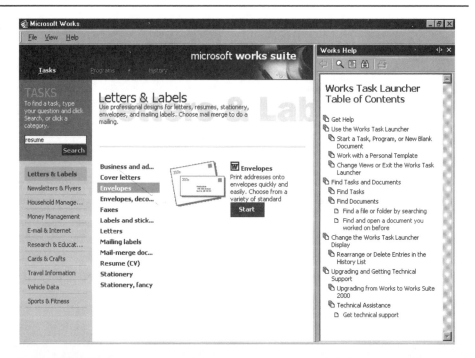

To display the Help Index, click the Index button on the Works toolbar. Then either start typing a word in the text box at the top of the Help pane to scroll down the index to entries beginning with those letters, or scroll the list box to the entry you're interested in, and select it. Works will display a list of topics in the Topics Found list box. Click the topic you want to access (see Figure 2.21).

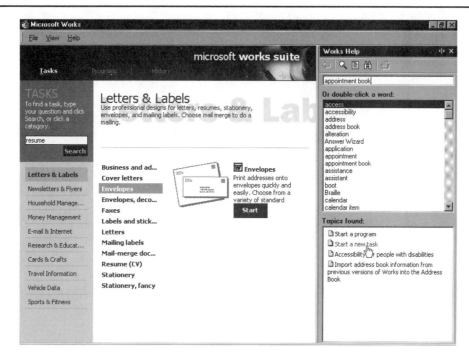

To print a Help topic, display it and click the Print button.
To close the Help pane, click its close button (the ∞ button in its upper-right corner).

Exiting the Task Launcher

To exit the Task Launcher, choose File ➢ Exit or press Alt+F4. Alternatively, right-click the Microsoft Works button in the Windows Taskbar and choose Close from the context menu.

CHAPTER **3**

Word 2000 Basics

In this chapter, you'll get started with Word. You'll start by setting up the screen so you're working comfortably and can see what you need to see. I'll discuss how to use the menus and the toolbars, and how to choose which toolbars to display on screen and how to change their shape and location. You'll start a basic document, so you have something to look at. Then I'll discuss the various views that Word provides for looking at your documents and when you may want to use each of these views. After that, I'll show you how you get Help when using Word. Finally, you'll exit Word.

Arguably the world's most popular word processor, Word is an integral part of Microsoft Office, Microsoft's suite of professional business applications. (Other Office applications include Excel, the spreadsheet; PowerPoint, the presentation software; and Access, the database.) As befits Office, Word is a heavy-duty word processor with a full set of features that enable you to create a wide variety of documents, from straightforward memos and manuscripts to mail-merge documents and professional publications.

Using Word to type a simple document such as a list can feel like taking a sledge-hammer to a walnut. If you need to create only simple documents and find Word too complex or too cumbersome, you may want to use the Works Word Processor instead. The Works Word Processor is included in the Typical installation of Works Suite, but it's hidden from view by default, perhaps to encourage you to use Word instead. Chapter 11 discusses how to find and use the Works Word Processor.

Starting Word

You can start Word in any of several ways:

- Choose Start ➤ Programs ➤ Microsoft Word to launch Word without involving the Works Task Launcher. (If you use Word frequently for much of your work, you may want to start Word this way.)

- On the Tasks page in the Task Launcher, select a task that creates a Word document, and then click the Start button.

- On the Programs page in the Task Launcher, select Word in the list of programs, and then click the Start A Blank Word Document link.

- On the Programs page in the Task Launcher, select Word in the list of programs, select a task, and then click the Start button.

- On the History page in the Task Launcher, click an entry for a Word document to start Word and open the document.

- Choose Start ➤ New Office Document to display the New Office Document dialog box (see Figure 3.1)

FIGURE 3.1
In the New Office
Document dialog box,
choose the type of
Word document you
want to create, and
then click the OK
button.

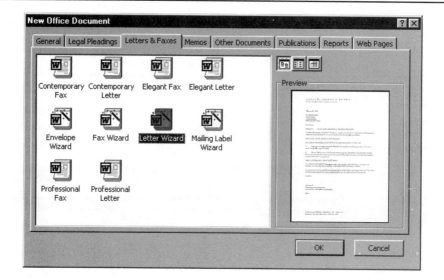

 TIP The quickest way to launch Word is usually to create a shortcut on the Quick Launch toolbar, because you can keep the Quick Launch toolbar available all the time you're working in Windows. To do so, choose Start ➤ Programs to display the Programs submenu. Then hold down the Ctrl key, click the Microsoft Word menu item, and drag it to the Quick Launch toolbar. Click the shortcut to launch Word.

 NOTE The first time you start Word after installing Works via the Typical installation procedure (discussed in the Appendix), Word will display the Microsoft Word 2000 User Information dialog box. Enter your username, your initials, and your organization (if appropriate). The program will suggest the username and organization to which your copy of Windows is assigned. Then enter the CD key (a 25-digit mixture of letters and numbers) in the CD Key text boxes at the bottom of the dialog box and click the OK button. (If you chose the Custom installation of Works, you will have had to supply this information during the installation, so you will not see this dialog box the first time you start Word.) After this, the Office 2000 Registration Wizard will offer to register your copy of Word; accept or decline as you see fit. And when Word starts, the Office Assistant will appear unbidden on your screen in its default character, an animated paperclip.

Setting Up Your Screen

Before you start working with documents, take a look at how Word appears on the screen (see Figure 3.2).

FIGURE 3.2
The Word window contains standard Windows elements and Word-specific items.

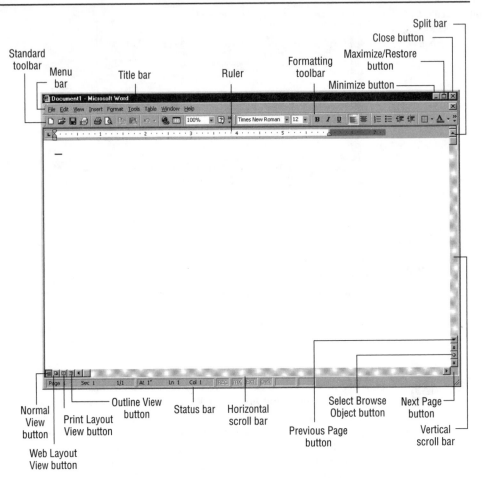

I'll examine most of these features in the rest of this chapter. The following list discusses the features that will be familiar if you've used other Windows applications and points to the discussion of the topics treated in more depth later in this chapter:

- The title bar shows the name of the document in the window, followed by *Microsoft Word*.

- The menu bar provides access to the commands on the menus.

- The toolbars provide access to assorted commands. You'll learn how to work with them a little later in this chapter.

- You use the Maximize/Restore, Minimize, and Close buttons to resize or close the Word window.

- Use the vertical scroll bar to move backward and forward in your document. You can click the up-arrow button and down-arrow button to scroll one line at a time. Alternatively, drag the scroll box (technically known as the *thumb*) to move quickly through the document. As you drag the scroll box, Word displays a ScreenTip showing the page number and the heading that you're scrolling by, as illustrated here.

- Use the horizontal scroll bar to move from side to side in your document. The horizontal scroll bar is useful in layout views when the page you're working on is too wide to fit on the screen at a readable magnification. As with the vertical scroll bar, you can either click the scroll buttons or drag the scroll box.

- The split bar lets you split the Word window into two so that you can see different parts of a document at the same time. I'll show you how to use this feature toward the end of this chapter.

- The status bar displays information about the position of the insertion point and about the document in the window. I'll discuss the status bar later in this chapter.

- The Next Page and Previous Page buttons display the next page and previous page of the document. The Select Browse Object button changes the behavior of the Next Page and Previous Page buttons from browsing by pages to browsing by another object. For example, instead of moving to the next page or previous page, you can move to the next table or previous table.

- The Normal View, Web Layout, Print Layout View, and Outline View buttons change the view. You'll learn about the three main views later in this chapter.

Using the Menus

To display a menu, click it with the mouse, or press the Alt key followed by the underlined letter on the menu (for example, press Alt and then F to display the File menu). To close a menu without choosing a command, click the menu's name again, or click in the document window, or press Alt again, or press Esc.

To choose an item from a menu, click it with the mouse, or press the key for the underlined letter, or use ↓ and ↑ to move the highlight to it and press Enter.

If a menu item is shown in gray embossed letters rather than black letters, it is currently unavailable. For example, the Footnotes item on the View menu will be unavailable until you create a footnote in the document.

Word's menus are *two-stage* and *adaptive*: They appear in two stages, and they change as you use them. Figure 3.3 illustrates a sample menu, the Tools menu, as it evolves and adapts. At first, when you display a menu, Word shows only the most-used commands on the menu to keep the menu as brief as possible, as in the illustration on the left of the figure. If you don't choose one of the items within a second or so, Word displays the rest of the menu, as in the middle illustration. This is disconcerting at first, but you may get used to it quickly. If you don't get used to it or if you don't like the effect, you can make Word display the menus normally, as you'll see in a moment.

FIGURE 3.3

Word's menus are two-stage and adaptive, as you can see in the three stages of Tools menu evolution shown here.

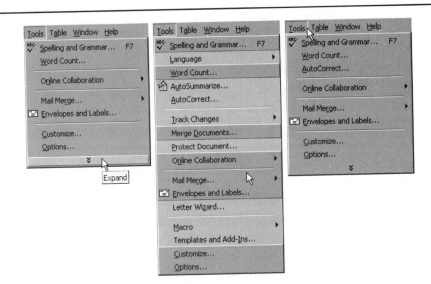

The last item on the short version of the menu has two arrows pointing downward, indicating that further menu items are available. You can either click this item to display the rest of the menu or wait for Word to display it, as described in the previous paragraph.

As you can see in the middle illustration in the figure, the most-used items on the menu are shown in the regular medium gray of most Windows menus, while the less-used items appear in a lighter gray. But the first time you use one of the lighter-gray items, Word promotes it to the regular gray and includes it in the short version of the menu from then on (as you can see in the right-hand illustration, in which the Auto-Correct item has joined the regulars on the menu). Word also promotes the menu items you use most frequently toward the top of the menu, changing the order of the menu items somewhat. If you're accustomed to regular menu behavior, this can make it harder for you to find the items you need on the menus.

Getting Full Menus and Non-Adaptive Menus

If you don't like the new two-stage, adaptive menus, you can make them behave like "normal" menus in previous versions of Word (and in most other Windows applications, including the other Works applications):

1. Choose Tools ➤ Customize to display the Customize dialog box.

2. Click the Options tab to display the Options page (if it isn't already displayed).

3. In the Personalized Menus And Toolbars area, clear the Menus Show Recently Used Commands First check box. This will gray out the Show Full Menus After A Short Delay check box, and will make Word show the full menu at once.

4. Click the Close button to close the Customize dialog box.

Using Toolbars

Word comes with a variety of toolbars containing buttons that give you quick access to actions—everything from italicizing your text to running a mail merge. To see what a button represents, you can display a ScreenTip by moving the mouse pointer over a button and holding it there for a moment.

By default, Word displays the Standard and Formatting toolbars, arranging them to share the screen with their most commonly used buttons visible (depending on the screen resolution and window size you are using). But you can easily choose to display other toolbars (such as the Tables And Borders toolbar or the Drawing toolbar) if you need them. Alternatively, you can hide the Standard and Formatting toolbars to give yourself more screen real estate.

Like many Windows applications, Word can display its toolbars and the menu bar as either *docked* panels attached to one side of the screen or as free-floating (or *undocked*) panels that you can drag anywhere on your screen. At the right-hand end of the visible part of any docked toolbar (or the lower end of a vertically docked toolbar), Word displays the More Buttons button—a minimal button with a single downward-pointing arrow. When part of a toolbar is hidden by another toolbar, Word displays >> on the

More Buttons button. Click the More Buttons button to display a panel containing the remaining buttons, as shown in Figure 3.4. In the figure, the mouse pointer is over the More Buttons button.

FIGURE 3.4

Click the More Buttons button at the right-hand end of a toolbar to display a panel containing the remaining buttons.

Like the menus, Word's toolbars are adaptive. When you use a button that was previously on a hidden part of a toolbar, Word will promote it to the displayed part of the toolbar. If two toolbars are sharing a row across the screen, part of the toolbar that the button was not on may be removed to make space for the button you used.

Displaying the Full Standard Toolbar and Formatting Toolbar

If you're used to using most of the buttons on the Standard toolbar and the Formatting toolbar in previous versions of Word (or in other applications), you may find it awkward to have them competing for space on the same line. Here's how to tell Word to display them separately:

1. Choose Tools ≻ Customize to display the Customize dialog box.

2. Click the Options tab to display the Options page (if it isn't already displayed).

3. Clear the Standard And Formatting Toolbars Share One Row check box.

4. Click the Close button to close the Customize dialog box.

One more thing you can do in the Customize dialog box is reset your toolbars and menus to their default settings. To do so, click the Reset My Usage Data button.

Displaying and Hiding Toolbars

To display and hide toolbars:

- With the mouse, right-click anywhere in the menu bar or in a displayed toolbar to display a list of toolbars. Check marks will appear next to those currently displayed. Click next to a displayed toolbar to hide it or next to a hidden toolbar to display it.

- With the keyboard (or the mouse), choose View ➤ Toolbars to display the list of toolbars. Again, check marks will appear next to those toolbars currently displayed. Use ↓ and ↑ (or move the mouse pointer) to move the highlight to the displayed toolbar you want to hide or the hidden toolbar you want to display, then press Enter (or click the highlighted item).

 TIP Unless you have a huge monitor or high screen resolution (or both), hide toolbars when you don't need immediate access to them, so that you have more of the screen available for your work.

Moving and Reshaping Toolbars

Word can display its toolbars and the menu bar either attached to one side of the screen or as free-floating. Docked toolbars can overlap each other, which means that you can arrange them to save space on screen. Figure 3.5 shows toolbars arranged somewhat improbably on screen, demonstrating the possibilities.

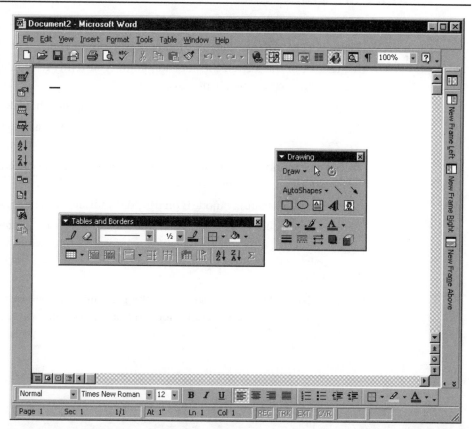

FIGURE 3.5
You can display your toolbars at any extremity of the Word screen, or you can place them plumb in the middle.

To move a toolbar or the menu bar from its current position, first click the move handle at its left end (or its top end, if it's positioned vertically) or in any space in the toolbar or menu bar not occupied by a button or menu item. Then drag the toolbar to where you want it—either to one of the edges, in which case it will snap into position, or to the middle of the screen.

To uncover more of a docked toolbar that is obscured by another docked toolbar, drag the move handle of the toolbar that is doing the obscuring.

 TIP You can dock a floating toolbar (or the floating menu bar) by double-clicking its title bar.

To reshape a floating toolbar or floating menu bar, move the mouse pointer over one of its borders until the pointer turns into a double-ended arrow, then click and drag to resize the toolbar. Because of the shape of their buttons or menu names, toolbars and the menu bar resize in jumps rather than smoothly like windows do.

Reading the Status Bar

The status bar (see Figure 3.6) provides the following information from left to right:

- The number of the page the insertion point is currently on.
- The number of the section the insertion point is currently in (you'll learn about sections and their use in Chapter 6).
- The current page number and the number of pages in the whole document.
- The vertical position of the insertion point from the top of the page (for example, *At 4.2"*).
- The column number—the number of characters between the current position of the insertion point and the left margin (for example, *Col 36*).
- Whether Macro Recording mode is on (the REC indicator will be darkened if it is).
- Whether change-tracking is on (the TRK indicator will be darkened if it is). Change-tracking, also known as *revision marking*, is useful when you have several people working on a document and you need to keep track of who did what when.
- Whether Extend Selection mode is on (the EXT indicator will be darkened if it is). I'll show you Extend Selection mode in the next chapter.

- Whether Overtype mode is on (the OVR indicator will be darkened if it is). You'll learn about Overtype mode in the next chapter as well.

- The language the current selection (or the text at the position of the insertion point) is formatted as—for example, *English (US)*.

- The state of spell-checking and grammar-checking in the document. While Word is checking the spelling and grammar as you work, you'll see a pen moving across the page on the icon. When Word has finished checking, you'll see a red cross on the right-hand page of the icon if there's a spelling or grammar problem, and a red check mark if Word considers all to be well.

FIGURE 3.6

The status bar provides information about the position of the insertion point, the document, and what Word is currently doing.

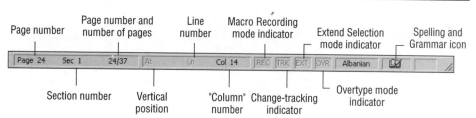

Displaying and Hiding the Status Bar and Scroll Bars

To adjust the amount of free space you have on screen, you can hide and redisplay the status bar and scroll bars as necessary. I find the status bar and vertical scroll bar more or less indispensable, but usually get rid of the horizontal scroll bar.

1. Choose Tools ➤ Options to display the Options dialog box.

2. Click the View tab to bring the View page (see Figure 3.7) to the front of the dialog box if it's not already displayed.

3. In the Show group box, clear the Status Bar, Horizontal Scroll Bar, and Vertical Scroll Bar check boxes to hide the status bar and scroll bars. Select these check boxes to display the status bar and scroll bars.

4. Click the OK button to close the Options dialog box.

TIP To maximize the amount of text displayed in the Word window in Normal view, Outline view, and Web Layout view, select the Wrap To Window check box in the Outline And Normal Options area of the View page of the Options dialog box.

FIGURE 3.7

*Use the View page of
the Options dialog box
to display and hide
the status bar and the
scroll bars.*

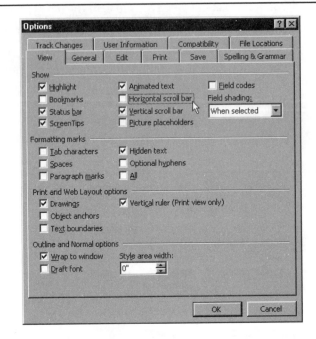

Displaying and Hiding the Rulers

To help you position your text optimally on the page, Word offers a horizontal ruler in Normal view and Web Layout view and both horizontal and vertical rulers in Print Layout view and Print Preview. The horizontal ruler displays margin stops and tab stops for the current paragraph or selected paragraphs. Chapter 5 covers how to set margins and tabs.

You can either display the ruler on your screen all the time or keep it hidden but available. To toggle the display of the ruler on and off, choose View ➤ Ruler. To pop up the horizontal ruler momentarily, move the mouse pointer to the thin, light-gray bar at the top of the current document window, as shown in the top part of Figure 3.8. The ruler will appear automatically so that you can view text positioning or work with tabs, as shown in the bottom part of Figure 3.8. The ruler will disappear when you move the mouse pointer away from it again.

FIGURE 3.8
When the ruler is hidden, you can pop it up by moving the mouse pointer to the thin, light-gray bar at the top of the document window (above), causing it to appear (below).

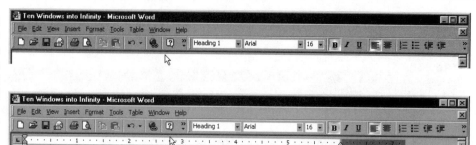

To pop up the vertical ruler in Print Layout view or Print Preview, move the mouse pointer to the thin light-gray bar at the left edge of the current document window. The vertical ruler will appear automatically and will disappear when you move the pointer away again.

 TIP   These pop-up rulers are controlled by the Provide Feedback With Animation check box on the General page of the Options dialog box. To prevent the rulers from popping up, select Tools ➢ Options to display the Options dialog box, click the General tab to display the General page, clear the Provide Feedback With Animation check box, and click OK.

Understanding and Arranging Windows

In this section, you'll learn how Word uses windows and how you work with them.

How Word Handles Windows

To work effectively in Word, you need to understand how Word handles windows when you have more than one document open. Word 2000 uses a different arrangement of windows than most other Windows applications, which keep all document windows within one main window, the application window. (Earlier versions of Word did this too.)

In Word 2000, each document appears in a separate document window, and each document window appears as a separate icon on the Taskbar, identified by the name of the document. For example, one document window might be identified as *September Report Memo*, another as *Letter to Mom*, and a third *Ode to the Bosnians*. This makes it easier to switch from one open document to another by using the Taskbar. However, not having an application window as such can make it confusing as to when you're closing a document and when you're closing Word itself. When you have only one document open, the Word menu bar grows a Close Window button at its right-hand end, as shown in Figure 3.9. By clicking this Close Window button, you can close the document rather than Word. (As soon as you open another document, the Close Window button disappears.) Clicking the Close button on the title bar of the last open Word window closes Word.

FIGURE 3.9

When only one document is open, Word displays a Close Window button at the right-hand end of the menu bar.

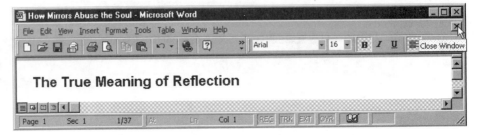

Switching from One Document Window to Another

If you have the Taskbar displayed, the easiest way to switch from one document window to another is to click the Taskbar icon for the window you want to activate. Alternatively, you can press Alt+Tab to *coolswitch* (switch quickly) through all the Word windows and other running applications. You can also use the Window menu in Word to move between document windows. The Window menu lists the first nine document windows you have open; you can activate any of these document windows by choosing its name from the menu. If you have more than nine documents open (under normal circumstances, you'll seldom need to), the Window menu will include a More Windows item that displays the Activate dialog box shown in Figure 3.10. Either double-click the listing for the window you want or select the listing and click the OK button.

FIGURE 3.10

When you have more than nine documents open, Word provides the Activate dialog box as a way of moving from one document to another.

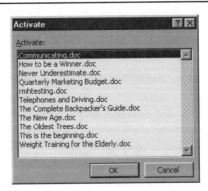

Arranging Windows

As with almost any Windows application, you can resize the Word document windows to any size that suits you by dragging the borders or corners of any window. This is the easiest way to get the windows you want to work with to a suitable size. (If a window is maximized, you need to restore it to a non-maximized state before you can resize it.) You can also arrange windows by choosing Window ➢ Arrange All. The Arrange All command *tiles* the windows on the Desktop, giving each as equal a share of space as possible. Unfortunately, Arrange All tiles two or three windows by dividing the screen horizontally rather than vertically, which typically makes them too small to do much work in. Figure 3.11 shows three windows tiled horizontally.

FIGURE 3.11
The Window ➢ Arrange All command tiles the windows horizontally.

You can also arrange Word document windows, together with any other windows of your choice, by using the Cascade Windows, Tile Windows Horizontally, and Tile Windows Vertically items on the context menu on the Windows Taskbar. (To display the context menu, right-click in an open space on the Taskbar.) These commands work on any windows that are not minimized. For example, to arrange two Word windows side by side, right-click in any open space on the Taskbar and choose Tile Windows Vertically from the context menu. Figure 3.12 shows two windows tiled vertically.

FIGURE 3.12
*You'll usually get better
results by using the Tile
Windows Vertically
command on the
Windows Taskbar
context menu.*

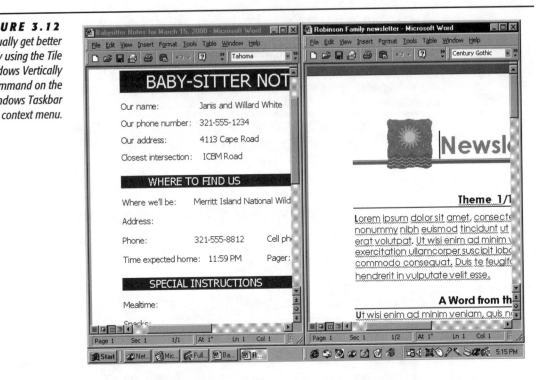

For most purposes, you'll usually do best to maximize the Word window so you have as much space as possible to work in. Unless you have a huge monitor (or need to see other applications while you work in Word), maximize the Word window by clicking the Maximize button on the title bar. Once you've maximized the Word window, Word will replace the Maximize button with the Restore button; click the Restore button to restore the window to the size it was before it was last maximized.

You may also want to use Zoom to enlarge or shrink the display. If so, skip ahead to the section titled "Zooming the View" later in this chapter.

Viewing the Document

Word offers five main ways of viewing your documents, each of which has its strengths and weaknesses: Normal view, Web Layout view, Print Layout view, Print Preview, and Outline view. In the following sections, I'll describe each view briefly. In conjunction with the five views, there are two features that you can use: split-screen view and the Document Map. You'll learn about these as well.

Normal View

Normal view provides the easiest view of the text and other elements on screen and is probably the view you'll spend most of your time using when creating and editing documents. In Normal view, Word approximates the fonts and other formatting that you'll see when you print your document, but adapts the document so that you can see as much of it as possible on your screen. In Normal view, you don't see the margins of the paper, the headers and footers, or the footnotes and comments. Word can also wrap the text horizontally to the size of the window so that no text disappears off the side of the screen.

To switch the document to Normal view, choose View ➤ Normal or click the Normal View button at the left end of the horizontal scroll bar.

Web Layout View

Web Layout view is designed for creating and reading online documents. Web Layout view (see Figure 3.13) splits the screen vertically, displaying the Document Map (a collapsible outline of the document) in the left pane and the document itself in the right pane at an easily readable size.

FIGURE 3.13
Web Layout view
provides special
features for working
with online documents.

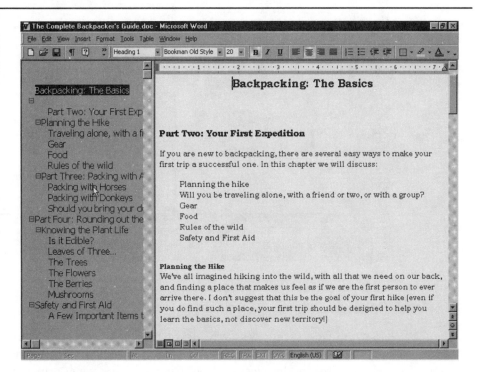

To switch to Web Layout view, choose View ➤ Web Layout or click the Web Layout View button on the horizontal scroll bar.

Print Layout View

Print Layout view is useful for getting an idea of how your documents will look when you print them. In Print Layout view, Word shows you the margins of the sheet or sheets of paper you're working on, any headers or footers, and any footnotes or comments. Word doesn't wrap text to the size of the window, as doing so would change the page from its print format.

To switch to Print Layout view, choose View ➤ Print Layout or click the Print Layout View button on the horizontal scroll bar. You'll see an approximation of the layout of your document, complete with margins (see Figure 3.14). If necessary, zoom to a more appropriate zoom percentage (see the section titled "Zooming the View" a page or two later in the chapter).

FIGURE 3.14
Print Layout view shows you where each element in your document will appear when printed.

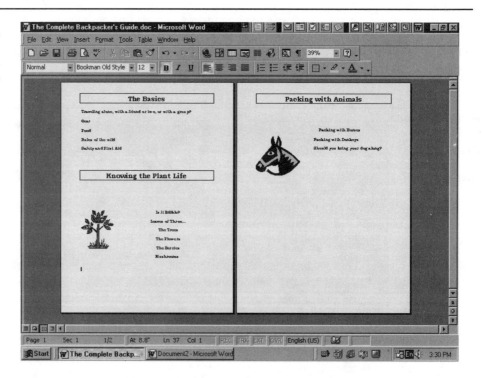

Print Preview

Word's Print Preview provides a way for you to scan your documents on screen for formatting mistakes before you commit them to paper. Print Preview shows you, as closely as Word can, the effect you'll get when you print your document on the currently selected printer. You'll learn how to use Print Preview in Chapter 8.

Outline View

Word's Outline view lets you collapse your documents to a specified number of heading levels—for example, you can choose to view only the first-level heads in your documents or the first three levels of heads, as demonstrated in Figure 3.15.

FIGURE 3.15
Outline view lets you collapse a document to different heading levels. In this example, the document is collapsed to show three levels of headings.

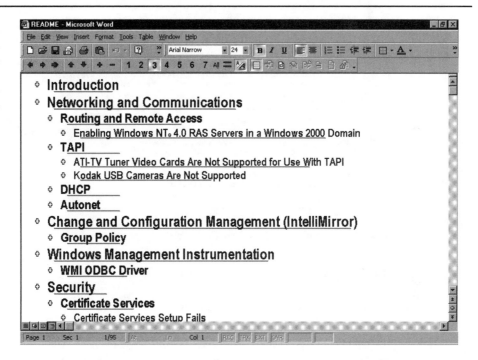

Outline view is very useful for structuring long documents and is much more complex than the other views. For information on Outline view and other advanced Word topics, consult a Word-specific book such as *Word 2000: No Experience Required* (also published by Sybex and written by me).

Split-Screen View

Word also offers split-screen view (see Figure 3.16), in which the screen is divided into two panes. You can use a different view in each pane, display a different part of the document in each pane, and zoom each pane to a different zoom percentage. Split-screen view is especially useful when you need to see two separate parts of a document (for example, the beginning and the end) on screen at the same time.

To split the screen, choose Window ➤ Split. The mouse pointer will change to a double-headed arrow pointing up and down and dragging a thick gray line. Move the line up or down the screen to where you want to split it, then click to place the line.

FIGURE 3.16
Choose Window ➤ Split to split the screen into two panes. You can then work in a different view or at a different zoom percentage in each pane.

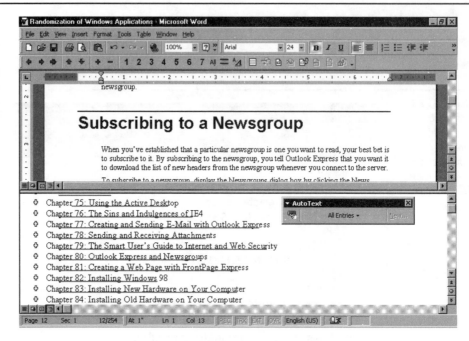

To reunite the split screen, choose Window ➤ Remove Split.

 TIP To split the window in half quickly, double-click the split bar—the tiny horizontal bar at the top of the vertical scroll bar. Double-click the bar dividing the screen to remove the split.

Document Map

The Document Map, shown in Figure 3.13 earlier in the chapter, is a prime component of Web Layout view. You can also use the Document Map with Normal view, Print Layout view, and Outline view (though it is largely redundant for Outline view). You cannot use the Document Map with Print Preview.

The Document Map consists of an outline pane that shows the outline of the document. The outline consists of the various levels of headings in the document (you define headings by using the Heading 1 through Heading 9 styles; I'll discuss styles in Chapter 6). You can collapse and expand the outline to show different levels of headings by clicking the plus sign or minus sign in the little box to the left of any heading that has subheadings. You can right-click in the Document Map to display a context menu of commands, including commands to collapse or expand the Document Map to show a specified number of levels of heading. For example, to display three levels of headings in the Document Map, right-click in it and choose Show Heading 3 from the context menu. You can click a heading in the Document Map to display that part of the document in the main pane of the Word window.

Zooming the View

In any of Word's views, you can use the Zoom feature to increase or decrease the size of the display. Word lets you set any zoom percentage between 10% and 500% of full size.

You can use either the Zoom box on the Standard toolbar or the Zoom dialog box to set the zoom percentage.

Zooming with the Zoom Box on the Standard Toolbar

To zoom the view with the Zoom box on the Standard toolbar:

1. Display the Standard toolbar if it isn't visible.

2. Click the button to the right of the Zoom box to display a drop-down list of zoom percentages.

3. Choose a zoom percentage from the drop-down list or type in a different percentage (between 10% and 500%).

Zooming with the Zoom Dialog Box

To zoom the view with the Zoom dialog box:

1. Choose View ➢ Zoom to display the Zoom dialog box (see Figure 3.17).

FIGURE 3.17
In the Zoom dialog box, choose the zoom percentage you want in the Zoom To box.

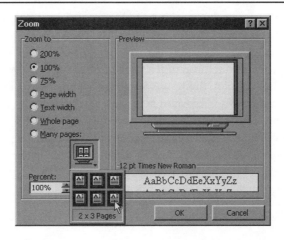

2. In the Zoom To box, choose the zoom percentage you want:

- To zoom to 200%, 100%, 75%, Page Width, Text Width, or Whole Page (which is available only in Print Layout view and Print Preview), click the appropriate option button in the Zoom To box.

- To display more than one page at a time (only in Print Layout view and Print Preview), click the monitor next to the Many Pages option button and drag through the grid it displays (as shown in the figure) to indicate the configuration of pages you want to view: 2∞2 pages, 2∞3 pages, and so on. You'll have more display options for a document that contains many pages than a document that contains only a few.

- To display the page or pages at a precise zoom percentage of your choosing, adjust the setting in the Percent box at the bottom-left corner of the Zoom dialog box.

3. Click the OK button to apply the zoom percentage to the document.

Getting Help

Word comes with a sophisticated Help system designed to answer questions you have about working with Word. You can get Help by using the Office Assistant or by accessing the Microsoft Word Help application directly.

The Office Assistant is the default face for Microsoft Office Help application. The Office Assistant consists of animated characters and graphics, such as Rocky the dog, seen in Figure 3.18. Click the Office Assistant to display the prompt balloon shown in the left part of the figure. (If the Office Assistant is hiding, you can summon it by pressing the F1 key, clicking the Microsoft Word Help button—the button with a blue question mark—on the Standard toolbar, or choosing Help ➤ Show The Office Assistant.)

Type your question, or relevant words, in the text box at the bottom of the Office Assistant balloon, then press Enter or click the Search button to display the list of topics that the Office Assistant associates with that topic.

If one of the Office Assistant's suggestions is suitable, click it to display the Microsoft Word Help window with instructions or advice for the procedure or topic you chose. If there's a See More button toward the bottom of the Office Assistant's balloon, you can click that to display further related topics.

FIGURE 3.18
Use the Office Assistant to access Word's Help system.

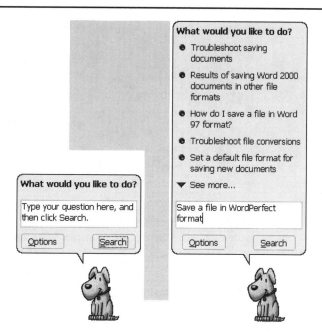

To find further topics from the Microsoft Word Help window, click the Show button to display the left panel of the Microsoft Word Help window (see Figure 3.19):

- The Contents tab of this panel contains a list of the topics in the Word Help file. To expand any topic, click the plus sign to the left of it. To collapse an expanded topic, click the minus sign to the left of it.

- The Answer Wizard tab provides a way to search for Help topics without using the Office Assistant. Enter your question, or relevant words, in the What Would You Like To Do? text box, then click the Search button. Double-click the topic in the Select Topic To Display list box to display the topic in the main part of the Microsoft Word Help window.

- The Index tab provides an alphabetical list of the keywords in the Help file. You can type one or more keywords in the Type Keywords text box and press Enter, or click the Search button, or select a keyword in the Or Choose Keywords list box. Double-click the topic you want in the Choose A Topic list box to display it in the main part of the Microsoft Word Help window.

To move backward and forward between the Help topics you've been working with, use the Back and Forward buttons on the toolbar of the Microsoft Word Help window. The Forward button will become available only when you've used the Back button.

To close the Microsoft Word Help application, click its Close button.

FIGURE 3.19
Use the left panel of the Microsoft Word Help application window to access further information.

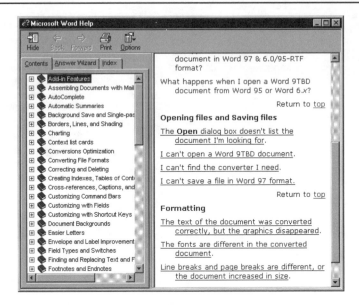

Getting Rid of the Office Assistant

If you prefer not to use the Office Assistant, you can turn it off by right-clicking it and choosing Options from the context menu to display the Office Assistant dialog box. On the Options page, clear the Use The Office Assistant check box, then click the OK button to close the Office Assistant dialog box. You can then click the Microsoft Word Help button or choose Help ➢ Microsoft Word Help to display the Microsoft Word Help window without the intervention of the Office Assistant.

To start using the Office Assistant again, choose Help ➢ Show The Office Assistant.

Exiting Word

When you finish working in Word, choose File ➢ Exit to exit and get back to the Windows Desktop. If you have unsaved documents, Word or the Office Assistant will prompt you to save them. For the moment, choose No, because in this chapter you've been working only with a scratch document.

CHAPTER 4

Creating Word Documents

n this chapter, you'll learn how to work with Word documents. You'll create a new Word document and save it to disk. After that, I'll discuss how to close a document you've been working on and how to reopen that document or open another document. Along the way, I'll discuss the most common things you'll want to do in documents you create: Enter text in them, undo mistakes you've made, and insert information such as dates or special characters.

Creating a New Document

You can create a new document in several different ways in Word, depending on what type of document you want to create and whether you're starting from Windows, from the Works Task Launcher, or from Word itself.

Starting Word with a New Blank Document

As you saw in Chapter 3, when you run Word by choosing Start ➤ Programs ➤ Microsoft Word or by clicking the Start A Blank Word Document link from the Programs page in the Task Launcher, it opens a new blank document and names it Document1.

Creating a New Document Based on the Default Template

 To create a new document based on the default template (Blank Document), click the New Blank Document button on the Standard toolbar or press Ctrl+N. Word will open a new document named Documentx—Document2, Document3, and so on.

Creating a New Document Based on Another Template

At other times when working in Word, you'll probably want to create a new document based on a template that already contains some text or that provides a different look and feel than the default template does. Word ships with a couple dozen templates for everything from a contemporary resume to several kinds of Web pages, and you access them as described in this section. In addition, Works provides a number of templates driven by wizards; I'll discuss these in the next section.

To create a new document based on a different template, follow these steps:

1. Choose File ➢ New ➢ More Templates. Word will display the New dialog box (see Figure 4.1).

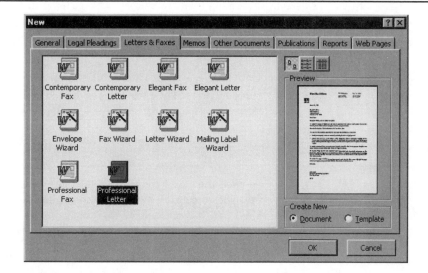

2. In the Create New group box at the lower-right corner of the New dialog box, make sure that the Document option button is selected rather than the Template option button. (You use the Template option button for creating a new template—the skeleton upon which a document is based.)

3. In the New dialog box, choose the tab that contains the type of document you want to create: General, Legal Pleadings, Letters & Faxes, Memos, Other Documents, Publications, Reports, or Web Pages.

   • If you didn't install all the templates that Word offers, you may not see all of these tabs in the New dialog box. Then again, if you or someone else has created more templates in another folder, you may see more tabs than those listed here.

   • To see a preview of a template in the tab you chose, click a template. The preview will appear in the box on the right side of the New dialog box.

NOTE A *template* is a special type of document that you use to produce documents that share the same look or contents. Templates can contain styles, AutoText entries, toolbars, and macros, all of which you'll learn about in later chapters. By basing a document on a different template, you can change its styles instantly, change its look completely, and virtually typeset it differently, in seconds. (Word calls this *attaching* a template to a document.) Take a look at the Preview box as you click some of the templates offered to get an idea of the different templates available.

• You can choose between three views of the templates available by clicking any of the three buttons above the Preview box. The leftmost button gives the Large Icons view, the second gives the List view, and the third gives the Details view.

 TIP The Details view offers the most information of the three views, and you can sort the templates by name, size, type, or date last modified by clicking the buttons at the top of the columns.

4. To start a document based on the template you chose, double-click the icon or listing for the template, or click it once and then click the OK button.

Creating a Document by Using a Works Wizard and Template

Your fourth option for creating a Word document is to use one of the templates that Works provides. (These templates are not included in regular distributions of Word—for example, those sold separately and those included with the Office 2000 application suite.) The Works templates are designed with the home or home office in mind, and most are driven by wizards that make them easy to use.

To create a document by using a Works wizard and template, follow these steps:

1. If you're working in Word, choose File ➤ New ➤ Works Task Launcher to display the Works Task Launcher with the Programs page foremost and Word selected in the list of programs. (If you're not working in Word, start or activate the Task Launcher, display the Programs page, and select Word.)

2. In the list of tasks, select the task that represents the type of document you want to create. Works will display information about the task and a blue Start button.

3. Click the Start button to start the wizard. Works will start Word (if it's not running) or activate it (if it is running) and will start the wizard running. Figure 4.2 shows the Works Menus Wizard, which helps you create menus (as in restaurants, not software).

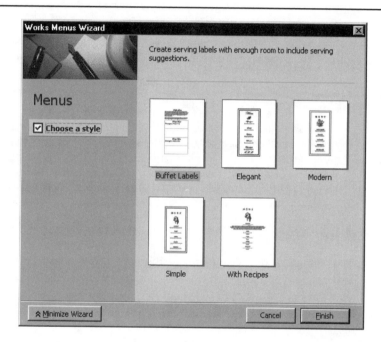

4. Choose options in the Wizard dialog box. The options available to you will vary depending on the type of document you're creating. As you choose options, the wizard will implement them in the Word window. Click the Minimize Wizard button (if there is one) on the wizard to reduce the wizard to a small window that lets you see more of the document; click the resulting Maximize Wizard button to restore the wizard window to its regular size.

5. Click the Finish button to close the wizard and create the document.

Working with Text

As in most word-processing applications, Word's basic unit is the paragraph. These aren't paragraphs as people generally understand them: A paragraph in Word consists of a paragraph mark (made by pressing the Enter key) and any text (or graphic) between it and the previous paragraph mark (or the beginning of the document). In other words, a paragraph consists of anything (text, a graphic, space, or even nothing at all) that appears between two paragraph marks, up to and including the second paragraph mark. Strange as it seems, a paragraph mark with nothing between it and the previous paragraph mark is considered a full paragraph. You can treat each paragraph as a unit for formatting with styles (which I'll cover in Chapter 6) or for moving and copying.

Each blank document you create contains one paragraph, which is located at the start of the document. You can add as many paragraphs to a document as you need.

 TIP If you're not seeing paragraph marks on your screen, click the ¶ button on the Standard toolbar. (If you have the Standard and Formatting toolbars displayed on the same row, you may have to display the More Buttons panel to access the ¶ button the first time.) This is the Show/Hide ¶ button, and it toggles the display of spaces, tabs, paragraph marks, and the like. Some people find it easier to work with these marks displayed; others find them distracting. You can also display and hide these marks by pressing Ctrl+Shift+8.

Entering Text

To enter text in your document, position the insertion point where you want the text to appear and type it in. Word will automatically wrap text as it reaches the end of a line, so you don't need to (and in fact shouldn't) press the Enter key at the end of a line. Press the Enter key when you need to start a new paragraph.

 NOTE If you're working in Normal view (discussed in Chapter 3), Word will adjust the display of the text to suit the screen and window size you are working with, rather than displaying the text as it will appear when you print it out. For precise layout, you'll need to work in Print Layout view (View ➤ Print Layout) rather than Normal view.

If you want to move to a new line without starting a new paragraph—for example, so there is no extra space between lines in poetry—press Shift+Enter to start a new line within the same paragraph. You shouldn't need to do this often—just for special effects.

As you reach the end of a page, Word will automatically break text onto the next page. If you want, you can start a new page at any point by inserting a page break. To do so, press Ctrl+Enter.

In Print Layout view, Web Layout view, and Print Preview, Word 2000 provides a new feature called Click and Type that enables you to double-click where you want to enter text on the page. Word automatically enters any blank paragraphs and tabs required to position the insertion point where you double-clicked and changes the alignment of the paragraph if necessary. (If there are already superfluous blank paragraphs or tabs beyond where you double-clicked, Word removes them automatically.)

For example, to create a centered heading one-third of the way down the fresh page in a new blank document, you could double-click one-third of the way down the page and in the middle of the line. Word will place the insertion point there, add blank paragraphs from the top of the page to the line of the heading, and apply center alignment. You can then create a right-aligned paragraph at the bottom of the page by double-clicking at the right margin toward the bottom of the page.

The mouse pointer displays the type of alignment that Click and Type will implement if you double-click in that area: centering around the horizontal middle of the page, right alignment near to the right margin, and left alignment everywhere else.

Insert and Overtype Modes

Word offers two *modes* (methods of behavior) for adding text to your documents: Insert mode and Overtype mode. In *Insert mode* (the default mode), characters you type are inserted into the text at the insertion point, pushing along any characters to the right of the insertion point. If you want to type over existing text in Insert mode, select the text using either the mouse or the keyboard (see the next section for instructions on selecting text) and type in the text you want to insert in its place. In Insert mode, the OVR indicator on the status bar is dimmed.

In *Overtype mode*, any character you type replaces the character (if any) to the immediate right of the insertion point. When Word is in Overtype mode, the OVR indicator on the status bar is active (darkened).

To toggle between Insert mode and Overtype mode, double-click the OVR indicator on the status bar or press the Insert key. Alternatively, choose Tools ➢ Options to display the Options dialog box, click the Edit tab to display it, select the Overtype Mode check box, and click the OK button.

Moving the Insertion Point

In Word, you can move the insertion point using the mouse, the keyboard, or a combination of the two. In most situations, you can use whichever means you prefer, though you will probably find the mouse easier for some operations and the keyboard easier for others.

Using the Mouse

To position the insertion point using the mouse, move the mouse pointer to where you want the insertion point, and click to place it there.

Use the vertical scroll bar to move up and down through your document (or, if you have an IntelliMouse or other scrolling mouse, use the mouse's roller). When you scroll with the scroll box (the *thumb*) in a multipage document, Word will display a small box next to the scroll bar showing which page and heading you're scrolling past. Use the horizontal scroll bar to move from side to side as necessary.

 TIP If you often need to scroll horizontally in Normal view to see the full width of your documents, turn on Word's Wrap To Window option, which makes the text fit into the current window size, regardless of width. To turn on Wrap To Window, choose Tools ➢ Options, click the View tab, and select the Wrap To Window check box. Click the OK button to close the Options dialog box.

Click the Next Page and Previous Page buttons at the foot of the vertical scroll bar to move to the next page and previous page. Make sure that these buttons are black, which indicates that Word is browsing by pages. If they're blue, Word is browsing by a different item, such as sections or comments; clicking the buttons while they are blue will take you to the next (or previous) section or comment in the document. To reset Word to browse by pages, click the Object Browser button between the Next and Previous buttons and choose the Browse By Page button in the Object Browser list, as shown in Figure 4.3.

 NOTE The Object Browser allows you to choose which type of item you want to navigate to in the document. You can move to the previous or next field, endnote, footnote, comment, section, page, Go To item, Find item, edit, heading, graphic, or table. This provides a way of moving quickly from one instance of an item to the next or previous instance. For example, if you need to check each table in a document, choose Table from the Object Browser list and then use the Previous and Next buttons to navigate from table to table.

FIGURE 4.3
Click the Select Word Object button and choose the object in the Object Browser list.

Using Keyboard Shortcuts

Word offers a number of keystroke combinations that let you move the insertion point swiftly through the document without removing your hands from the keyboard. Besides ← to move left one character, → to move right one character, ↑ to move up one line, and ↓ to move down one line, you can use the following:

Keystroke	Action
Ctrl+→	One word to the right
Ctrl+←	One word to the left
Ctrl+↑	To the beginning of the current paragraph or (if the insertion point is at the beginning of a paragraph) to the beginning of the previous paragraph
Ctrl+↓	To the beginning of the next paragraph
End	To the end of the current line
Ctrl+End	To the end of the document
Home	To the start of the current line
Ctrl+Home	To the start of the document
PageUp	Up one screen's worth of text
PageDown	Down one screen's worth of text
Ctrl+PageUp	To the first character on the current screen
Ctrl+PageDown	To the last character on the current screen

 TIP You can quickly move to the last three places you edited in a document by pressing Shift+F5 (Go Back) once, twice, or three times. This is especially useful when you open a document and need to return to the point at which you were last working.

Selecting Text

Word offers a number of different ways to select text: You can use the keyboard, the mouse, or the two in combination. You'll find that some ways of selecting text work better than others with certain equipment; experiment to find which are the fastest and most comfortable methods for you.

Selected text appears highlighted in reverse video—for example, if your normal text is black on a white background, selected text will be white on a black background.

Selecting Text with the Mouse

The simplest way to select text with the mouse is to position the insertion point at the beginning or end of the block you want to select, then click and drag to the end or beginning of the block.

Understanding the Automatic Word-Selection Feature

Word offers an automatic word-selection feature to help you select whole words more quickly with the mouse. When this feature is switched on, as soon as you drag the mouse pointer from one word to the next, Word will select the whole of the first word and the whole of the second; when the mouse pointer reaches the third, it selects that too, and so on.

To temporarily override automatic word selection, hold down the Alt key before you click and drag.

To turn off automatic word selection, first choose Tools ➤ Options to display the Options dialog box. Click the Edit tab to bring the Edit page to the front of the dialog box, and clear the When Selecting, Automatically Select Entire Word check box. Then click the OK button. To turn on automatic word selection, select the When Selecting, Automatically Select Entire Word check box.

You can also select text with multiple clicks:

- Double-click in a word to select it.
- Triple-click in a paragraph to select it.
- Ctrl-click in a sentence to select it.

In the *selection bar* on the left side of the screen (where the insertion point turns from an I-beam to an arrow pointing up and to the right), you can click to select text as follows:

- Click once to select the line the arrow is pointing at.
- Double-click to select the paragraph the arrow is pointing at.
- Triple-click (or Ctrl-click once) to select the entire document.

Selecting Text with the Keyboard

To select text with the keyboard, hold down the Shift key and move the insertion point by using the keyboard shortcuts listed in the section titled "Using Keyboard Shortcuts" earlier in this chapter.

Selecting Text with the Extend Selection Feature

You can also select text by using Word's Extend Selection feature, though for most uses it's slow and clumsy. Press the F8 key once to enter Extend Selection mode; you'll see EXT appear undimmed on the status bar. Press F8 a second time to select the current word, a third time to select the current sentence, a fourth time to select the current paragraph, and a fifth time to select the whole document. Then press the Esc key to turn off Extend Selection mode.

Extend Selection also works with other keys on the keyboard: To select a sentence, press F8 at the beginning of the sentence and then press the punctuation mark that appears at the end of the sentence. To select some text, position the insertion point at the beginning of that text, press F8, and then press the letter up to which you want to select. If there is another instance of the letter before the one you want to select, press the letter again.

To select a paragraph, place the insertion point at the start of the paragraph, press F8, and then press the Enter key.

Selecting Text with the Mouse and Keyboard

Word also offers ways to select text using the mouse and keyboard together. These techniques are well worth trying out, as you can quickly select awkward blocks of text—for example, if you want to select a few sentences from a paragraph or to select columns of characters.

To select a block of text using the mouse and the keyboard, position the insertion point at the start (or end) of a block and click. Then move the insertion point to the end (or start) of the block—scroll if necessary with the mouse roller or the scroll bar, but don't use the keyboard—hold down the Shift key, then click again.

To select columns of characters, hold down the Alt key, click, and drag from one end of the block to the other (see Figure 4.4). This technique can be very useful for getting rid of extra spaces or tabs used to align text.

FIGURE 4.4

To select columns of characters without selecting whole lines, hold down the Alt key and drag through the block.

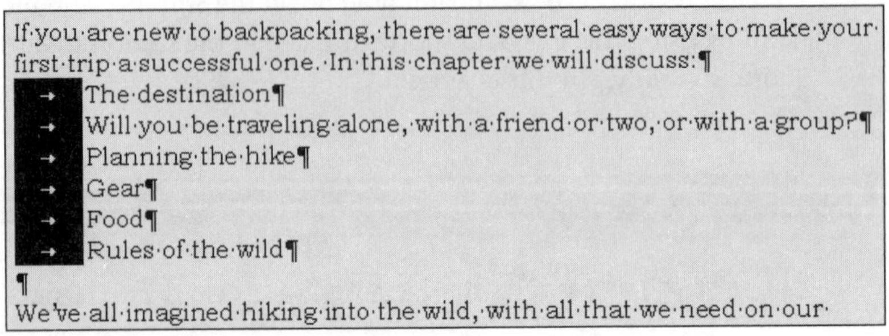

> If·you·are·new·to·backpacking,·there·are·several·easy·ways·to·make·your·
> first·trip·a·successful·one.·In·this·chapter·we·will·discuss:¶
> → The·destination¶
> → Will·you·be·traveling·alone,·with·a·friend·or·two,·or·with·a·group?¶
> → Planning·the·hike¶
> → Gear¶
> → Food¶
> → Rules·of·the·wild¶
> ¶
> We've·all·imagined·hiking·into·the·wild,·with·all·that·we·need·on·our·

Deleting Text

Word lets you delete text swiftly and easily:

- To delete a block of text, simply select it and press the Delete key.
- To delete the character to the left of the insertion point, press the Backspace key.
- To delete the character to the right of the insertion point, press the Delete key.
- To delete the word to the right of the insertion point, press Ctrl+Delete. This actually deletes from the insertion point to the beginning of the next word (or the end of the line, if the current word is the last one in the line), so if the insertion point is in a word when you press Ctrl+Delete, you won't delete the whole word.
- To delete the word to the left of the insertion point, press Ctrl+Backspace. Again, if the insertion point isn't at the end of the word, only the part of the word to the left of the insertion point will be deleted.

TIP You can also delete selected text by choosing Edit ➢ Clear or by right-clicking in the selection and choosing Cut from the context menu that appears. (Some context menus—which are different for the various elements of Word documents—don't have a Cut command.)

Cutting, Pasting, and Moving Text

You can easily copy and move text (and graphics) around your document either by using the Cut, Copy, and Paste commands or by using Word's drag-and-drop feature, which lets you copy or move text using your mouse.

Word 2000 brings with it the Office 2000 Clipboard, which can contain up to 12 different copied or cut items, rather than relying on the Windows Clipboard, which can contain only one text item and one graphical item at a time. This new Office Clipboard is implemented as a toolbar in Word (and in the other Office 2000 applications, if you have them), and its contents are available to Word but not to the other Works applications. As shown in Figure 4.5, the Office Clipboard uses icons to indicate the type of information each of the 12 storage containers holds: Here, the first two storage containers contain textual information (taken from a Works Spreadsheet spreadsheet), while the third and fourth contain material copied from a Word document.

 NOTE The Clipboard automatically appears when you copy or cut two items in succession. You can display it as you would any toolbar by choosing View ➤ Toolbars ➤ Clipboard, and dismiss it either the same way or by clicking its close button.

As you cut or copy items, they are added to the Office Clipboard until it contains 12 items. When you cut or copy a thirteenth item, Word (or the Office Assistant) will warn you that copying this item will drop the first item from the Clipboard. Click OK or Cancel.

 NOTE You can't clear an individual item from the Clipboard, so once you've placed an item on the Clipboard, it's there until you clear the Clipboard completely or copy (or cut) enough items to push the current items off it.

You can paste any individual item from the Office Clipboard to the current position of the insertion point in a Word document by clicking the item. Alternatively, you can paste in all the items from the Clipboard by clicking the Paste All button on the Clipboard's toolbar. The Paste All command is useful for gathering a number of items in sequence—for example, you might want to cull a dozen headings or paragraphs from a report to create a summary.

When the Office Clipboard is full, or nearing full, you can remove all the items from the Office Clipboard by clicking the Clear Clipboard button on the Office Clipboard's toolbar.

The most recent text item or graphical item on the Office Clipboard is also placed on the Windows Clipboard, so that you can transfer information to and from non-Office programs much as before. Likewise, the current text or graphical item on the Windows Clipboard is also placed on the Office Clipboard.

Cut

The Cut command removes the selected text (or graphics) from the Word document and places it on the Office Clipboard and Windows Clipboard. From there, you can paste it into another part of the document, into another document, or into another application. To cut the current selection, click the Cut button, then right-click and choose Cut from the context menu, choose Edit ➢ Cut, or press Ctrl+X.

Copy

The Copy command copies the selected text (or graphics) to the Office Clipboard and the Windows Clipboard. From there, you can paste it into another part of the document, into another document, or into another application. To copy the current selection, click the Copy button, then right-click and choose Copy from the context menu, choose Edit ➢ Copy, or press Ctrl+C.

Paste

The Paste command pastes a copy of the Windows Clipboard's contents into your Word document at the insertion point. To paste the contents of the Windows Clipboard, right-click and choose Paste from the context menu, click the Paste button, choose Edit ➢ Paste, or press Ctrl+V.

Using Undo and Redo

Word provides an Undo feature that can undo one or more of the last actions that you've taken, and a Redo feature that can redo anything that you've just chosen to undo.

To undo the last action you've taken, click the Undo button on the Standard toolbar, press Ctrl+Z, or choose Edit ➢ Undo.

To undo more than one action, click the arrow to the right of the Undo button and choose the number of actions to undo from the drop-down list, as shown in Figure 4.6.

FIGURE 4.6

You can undo more than one action at once by clicking the arrow to the right of the Undo button and choosing the actions to undo from the drop-down list.

To redo a single action, click the Redo button on the Standard toolbar, press Ctrl+Y, or choose Edit ➢ Redo. (Often, the Redo button is on the part of the Standard toolbar that is covered by the Formatting toolbar.) To redo more than one action, click the arrow to the right of the Redo button and choose the number of actions to redo from the drop-down list.

When there is no action that can be undone, the Undo button will be dimmed and unavailable. When there is no undone action that can be redone, the Redo button will be dimmed and unavailable.

WARNING There are a few actions that Word *can't* undo, including File ➢ Save, File ➢ Close, and a number of others. If you find yourself needing to undo an action that Word says it cannot undo, you may have to resort to closing the document without saving changes to it. You will lose all changes made since the last time you saved it—but if you've done something truly horrible to the document, this sacrifice may be worthwhile. (This is another argument for saving your documents frequently, preferably after just enough reflection to be sure you haven't ruined them.)

Inserting a Date

To insert a date in a document:

1. Position the insertion point where you want the date to appear. (If necessary, use the Click and Type feature to position the insertion point.)

2. Choose Insert ➢ Date And Time to display the Date And Time dialog box (see Figure 4.7).

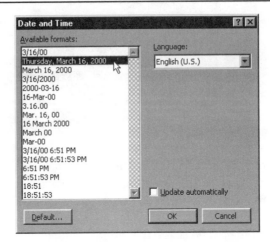

FIGURE 4.7
*Use the Date And Time
dialog box to quickly
insert a date in a
document.*

3. In the Available Formats list box, choose the date format that you want to use.

   • The Language drop-down list box will show the language you're currently working in. You can choose another language—for example, *English (Australian)* instead of *English (US)*—to see the date formats available for that language.

   • If you want to make the date format in the Available Formats list box the default date format, click the Default button, and then click the Yes button in the confirmation dialog box that appears. Word will then select that date format automatically every time you display the Date And Time dialog box.

4. If you want the date to be updated every time the document is opened, select the Update Automatically check box. Automatic updating is useful for documents such as reports, which you often want to bear the date (and perhaps the time) on which they were printed, not the date on which they were created. For documents such as business letters and memos, on the other hand, you usually will want to make sure this check box is cleared, so the date you insert remains the same no matter when you open or print the document.

5. Click the OK button to insert the date in your document.

Inserting Symbols and Special Characters

Word offers enough symbols and special characters for you to typeset almost any document. Symbols can be any character from multiplication or division signs to the fancy ➤ arrow Sybex uses to indicate menu commands. Special characters are a subset of symbols that include em dashes (—) and en dashes (–), trademark symbols (™), and the like—symbols that Microsoft thinks you might want to insert more frequently and with less effort than the symbols relegated to the Symbols tab.

To insert a symbol or special character at the insertion point or in place of the current selection:

1. Choose Insert ➤ Symbol to display the Symbol dialog box (see Figure 4.8).

FIGURE 4.8
In the Symbol dialog box, choose the symbol or special character to insert and then click the Insert button.

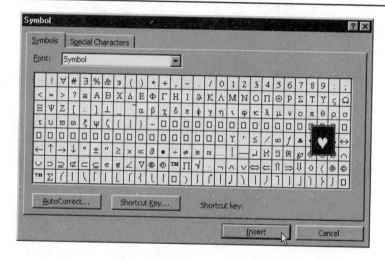

2. To insert a symbol, click the Symbols tab to bring it to the front of the dialog box if it isn't already there, and then choose the symbol to insert from the box.

- Use the Font drop-down list to pick the font you want to see in the dialog box. For some fonts, a Subset drop-down list will appear to the right of the Font drop-down list; you can also choose a different subset of the font from this drop-down list.

- To enlarge a character so you can see it more clearly, click it once. An enlarged version of it will pop out at you. You can then move the zoom box around the Symbols dialog box by using ↑, ↓, ←, and →, or by clicking it and dragging with the mouse.

NOTE Word will display a shortcut key for the symbol (if there is one) to the right of the Shortcut Key button. If you're often inserting a particular symbol, you can use the shortcut key instead—or you can create a shortcut key of your own, as you'll see in the next section. You can also create an AutoCorrect entry, which can be a handy way of inserting symbols in text. You'll learn how to do this in Chapter 6.

3. To insert a special character, click the Special Characters tab to bring it to the front (unless it's already there). Choose the character to insert from the list box (see Figure 4.9).

FIGURE 4.9

Choose a special character from the Special Characters tab of the Symbol dialog box, and then click the Insert button.

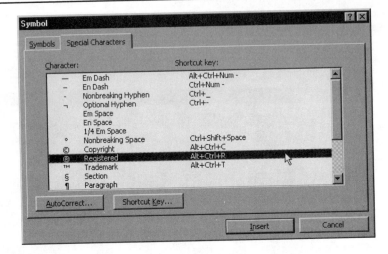

4. To insert the symbol or special character, click the Insert button. Word will insert the character, and the Cancel button will change to a Close button.

   • You can also insert a symbol or special character by double-clicking it.

5. To insert more symbols or special characters, repeat steps 2 through 4.

6. Click the Close button to close the Symbol dialog box.

If you find yourself inserting a particular symbol or special character frequently, you can create a shortcut key combination (by selecting the symbol or special character, clicking the Shortcut Key button, and using the Customize Keyboard dialog box to create the shortcut key combination) for placing it more quickly. As you can see in the Symbol dialog box, many of the symbols and special characters already have shortcut keys assigned, but you can replace these with more convenient keyboard shortcuts of your own if you prefer.

Saving a Word Document

The first time you save a Word document, you assign it a name and choose the folder in which to save it. Thereafter, when you save the document, Word uses that name and folder and does not prompt you for changes to them—unless you decide to save the file under a different name or in a different folder, in which case you need to use the File ➤ Save As command rather than File ➤ Save. I'll discuss this in a moment.

Saving a Document for the First Time

To save a Word document for the first time:

1. Click the Save button or choose File ➤ Save. Word will display the Save As dialog box (see Figure 4.10).

NOTE In dialog boxes that show filenames, you'll see file extensions (for example, .doc at the end of a Word filename) only if you chose to see them in Windows Explorer. To display extensions in Explorer, choose View ➤ Options and clear the Hide MS-DOS File Extensions For File Types That Are Registered check box on the View page of the Options or Folder Options dialog box, then click the OK button.

FIGURE 4.10
In the Save As dialog box, choose the folder in which to save your file, then enter a name for the file.

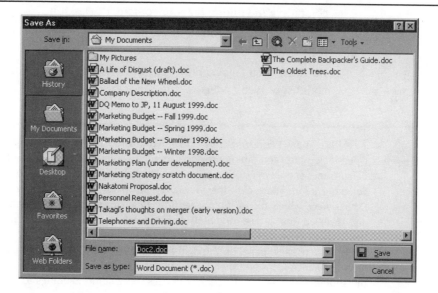

2. In the Save In box at the top of the Save As dialog box, choose the folder in which to save the document.

- Click the drop-down list button to the right of the Save In box to display the drop-down list of computers, folders, and locations accessible from your computer.

- Click the Up One Level button (or press the Backspace key with the focus on the folder list) to move up one level of folders, or double-click a folder to open it and display its contents.

- Click the Back button (the button with the blue arrow pointing to the left) to move to the folder you were in previously. This button works like the Back button in Internet Explorer (or any other Web browser). When you display the ScreenTip for this button, it will show the name of the folder to which clicking the button will take you.

- Click the History button in the left panel of the dialog box to display the list of documents and folders you've worked with recently. (This list of documents is stored as links in the \Office\Recent\ folder.)

- Click the My Documents button in the left panel of the dialog box to display the \My Documents\ folder.

- Click the Desktop button in the left panel of the dialog box to display the computers and folders on your computer's Desktop.

- Click the Favorites button in the left panel of the dialog box to display your list of Favorite folders and documents.

- Click the Web Folders button in the left panel of the dialog box to display your list of Web folders.

TIP Like many Windows dialog boxes that provide access to files, Word's Save dialog box, Open dialog box, and others provide various ways in which to view and sort the files. The default view, shown in Figure 4.10, is List view, which shows an unadorned list of filenames. For more information, click the View drop-down list button and choose Details to show Details view, which shows the Name, Size, Type (for example, Microsoft Word Document), and Modified (that is, last-modified) date for each file. You can also choose View ➢ Properties to show a panel of properties on the right-hand side of the dialog box or View ➢ Preview to display a preview panel on the right-hand side of the dialog box. To sort the files, choose View ➢ Arrange Icons and then By Name, By Type, By Size, or By Date, as appropriate, from the submenu. In Details view, you can click the column headings to sort the files by that column: Click once for ascending sort order, and click again to reverse the order.

3. In the File Name text box, enter a name for your file.

- You can enter a thorough and descriptive name—up to 255 characters, including the path to the file (the name of the folder or folders in which to save the file).

- You can't use the following characters in filenames (if you do try to use one of these, Word will advise you of the problem):

Colon	:
Backslash	\
Forward slash	/
Greater-than sign	>
Less-than sign	<
Asterisk	*
Question mark	?
Double quotation mark	"
Pipe symbol	|

4. Click the Save button to save the file.

5. If Word displays a Properties dialog box for the document (see Figure 4.11), you can enter identifying information on the Summary tab.

- In the Title text box, Word displays the first paragraph of the document (or a section of it, if it's long). You'll often want to change this.

- In the Author and Company text boxes, Word displays the username from the User Information page of the Options dialog box.

- Use the Subject text box to describe the subject of the document, and enter any keywords that will help you remember the document in the Keywords text box.

- Fill in other text boxes as desired, then click the OK button to close the Properties dialog box and save the file.

FIGURE 4.11

You can enter identifying information in the Properties dialog box.

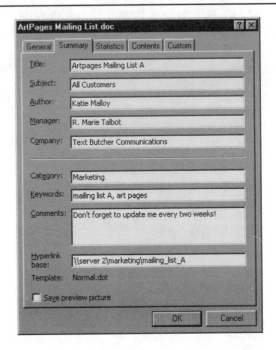

 NOTE Whether the Properties dialog box appears depends on the Prompt For Document Properties setting on the Save page of the Options dialog box. To have Word automatically prompt you for summary information, choose Tools ➢ Options, click the Save tab to display the Save page, select the Prompt For Document Properties check box, and click OK.

 TIP To save all open documents at once, hold down one of the Shift keys on your keyboard, then, with your mouse, choose File ➢ Save All. Word will save each document that contains unsaved changes, prompting you for filenames for any document that has never been saved. If you have made changes to any of the templates on which the documents are based, Word will prompt you to save the template as well.

Saving a Document Again

 To save a document that you've saved before, click the Save button, choose File ➤ Save, or press Ctrl+S (the shortcut for Save). Word will save the document without consulting you about the location or filename.

Saving a Document under Another Name

One of the easiest ways to make a copy of a Word document is to open it and save it under a different name. This technique can be particularly useful if you've made changes to the document but don't want to replace the original document—for example, if you think you might need to revert to the original document and you've forgotten to make a backup before making your changes. The Save As command can also be useful for copying a document to a different folder or drive—for example, if you want to copy a document to a floppy drive or to a network drive.

To save a document under a different name or to a different folder:

1. Choose File ➤ Save As to display the Save As dialog box.

2. Enter a different name for the document in the File Name box or choose a different folder in the Save In area.

3. Click the Save button to save the document.

If the folder you chose already contains a document of the same name, Word will ask whether you want to overwrite it. Click Yes or No. If you choose No, Word will return you to the Save As dialog box so that you can select a different name or different folder.

Saving a Word Document in a Different Format

Word lets you save documents in formats (file types) other than Word—for example, the file formats of other word processors. To save a file in a different format, you need to have Word's converter file for that format installed on your computer. If you don't, Word will prompt you to install the converter. Click the Yes button, and the Windows Installer will install the converter in question and notify you when it has finished doing so.

To save an existing file in a different format:

1. Choose File ➤ Save As. Word will display the Save As dialog box.

2. Scroll down the Save As Type drop-down list and choose the file type you want to save the current document as.

3. If you want, enter a different filename for the file.

4. Click the Save button or press Enter.

 NOTE If you haven't saved the file before, you can choose File ➢ Save instead of File ➢ Save As to open the Save As dialog box. You'll also need to specify a name for the document.

Closing a Document

To close the current document, choose File ➢ Close, press Ctrl+F4, or click the Close button on the document window. If the document contains unsaved changes, Word will prompt you to save them (see Figure 4.12) and will close the document when you've finished.

FIGURE 4.12
If the document you're closing contains unsaved changes, Word will prompt you to save them.

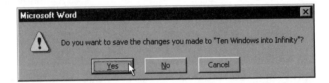

If the document has been saved before and if there are no new changes, Word will simply close the document. If you've created a new document but never changed it (for example, by typing something into it) or saved it, Word will close it without prompting you to save it.

 TIP To close all open documents at once, hold down one of the Shift keys on your keyboard, then, with your mouse, choose File ➢ Close All.

Opening a Word Document

To open a Word document:

 1. Click the Open button on the Standard toolbar, choose File ➢ Open, or press Ctrl+O. Word will display the Open dialog box (see Figure 4.13). The Open dialog box provides several methods of navigating to the folder and file you want to open.

FIGURE 4.13

In the Open dialog box, use the Look In box to navigate to the folder that contains the document you want to open, then highlight the document and click the Open button.

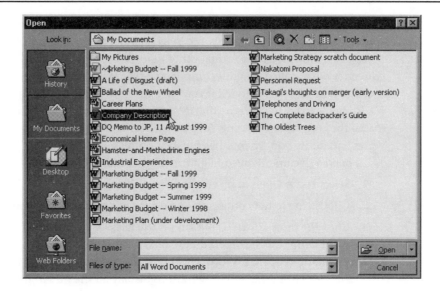

2. If you're already in the right folder, proceed to Step 3. If not, use the techniques described for the Save As dialog box in the section titled "Saving Documents for the First Time" to navigate to the folder holding the document you want to open. You'll notice that the Open dialog box has a Look In drop-down list rather than a Save In drop-down list, but otherwise everything works the same.

3. Choose the document or documents you want to open.

   • To open several documents at once, click the first one in the Open dialog box to select it. Then, to select contiguous documents, hold down Shift and click the last document in the sequence to select it and all the ones between it and the first document. To select noncontiguous documents, hold down Ctrl and click each document you want to open.

   • You can also combine the two methods of selection: First use Shift+click to select a sequence of documents, then use Ctrl+click to select others. To deselect documents within the range you have selected, use Ctrl+click.

4. Click the Open button to open the document or documents.

 TIP You can also open Word documents by using the History page of the Works Task Launcher or by choosing Start ➤ Documents and choosing a recent document off the list of recent documents that Windows maintains.

Opening a Non-Word Document

Word can open files saved in a number of other formats, from plain-text ASCII files to spreadsheets (for example, Lotus 1-2-3) to calendar and address books.

To open a file saved in a format other than Word, you need to have the appropriate converter file installed on your computer so that Word can read the file. Generally speaking, the easiest way to tell if you have the right converter installed for a particular file format is to try to open the file; if Word cannot open the file, it will prompt you to install the converter. Click the Yes button. The Windows Installer will install the converter and notify you when it has finished doing so.

To open a document saved in a format other than Word:

1. Select File ➢ Open to display the Open dialog box.

2. Choose the folder containing the document you want to open.

3. Click the drop-down list button on the Files Of Type list box at the bottom left-hand corner of the Open dialog box. From the list, select the type of file that you want to open. If Word doesn't list the file that you want to open, choose All Files (*.*) from the drop-down list to display all the files in the folder.

4. Choose the file in the main window of the Open dialog box, then click the Open button or press Enter to open the file.

CHAPTER <u>5</u>

Simple Formatting

Word supplies you with enough formatting options to create anything from simple, typewriter-style documents up to a complex newsletter or book. The basic types of formatting options start with character formatting (how the individual letters look) and move through paragraph formatting (how paragraphs appear on the page) to style formatting (a combination of character and paragraph formatting, among other formatting) and finally page setup. In this chapter, you'll learn about character formatting, paragraph formatting, and page setup. In the next chapter, you'll add styles to the mix.

Character Formatting

Character formatting is formatting that you can apply to one or more characters. A character is a letter, a number, a symbol, a space, or an object (such as a graphic). Character formatting consists of:

- character attributes (properties), such as bold, italic, underline, and strikethrough (among others)
- fonts (also known as typefaces), such as Courier New, Times New Roman, and Arial
- point size—the size of the font
- character spacing, such as superscripts and subscripts (vertical spacing) and kerning (horizontal spacing)

You can apply character formatting in several ways: by using the Font dialog box, keyboard shortcuts, or the Formatting toolbar. Each of these methods has advantages and disadvantages depending on what you're doing when you decide to start applying formatting and how much of it you need to apply. To work most efficiently in Word, you need to know all the ways of applying formatting.

Character Formatting Using the Font Dialog Box

The Font dialog box offers you the most control over font formatting, providing all the character-formatting options together in one handy location.

To set character formatting using the Font dialog box:

1. Select the text whose formatting you want to change. If you want to change the formatting of just one word, place the insertion point inside it.

2. Right-click in the text and choose Font from the context menu, or choose Format ➤ Font, to display the Font dialog box (see Figure 5.1). If the Font page isn't displayed, click its tab to bring it to the front of the dialog box.

FIGURE 5.1
*The Font dialog box
gives you quick access
to all the character
formatting options
Word offers.*

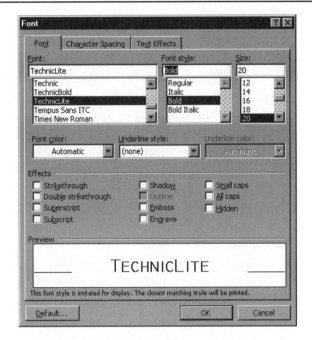

3. Choose the formatting options you want from the Font page:

   • In the Font list box, choose the font for the text.

   • In the Font Style list box, choose the font style: Regular, Italic, Bold, or Bold Italic.

TIP Watch the Preview box at the bottom of the dialog box to see approximately how your text will look.

   • In the Size box, choose the font size you want. To choose a font size that Word doesn't list, type it in the top Size box—for example, enter **13** to produce 13-point text. (Word offers 12-point and 14-point options in the list box.)

   • In the Underline box, choose the underlining style you want. The styles are mostly self-explanatory, with the possible exception of these two: None removes any existing underline, while Words Only adds a single underline underneath words, with no underline underneath spaces. If you apply underlining, you can select the color for the underline by using the Underline Color drop-down list. Automatic applies the default color (typically that of the current font). For colors beyond those shown on the drop-down panel, click the More Colors button on the panel, select the color you want on either the Standard page or the Custom page of the Colors dialog box, and click the OK button to apply the color.

- For any special effects, select the check boxes in the Effects area for Strikethrough, Double Strikethrough, Superscript, Subscript, Shadow, Outline, Emboss, Engrave, Small Caps, All Caps, or Hidden. (Hidden text is invisible under normal viewing conditions and does not print unless you choose to include it.)

- Finally, choose a color for your text from the Font Color drop-down list. This will affect the text on screen—and on printouts if you have a color printer. Again, you can choose colors other than those on the drop-down palette by clicking the More Colors button to display the Colors dialog box.

4. For special effects, adjust the settings on the Character Spacing page of the Font dialog box.

- The Scale drop-down list controls the horizontal scaling of the text. By default, this is set to 100%—full size. You can change this value to anything from 1% to 600% to squeeze or stretch the text horizontally.

- The Spacing option controls the horizontal placement of letters relative to each other—closer to each other or farther apart—by adjusting the space between the letters. From the Spacing drop-down list, you can choose Expanded or Condensed, then use the up and down spinner arrows in the By box to adjust the degree of expansion or condensation. (Alternatively, simply click the spinner arrows and let Word worry about making the Spacing drop-down list match your choice.) Again, watch the Preview box for a simulation of the effect your current choices will have.

- The Position option controls the vertical placement of letters relative to the baseline they're theoretically resting on. From the Position list, you can choose Normal, Raised, or Lowered, then use the spinner arrows in the By box to raise or lower the letters—or simply click the spinner arrows and let Word determine whether the text is Normal, Raised, or Lowered.

- To turn on automatic kerning for fonts above a certain size, select the Kerning For Fonts check box and adjust the point size in the Points And Above box if necessary.

 NOTE *Kerning* is adjusting the space between letters so that no letter appears too far from its neighbor. For example, if you type WAVE in a large font size without kerning, Word will leave enough space between the W and the A, and the A and the V, for you to drive a small truck through. With kerning, you'll only be able to get a motorcycle through the gap.

5. To really enliven a document, try one of the six options on the Text Effects page of the Font dialog box: Blinking Background, Las Vegas Lights, Marching Black Ants, Marching Red Ants, Shimmer, and Sparkle Text. Use these options in moderation for best effect on Web pages, and be aware that they can look bad in printed documents. To remove an animation, select None in the Animations list box.

6. When you've finished making your choices in the Font dialog box, click the OK button to close the dialog box and apply your changes to the selected text or current word.

Setting a New Default Font

To set a new default font for all documents based on the current template, make all your choices on the Font and Character Spacing pages (you probably won't want to set any Text Effects options as defaults) of the Font dialog box, then click the Default button (on any page). Word will display the message box shown in Figure 5.2 to confirm that you want to change the default font. Click the Yes button to make the change.

FIGURE 5.2
To set a new default font for all documents based on the current template, click the Default button in the Font dialog box, and then click the Yes button in this message box.

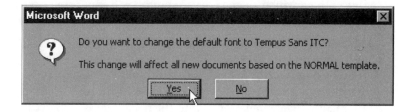

Character Formatting Using the Formatting Toolbar

The Formatting toolbar, shown in Figure 5.3, offers a quick way to apply some of the most-used character formatting options: font, font size, bold, italic, underline, highlighting, and font color.

FIGURE 5.3
The Formatting toolbar provides a quick way to apply formatting to your documents.

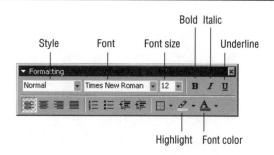

To change fonts with the Formatting toolbar, select the text you want to affect, then click the drop-down list button on the Font box and select the new font from the list that appears:

- The fonts you've used most recently will appear at the top of the list, with an alphabetical listing of all the fonts underneath.
- To move quickly down the list of fonts, type the first letter of the font's name.

To change the font size, select the text to change, then click the drop-down list button on the Font Size box and select the font size from the list that appears. To choose a font size that Word doesn't list, type it in the Font Size box and press Enter.

 TIP To change the font or font size of just one word, you don't need to select it—just placing the insertion point within the word does the trick.

To apply bold, italic, or underline, select the text you want to emphasize, then click the Bold, Italic, or Underline button on the Formatting toolbar. When you've applied one of these attributes, the relevant button will appear to be pushed in.

To remove bold, italic, or underline, select the emphasized text, then click the Bold, Italic, or Underline button again to remove the formatting.

To apply highlighting to one instance of text, select the text, then click the Highlight button. To apply highlighting to several instances of text easily, click the Highlight button before selecting any text. Your mouse pointer will take on a little highlighter pen when moved into the document window. Click and drag this pen over text to highlight it.

To turn off the highlighting, click the Highlight button again or press the Esc key. To change the color of the highlighting from its default fluorescent yellow, click the drop-down list arrow next to the Highlight button and choose another color from the list. To remove highlighting, click and drag the highlighter pen over the highlighted text.

To change the font color of the current selection or current word, click the Font Color drop-down palette button and choose the color you want from the palette. You can then apply that color quickly to selected text by clicking the Font Color button.

Character Formatting Using Keyboard Shortcuts

Word offers the following keyboard shortcuts for formatting text with the keyboard. For all of them, select the text you want to affect first, unless you want to affect only the word in which the insertion point is currently resting.

Action	Keyboard Shortcut
Increase font size (in steps)	Ctrl+Shift+.
Decrease font size (in steps)	Ctrl+Shift+,
Increase font size by 1 point	Ctrl+]
Decrease font size by 1 point	Ctrl+[
Change case (cycle)	Shift+F3
All capitals	Ctrl+Shift+A
Small capitals	Ctrl+Shift+K
Bold	Ctrl+B
Underline	Ctrl+U
Underline (single words)	Ctrl+Shift+W
Double-underline	Ctrl+Shift+D
Hidden text	Ctrl+Shift+H
Italic	Ctrl+I
Subscript	Ctrl+=
Superscript	Ctrl+Shift+= (i.e., Ctrl++)
Remove formatting	Ctrl+Shift+Z
Change to Symbol font	Ctrl+Shift+Q

Paragraph Formatting

With paragraph formatting, you can set a number of parameters that influence how your paragraphs look: alignment, indentation, line spacing, text flow, and tabs. The following sections of this chapter discuss each of these paragraph-formatting options.

Setting Alignment

Word provides the standard four kinds of paragraph alignment: left-aligned (the default and normal alignment), centered, right-aligned (aligned with the right margin), and justified (aligned with both the left margin and the right margin). Alignment is also called *justification*.

There are several ways to set paragraph alignment: You can align a new paragraph quickly in Print Layout view by using the alignment buttons on the Formatting toolbar, the keyboard shortcuts, or the options in the Paragraph dialog box. Using the buttons on the Formatting toolbar is the easiest way of aligning existing text.

Aligning New Text by Using Click and Type

If you need to quickly align a new paragraph you're adding to a page, your best bet is to use the Click and Type feature, which you learned about in Chapter 4. Double-click to place the insertion point where you want it in blank space on the page, and Word handles the intervening paragraphs, any necessary tabs, and the alignment automatically.

Setting Alignment Using the Formatting Toolbar

To set alignment using the Formatting toolbar:

1. Place the insertion point in the paragraph that you want to align. To align more than one paragraph, select all the paragraphs you want to align.

2. Click the Align Left, Center, Align Right, or Justify button on the Formatting toolbar (see Figure 5.4).

FIGURE 5.4
To align the current paragraph or selected text quickly, click the appropriate button on the Formatting toolbar.

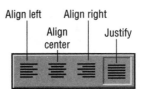

Setting Alignment Using Keyboard Shortcuts

When you're typing, the quickest way to set the alignment of paragraphs is by using these keyboard shortcuts:

Shortcut	Effect
Ctrl+L	Align left
Ctrl+E	Center
Ctrl+R	Align right
Ctrl+J	Justify

Setting Alignment Using the Paragraph Dialog Box

The third way to set alignment is to use the Paragraph dialog box. Using the Paragraph dialog box is usually slower than the other ways of setting alignment, but when you're making other formatting changes in the Paragraph dialog box, you may want to set alignment there too.

To set alignment using the Paragraph dialog box:

1. Place the insertion point in the paragraph you want to align. To align several paragraphs, select all the paragraphs you want to align.

2. Right-click and choose Paragraph from the context menu, or choose Format ➢ Paragraph, to display the Paragraph dialog box (see Figure 5.5).

FIGURE 5.5
In the Paragraph dialog box, you can set many paragraph-formatting options, including alignment.

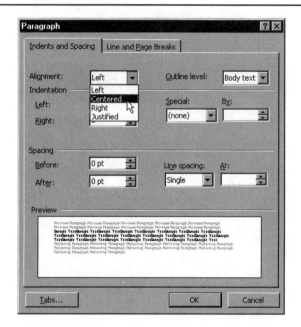

3. On the Indents And Spacing page, choose the alignment you want from the Alignment drop-down list.

4. Click the OK button to close the Paragraph dialog box.

Setting Indents

As with setting alignment, you can set indents in more than one way. Again, the quickest way is with the ruler, but you can also use the Paragraph dialog box and keyboard shortcuts.

Before you get into setting indents, you need to know a little about how Word handles them. Briefly, the size of the page you're working with is set via the Page Setup dialog box, which I'll discuss in the section titled "Page Setup" later in this chapter. For most documents, Word starts you off with an 8 1/2-inch × 11-inch page—standard letter-sized paper. You can then set top, bottom, left, and right margins for the page. Again,

Word starts you off with default margins, but you can set your own margins whenever you want (I'll discuss this in "Page Setup" too). Any indents you set are relative to the margins, not to the edges of the page. You can set both positive indents (in from the margin) and negative indents (out from the margin).

Setting Indents with the Ruler

To set indents using the ruler, click and drag the indent markers on it (see Figure 5.6).

- The first-line indent marker (the downward-pointing arrow) specifies the indentation of the first line of the paragraph (this could be a hanging indent).

- The left indent marker (the upward-pointing arrow) specifies the position of the left indent.

 TIP To move the left indent marker and first-line indent marker together, drag the left indent marker by the square box at its base rather than by the upward-pointing mark. Dragging by the upward-pointing mark will move the left indent marker but leave the first-line indent marker where it was.

- The right indent marker specifies the position of the right indent.

Setting Indents with the Paragraph Dialog Box

Depending on whether you have a graphical or literal mindset, you may find setting indents in the Paragraph dialog box easier than setting them with the ruler.

To set paragraph indents with the Paragraph dialog box:

1. Place the insertion point in the paragraph for which you want to set indents. To set indents for several paragraphs, select all the paragraphs you want to set indents for.

2. Right-click and choose Paragraph from the context menu, or choose Format ➢ Paragraph, to display the Paragraph dialog box.

3. Make sure the Indents And Spacing page is selected (if it's not visible, click its tab to bring it in front of the Line And Page Breaks page).

4. In the Left box, enter the distance to indent the paragraph from the left margin.

5. In the Right box, enter the distance to indent the paragraph from the right margin.

6. In the Special box, choose from None, First Line, and Hanging:

   - None formats the paragraph as a regular paragraph, with indents controlled solely by the Left and Right settings.

   - First Line adds an indent to the first line of the paragraph. This indent is in addition to the Left setting. For example, if you choose a Left setting of 0.5 inch and a First Line setting of 0.5 inch, the first line of the paragraph will be indented one inch. By using a first-line indent, you can avoid having to type a tab at the beginning of a paragraph.

   - Hanging makes the first line of the paragraph hang out to the left of the rest of the paragraph. (This is sometimes referred to as an *outdent*.) Hanging indents are great for bulleted or numbered paragraphs—the bullet or number hangs out to the left of the paragraph, and the wrapped lines of the paragraph align neatly with the first line.

7. Figure 5.7 illustrates the different types of indentation Word provides for paragraphs.

FIGURE 5.7
Word provides these different types of indentation for formatting paragraphs.

This paragraph is **not indented at all** and looks suitably dense as a result. If you are going to use no indentation, set extra space between paragraphs so that the reader can tell where a paragraph begins and ends.

   First-line indents save you from having to create an indent at the start of each new paragraph by pressing the Tab key or typing a few spaces. The lines that follow a first-line indent are flush left.

   - Hanging indents are most useful for bulleted lists and the like; the bullet stands clear of the text.

     To set off a quotation, you can indent it from both margins. This way, the reader's eye can easily identify it as quoted material. Common practice is to run short sections of quoted material into paragraphs (using quotation marks) but to place longer quotes self-standing, with a smaller font size.

8. If you chose a Special setting of First Line or Hanging, enter a measurement in the By box.

9. Click the OK button to close the Paragraph dialog box.

TIP When setting indents, you can use negative values for left and right indents to make the text protrude beyond the margin. Negative indents can be useful for special effects, but if you find yourself using them all the time, you probably need to adjust your margins. One other thing—for obvious reasons, you can't set a negative hanging indent, no matter how hard you try.

Setting Indents by Using Keyboard Shortcuts

Here are the keyboard shortcuts for setting indents:

Indent from the left	Ctrl+M
Remove indent from the left	Ctrl+Shift+M
Create (or increase) a hanging indent	Ctrl+T
Reduce (or remove) a hanging indent	Ctrl+Shift+T
Remove paragraph formatting	Ctrl+Q

Choosing Measurement Units

You may have noticed that the measurement units (inches, centimeters, etc.) in the Paragraph dialog box on your computer are different from those in the screens shown here—for example, you might be seeing measurements in centimeters or picas rather than in inches. If you're using Word's Web features (which you'll learn about in Chapter 24), you may even be seeing measurements in pixels (abbreviated *px*). A pixel is one of the tiny glowing phosphors that goes to make up a monitor screen.

If so, don't worry. Word lets you work in any of four measurements: inches, centimeters, points, and picas. Points and picas—$1/72$ of an inch and $1/6$ of an inch, respectively—are most useful for page layout and typesetting, but if you're not doing those, you might want to switch between inches and centimeters.

To change your measurement units:

1. Choose Tools ➤ Options to display the Options dialog box.

2. Click the General tab to bring the General page of the dialog box to the front.

3. Choose Inches, Centimeters, Millimeters, Points, or Picas as your measurement unit from the Measurement Units drop-down list.

4. Click the OK button to close the Options dialog box.

Setting Line Spacing

In most documents, Word starts you off with single-spaced lines, with only enough spacing between the lines to prevent the descenders on characters on one line from touching the ascenders on characters in the next line. You can change the line spacing of all or part of a document by using either the Paragraph dialog box or keyboard shortcuts:

1. Place the insertion point in the paragraph you want to adjust or select several paragraphs whose line spacing you want to change. To select the whole document quickly, choose Edit ➤ Select All, or hold down the Ctrl key and click once in the selection bar at the left edge of the Word window. Alternatively, press Ctrl+5 (that's the 5 on the numeric keypad, not the 5 above the letters R and T).

2. Right-click in the selection and choose Paragraph from the context menu, or choose Format ➤ Paragraph, to display the Paragraph dialog box (shown in Figure 5.5 earlier in this chapter).

3. If the Indents And Spacing page isn't at the front of the Paragraph dialog box, click its tab to bring it to the front.

4. Use the Line Spacing drop-down list to choose the line spacing you want. The list below shows your options:

Line Spacing	Effect
Single	Single spacing, based on the point size of the font.
1.5 lines	Line-and-a-half spacing, based on the point size of the font.
Double	Double spacing, based on the point size of the font.
At least	Sets a minimum spacing for the lines, measured in points. This can be useful for including fonts of different sizes in a paragraph or for including inline graphics. If you use fonts larger than the At Least size, Word will increase the line spacing to accommodate the tallest character.
Exactly	Sets the exact spacing for the lines, measured in points.
Multiple	Multiple line spacing, set by the number in the At box to the right of the Line Spacing drop-down list. For example, to use triple line spacing, enter **3** in the At box; to use quadruple line spacing, enter **4**.

5. If you chose At Least, Exactly, or Multiple from the Line Spacing drop-down list, adjust the setting in the At box if necessary.

6. Click the OK button to apply the line spacing setting to the chosen text.

 TIP To set line spacing with the keyboard, press Ctrl+1 to single-space the selected paragraphs, Ctrl+5 to set 1.5-line spacing, and Ctrl+2 to double-space paragraphs.

Setting Spacing Before and After Paragraphs

As well as setting the line spacing within any paragraph, you can adjust the amount of space before and after any paragraph to position it more effectively on the page. So instead of using two blank lines (that is, two extra paragraphs with no text) before a heading and one blank line afterward, you can adjust the paragraph spacing to give the heading plenty of space without using any blank lines.

 TIP The easiest way to set consistent spacing before and after paragraphs of a particular type is to use Word's *styles*, which you'll learn about in the next chapter.

To set the spacing before and after a paragraph:

1. Place the insertion point in the paragraph whose spacing you want to adjust, or select several paragraphs to adjust their spacing all at once.

2. Right-click and choose Paragraph from the context menu, or choose Format ➢ Paragraph, to display the Paragraph dialog box (shown in Figure 5.5, earlier in the chapter).

3. Make sure the Indents And Spacing page is foremost. If it isn't, click its tab to bring this page to the front.

4. In the Spacing box, choose a Before setting to specify the number of points of space before the selected paragraph. Watch the Preview box for the approximate effect this change will have.

5. Choose an After setting to specify the number of points of space after the current paragraph. Again, watch the Preview box.

 NOTE The Before setting for a paragraph adds to the After setting for the preceding paragraph; it does not change the After setting. For example, if the previous paragraph has an After setting of 12 points and you specify a Before setting of 12 points for the current paragraph, you'll end up with 24 points of space between the two paragraphs (in addition to whatever line spacing you've set).

6. Click the OK button to close the Paragraph dialog box and apply the changes.

TIP To quickly add or remove one line worth of space before a paragraph, select the paragraph or place the cursor within it and press Ctrl+0 (Ctrl+zero).

Using the Text Flow Options

Word offers six options for controlling how your text flows from page to page in the document. To select these options, click in the paragraph you want to apply them to or select a number of paragraphs. Then choose Format ➤ Paragraph to display the Paragraph dialog box, click the Line And Page Breaks tab to bring the Line And Page Breaks page to the front of the dialog box (unless it's already at the front), and select the options you want to use. Figure 5.8 shows the Line And Page Breaks page of the Paragraph dialog box.

FIGURE 5.8
You can set text flow options on the Line And Page Breaks page of the Paragraph dialog box.

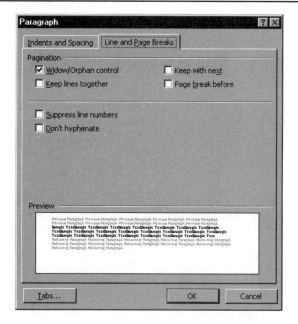

The list below shows the options available in the Line And Page Breaks dialog box:

Widow/Orphan Control	A *widow* (in typesetting parlance) is when the last line of a paragraph appears by itself at the top of a page; an *orphan* is when the first line of a paragraph appears by itself at the foot of a page. Leave the Widow/Orphan Control box selected to have Word rearrange your documents to avoid widows and orphans.
Keep Lines Together	Tells Word to prevent the paragraph from breaking over a page. If the whole paragraph will not fit on the current page, Word moves it to the next page. If you write long paragraphs, choosing the Keep Lines Together option can produce painfully short pages.
Keep With Next	Tells Word to prevent a page break from occurring between the selected paragraph and the next paragraph. This option can be useful for making sure that a heading appears on the same page as the paragraph of text following it or that an illustration appears together with its caption—but be careful not to set Keep With Next for body text paragraphs or other paragraphs that will need to flow normally from page to page.
Page Break Before	Tells Word to force a page break before the current paragraph. This is useful for making sure that, for example, each section of a report starts on a new page.
Suppress Line Numbers	Tells Word to turn off line numbers for the current paragraph. This applies only if you are using line numbering in your document.
Don't Hyphenate	Tells Word to skip the current paragraph when applying automatic hyphenation.

When you've chosen the options you want, click the OK button to apply them to the paragraph or paragraphs.

Setting Tabs

To align the text in your documents, Word provides five kinds of tabs: left-aligned; centered; right-aligned; decimal-aligned; and bar, which produces a vertical line at the tab's position.

Setting Tabs Using the Ruler

The quickest way to set tabs for the current paragraph, or for a few paragraphs, is to use the ruler. If the ruler isn't visible, choose View ➤ Ruler to display it, or simply pop it up by sliding the mouse pointer onto the gray bar at the top of the screen once you've selected the paragraphs you want to work on.

To add a tab:

1. Display the ruler if necessary.
2. Place the insertion point in a single paragraph or select the paragraphs to which you want to add the tab.
3. Choose the type of tab you want by clicking the tab selector button shown here at the left end of the ruler to cycle through left tab, center tab, right tab, and decimal tab.
4. Click on the ruler in the location where you want to add the tab. The tab mark will appear in the ruler, as shown in Figure 5.9.

FIGURE 5.9
Click in the ruler where you want to place a new tab.

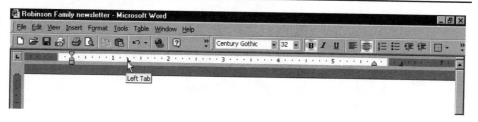

 TIP When adding a tab, you can click with either the left or the right mouse button. For moving or removing a tab, only the left button works.

To move a tab, display the ruler if necessary, then click the tab marker and drag it to where you want it.

To remove a tab, display the ruler if it's not visible, then click the marker for the tab you want to remove and drag it into the document. The tab marker will disappear from the ruler.

Setting Tabs Using the Tabs Dialog Box

When you need to check exactly where the tabs are in a paragraph, or if you set too many tabs in the ruler and get confused, you can turn to the Tabs dialog box to clear everything up.

First, place the insertion point in a single paragraph or select the paragraphs whose tabs you want to change. Then choose Format ➢ Tabs to display the Tabs dialog box, shown in Figure 5.10, and follow the procedures described in the next sections.

FIGURE 5.10

The Tabs dialog box gives you fine control over the placement and types of tabs in your document.

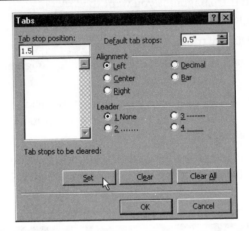

TIP To quickly display the Tabs dialog box, double-click on an existing tab in the bottom half of the ruler. (If you double-click in any open space in the bottom half of the ruler, the first click will place a new tab for you; if you double-click in the top half of the ruler, Word will display the Page Setup dialog box.) You can also get to the Tabs dialog box quickly by clicking the Tabs button on either panel of the Paragraph dialog box.

To set different spacing for default tabs, adjust the setting in the Default Tab Stops box at the top of the Tabs dialog box. For example, a setting of 1 inch will produce tabs at 1 inch, 2 inch, 3 inch, and so on.

To set tabs:

1. Enter a position in the Tab Stop Position box.

   • If you're using the default unit of measurement set for Word, you don't need to specify the units.

   • If you want to use another unit of measurement, specify it—for example, **2.3"**, **11 cm**, **22 pi**, **128 pt**, or **66px**.

2. Specify the tab alignment in the Alignment box: Left, Center, Right, Decimal, or Bar. (Bar inserts a vertical bar—|—at the tab stop.)

3. In the Leader area, you can specify a tab leader—periods, hyphens, or underlines leading up to the tabbed text. (Periods are often used as tab leaders for tables of

contents, between the heading and the page number.) Choose the None option button to remove leaders from a tab.

4. Click the Set button.

5. Repeat steps 1 through 4 to specify more tabs if necessary.

6. Click the OK button to close the Tabs dialog box and apply the tabs you set.

To clear a tab, select it in the Tab Stop Position list and click the Clear button. Word will list the tab you chose in the Tab Stops To Be Cleared area of the Tabs dialog box. Choose other tabs to clear if necessary, then click the OK button.

To clear all tabs, simply click the Clear All button, then click the OK button.

To move tabs using the Tabs dialog box, you need to clear them from their current position and then set them elsewhere—you can't move them as such. (To move tabs easily, use the ruler method described earlier in this chapter.)

Language Formatting

You can format text as being written in a language other than English. Applying this formatting doesn't change the text (if it's in English, it will still be in English; if it's Greek, it will still be Greek), but it does change the language that Word believes the text to be in.

Once you've applied language formatting, you can not only spell-check text written in other languages, but you can use the Find feature to search for text formatted in those languages for quick reference.

To format selected text as another language:

1. Choose Tools ➤ Language ➤ Set Language to display the Language dialog box, shown in Figure 5.11.

FIGURE 5.11
In the Language dialog box, choose the language in which to format the selected text, then click OK.

2. In the Mark Selected Text As list box, choose the language in which to format the text.

   • Selecting the Do Not Check Spelling Or Grammar check box tells Word not to use the spell-checker and other proofing tools on the selected text. This can be useful for one-off technical terms that you don't want to add to your custom dictionaries. But if you find the spell-checker suddenly fails to catch blatant spelling errors, check to see whether the Do Not Check Spelling Or Grammar check box is selected for the text in question.

3. Click the OK button to apply the language formatting to the selected text.

WARNING If Word does not have the dictionary files installed for a language that you have formatted text as, it will display a warning message box when you run a spelling check on the text. After checking other text formatted as languages whose dictionaries it does have, Word will then tell you that the spelling check is complete. This can be deceptive, because it will not have checked the text for whose language it does not have the dictionary.

Page Setup

If you're ever going to print a document, you need to tell Word how it should appear on the page. You can change the margins, paper size, layout of the paper, and even which printer tray the paper comes from.

NOTE The best time to set paper size is at the beginning of a project. While you can change it at any time during a project without trouble, having the right size (and orientation) of paper from the start will help you lay out your material.

To alter the page setup, double-click in the top half of the horizontal ruler (or anywhere in the vertical ruler) or choose File ➤ Page Setup to display the Page Setup dialog box, then follow the instructions for setting margins, paper size, and paper orientation in the next sections. If you want to change the page setup for only one section of a document, place the insertion point in the section you want to change before displaying the Page Setup dialog box. Alternatively, you can choose This Point Forward from the Apply To drop-down list on any tab of the Page Setup dialog box to change the page setup for the rest of the document.

Setting Margins

To set the margins for your document, click the Margins tab in the Page Setup dialog box to display the Margins page, shown in Figure 5.12. In the boxes for Top, Bottom, Left, and Right margins, use the spinner arrows to enter the measurement you want for each margin; alternatively, type in a measurement.

FIGURE 5.12
Set margins for your documents on the Margins page of the Page Setup dialog box.

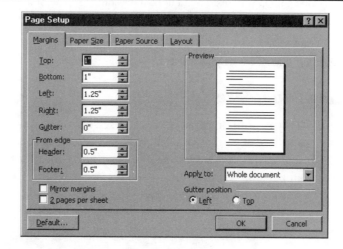

If you're typesetting documents (rather than simply using the word processor to put them together), you may want to select the Mirror Margins check box. This makes the two inner-margin measurements the same and the two outer-margin measurements the same. It also changes the Left and Right settings in the column under Margins in the Page Setup dialog box to Inside and Outside, respectively. (If you're having trouble visualizing the effect that mirror margins produce, try opening a few books on your bookshelf and looking to see whether the margins will mirror each other when the book is closed. This book doesn't use mirror margins, but many others do.)

To print two pages per sheet of paper, select the 2 Pages Per Sheet check box. This is especially useful with the Landscape paper orientation (discussed in the section later in this chapter titled "Setting Paper Orientation") for creating folded booklets on standard letter-sized paper. When you select 2 Pages Per Sheet, the Mirror Margins check box becomes dimmed and unavailable.

The *gutter measurement* is the space that your document will have on the inside of each facing page. For example, if you're working with mirror-margin facing pages, you could choose to have a gutter measurement of 1 inch and inside and outside margins of 1.25 inches. That way, your documents would appear with a 1.25-inch left margin on left-hand pages, a 1.25-right margin on right-hand pages, and a 2.25-inch margin on the inside of each page (the gutter plus the margin setting). The two Gutter Position option buttons (Left and Top) control where Word positions the gutter margin on your pages. The default position of the gutter margin is left, but you can change the gutter margin to the top by selecting the Top option button. When Top is selected, the Mirror Margins and 2 Pages Per Sheet check boxes are dimmed and unavailable.

 TIP Use gutters for documents you're planning to bind. That way, you can be sure that you won't end up with text bound unreadably into the spine of the book.

The Preview box in the Page Setup dialog box gives you an idea of how your document will look when you print it.

Setting Paper Size

Word lets you print on paper of various sizes, offering a Custom option to allow you to set a paper size of your own, in addition to various standard paper and envelope sizes.

To change the size of the paper you're printing on, click the Paper Size tab of the Page Setup dialog box to display the Paper Size page, shown in Figure 5.13.

FIGURE 5.13

Use the Paper Size page of the Page Setup dialog box to change the size of the paper you're printing on.

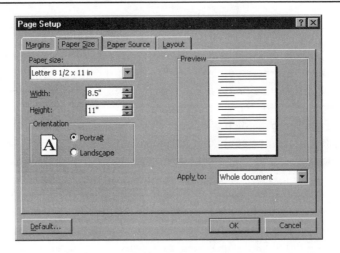

In the Paper Size drop-down list box, choose the size of paper you'll be working with (for example, Letter 8 $^1/_2$ × 11 in). If you can't find the width and height of paper you want, use the Width and Height boxes to set the width and height of the paper you're using; Word will automatically set the Paper Size box to Custom Size.

Setting Paper Orientation

To change the orientation of the page you're working on, click the Paper Size tab of the Page Setup dialog box and choose Portrait or Landscape in the Orientation group box. (Portrait is taller than it is wide; Landscape is wider than it is tall.)

Borders and Shading

If a part of your document—whether it be text, a graphic, or an entire page—needs a little more emphasis, you can select it and add borders and shading by using either the Tables And Borders toolbar or the Borders And Shading dialog box. In general, the Tables And Borders toolbar is easier to use, because you can immediately see the effects it's producing.

Adding Borders and Shading Using the Tables And Borders Toolbar

To display the Tables And Borders toolbar, right-click the menu bar or any displayed toolbar and choose Tables And Borders from the context menu. Figure 5.14 shows the Tables And Borders toolbar with the buttons related to borders and shading identified.

FIGURE 5.14
Use the border-related buttons on the Tables And Borders toolbar to apply borders.

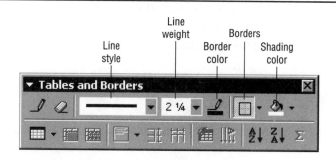

First, choose the style of border you want to apply:

- Click the Line Style button and choose a suitable style of line from the drop-down list: single, dotted, dashed, dotted-and-dashed, multiple lines, and so on.

- Click the Line Weight button and choose a suitable weight from the drop-down list.

- Click the Border Color button and choose a color from the palette of available colors. The Automatic choice applies the default color of border for the font color of the text or object selected. To see more colors, click the More Line Colors button to display the Colors dialog box, select a color on either the Standard page or the Custom page, and click the OK button to apply it.

Next, apply the border:

- To apply the current style of border to the current selection, click the Border button.
- To apply a different style of border, click the drop-down list button and choose a type of border from the Border palette. If you're not clear which style of border one of the buttons on the palette represents, hover the mouse pointer over it to display the ScreenTip for the button.
- To remove the border from the current selection, click the No Border button on the border palette.

Then apply shading if you want to:

- To apply the current shading color to the selection, click the Shading Color button.
- To change the current shading color, click the drop-down list button and choose a color from the palette. To see more fill colors, click the More Fill Colors button to display the Colors dialog box, select a color on either the Standard page or the Custom page, and click the OK button to apply it.
- To remove shading from the current selection, click the No Fill button on the Shading Color palette.

Adding Borders and Shading Using the Borders And Shading Dialog Box

For more control over the borders and shading you apply, use the Borders And Shading dialog box:

1. Select the text or objects to which you want to apply borders or shading and choose Format ➢ Borders And Shading to display the Borders And Shading dialog box, shown in Figure 5.15.

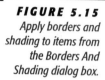

FIGURE 5.15

Apply borders and shading to items from the Borders And Shading dialog box.

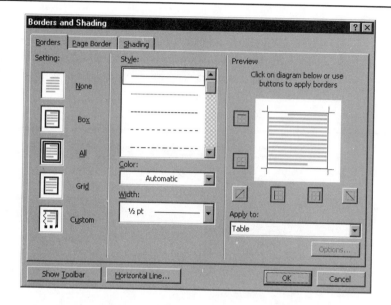

2. On the Borders page, choose the type of border you want to add from the options displayed:

   - In the Setting area, choose one of the settings: None, Box, Shadow (for some items only), Grid (for tables and cells), 3-D (not available for tables and cells), All (for some items only), or Custom. Watch the effect in the Preview box.

   - Next, choose the type of line you want from the Style list, choose a color from the Color drop-down list, and choose a weight from the Width drop-down list. To change one of the lines, click the appropriate icon in the Preview area to apply it or remove it.

   - For text, you can choose Text or Paragraph from the Apply To drop-down list below the Preview area. If you apply the border to a paragraph, you can specify the distance of the border from the text by clicking the Options button and specifying Top, Bottom, Left, and Right settings in the Border And Shading Options dialog box. Then click the OK button.

3. On the Page Border page (shown in Figure 5.16), choose the type of border you want to add to the page. The controls on this page work in the same way as

those described in step 2. The important difference is that the Apply To drop-down list allows you to choose between the Whole Document, This Section, This Section—First Page Only, and This Section—and All Except First Page. Again, clicking the Options button displays the Border And Shading Options dialog box, which allows you to place the border precisely on the page. The Art drop-down list provides decorative page borders suitable for cards, notices, and the like.

FIGURE 5.16
Choose the type of border you want on the Page Border page of the Borders And Shading dialog box.

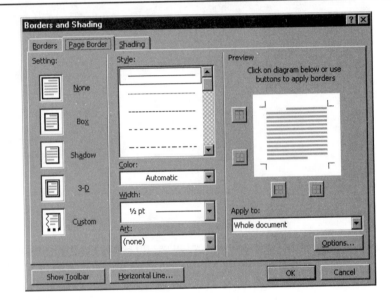

4. On the Shading page (shown in Figure 5.17), choose the type of shading to add:

   - Choose the color for the shading from the Fill palette.

   - Choose a style and color for the pattern in the Style and Color drop-down list boxes in the Patterns area.

   - Finally, use the Apply To list to specify whether to apply the shading to the paragraph or just to selected text.

 WARNING Go easy with shading on printed documents, especially if you're using a monochrome printer. Any shading over 20 percent will completely mask text on most black-and-white printouts (even if it looks wonderfully artistic on screen). For Web documents, you can be a little more liberal with shading, but be careful not to make the pages difficult to read.

FIGURE 5.17
Choose shading as appropriate on the Shading page of the Borders And Shading dialog box.

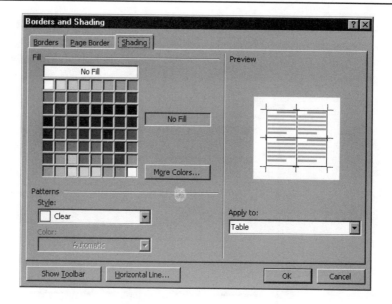

5. Click OK to close the Borders And Shading dialog box and apply your changes to the selection.

Removing Borders and Shading

To remove borders and shading, select the item, then choose Format ➢ Borders And Shading to display the Borders And Shading dialog box. Then:

- To remove a border, choose None in the Setting area on the Borders page.
- To remove a page border, choose None in the Setting area on the Page Border page.
- To remove shading, choose No Fill in the Fill palette and Clear from the Style drop-down list on the Shading page.
- Click OK to close the Borders And Shading dialog box.

Inserting Decorative Horizontal Lines

To insert a decorative horizontal line in a document:

1. Choose Format ➢ Borders And Shading to display the Borders And Shading dialog box.
2. Click the Horizontal Lines button on any one of the three pages. Word will close the Borders And Shading dialog box and display the Horizontal Line dialog box (see Figure 5.18).

FIGURE 5.18
Use the Horizontal Line dialog box to apply a horizontal line to a page.

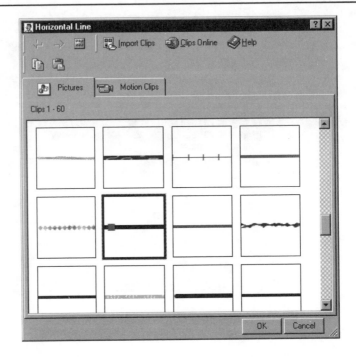

3. On the Pictures page, click to select the style of line you want.

4. Either click the Insert Clip button on the context menu that appears when you click the style of line, or click the OK button to insert the line and close the Horizontal Line dialog box.

Figure 5.19 shows a horizontal line inserted in a document.

FIGURE 5.19
Horizontal lines can add spice to your documents.

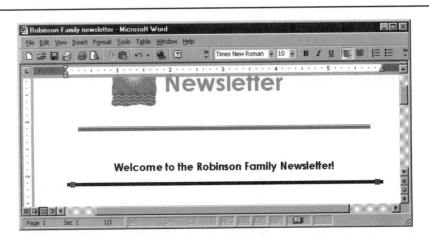

CHAPTER **6**

Using Styles and Advanced Formatting

In this chapter, you'll learn about the more complex formatting options that Word provides for making your documents look as you want them to. I'll start by discussing styles, which draw together the different types of formatting that you learned about in the previous chapter. Styles are a powerful tool for applying complex, frequently used formatting. From there, you'll see how you can use sections to apply substantially different formatting to different parts of the same document. After that, I'll show you how to use two key automation features: Word's automatic bullets and numbering for creating quick lists, and the AutoCorrect feature, which enables you to correct misspellings automatically and expand designated abbreviations.

Style Formatting

Word's *paragraph styles* bring together all the formatting elements discussed in Chapter 5—character formatting, paragraph formatting (including alignment), tabs, language formatting, and borders and shading. Each style contains complete formatting information that you can apply with a click of the mouse or a single keystroke.

 NOTE Word also offers *character styles*, which are similar to paragraph styles but contain only character formatting. Character styles are suitable for picking out elements in a paragraph formatted with paragraph styles.

Using styles not only gives your documents a consistent look—every Heading 1 paragraph will appear in the same font and font size, with the same amount of space before and after it, and so on—but also saves you a great deal of time in formatting your documents.

You can either use Word's built-in styles (which are different in Word's various predefined templates, and in the templates that Works provides) or create your own styles. Every paragraph in Word uses a style. Word starts you off in the Normal style unless the template you're using dictates otherwise.

Applying Styles

To apply a style, place the insertion point in the paragraph or select a number of paragraphs, then click the Style drop-down list button on the Formatting toolbar and choose the style you want from the list, as shown in Figure 6.1.

FIGURE 6.1

The easiest way to apply a style is to use the Style drop-down list on the Formatting toolbar.

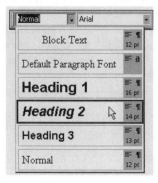

 TIP Some of the most popular styles have keyboard shortcuts: Ctrl+Shift+N for Normal style; Ctrl+Alt+1 for Heading 1, Ctrl+Alt+2 for Heading 2, Ctrl+Alt+3 for Heading 3; and Ctrl+Shift+L for List Bullet style.

You can also apply a style by choosing Format ➤ Style to display the Style dialog box (see Figure 6.2), choosing the style in the Styles list box, and clicking the Apply button.

FIGURE 6.2

To apply a style, choose it in the Styles list box and click the Apply button.

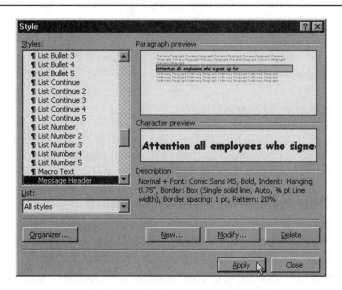

TIP If you have many styles defined or a slow computer (or both), the style list may be slow to appear the first time you summon it for any given document. To speed this up, you can make Word display styles in a standard font. Choose Tools ➢ Customize to display the Customize dialog box, click the Options tab to display the Options page, clear the List Font Names In Their Font check box, and click the OK button. This also speeds up the display of the Font drop-down menu.

To see which style paragraphs are in, you can display the *style area*, a vertical bar at the left side of the Word window that displays the style name for each paragraph, as shown in Figure 6.3. You can display the style area in Normal view and Outline view, but not in Web Layout view, Print Layout view, or Print Preview.

FIGURE 6.3
The style area at the left side of the Word window displays the name of the style in use for each paragraph.

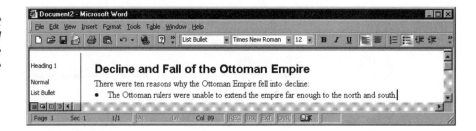

To display the style area, choose Tools ➢ Options to display the Options dialog box and click the View tab to bring the View page to the front. Enter a measurement in the Style Area Width box in the Window area and then click the OK button.

To alter the width of the style area once you've displayed it, click and drag the dividing line. To remove it, drag the dividing line all the way to the left of the Word window.

Creating a New Style

As you can see in the Styles list box shown in Figure 6.2, Word's templates come with a number of built-in styles. If they're not enough for you, you can create your own styles in three ways: by example, by definition, or by having Word do all the work for you.

Creating a New Style by Example

The easiest way to create a style is to set up a paragraph of text with the exact formatting you want for the style—character formatting, paragraph formatting, borders and shading, bullets or numbers, and so on. Then click the Style drop-down list, type the name for the new style in the text box that displays the current style's name (as shown in Figure 6.4, which shows me creating a style named *Dramatic* based on the selected paragraph), and press Enter. Word will create the style, which you can immediately select from the Style drop-down list and apply to other paragraphs as necessary.

Creating a New Style by Definition

The more complex way of creating a style is by definition:

1. Choose Format ➢ Style to display the Style dialog box.

2. Click the New button. Word will display the New Style dialog box (see Figure 6.5).

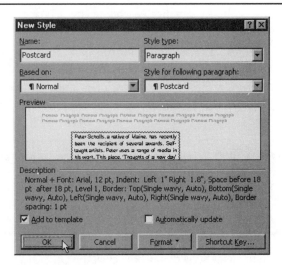

3. Specify the information for your new style:

  • In the Name box, enter a name for the style. Word will accept style names over 100 characters, but you'll do better to keep them short enough to fit in the Style box on the Formatting toolbar. If your style name is over 20 characters long, you should probably rethink your naming conventions.

- From the Based On drop-down list, choose the style on which you want to base the new style. Bear in mind that if you change the base style later, the new style will change too. The Preview box will show what the Based On style looks like.

- In the Style Type box, choose whether you want a paragraph style or a character style.

- In the Style For Following Paragraph box (which is not available for character styles), choose the style that you want Word to apply to the paragraph immediately after this style. For example, after the Heading 1 style, you might want Body Text, or after Figure, you might want Caption. But for many styles, you'll want to continue with the style itself.

4. To adjust the formatting of the style, click the Format button and choose Font, Paragraph, Tabs, Border, Language, Frame, or Numbering from the drop-down list. This will display the dialog box for that type of formatting. When you've finished, click the OK button to return to the New Style dialog box.

5. Repeat step 4 as necessary, selecting other formatting characteristics for the style.

6. Select the Add To Template check box to add the new style to the template.

7. Select the Automatically Update check box if you want Word to automatically update the style when you change it. (I'll discuss this option more in a minute.)

8. To set up a shortcut key for the style, click the Shortcut Key button. Word will display the Customize Keyboard dialog box. With the insertion point in the Press New Shortcut Key box, press the shortcut key combination you'd like to set, click the Assign button, then click the Close button.

 WARNING Watch the Currently Assigned To area of the Customize Keyboard dialog box (which you'll see after typing in the combination) when selecting your shortcut key combination. If Word already has assigned that key combination to a command, macro, or style, it will display its name there. If you choose to assign the key combination to the new style, the old assignment for that combination will be deactivated.

9. In the New Style dialog box, click the OK button to return to the Style dialog box.

10. To create another new style, repeat steps 2 through 9.

11. To close the Style dialog box, click the Apply button to apply the new style to the current paragraph or current selection, or click the Close button to save the new style without applying it.

Having Word Create Styles Automatically

Creating styles yourself can get tedious—why not have Word create them for you? And when you change the formatting of a paragraph that has a certain style, you can have Word update the style for you, so that every other paragraph that has the same style takes on that formatting too.

To have Word automatically create styles for you:

1. Choose Tools ➢ AutoCorrect to display the AutoCorrect dialog box.

2. Click the AutoFormat As You Type tab to display its page.

3. In the Automatically As You Type area at the bottom of the page, select the Define Styles Based On Your Formatting check box. (This is selected by default.)

4. Click the OK button to close the AutoCorrect dialog box.

Once you've set this option (or if it was set already), Word will attempt to identify styles you're creating and will supply names for them. For example, if you start a new document (with paragraphs in the Normal style, as usual) and bold and center the first paragraph, Word may define that bolding and centering as a Title style; if you simply increase the font size, Word may define that paragraph as Heading 1 instead. This sounds unsettling but works surprisingly well—and if it doesn't suit you, you can easily turn it off by clearing the Define Styles Based On Your Formatting check box.

Modifying a Style

You can modify a style by example and by definition. You can also choose to have Word automatically identify and apply changes you make to the style.

Modifying a Style by Example

To modify a style by example, change the formatting of a paragraph that currently has the style assigned to it, then choose the same style again from the Style drop-down list. Word will display the Modify Style dialog box, shown in Figure 6.6. Make sure the Update The Style To Reflect Recent Changes option button is selected, then click the OK button to update the style to include the changes you just made to it. If you want Word to automatically update the style without displaying this dialog box when you make changes in the future, select the Automatically Update The Style From Now On check box first.

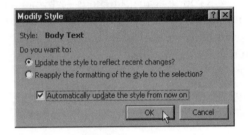

Modifying a Style by Definition

Modifying a Word style by definition is similar to creating a new style, except that you work in the Modify Style dialog box, which offers one fewer option than the New Style dialog box offers (you don't get to choose whether the style is a paragraph style or a character style because Word already knows which it is).

Open the Style dialog box by choosing Format ➤ Style, then choose the style you want to work on from the Styles list. (If you can't see the style you're looking for, make sure the List box at the bottom-left corner of the Style dialog box is showing All Styles rather than Styles In Use or User-Defined Styles.)

Click the Modify button. Word will display the Modify Style dialog box. From there, follow steps 3 through 9 in the section titled "Creating a New Style by Definition" (except for selecting the style type) to modify the style and step 11 to exit the Style dialog box.

Removing a Style

Removing a style is much faster than creating one. Simply open the Style dialog box by choosing Format ➤ Style, select the style to delete in the Styles list, and click the Delete button. Word will display a message box asking you to confirm that you want to delete the style; click the Yes button.

You can then delete another style in the same way, or click the Close button to leave the Style dialog box.

TIP Keep in mind that you can't delete a Heading style once you've started using it. Also, when you delete a style that's in use (other than a Heading style), Word applies the Normal style to those paragraphs. (If you do this by mistake, choose Edit ➤ Undo Style to make Word both restore the style to the list of available styles and reapply it to the paragraphs it was previously applied to.)

Styles and Templates

A template is a special type of document on which you can base other documents. In fact, every document you create in Word is based on a template. If you do not specify a particular template when you create a new document, Word bases the document on a default template called the Normal template, which in essence creates a blank document. If you need to, you can subsequently attach a different template to the document; I'll describe how to do this in the next section.

When you create a document, it inherits the styles in the template. You can subsequently create new styles in the document itself or in the template.

Each template has a built-in set of styles. You can modify these styles or create new styles, as described in the preceding sections. You can also copy styles from one template to another, as described in the next section.

Changing the Template a Document Is Based On

To change the template attached to a document:

1. Choose Tools ➤ Templates And Add-Ins to display the Templates And Add-Ins dialog box (see Figure 6.7). The template currently attached to the document appears in the Document Template text box.

FIGURE 6.7

The Templates And Add-Ins dialog box displays the name of the template currently attached to the document. To attach a different template to the document, click the Attach button. Word will display the Attach Template dialog box.

2. Click the Attach button to display the Attach Template dialog box.

3. Select the template you want to attach to the document. (You may need to navigate to a different location to find the template.)

4. Click the Open button. Word will close the Attach Template dialog box, returning you to the Templates And Add-Ins dialog box.

5. If you want the document to take on the styles contained in the new template, select the Automatically Update Document Styles check box. (This is usually a good idea.)

6. Click the OK button to close the Templates And Add-Ins dialog box.

Copying Styles from One Document or Template to Another

To copy styles from one document or template to another:

1. Choose Tools ➤ Templates And Add-Ins to display the Templates And Add-Ins dialog box.

2. Click the Organizer button to display the Organizer dialog box (see Figure 6.8).

FIGURE 6.8
Use the Organizer dialog box to copy styles from one template to another.

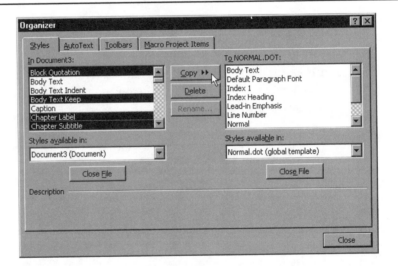

3. If the Styles page of the Organizer dialog box isn't displayed, click its tab to display it.

4. Open the document or template from which you want to copy the styles in one of the two list boxes and the document or template to which you want to copy the styles in the other list box. (It doesn't matter which is in the left-hand list box and which is in the right-hand list box.)

• The left-hand list box at first displays the active document, and the right-hand list box displays the Normal template. If the active document is attached to a template other than the Normal template, you can select it in the Styles Available In drop-down list.

• To close the document or template currently open in a list box, click the corresponding Close File button. The Close File button will become an Open File button.

- To open a document or template, click the Open button. Word will display the Open dialog box. Navigate to the document or template and open it.

5. In one list box, select the styles you want to copy. Use Shift+click to select multiple contiguous styles, or Ctrl+click to select multiple noncontiguous styles.

6. Click the Copy button to copy the styles to the other template.

7. When you've finished copying styles, click the Close button to close the Organizer dialog box:

   - If you've made changes to a template that currently does not have a document open, or a document that was not open, Word will prompt you to save the changes to the template or document.

   - If you've made changes to a template that is attached to an open document, Word will prompt you to save the changes the next time you save the document.

   - If you've made changes to a document that is open, Word will save those changes the next time you save the document.

Using Themes

Word provides a large number of themes that you can apply to your documents to give them a particular look. A *theme* is essentially a design scheme and color scheme for a document. A theme typically consists of a background color or background graphic; horizontal lines or other design elements; and fonts, colors, and sizes for regular items such as heading styles, body text styles, and bullets. Some themes have different colors for hyperlinks and table borders as well. When you apply a theme to a document, Word applies these colors, fonts, and graphics to the document, changing (and perhaps unifying) its look.

As you may have noticed from the previous description, themes have a certain amount of overlap with templates in that they affect the look of the document you apply them to. Themes are different from templates in that templates can contain customized toolbars, menus, and keyboard shortcuts. Furthermore, templates can contain default text and AutoText entries, while themes cannot.

Usually, the best way to work with themes is to start a document based on a particular template and then apply a suitable theme to the document to achieve a certain look. By using a consistent theme, you can provide a degree of unity among documents that are based on different templates. As you might imagine, themes are especially useful for Web pages.

To apply a theme to a document:

1. Choose Format ➢ Theme to display the Theme dialog box (see Figure 6.9).

FIGURE 6.9
Use the Theme dialog box to apply a theme (a unified look) to a document.

2. Select a theme in the Choose A Theme list box. The Sample Of Theme box will display a preview of how the theme will look.

NOTE Many themes are not installed in Works Suite's default installation of Word. When you choose a theme in the Choose A Theme list box that is not installed, Word will display a message in the preview area telling you this and providing an Install button that you can click to install the theme.

3. Below the Choose A Theme list box, select options for the theme. Watch the preview as you try these options:

• The Vivid Colors check box applies higher-contrast colors to the theme. This check box is cleared by default.

• The Active Graphics check box controls whether the theme displays any animated graphics it contains when viewed with a Web browser.

• The Background Image check box controls whether the theme uses its background image for this document.

4. Click the OK button to apply the theme to the document.

To change the theme of a document, repeat the above procedure and choose a different theme.

To remove a theme from a document, choose Format ➤ Theme, select the (No Theme) option at the top of the Choose A Theme list box, and click the OK button.

Using the Style Gallery

Word provides the Style Gallery to give you a quick overview of its many templates and the myriad styles they contain. To open the Style Gallery, choose Format ➤ Theme to display the Theme dialog box, then click the Style Gallery button. Word will display the Style Gallery dialog box, shown in Figure 6.10.

FIGURE 6.10
The Style Gallery dialog box gives you a quick view of the styles in Word's templates.

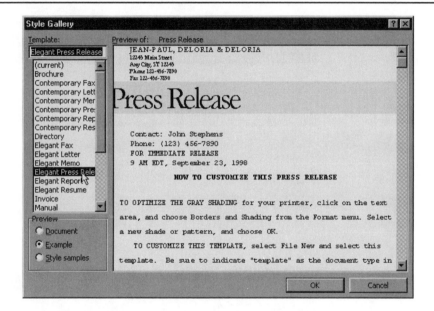

To preview a template in the Preview Of box, select it in the Template list box. Then choose the preview you want in the Preview box:

- Document shows you how your current document looks with the template's styles applied.
- Example shows you a sample document that uses the template's styles.
- Style Samples shows each of the styles in the document.

NOTE   If the template you select in the Template list box is not yet installed on your computer, Word will prompt you to install it by clicking the OK button in the Style Gallery dialog box.

To apply the template you've chosen to your document, click the OK button.

Section Formatting

Often you'll want to create documents that use different page layouts, or even different sizes of paper, for different pages. Word handles this by letting you divide documents into *sections*, each of which can have different formatting characteristics. For example, you could use sections to set up a document to contain both a letter and an envelope, or to have one-column text and then multi-column text, and so on. The top part of Figure 6.11 shows an envelope and the beginning of a letter in Normal view, in which you get to see the section break between the two. The bottom part of Figure 6.11 shows the same envelope and letter in Page Layout view, showing the different layouts that they have.

FIGURE 6.11

Word uses sections to implement different page layouts, or different sizes of paper, for different pages.

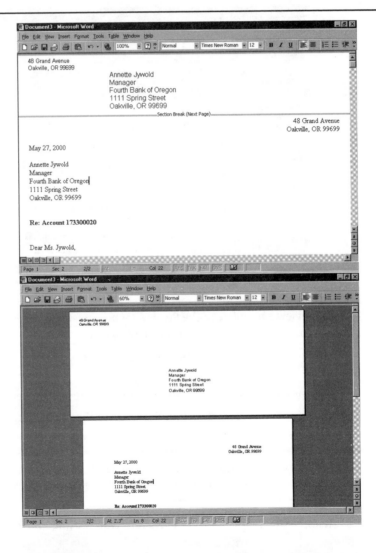

Creating a Section

To create a section:

1. Place the insertion point where you want the new section to start.

2. Choose Insert ➤ Break. Word will display the Break dialog box, shown in Figure 6.12.

3. Choose the type of section break to insert by clicking an option button in the Section Break Types area:

    • Next Page starts the section on a new page. Use this when you have a drastic change in formatting between sections—for example, an envelope on one page and a letter on the next.

    • Continuous starts the section on the same page as the preceding paragraph. This is useful for creating layouts with differing numbers of columns on the same page.

    • Even Page starts the section on a new even page.

    • Odd Page starts the section on a new odd page. This is useful for chapters or sections that should start on a right-hand page for consistency.

4. Click the OK button to insert the section break. It will appear in Normal view and Outline view as a double dotted line across the page containing the words *Section Break* and the type of section break, as you saw in the upper part of Figure 6.11.

The Sec indicator on the status bar will indicate which section the insertion point is currently in.

TIP If you need to try a different type of section break (for example, Next Page instead of Continuous), you can change the type of section break on the Layout page of the Page Setup dialog box: Place the insertion point in the relevant section, then choose File ➢ Page Setup, select the type of section you want from the Section Start drop-down list on the Layout page, and click the OK button. The advantage of changing the break rather than deleting it and then creating a new break of a different type is that changing the break does not affect the formatting of the section, while deleting the break does (as I'll explain next).

Deleting a Section

To delete a section break, place the insertion point at its beginning (or select the section break) and press the Delete key.

 WARNING When you delete a section break, the section before the break will take on the formatting characteristics of the section after the break.

Automatic Bullets and Numbering

In this section, you'll learn about the options Word offers for adding automatic bullets and numbering to your documents.

The bullets and numbering that Word applies automatically are paragraph formatting rather than individual characters on the page. In other words, once you've added a bullet to a list, you can't just select the bullet and delete it as you might delete a character—you have to remove it from the paragraph's formatting. I'll discuss this process later in the section titled "Removing Bullets and Numbering."

Adding Bullets and Numbering

You can add straightforward bullets and numbering to existing text by using the buttons on the Formatting toolbar.

 To add bullets, first select the paragraphs you want to add bullets to and then click the Bullets button on the Formatting toolbar. Word will add the bullets and apply a hanging indent to each of the paragraphs but leave the paragraphs in their current style.

 TIP To continue a numbered or bulleted list, press Enter at the end of the list. To discontinue the list, press Enter twice at the end of the list.

To add numbers, select the paragraphs you want to number and then click the Numbering button on the Formatting toolbar.

For a variety of styles of bullets and numbering, select the paragraphs you want to apply them to, then either right-click in the selection and choose Bullets And Numbering from the context menu or choose Format ➢ Bullets And Numbering to open the Bullets And Numbering dialog box (see Figure 6.13).

FIGURE 6.13
The Bullets And Numbering dialog box gives you plenty of choices for bulleting and numbering your lists.

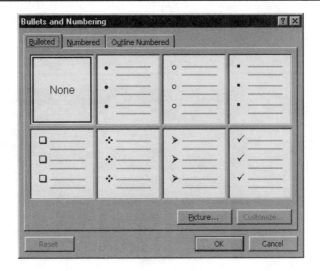

Choose the page that corresponds to the type of list you want to create: Bulleted, Numbered, or Outline Numbered, then click the style that suits you best. Click the OK button to apply the bullets or numbering and close the Bullets And Numbering dialog box.

Removing Bullets and Numbering

To remove bullets or numbering from selected paragraphs, either click the Bullets button or the Numbering button, or choose Format ➢ Bullets And Numbering to display the Bullets And Numbering dialog box. Select the None option and click the OK button.

Modifying the Bullets and Numbering Styles

If you find the choices offered in the Bullets And Numbering dialog box inadequate for your needs, you can create your own bullets or numbers to adorn your text.

To create your own styles of bullets and numbering:

1. Select the paragraphs to which you want to add bullets or numbers (or both).

2. Right-click and select Bullets And Numbering from the context menu, or choose Format ≻ Bullets And Numbering, to display the Bullets And Numbering dialog box.

3. Select the appropriate page and the format that suits you best, then click the Customize button. Word will display the Customize Bulleted List dialog box, the Customize Numbered List dialog box, or the Customize Outline Numbered List dialog box as appropriate. Figure 6.14 shows the Customize Bulleted List dialog box, and the steps that follow discuss the options available in this dialog box. The Customize Numbered List dialog box and Customize Outline Numbered List dialog box look a little different, but the options work in similar ways.

FIGURE 6.14
In the Customize Bulleted List dialog box, you can choose almost any bullet character that your computer can produce.

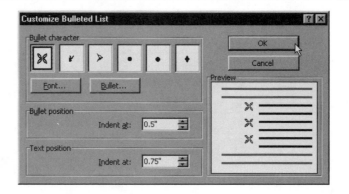

4. In the Bullet Character group box, choose from one of the six bullets displayed, or click the Bullet button to open the Symbol dialog box, choose a character, and click OK to return to the Customize Bulleted List dialog box. Then click the Font button to display the Font dialog box and choose a suitable font, font size, and other formatting for the bullet. Click the OK button to close the Font dialog box and return to the Customize Bulleted List dialog box.

5. In the Bullet Position group box, use the Indent At measurement to specify any indent the bullet should receive.

6. In the Text Position group box, use the Indent At measurement to specify the indent of the text. Usually, you'll want this to be more than the indent for the bullet.

7. Click the OK button to apply the formatting to your list.

NOTE You can also customize a bulleted list by using pictures for bullets. To do so, click the Picture button in the Bullets And Numbering dialog box to display the Picture Bullet dialog box. On the Pictures page, select the type of bullet you want to use, then click the OK button to apply the bullet to the current selection.

AutoCorrect

AutoCorrect offers five features that help you quickly enter your text in the right format. Every time you finish typing a word and press the spacebar, press Enter, press Tab, or type any form of punctuation (comma, period, semicolon, colon, quotation marks, exclamation point, question mark, or even a % sign), Word checks it to see whether it needs AutoCorrect action and, if it does, corrects it appropriately.

The first four of AutoCorrect's features are straightforward; the fifth is a little more complex:

- Correct TWo INitial CApitals stops you from typing an extra capital at the beginning of a word. If you need to type technical terms that need two initial capitals, clear the check box to turn off this option or create AutoCorrect exceptions for them. You'll learn about exceptions later in this chapter.

 TIP If you type three initial capitals in a word, Word will not try to correct the second and third, figuring you're typing an acronym of some sort. (It will still query the spelling of the word if it doesn't recognize it.)

- Capitalize First Letter Of Sentences does just that. If you and Word disagree about what constitutes a sentence, turn off this option by clearing the check box. For example, if you start a new paragraph without ending the one before it with a period, Word will not capitalize the first word. On the other hand, if you want to create a sentence fragment that shouldn't start with a capital but that comes after a period, you're out of luck—Word will capitalize the first word.

- Capitalize Names Of Days does just that.

- Correct Accidental Usage Of cAPS lOCK key is a neat feature that works most of the time. If Word thinks you've got the Caps Lock key down and you don't know it, it will turn Caps Lock off and change the offending text from upper to lower case and vice versa. Word usually decides that Caps Lock is stuck when you start a new sentence with a lowercase letter and continue with uppercase letters; however, the end of the previous sentence may remain in the wrong case.

- Replace Text As You Type is the best of the AutoCorrect features. You'll learn about it in detail in the next section.

Replace Text As You Type

The AutoCorrect Replace Text As You Type feature keeps a list of AutoCorrect entries. Each time you finish typing a word, AutoCorrect scans this list for that word. If the word is on the list, Word substitutes the replacement text for the word. AutoCorrect keeps a separate list of entries for each language that you use in your document via language formatting (Tools ➤ Language ➤ Set Language). When you display the AutoCorrect dialog box, it identifies itself by the current language: **AutoCorrect: English (U.S.)**, **AutoCorrect: French**, and so on.

Replace Text As You Type is a great way of fixing typos you make regularly, and Word comes with a decent list of AutoCorrect entries already configured—if you type *awya* instead of *away* or *disatisfied* instead of *dissatisfied*, Word will automatically fix the typo for you. But AutoCorrect is even more useful for setting up abbreviations for words or phrases that you use frequently, saving you not only time and keystrokes but also the effort of memorizing complex spellings or details. For example, suppose you write frequently to your bank manager demanding an explanation of charges to your account: You could set up one AutoCorrect entry containing the address and salutation, another containing your account details, a third containing your ritual complaint, and a fourth containing your name and signature. You would have the bulk of the letter written in a fourfold flurry of keystrokes. (You could also use a template to achieve a similar savings of time.)

You can add AutoCorrect entries to Word's list in two ways—either automatically while running a spelling check, or manually at any time.

Adding AutoCorrect Entries while Spell-Checking

Adding AutoCorrect entries while spell-checking a document is a great way to teach Word the typos you make regularly. When the spell-checker finds a word it doesn't like, make sure the appropriate replacement word is highlighted in the Suggestions box; if the word selected in the Suggestions box isn't the appropriate one, type in the right word. Then click the AutoCorrect button in the Spelling dialog box. Word will add the word from the Not In Dictionary box to the Replace list in AutoCorrect and the word selected in the Suggestions box to the With list in AutoCorrect. This way, you can build an AutoCorrect list tailored precisely to your typing idiosyncrasies.

You can also add AutoCorrect entries during on-the-fly spell-checks by choosing AutoCorrect from the context menu and selecting the word to map the current typo to in the submenu that appears. Figure 6.15 illustrates adding an AutoCorrect entry on the fly.

FIGURE 6.15
You can add an AutoCorrect entry while spell-checking a word.

Adding AutoCorrect Entries Manually

Adding AutoCorrect entries while spell-checking is great for building a list of your personal typos in Word, but it's of little use for setting up AutoCorrect with abbreviations that will increase your typing speed dramatically. For that, you need to add AutoCorrect entries manually.

To add AutoCorrect entries manually:

1. If the replacement text for the AutoCorrect entry is in the current document, select it.

 TIP To create an AutoCorrect entry that contains formatting—bold, italic, paragraph marks, tabs, and so on—or a graphic, you need to select the formatted text (or the graphic) in a document before opening the AutoCorrect dialog box.

2. Choose Tools ➢ AutoCorrect to display the AutoCorrect dialog box, shown in Figure 6.16.

FIGURE 6.16
You can add AutoCorrect entries manually in the AutoCorrect dialog box.

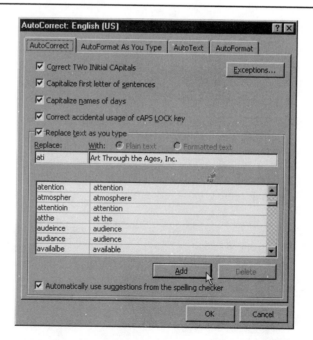

3. Make sure that the Replace Text As You Type check box is selected.
4. Enter the typo or abbreviation to replace in the Replace box.

TIP When choosing the Replace text for an abbreviated AutoCorrect entry, avoid using a regular word that you might type in a document and not want to have replaced. Try reducing the word or phrase to an abbreviation that you'll remember—for example, omit all the vowels and include only the salient consonants.

5. Enter the replacement text in the With box.

   • If you selected text before opening the AutoCorrect dialog box, that text will appear in the With box. If the text needs to retain its formatting, make sure the Formatted Text option button has been selected. (The Formatted Text option button also needs to be selected if your selection contains a paragraph mark or tab—that counts as formatting.)

6. Click the Add button or press Enter to add the AutoCorrect entry to the list.

   • If Word already has an AutoCorrect entry stored for that Replace text, you'll see a Replace button instead of the Add button. When you press Enter or click this button, Word will display a confirmation dialog box to make sure that you want to replace the current AutoCorrect entry.

7. To add another AutoCorrect entry, repeat steps 3 through 6.

8. To close the AutoCorrect dialog box, click the Close button.

Getting Creative with AutoCorrect Entries: Including Graphics

You can include inline graphics, text boxes, borders, and so on in AutoCorrect entries. (In the next chapter, you'll learn how to incorporate graphics into Word documents.) For example, you can easily include your company's logo in an AutoCorrect entry for the company address for letterhead:

1. Enter the text of your company's address and format it as appropriate.

2. Position the insertion point where you want the graphic to appear in the Auto-Correct entry text.

3. Choose Insert ➤ Picture ➤ Clip Art to display the Microsoft Clip Gallery application.

4. Make sure the Pictures page is displayed. (If it isn't, click its tab to display it.)

5. Select one of the categories in the list box to display its contents.

Continued ▶

6. Click the picture you want, then choose the Insert Clip item (the top item) from the context menu to insert the picture in the document at the insertion point.

7. Resize the picture if necessary, crop it, or add a border to it.

8. Select the text and the picture of the address.

9. Choose Tools ➤ AutoCorrect. Word will display the AutoCorrect dialog box with the selected text and picture in the With text box. It will select the Formatted Text option button, because the picture counts as formatting.

10. Enter the abbreviation for the address and picture in the Replace text box.

11. Click the Add button to add the AutoCorrect entry.

12. Click the OK button to close the AutoCorrect dialog box.

Now you can enter the address and its picture in a document by typing the text of the abbreviation and then pressing a punctuation key. Be imaginative like this, and Auto-Correct can save you plenty of time in your work, a few seconds at a time.

The Automatically Use Suggestions From The Spelling Checker check box controls whether AutoCorrect includes suggestions from the spell-checker in the list of words it provides when you right-click a misspelled word and choose AutoCorrect from the context menu.

Deleting AutoCorrect Entries

To delete an AutoCorrect entry, choose Tools ➤ AutoCorrect to open the AutoCorrect dialog box, and select the entry from the scroll list at the bottom of the dialog box. (You can type the first few letters of an entry's Replace designation in the Replace box to scroll to it quickly.) Then click the Delete button.

You can then either delete further AutoCorrect entries or click the OK button to close the AutoCorrect dialog box.

Using AutoCorrect Exceptions

If you've already managed to think up a couple of things that could cause problems with AutoCorrect, hold up a moment: AutoCorrect has an Exceptions feature that you can use to prevent specific items from triggering AutoCorrect corrections.

On the AutoCorrect page of the AutoCorrect dialog box, click the Exceptions button to display the AutoCorrect Exceptions dialog box, shown in Figure 6.17.

When Word doesn't recognize an abbreviation, it will think the period that denotes the abbreviation is the end of a sentence instead. On the First Letter page, you can prevent this from happening by adding to the list of abbreviations any abbreviation that Word does not recognize. Simply type the word in the Don't Capitalize After text box and click the Add button.

FIGURE 6.17
In the AutoCorrect Exceptions box, you can set exceptions to prevent specific terms you use from being corrected automatically.

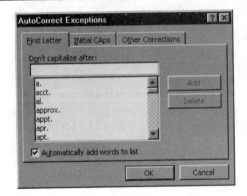

When the Automatically Add Words To List check box at the bottom of the First Letter page is selected, Word will automatically add first-letter exceptions to the list when you use Backspace to undo AutoCorrect's correction of them. For example, say you're writing about syntax and you need to use the abbreviation *prep.* for *preposition.* If you type *prep. used*, AutoCorrect will change *used* to *Used* because it thinks the period ends a sentence. But if you now use Backspace to delete *Used* and then type in *used* to replace it, Word will create a first-letter exception for *prep.*

To delete a first-letter exception, select it in the Don't Capitalize After list box and click the Delete button.

On the INitial CAps page, you can create exceptions for those rare terms that need two initial capitals (for example, IPng, the next-generation Internet Protocol). Enter the text in the Don't Correct text box, then click the Add button.

To delete an initial-cap exception, select it in the Don't Correct list box and click the Delete button.

When the Automatically Add Words To List check box at the bottom of the INitial CAps page is selected, Word will automatically add two–initial-cap words to the list when you use Backspace to undo AutoCorrect's correction of them and then retype them. For example, if you're writing about the next-generation Internet protocol and you type *IPng* and a space, AutoCorrect will change *IPng* to *Ipng.* But if you press Backspace four times (once for the space, once for the *g*, once for the *n*, and once for the *p*, leaving the *I* there) and then type *Png* and a space, Word will create a two–initial-cap exception for *IPng* and will cease and desist from lowercasing the second letter.

On the Other Corrections page, you can create exceptions for other words. Type the word in the Don't Correct text box, then click the Add button. To delete an entry, select it in the list box and click the Delete button.

When the Automatically Add Words To List check box on the Other Corrections page is selected, Word will automatically add other words to the list when you correct AutoCorrect's correction of them by backspacing over the correction and retyping the word.

CHAPTER <u>7</u>

Using Graphical Elements and Text Boxes

In this chapter, you'll learn how to use graphical elements and text boxes in your documents. Graphical elements include pictures and videos (as you might imagine), and AutoShapes, which are graphical objects that you create using Word's drawing tools.

A text box is a box that you can place anywhere you choose on a page, rather than being constrained by the margin settings for the page. Despite their name, text boxes can contain not only text but also graphics and other objects.

Along the way, I'll discuss how to work with the Clip Gallery, Microsoft's repository of clip art, sound clips, and video clips.

Inserting, Sizing, and Positioning Graphical Objects

You can easily insert graphical objects of various types into Word documents. Once you've inserted them, you can resize them, move them, and crop them as necessary. In this section, I'll discuss graphical objects using pictures as the examples, but the techniques apply to other graphical objects (such as shapes and video clips) as well. The inserting and positioning skills even apply to sound clips, which you can also insert in your documents and position where you need them to appear.

Inserting a Picture

To insert a picture at the insertion point:

1. Choose Insert ➢ Picture to display the Picture submenu.

2. Choose from the six options for inserting a picture: Clip Art, From File, AutoShapes, WordArt, From Scanner Or Camera, or Chart. The process is a little different for each of the options. In this example, choose Clip Art, because it's the one you're most likely to want to use first; it demonstrates the Microsoft Clip Gallery and also shows some of the other items you may want to insert in your documents. Word starts the Microsoft Clip Gallery application, which manifests itself as the Insert ClipArt window (see Figure 7.1).

3. On the Pictures page, select the category of clip you want to insert in the document. Scroll down to see categories of clips beyond those that fit in the dialog box. In this example, choose Animals. The Pictures page will change to show the clips available in that category (see Figure 7.2). Again, scroll to see more clips than those that initially appear in the window.

FIGURE 7.1
In the Insert ClipArt window, choose the category of clip you want to insert.

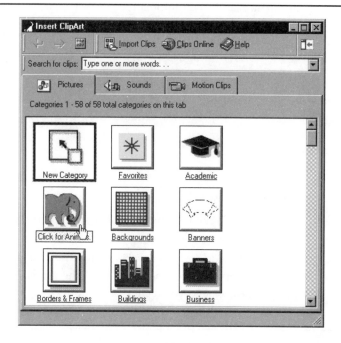

FIGURE 7.2
Next, choose the clip you're interested in.

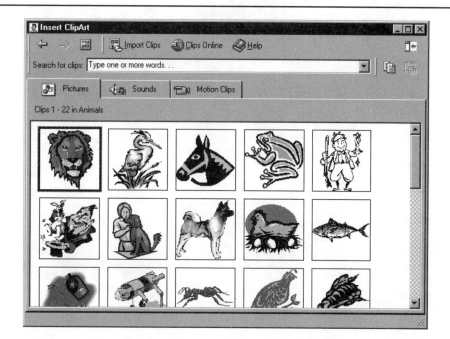

4. Select the clip you want to use. You can then choose from the following options on the menu that the clip automatically displays when you click it (see Figure 7.3):

FIGURE 7.3

Use the clip's automatic menu to tell Word what you want to do with the clip.

- Click the Insert Clip button (the top button) to insert the clip in the document.
- Click the Preview Clip button (the second button) to display a preview window that shows an enlarged version of the clip.
- Click the Add Clip To Favorites Or Other Category button to display a pop-out panel with a drop-down list of the categories, as shown in Figure 7.4. Select the category and click the OK button.

FIGURE 7.4

You can add the clip to your list of Favorites, or to another category, by clicking the third button on the Add Clip To Favorites Or Other Category pop-out panel.

- Click the Find Similar Clips button to display a pop-out panel (see Figure 7.5) that you can use to search for best-matching clips or for clips with keywords associated with the current clip's keywords.

FIGURE 7.5

Click the Find Similar Clips button and use the pop-up panel to search for clips associated with the same keywords as the current clip.

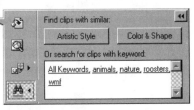

TIP Use the Back and Forward buttons at the top of the Insert ClipArt window to move backward and forward as you navigate through the categories of clips and the clips themselves. Click the All Categories button to return to the topmost level of categories (the categories you see when you initially display the Insert ClipArt dialog box).

5. Insert further clips as necessary. Then click the Close button to close the Insert ClipArt application, or click in the Word window to continue working in Word while leaving the Insert ClipArt application running so that you can insert further pictures or objects easily.

Resizing and Cropping a Picture

To resize a picture quickly, first click it to select it. Word will display the Picture toolbar (shown in Figure 7.6) and an outline around the picture with eight handles, one at each corner and one in the middle of each side. Drag a corner handle to resize the image proportionally; drag a side handle to resize the image only in that dimension (horizontally or vertically).

FIGURE 7.6
The Picture toolbar contains buttons for manipulating pictures quickly.

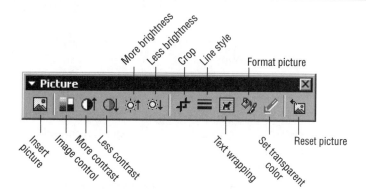

To crop a picture quickly (cutting off part of it), click the picture to select it, then click the Crop button to select the cropping tool. The mouse pointer will change into cropping handles. Move the mouse pointer over one of the picture's handles, then drag inward or outward to crop the picture.

To resize or crop a picture more precisely:

1. Click the picture to display the outline and handles around it.

2. Click the Format Picture button, double-click the picture, right-click and choose Format Picture from the context menu, or choose Format ➢ Picture. Word will display the Format Picture dialog box (see Figure 7.7).

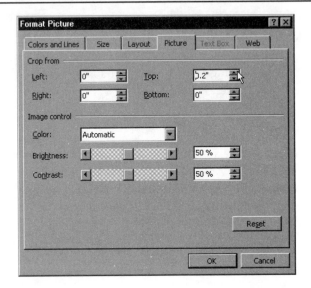

3. To crop a picture, make sure the Picture page is displayed (click its tab if it isn't). Enter the amount you want to crop in the Left, Right, Top, and Bottom boxes in the Crop From area.

4. To resize the picture, click the Size tab to display the Size page. Then either set Width and Height percentages in the Scale area, or enter the desired width and height, such as 1.46" by 1.74", in the Width and Height boxes in the Size And Rotate area.

 TIP The Lock Aspect Ratio check box in the Scale area of the Size page controls whether the Height and Width boxes act in concert or independently.

5. Click the OK button to close the Format Picture dialog box and apply your changes.

To reset a picture to its original size, click the Reset button on the Size page of the Format Picture dialog box. To reset a picture to its original coloring, click the Reset button on the Picture page of the Format Picture dialog box. To reset a picture to both its original size and its original coloring, click the Reset button on the Picture toolbar.

Positioning a Picture

Once you've inserted a picture, you can position it exactly where you want it to appear. To position a picture effectively, you need to understand how pictures (and other objects) can be positioned in relation to the text on the page.

The text in a Word document is contained in the main layer of the document, the *text layer*. You can place pictures in the text layer, either inline with the text (as if they were just another character) or with the text wrapping around them. For greater freedom of placement, you can also place pictures behind the text layer (so that any text that occupies the same space appears superimposed on the picture) or in front of the text layer, where the picture will block out anything that is positioned behind it.

Each graphical object that is not inline in a Word document is secured by an *anchor*, which represents the point in the text to which the object is attached (as shown in Figure 7.8). Anchors are normally hidden, but you can display them by choosing Tools ➢ Options, displaying the View page of the Options dialog box, and selecting the Object Anchors check box in the Print And Web Layout Options area.

FIGURE 7.8
Word displays an anchor symbol to indicate the point in the text to which a graphical object is attached.

To position a picture, click it to select it, then click the Text Wrapping button on the Picture toolbar to display the menu of wrapping choices. Figure 7.9 shows this menu. Select the appropriate choice: Square (with text around it), Tight (with text tight around it), Behind Text, In Front Of Text, Top And Bottom (no text alongside the picture), or Through (text fills in white space in the picture). Then click the picture and drag it vertically to where you want it to appear in the document.

FIGURE 7.9
*Use the Text Wrapping
button on the Picture
toolbar to specify text
wrapping for a picture.*

To change the wrapping and horizontal alignment of a picture:

1. Right-click the picture and choose Format Picture from the context menu, or select the picture and click the Format Picture button on the Picture toolbar, to display the Format Picture dialog box.

2. Click the Layout tab to display the Layout page (see Figure 7.10).

FIGURE 7.10
*Use the Layout page of
the Format Picture
dialog box to set
layout and horizontal
alignment for a picture.*

3. In the Wrapping Style area, choose the wrapping option for the picture.

4. In the Horizontal Alignment area, select the horizontal alignment for the picture: Left, Center, Right, or Other.

5. For more alignment options, click the Advanced button to display the Advanced Layout dialog box (see Figure 7.11).

FIGURE 7.11
Use the Advanced Layout dialog box to specify advanced alignment options for a picture.

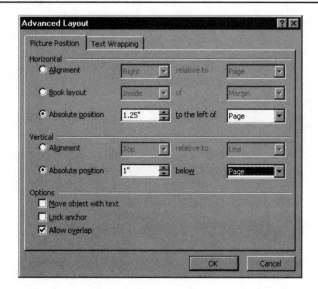

• On the Picture Position page, you can specify horizontal and vertical alignment options. One of the most useful capabilities here is to specify an absolute position (horizontal, vertical, or both) for a picture relative to the page. The Move Object With Text check box controls whether the picture can move along with the text to which it is anchored. The Lock Anchor check box controls whether the anchor for the picture can be moved; once you've positioned a picture carefully, you can lock the anchor to make sure no one moves the picture by accident. The Allow Overlap check box controls whether the picture can be overlapped by other pictures.

• On the Text Wrapping page, select a wrapping style in the Wrapping Styles area. In the Wrap Text area, select how to wrap the text: Both Sides, Left Only, Right Only, or Largest Only. Finally, you can specify the distance between the picture and the text that wraps around it by entering values in the Top, Bottom, Left, and Right text boxes in the Distance From Text area. Click the OK button when you've finished.

6. Click the OK button to apply the wrapping and alignment to the picture.

Finer Movements: Nudging a Graphical Object into Place

When you need to move a graphical object only a small amount, it can be difficult to achieve the necessary precision with the mouse, particularly if you've had too much coffee. Word provides a Nudge tool for moving an object a little at a time.

The easiest way to nudge an object is with the keyboard. Select the object, then press the appropriate arrow key to move the object just a fraction.

You can also nudge a graphical object with the mouse, but the process is a little more protracted. Select the object, then choose Draw ➢ Nudge from the Drawing toolbar to display the Nudge submenu. Choose the direction in which to nudge the object (Up, Down, Left, or Right).

Importing Clips into the Clip Gallery

You can add to the clips in the Clip Gallery by either downloading clips from the Microsoft Web site or by importing clips stored elsewhere (for example, on a local hard drive or on a network).

Downloading Clips Online

To download clips from the Microsoft Web site:

1. Choose Insert ➢ Picture ➢ Clip Art to display the Insert ClipArt application window (if it isn't already displayed).

2. Click the Clips Online button. The Clip Gallery will display the Connect To Web For More ClipArt, Photos, Sounds dialog box.

3. Select the Don't Show This Message Again check box to suppress future appearances of this dialog box, then click the OK button. The Clip Gallery will start your default browser (Internet Explorer, unless you've designated a different default browser), fire up your Internet connection, and display the Microsoft Clip Gallery Live Site. Read the End User License agreement, and click the Accept button if you agree to be bound by its terms.

4. Navigate to the category of clips you want and download the clips. The Clip Gallery will add them to its repertoire.

Importing Clips from Other Locations

To import clips into the Clip Gallery:

1. Choose Insert ➤ Picture ➤ Clip Art to display the Insert ClipArt window (if it isn't already displayed).

2. Select the tab for the page containing the type of clip you want to import. For example, if you want to import video clips, select the Motion Clips tab to display the Motion Clips page.

3. Click the Import Clips button to display the Add Clip To Clip Gallery dialog box (see Figure 7.12).

FIGURE 7.12

In the Add Clip To Clip Gallery dialog box, choose which clips to import into the Clip Gallery and how to import them.

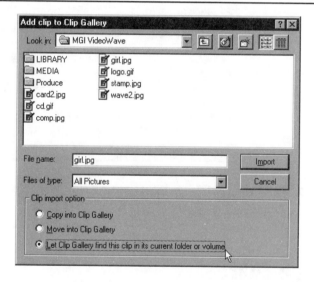

4. Navigate to the clips using the usual Windows techniques and select the clips.

5. In the Clip Import Option group box, choose how to import the clips:

   • Choose the Copy Into Clip Gallery option button (the default) to copy the clips to the Clip Gallery. It's best not to use this option if the files are on your computer's hard drive, as it will make them take up twice as much space as they need.

   • Choose the Move Into Clip Gallery option button (if it's available) to move the clips. Use this option if the clips are on your computer's hard drive and you want to manage all your clips through the Clip Gallery.

   • Choose the Let Clip Gallery Find This Clip In Its Current Folder Or Volume option button if you prefer to leave the clips where they are but let the Clip Gallery learn about their location.

6. Click the Import button to import the clips. The Clip Gallery will then display the Clip Properties dialog box (see Figure 7.13) for each clip in turn. Enter a description on the Description page, choose one or more categories on the Categories page, and select one or more keywords on the Keywords page if you want. Select the Mark All Clips With The Same Properties check box if you want to give the same properties to each of the clips you're importing. (This check box appears on each page in the dialog box when you have selected multiple clips.)

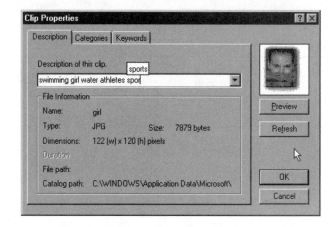

FIGURE 7.13
In the Clip Properties dialog box, add a description, choose categories, and select keywords for the clips you're importing.

7. Click the OK button to import the clip. The Clip Gallery will display the Clip Properties dialog box for the next clip (if there is one); if not, it will return you to the Insert ClipArt window, which will show the clips you imported.

Inserting a Chart

To insert a chart in a document:

1. If you have columnar text or a table from which you want to create the chart, select it. Otherwise, place the insertion point where you want the chart to appear.

2. Choose Insert ➤ Picture ➤ Chart to start the Microsoft Graph charting application. Word will add a prototype column chart to the document, together with a datasheet for entering information for the chart (see Figure 7.14). If you chose data in step 1, the datasheet and the chart will reflect your data; otherwise, they will show sample information.

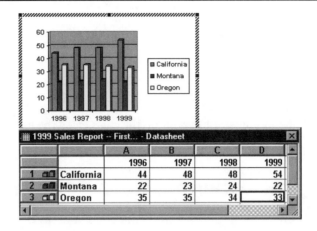

3. Enter your data in the datasheet, or adjust your data as necessary. The chart will show the data you enter in the datasheet.

4. Right-click the chart and choose Chart Type from the context menu to display the Chart Type dialog box (see Figure 7.15).

5. To create a standard type of chart, select the type of chart in the Chart Type list box on the Standard Types page, then select a suitable subtype in the Chart Sub-Type list box. To see a sample of how the chart will look with the data in your

datasheet, click the Press And Hold To View Sample button and hold the mouse button down until the sample appears in place of the chart sub-types.

6. To create a custom chart, select the Custom Types tab to display the Custom Types page. Select the chart type in the Chart Type list box.

7. If you want to create this type of chart regularly, click the Set As Default Chart button.

8. Click the OK button to apply your choice of chart type to the chart.

You can now size and position the chart using the techniques described for pictures earlier in this chapter.

Changing the Background of a Document

For most of the documents you print, you'll want to keep the default white background that Word uses in most of its templates. But for online documents and Web pages, you might want to apply a colored background or a fill effect.

You can change the background of a document by choosing Format ➤ Background and selecting a fill color from the color panel that appears. If none of the colors appeals to you, select the More Colors item to display the Colors dialog box. Select the color you want on either the Standard page or the Custom page and click the OK button to apply it.

To apply a fill effect to the background of a document, choose Format ➤ Background ➤ Fill Effects to display the Fill Effects dialog box. Select a suitable fill effect on the Gradient page, the Texture page, the Pattern page, or the Picture page, and click the OK button to apply it to the document.

 TIP One of the easiest ways of changing the background of a document is to apply a different theme to the document, as discussed in Chapter 6.

Working with the Drawing Tools

 Word provides a full set of drawing tools for creating drawing objects in your documents, annotating the documents, and so on. To access the drawing tools, display the Drawing toolbar (see Figure 7.16) by clicking the Drawing button on the Standard toolbar, or by right-clicking the menu bar or any displayed toolbar and choosing Drawing from the context menu of toolbars.

FIGURE 7.16

The Drawing toolbar provides you with the means of adding drawings, lines, and shapes to your documents.

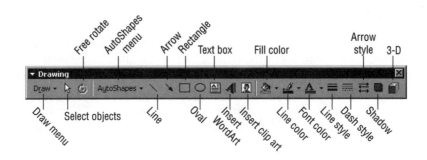

The drawing tools are largely self-explanatory. For example, to create a rectangle, you click the Rectangle button, then click where you want one corner of the rectangle to be, and drag until the rectangle is the size you want it. To change the lines of the rectangle to red, select the rectangle, click the Line Color drop-down list button, and choose the color you want from the color palette. To apply 3-D effects to the rectangle, select the rectangle, click the 3-D button, and choose a suitable effect from the drop-down panel.

That said, there are a number of techniques that are less immediately apparent:

- Click the Select Objects button, then click and drag to select multiple objects.

- Hold down Shift as you drag to constrain a rectangle to a square and an oval to a circle.

- Hold down Ctrl as you drag to center the object you create on the point at which you started to drag.

- Hold down Ctrl and Shift as you drag to create a square or a circle centered on the point at which you started to drag.

- Use the commands on the Draw ➢ Order submenu to rearrange layers of objects: Bring To Front, Send To Back, Bring Forward, Send Backward, Bring In Front Of Text, and Send Behind Text.

- Word places drawing objects according to an underlying grid that is normally invisible. You can display the grid, or adjust it, by choosing Draw ➢ Grid and selecting settings in the Drawing Grid dialog box. To adjust the grid, choose horizontal and vertical spacing in the Grid Settings area. To display the grid on screen (which makes it easier to place objects precisely but makes your documents look like graph paper), select the Display Gridlines On Screen check box and the Horizontal Every check box, and set the number of units (whose measurements are defined in the Grid Settings area) in the Horizontal Every and Vertical Every text boxes. Click the OK button to apply your choices.

Two of the more complex and useful drawing elements are AutoShapes and text boxes. I'll discuss how to use these in the upcoming sections.

Working with AutoShapes

An AutoShape is any of a number of regular or semi-regular shapes that Word provides. AutoShapes include circles, rectangles, stars, and speech balloons. As with other graphical objects, you can format AutoShapes to your heart's content. You can also add text to AutoShapes.

Inserting an AutoShape

To insert an AutoShape:

1. Click the AutoShapes button on the Drawing toolbar to display the AutoShapes drop-down menu.

2. Choose one of the categories of shapes—Lines, Basic Shapes, Block Arrows, Flowchart, Stars And Banners, or Callouts—to display a submenu of shapes, as shown in Figure 7.17.

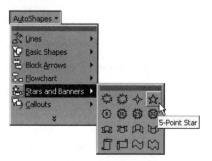

FIGURE 7.17
Choose an AutoShape from the AutoShape drop-down menu.

3. Click the shape you want. Word will change the mouse pointer to a cross and the view to Print Layout view if it is not currently in Print Layout view.

4. Click in the document at the point where you want one extreme of the AutoShape to appear, then drag to create the size of shape you want.

Now that you've inserted the AutoShape, you can format it by using the formatting options on the Drawing toolbar, as discussed earlier in this chapter.

Adding Text to an AutoShape

To add text to an AutoShape, right-click the AutoShape and choose Add Text from the context menu. Word will select the AutoShape and position the insertion point inside it. Type the text you want the AutoShape to have. You can then select the text and choose Format ➤ Font to display the Font dialog box or Format ➤ Paragraph to display the Paragraph dialog box. Then apply font or paragraph formatting as discussed in Chapter 5.

Changing an AutoShape to a Different Type

You can change an AutoShape you've created to another type of AutoShape. Click the AutoShape to select it, then choose Draw ➢ Change AutoShape from the Drawing toolbar to display the submenu of shape categories. Select the category of shape you want and then select the shape from the submenu that appears.

Inserting, Positioning, and Formatting Text Boxes

To precisely position text or a picture in a document, use a text box. A *text box* is a container that Word uses to position items (pictures, text, etc.) in an exact place on the page; you can use text boxes for positioning text such as sidebars in a newspaper layout or captions (also known as *callouts*) in an annotated figure.

You can position a text box relative to a paragraph (so that it moves with the text when the paragraph moves) or relative to the margin or page (so that it remains in place even if the paragraph moves). The advantage of positioning a text box relative to the page rather than relative to one of the margins is that you can adjust the margins without the text box moving. Text boxes are held in place by anchors.

Inserting a Text Box

To insert a text box:

1. Choose Insert ➢ Text Box. Word will change the insertion point to a large + sign and, if you are in Normal view or Outline view, will switch to Print Layout view.

2. Click and drag in the document to create a text box of the size you want, as shown in Figure 7.18. The text box will appear with a thick shaded border, and Word will display the Text Box toolbar.

Now either enter text in the text box or insert a picture in it as described earlier in this chapter.

Sizing and Positioning a Text Box

To resize a text box quickly, click in it to display the text box border and then drag one of the sizing handles.

To position a text box quickly:

1. Click inside the text box to display the text box border and handles. Make sure that you've selected the text box rather than any picture in it.

2. Move the mouse pointer onto the shaded border of the text box so that the pointer becomes a four-headed arrow attached to the normal mouse-pointer arrow.

3. Click and drag the text box to wherever you want to place it on the page. Figure 7.19 demonstrates dragging a text box and its contents.

FIGURE 7.19
*Click and drag a text
box to reposition it.*

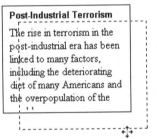

To resize and position a text box exactly:

1. Right-click the border of the text box and choose Format Text Box from the context menu to display the Format Text Box dialog box (see Figure 7.20).

2. To resize the text box, click the Size tab to display the Size page. You can then set the height and width either by entering measurements in the Height and Width boxes in the Size And Rotate area or by entering percentages in the Height and Width boxes in the Scale area. To resize the image proportionally, select the Lock Aspect Ratio check box; to resize the image differently in each dimension, clear the check box.

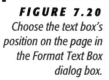

FIGURE 7.20
*Choose the text box's
position on the page in
the Format Text Box
dialog box.*

3. To reposition the text box, click the Layout tab to display the Layout page. Choose the wrapping style for the text box in the Wrapping Style area, then choose the horizontal alignment of the text box in the Horizontal Alignment area. To specify a more precise position for the text box, click the Advanced button to display the Advanced Layout dialog box. On the Picture Position page, specify the position for the text box using the techniques discussed for the Format Picture dialog box earlier in this chapter.

- To allow the text box to move when the text it is attached to moves, select the Move Object With Text check box. For example, if you position a text box relative to a paragraph, select this check box; if you position a text box relative to the page, clear this check box.

- To lock the text box to the paragraph it belongs with (so you can't move it by accident to another paragraph), select the Lock Anchor check box.

- To allow the text box to be overlapped by another text box or a graphical object, select the Allow Overlap check box.

4. Click the OK button to apply your choices to the text box.

Linking Text Boxes

If you're presenting text in a series of text boxes, you can link the text boxes together so that text flows from the end of the first to the beginning of the next. Doing so is much easier than dividing your text into separate chunks for each text box—particularly when you resize a text box so that it can contain a different amount of text.

 To create a text box link, right-click the first text box and choose Create Text Box Link from the context menu. The mouse pointer will change to a pitcher of text, as shown here. Click this pitcher-pointer on the next text box to pour the text into it. To link this text box to another text box, repeat the procedure.

To move from one linked text box to another, right-click the border of the current text box and choose Next Text Box or Previous Text Box from the context menu, as appropriate.

To remove a text box link, right-click the border of the text box and select Break Forward Link from the context menu.

Removing a Text Box

To delete a text box, select it by clicking on its border, then press the Delete button. This deletes both the text box and its contents. To preserve the contents of the text box, copy and paste them into the document before deleting the text box.

CHAPTER **8**

Printing a Word Document

O nce you've written, set up, and formatted your documents, you'll probably want to print them. As it does with its other features, Word offers a wealth of printing options. Printing can be as simple as clicking one button to print a whole document, or as complicated as choosing which parts of your document to print, what to print them on, how many copies to print, and even what order to print them in.

In this chapter, you'll learn first how to use Word's Print Preview mode to nail down any glaring deficiencies in your text before you print it. Second, you'll tackle straightforward printing. After that, I'll show you how to change your default paper source, in case you find yourself working with the wrong type of paper and constantly needing to change it.

Using Print Preview

Before you print any document, you'll do well to use Word's Print Preview mode to establish that the document looks right before you print it.

 To use Print Preview, click the Print Preview button or choose File ➤ Print Preview. Word will display the current document in Print Preview mode (see Figure 8.1).

FIGURE 8.1

In Print Preview mode, Word displays your document as it will appear when you print it.

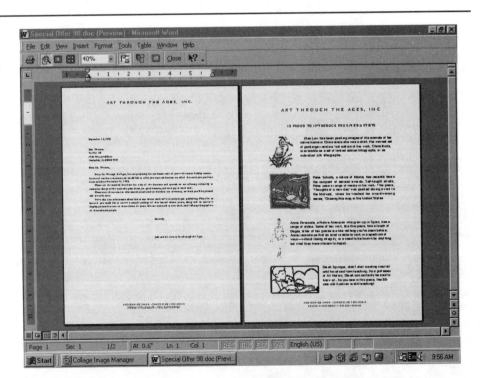

In Print Preview mode, Word displays the Print Preview toolbar (see Figure 8.2), which has the following buttons:

Print	Prints the current document using the default print settings.
Magnifier	Switches between Magnifier mode and Editing mode. In Magnifier mode, the pointer appears as a magnifying glass containing a plus sign (when the view is zoomed out) or a minus sign (when the view is zoomed in). In Editing mode, the pointer appears as the insertion point, and you can use it to edit as usual.
One Page	Zooms the view to one full page.
Multiple Pages	Zooms the view to multiple pages. When you click the Multiple Pages button, Word displays a small grid showing the possible display combinations—one full page; two pages side by side; three pages side by side; two pages, one on top of the other; four pages, two on top, two below; and so on. Click the arrangement of pages you want. Click and drag to the right or bottom to extend out to more columns or rows of pages.
Zoom Control	Determines the size at which you view the document. Use the drop-down list to choose the zoom percentage that suits you.
View Ruler	Toggles the display of the horizontal and vertical rulers on and off.
Shrink To Fit	Attempts to make your document fit on one fewer page (by changing the font size, line spacing, and margins). This is useful when your crucial fax strays a line or two on to an additional page and you'd like to shrink it down.
Toggle Full Screen View	Maximizes Word and removes the menus, status bar, scroll bars, etc., from the display. This is useful for clearing more screen real estate to see exactly how your document looks before you print it.
Close Preview	Closes Print Preview, returning you to whichever view you were in before.
Help	Adds a question mark to the pointer so that you can click any screen element and receive pop-up help.

FIGURE 8.2
*The Print Preview
toolbar offers quick
access to the Print
Preview features.*

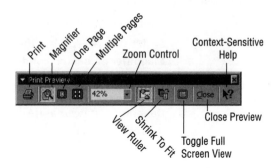

You can explore Print Preview on your own, but here's one thing to try: Click and drag the gray margin borders in the rulers to quickly adjust the page setup of the document, or double-click in these borders to display the Page Setup dialog box. Print Preview will show you how the document will look on the printer you're currently using. If you're using Print Preview to check that your documents look okay before you print them, make sure that you've already selected the printer you're going to use for the document.

To exit Print Preview, click the Close button on the Print Preview toolbar to return to the view you were in before you entered Print Preview, or choose File ➤ Print Preview, or press the Esc key.

Printing a Document

Once you've checked a document in Print Preview and fixed any aberrations, you're ready to print it. Next, you need to choose whether to print the whole document at once or just part of it.

Printing a Whole Document

The easiest way to print a document in Word is simply to click the Print button on the Standard toolbar. This prints the current document without offering you any options—to be more precise, it prints one copy of the entire document in page-number order (1, 2, 3) to the currently selected printer.

You can also print an entire document by using the procedure described in the next section and choosing All in step 2.

Printing a Document with Options

If you want to print only part of a document, don't click the Print button. Instead, choose File ➤ Print to display the Print dialog box (see Figure 8.3). Then:

1. Make sure the printer named in the Name drop-down list of the Printer group box is the one you want to use. If it's not, use the drop-down list to select the right printer.

 TIP The keyboard shortcuts for the Print command are Ctrl+P and Ctrl+Shift+F12. Ctrl+P is usually easier to remember.

FIGURE 8.3
In the Print dialog box, choose the printer you want to use, which pages you want to print, the number of copies you want, and any zoom effects you want to apply. Then click the OK button to print.

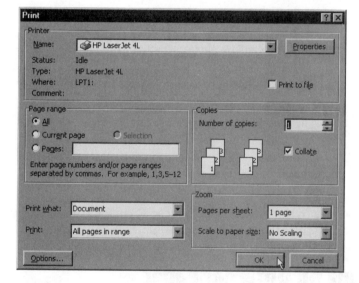

2. Choose which pages to print in the Page Range group box by clicking one of the option buttons:

- All prints the whole document.

- Current Page prints the page on which the insertion point is currently located.

- Selection prints only the selected text in your document. (If you haven't selected any text, this option button will be dimmed and unavailable.)

- Pages lets you print individual pages by number or a range (or ranges) of pages. Type the page number or numbers into the text box, and Word will automatically select the Pages option button. Use commas to separate the page numbers (for example, **1, 11, 21**) and a hyphen to indicate page ranges (for example, **31-41**). You can also combine the two: **1, 11, 21-31, 41-51, 61**, and so on.

TIP To print from a particular page to the end of the document, you don't need to know the number for the last page of the document—simply enter the page number followed by a hyphen (for example, **11-**).

3. Make sure that Document appears in the Print What box. If it doesn't, select Document from the Print What drop-down list.

   • If you want to print a peripheral part of the document, such as Document Properties or Comments, select it from the Print What drop-down list.

4. If you want to print only odd pages or even pages, use the Print drop-down list at the bottom-left corner of the Print dialog box to specify Odd Pages or Even Pages instead of All Pages In Range. This option can be useful for printing two-sided documents.

5. Choose how many copies of the document you want to print by using the Number Of Copies box in the Copies group box.

   • You can also choose whether to collate the pages—if you collate them, Word prints the first set of pages in order (1, 2, 3, 4, 5) and then prints the next set and subsequent sets; if you don't collate them, Word prints all the copies of page 1, then all the copies of page 2, and so on.

6. In the Zoom group box, you can choose whether to shrink the document down so that multiple pages fit on one sheet of paper. Choose the number of pages from the Pages Per Sheet drop-down list and select an option from the Scale To Paper Size drop-down list. For regular documents, you'll want to stick with 1 Page Per Sheet and No Scaling.

7. When you've made your choices in the Print dialog box, click the OK button to send the document to the printer.

Printing on Different Paper

So far you've learned only about printing on your default-sized paper (for example, $8 \frac{1}{2} \times 11$-inch paper). Sooner or later you're going to need to print on a different size of paper, be it to produce a manual, an application to some bureaucracy, or a trifold birthday card. Not only can you use various sizes of paper with Word, but you can also use different sizes of paper for different sections of the same document. (Chapter 6 discusses sections.)

When you want to print on paper of a different size, you will need to set up your document suitably—paper size, margins, and orientation. (You'll find details on this in the "Page Setup" section of Chapter 5.

Next, choose the paper source for each section of your document.

Choosing a Paper Source

If you're writing a letter or a report, you may want to put the first page on special paper. For example, the first page of a letter might be on company paper that contains the company's logo, name, address, and URL, while subsequent pages might be on paper that contains everything but the URL.

To choose the paper source for printing the current section of the current document:

1. Choose File ➤ Page Setup or double-click in the top half of the horizontal ruler or anywhere in the vertical ruler to display the Page Setup dialog box, then click the Paper Source tab to display the Paper Source page (see Figure 8.4).

FIGURE 8.4

Choose the printer trays for the various sections of a document on the Paper Source page of the Page Setup dialog box.

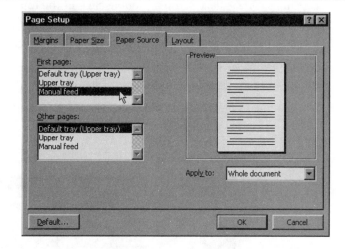

2. In the First Page list box, choose the printer tray that contains the paper for the first page. (If your printer has only one tray, choose Manual Feed so that you can feed the page of different paper separately from the main tray.)

3. In the Other Pages list box, choose the printer tray that contains the paper you want to use for the remaining pages of the document. Usually, you'll want to choose Default Tray here, but on occasion you may want to use either another tray or Manual Feed for special effects.

4. From the Apply To drop-down list, choose the section of the document that you want to print on the paper you chose. (The default is Whole Document unless the document contains sections, in which case the default is This Section. You can also choose This Point Forward to print from the insertion point through the rest of the document on the paper you chose, the page containing the insertion point being the "first page" and the rest of the document being the "other pages.")

5. Click the OK button to close the Page Setup dialog box and save your changes.

TIP To set the paper source for another section of the document, click in that section and repeat the preceding steps.

Setting a Default Paper Source

If you always print from a different paper tray than your copy of Word is set up to use, you'd do well to change it. This might happen if you always need to use letterhead on a networked printer that has a number of paper trays, and your colleagues keep filling the default paper tray with flavorless white bond.

To set your default paper source:

1. Choose File ➤ Page Setup or double-click in the top half of the horizontal ruler (or anywhere in the vertical ruler) to display the Page Setup dialog box.

2. Click the Paper Source tab to display the Paper Source page.

3. Make your selections in the First Page and Other Pages list boxes.

4. Choose an option from the Apply To drop-down list if necessary.

5. Click the Default button. Word will display a message box asking for confirmation of your choice, as shown in Figure 8.5.

FIGURE 8.5
When you choose a different default paper source, Word checks to make sure you know what you're doing. Click the Yes button.

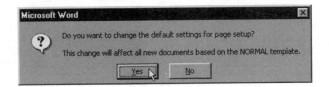

6. Click the Yes button. Word will close the Page Setup dialog box and make the change.

CHAPTER <u>9</u>

Creating Headers, Footers, and Watermarks

Headers and footers give you an easy way to repeat identifying information on each page of your document. For example, in a header (text placed at the top of each page) you might include the title of a document and the name of the author, while in a footer (text placed at the bottom of each page) you might include the filename, the date, and the page number out of the total number of pages in the document (for example, *Page 1 of 9*).

You can repeat the same header and footer throughout all the pages of your document, or you can vary them from page to page. For example, if a proposal has two different authors, you might want to identify in the header which author wrote a particular part of the proposal; or if you want to identify in the header the different part titles, you can easily arrange that, too. You can also arrange for odd pages to have different headers and footers from those on even pages, or for the first page in a document to have a different header and footer than subsequent pages.

Setting Headers and Footers

To include a header in your document:

1. Choose View ➤ Header And Footer. Word will display the page in Page Layout view and will display the Header And Footer toolbar (see Figure 9.1).

FIGURE 9.1

The Header And Footer toolbar offers 13 buttons that help you produce headers and footers quickly and easily, including a Close Header And Footer button to get you out of the header or footer.

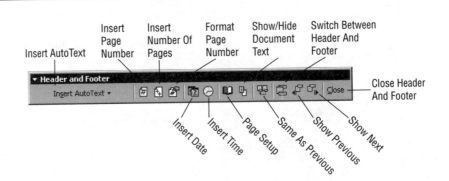

Insert AutoText   Insert Page Number   Insert Number Of Pages   Format Page Number   Show/Hide Document Text   Switch Between Header And Footer

Insert Date   Insert Time   Page Setup   Same As Previous   Show Previous   Show Next

Close Header And Footer

NOTE You can work with headers and footers only in Print Layout view and Print Preview. If you choose View ➤ Header And Footer from Normal view, Web Layout view, or Outline view, Word will switch you to Page Layout view. When you leave the Header or Footer area, Word will return you to the view you were in before.

2. Enter the text (and graphics, if you like) for the header in the Header area at the top of the page. Use the buttons on the Header And Footer toolbar to speed your work:

- Insert AutoText provides a drop-down menu of predefined header and footer text, including the filename and path and *Page X of Y* (for example, Page 3 of 34).

- Insert Page Number inserts a field code for the current page number at the insertion point.

- Insert Number Of Pages inserts a field code for the number of pages in the document.

- Format Page Number displays the Page Number Format dialog box (see Figure 9.2). From the Number Format drop-down list, choose the type of numbering you want: 1, 2, 3; a, b, c; etc. If you want to include chapter numbers in the page numbering, select the Include Chapter Number check box. Then, from the Chapter Starts With Style drop-down list, choose the Heading style with which each chapter in the document starts. From the Use Separator drop-down list, choose a separator character for the numbering. Finally, in the Page Numbering area, choose whether to continue the page numbering from the previous section of the document (if there is a previous section) or to start at a number of your choosing. Click the OK button when you've made your selections.

FIGURE 9.2

In the Page Number Format dialog box, choose formatting and numbering options for the page numbers.

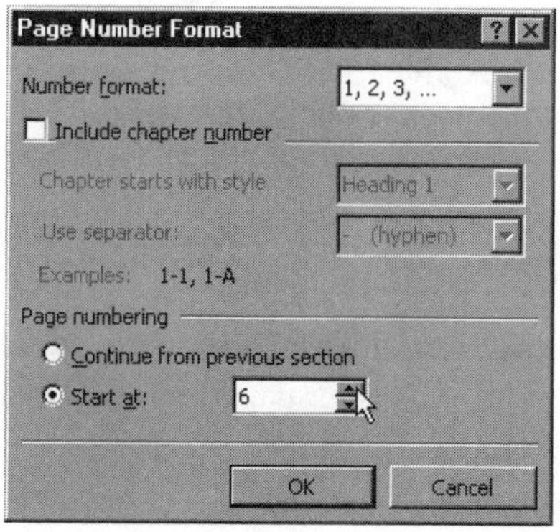

- Insert Date inserts a code for the current date in the document.

- Insert Time inserts a code for the current time in the document.

- Page Setup displays the Page Setup dialog box with the Layout page at the front.

- Show/Hide Document Text displays and hides the document text. Its purpose is a little esoteric: You probably won't want to hide your document's text unless you're trying to place a header or footer behind the text. For example, you might want to add a watermark behind the text on a business letter or a brochure. (For information on creating a watermark, see the section titled "Creating a Watermark" later in this chapter.)

 WARNING   Unwittingly clicking the Show/Hide Document Text button can lead you to think you've lost all the text in your document. If your text suddenly disappears under suspicious circumstances, check to see if the Show/Hide Document Text button is selected. If it is, restore the display of the document text by clicking the Show/Hide Document Text button again. If the Show/Hide Document Text button isn't the culprit and your text has really vanished, try undoing the last action by choosing Edit ➢ Undo or pressing Ctrl+Z. You can also try closing the document without saving changes.

- Same As Previous makes the current header or footer the same as the header or footer in the previous section (if there is a previous section) or page (if you're using a different header and footer on the first page). If there is no previous section, this button will not be available (I'll discuss headers and footers in relation to sections in a moment).

- Switch Between Header And Footer moves the insertion point between header and footer. Alternatively, you can use the up and down arrow keys to move between the two.

- Show Previous moves the insertion point to the header or footer in the previous section (if there is a previous section) or page (if you're using different headers and footers on the first page, or different headers and footers for odd and even pages).

- Show Next moves the insertion point to the header or footer in the next section (if there is a next section) or page (if you're using a different header and footer on the first page).

- Close Header And Footer hides the Header And Footer toolbar, closes the header and footer panes, and returns you to whichever view you were using before.

3. To return to your document, click the Close Header And Footer button or choose View ➢ Header And Footer again. You can also double-click anywhere in the main document as long as the Show/Hide Document Text button is not selected.

Formatting Headers and Footers

Despite their special position on the page, headers and footers contain regular Word elements (text, graphics, text boxes, and so on), and you work with them as described in the previous chapters.

By default, Word starts you off with the Header style in the Header area and the Footer style in the Footer area. You can modify these styles (as described earlier in this chapter), choose other styles (including Header First, Header Even, and Header Odd—which Word provides in some templates) from the Styles drop-down list on the Formatting toolbar (or by choosing Format ➤ Style and using the Styles dialog box), or apply extra formatting.

 TIP Headers and footers aren't restricted to the Header and Footer areas that appear on your screen. You can use headers and footers to place repeating text anywhere on your page. While in the Header or Footer area, you can insert a text box at a suitable location on the page, then insert text, graphics, and so on inside the text box.

Producing Different Headers and Footers for Different Sections

Often you'll want different headers and footers on different pages of your documents. Word gives you three options:

- A header and footer on the first page of a document that is different from the header and footer on subsequent pages

- A header and footer on odd pages that is different from the header and footer on even pages (combined, if you like, with a header and footer on the first page that is different from the header and footer on subsequent pages)

- A different header and footer for different sections (combined, if you like, with the two previous options)

Different First Page Headers and Footers

To produce a header and footer on the first page of a document that is different from the header and footer on subsequent pages:

1. Choose File ➤ Page Setup to display the Page Setup dialog box, then click the Layout tab to bring the Layout page to the front (see Figure 9.3). If you have headers or footers displayed already, you can click the Page Setup button on the Headers And Footers toolbar instead.

2. In the Headers And Footers group box, select the Different First Page check box.

3. Click the OK button to close the Page Setup dialog box.

After setting up your header and footer for the first page of the document, move to the second page and set up the header and footer for that page and subsequent pages.

FIGURE 9.3

Specify options for your headers and footers on the Layout tab of the Page Setup dialog box.

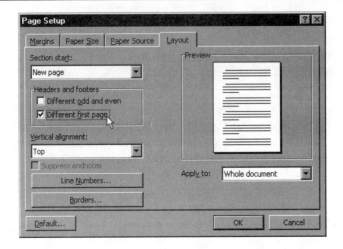

Different Headers and Footers on Odd and Even Pages

To create a header and footer on odd pages that is different from the header and footer on even pages, select the Different Odd And Even check box in the Headers And Footers box on the Layout page of the Page Setup dialog box (File ➤ Page Setup). Move the insertion point to an odd page and set its header and footer, then move to an even page and set its header and footer.

Different Headers and Footers in Different Sections

To set different headers and footers in different sections of a document, create the document and divide it into sections as described in "Section Formatting" in Chapter 6. To adjust the header or footer for any section, click in that section and choose View ➤ Header And Footer to display the Header area of the document.

By default, when a document consists of more than one section, Word sets the header and footer for each section after the first to be the same as the header and footer in the previous section; so the Same As Previous button on the Header And Footer toolbar will appear pushed in, and the legend Same As Previous will appear at the top-right corner of the header or footer area. To change this, click the Same As Previous button on the Header And Footer toolbar and then enter the new header or footer in the Header or Footer area.

To move through the headers or footers in the various sections of your document, click the Show Previous and Show Next buttons on the Header And Footer toolbar.

Creating a Watermark

A useful but little-used capability of Word is creating watermarks—text or graphics that appear behind or in front of the main text in a document. For example, you might want to stamp DRAFT across a report you were creating.

To create a watermark, you work with the header or footer for the appropriate page or section of a document. The header or footer is the mechanism that Word uses for creating the watermark so that it appears on each page, but the watermark can appear anywhere on the page; it's not limited to the Header or Footer area.

To create a watermark:

1. Choose View ➤ Header And Footer to display the Header area of the current page.

2. Insert a picture (or an AutoShape or a piece of WordArt, as in Figure 9.4) or a text box and position it where you want it to appear on the page. If you created a text box, enter the text in it.

FIGURE 9.4
You can place the contents of the watermark (in this case, a piece of WordArt) anywhere on the page—not just in the normal header area or footer area.

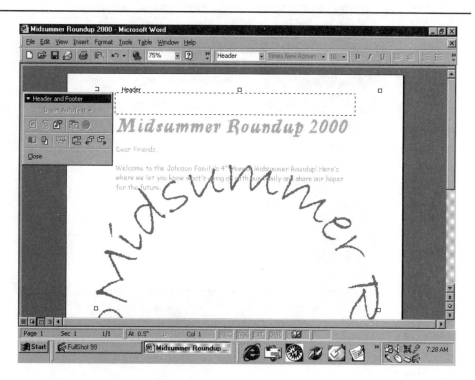

TIP To clear the screen so that you can better see what you're doing, click the Show/Hide Document Text button on the Header And Footer toolbar to hide the document text.

3. Format the item as appropriate. For example, if you place a drawing object behind the main text of a document, you may want to color it gray so that it shows faintly through the text rather than obscuring it completely. To lighten a picture, right-click it and choose Format Picture from the context menu to display the Format Picture dialog box. Click the Picture tab to display the Picture page, then choose Watermark from the Color drop-down list in the Image Control area; alternatively, adjust the Brightness and Contrast sliders until the picture takes on a suitable hue. Then, on the Layout page, choose the Behind Text option or the In Front Of Text option in the Wrapping Style area, as appropriate. Click the OK button to apply the effect.

4. Click the Close button on the Header And Footer toolbar (or choose View ➢ Header And Footer, or press Alt+Shift+C) to close the header and footer.

Figure 9.5 shows a completed watermark behind the text of a document.

FIGURE 9.5

This example shows a completed watermark behind the text of a document.

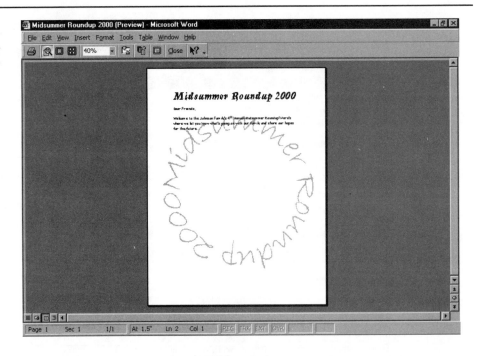

CHAPTER 10

Creating Mail-Merge Documents

Mail merge strikes terror into the hearts of many office workers. It gained its notoriety quite deservedly in the early days of word processing, when brave souls using WordStar, SuperScripsit, and other pioneering programs fought their way through truly incomprehensible instructions only to produce memorable letters beginning like this:

```
Mr. Dear 8671 Laurel Street
RonaldQGeldofsson    #2
```

You have probably received a few such letters in the past, and from what I can see, Publishers Clearing House is still heroically churning them out. But nowadays you can do better than that with far less effort.

Mail merge today is comparatively easy and friendly; with practice, it can even be fun. With just a little attention to the details of what you're doing, you can whip together merged letters, forms, envelopes, labels, or catalogs. Word's Mail Merge Helper smoothes out many of the potential speed bumps in the process.

 NOTE The version of Word 2000 that you install with Works Suite 2000 includes a component called the Word Add-In that provides a different interface for Mail Merge than the basic version of Word that comes with Microsoft Office. If you're used to regular Word merges, choose Tools ➤ Mail Merge ➤ Options to display the Mail Merge Helper dialog box, then proceed as usual.

How Mail Merge Works

Before I show you any of the specifics of mail merge with Word, you need to know the basic principles and the terminology of mail merge.

To perform a mail merge, you need a main document and a data source:

- The *main document* is the file that contains the skeleton into which you fit the variable information from the data file. The skeleton consists of the text that stays the same in each of the letters, catalogs, or whatever, and the *merge fields* that receive the information from the data file. For example, if you want to create mail-merged letters to a number of people, you'll create the letter as the main document. You'll enter in it the text that won't change from letter to letter, together with merge fields for the information that will change—the recipients' names and addresses, the salutation, their account number, the product you're trying to sell them, and so on.

- The *data source* or *data file* contains the information that will fit into the merge fields when the documents are merged. For example, in those mail-merged letters I mentioned, the data source will contain the name and address of each recipient, the salutation, the account number, that product you're trying to foist on them, and so on. This information could come from your personal Address Book or from another file, such as Works Database. If you were merging to create a catalog, the data source would contain the details of each product in the catalog—its code number, its name, the advertising blurb, the price, the specs, the weight, and so on.

In a typical mail merge, you'll specify the main document first, so that Word knows (and you know) what type of document you're trying to create. Next, you'll select the data source, which tells Word the available fields (units of information) for the merge. Once Word has that list of fields, you can insert them in the appropriate places in the main document.

At this stage, you can go ahead and perform the merge with all the records in your data source. Alternatively, you can sort your records into a particular order (for example, so that your merged letters are sorted by zip code, state, or town) or filter the records so that you use only those records that meet certain criteria (for example, only mailing to customers in Wyoming or customers interested in dog-related products). Once you've set everything up as you want it, you perform the merge—either to a new document, or directly to your printer, or to e-mail. (You can also simulate the merge before actually performing it, to make sure that nothing will go horribly wrong.)

Now that you have an overview of the mail-merge process, you're ready to learn the specifics.

Specifying the Main Document

The first step in mail merge is to specify your main document.

If you want to use an existing document as the main document for the mail merge, open that document. Otherwise, create a new document. (Word makes the Mail Merge command unavailable unless at least one document is open.)

Choose Tools ➢ Mail Merge ➢ Document Type to display the Document Type dialog box, shown in Figure 10.1. The Select Document Type For Mail Merge option button will be selected, and the Return To Original Document option button will be dimmed and unavailable, as you see in the figure.

FIGURE 10.1

Use the Document Type dialog box to specify the type of merge document you want to create.

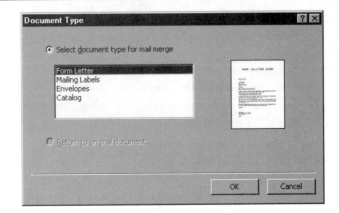

In the list box, select the type of merge document you want to create. The graphic to the right of the list box will show a crude representation of the type of document. I'll choose Form Letter in this example, because form letters still seem to be the most popular type of document created via mail merge. Click the OK button to dismiss the Document Type dialog box. Word will display the first Open Data Source dialog box (as you'll see in a moment, there are two dialog boxes with this name).

Specifying the Data Source

The first Open Data Source dialog box (shown in Figure 10.2) is part of the Works add-in for Word: It does not appear in the standard version of Word that ships with Microsoft Office. It offers you a simple choice: merge information from your Address Book, or merge information from another data source.

FIGURE 10.2

Use the Open Data Source dialog box to specify the data source for the mail merge.

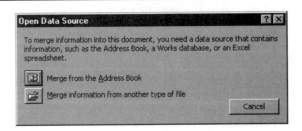

To create merge documents using information from your Address Book, click the Merge From The Address Book button. Word will remove the Open Data Source dialog box from the screen and will return you to your document with the Mail Merge toolbar displayed. Skip ahead to the next section, "Adding Merge Fields to the Main Document."

To create merge documents from another information source, such as a spreadsheet or database, click the Merge Information From Another Type Of File button. Word will display another Open Data Source dialog box, as shown in Figure 10.3. (This is the regular Open Data Source dialog box that comes with the standard version of Word.)

FIGURE 10.3
In the second Open Data Source dialog box, select the data source you want to use and click the Open button.

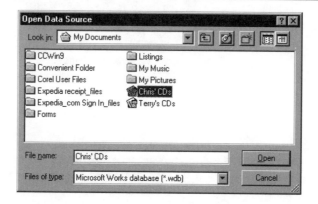

From the Files Of Type drop-down list, choose the type of file that contains your data source. For example, to use a Works Database database, choose the Microsoft Works Database item from the drop-down list.

Use the Look In drop-down list and list box to navigate to and select your data source, then click the Open button. If all is well, Word will close the Open Data Source dialog box and will return you to your main document with the Mail Merge toolbar displayed.

Adding Merge Fields to the Main Document

By this point, you should have specified the type of main document you're trying to create and designated the data source that you want to use for the merge. Word should have closed the Open Data Source dialog box, returned you to your main document, and displayed the Mail Merge toolbar, which provides buttons for inserting merge fields and Word fields into the main document. Figure 10.4 shows the buttons on the Mail Merge toolbar.

You're now ready to insert merge fields in your main document. If you're starting a main document from scratch, add the merge fields as you write it. If you started off with the basis of your merge document already written, you just need to add the merge fields to it.

FIGURE 10.4
The Mail Merge toolbar appears automatically when the merge has reached a stage at which you need its commands.

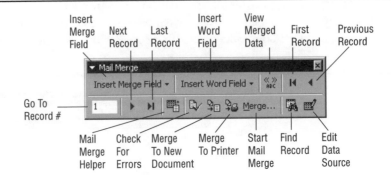

When Merges Go Bad I: You're Missing the Right Kind of Data

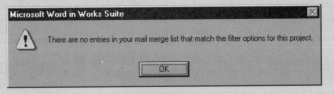

If you see the Microsoft Word In Works Suite message box shown in the illustration below telling you that there are no entries in your mail-merge list that match the filter options for the project, and you're not aware of having set any filters, chances are you've chosen the wrong data source. Click the OK button to get rid of this message box, then check your data source. (Restart the mail merge if necessary.)

To insert a merge field, click the Insert Merge Field button and choose the merge field from the drop-down list of merge fields in the data source you created or chose. Figure 10.5 demonstrates this process. For example, to enter an address from your Address Book, choose the Title field; Word will insert a field saying <<Title>> in the document. Follow that with a space, insert the First_Name field and another space, and then insert the Surname field. Press Enter and start entering the address fields. Remember the spaces and punctuation that the words will need—they're easy to forget when you're faced with a large number of fields, but the merged documents will look grotesque if you forget them.

If you're using a data source that doesn't have field names, Word will represent the fields as F1, F2, F3, and so on. (Usually, you'll find it easier to keep your merges straight if you use field names in your data sources, but you may occasionally find you need to use a quick-and-dirty data source that has none.)

FIGURE 10.5
Insert merge fields in your document, including any spaces, punctuation, and text that the fields will need in order to be laid out properly when the data is inserted in them.

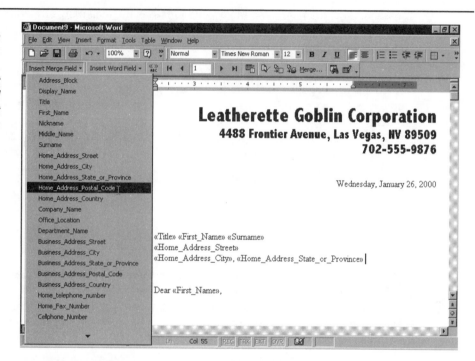

 TIP The Insert Word Fields button produces a drop-down list of special fields for use in complex merges, such as Ask, If... Then... Else..., and Fill-in. These fields, which provide you with a way to customize your merge documents so that they prompt the user for keyboard input, act in different ways depending on what kind of data they find in merge fields, and so on. They're far beyond the scope of this book, but if you do a lot of complex mail merges, you'll probably want to learn how to use them.

Once you've entered the merge fields in your document, you've got the components of the merge in place—a data source with records and a main document with field codes that match the header names in the data source. Next, you can specify options for the merge—filtering and sorting, error checking, and more—or just damn the torpedoes and merge the documents. If you want to specify options, read the next couple of sections; if not, skip ahead to the section titled "Merging Your Data" to learn how to perform the merge.

When Merges Go Bad II: Avoiding the Microsoft Query Twilight Zone

In many ways, the Works add-in for Word improves the mail-merge experience, making it easy to create merged documents using your Address Book, a Works database, an Excel spreadsheet, or an Access database as a data source.

But in one way, the Works add-in for Word makes merging more difficult—namely, that when you're using the Works add-in, it's not a good idea to click the Edit Data Source button from your main document to access your data source. Chances are, you'll see the Microsoft Word message box shown below, inviting you to edit a code number (PJ30717 in the illustration) that you don't recognize with Microsoft Query, an application that you probably don't know.

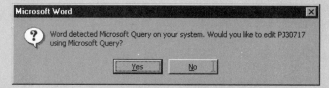

Click the No button. When you reject Microsoft Query's overture like this, you'll see a Microsoft Word dialog box such as the one shown below, threatening to break the link to the code number. Click the Cancel button to escape from the Twilight Zone of Microsoft Query back into your document without breaking the link between the main document and the Address Book.

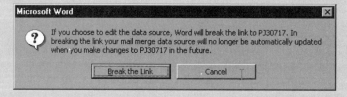

Setting Merge Options

In this section, I'll show you how you can filter and sort merge documents so that you can perform a merge without producing documents for every single record in your data source. If you don't want to try filtering or sorting, go straight on to the section titled "Merging Your Data."

Filtering the Records to Be Merged

By filtering your records, you can restrict the scope of your mail merges to just the appropriate part of your data source rather than creating a label, catalog entry, or form letter for every single record. For example, you can filter your records so that you print labels of only your customers in California and Arizona, or so that you send a letter extolling your pine-colored leatherette goblins only to people called Green (first name or last).

Here's how to filter the records you'll be merging:

1. Choose Tools ➤ Mail Merge ➤ Filter And Sort to display the Query Options dialog box.

2. Click the Filter Records tab to bring the Filter Records page to the front if it isn't already displayed. Figure 10.6 shows the Filter Records page of the Query Options dialog box.

FIGURE 10.6
On the Filter Records
page of the Query
Options dialog box,
choose how to filter the
records you'll be
merging.

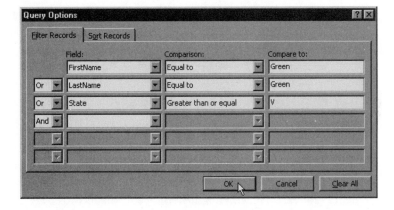

3. In the Field drop-down list in the top row, choose the field you want to use as the first filter.

4. In the Comparison drop-down list in the top row, choose the filtering operator to specify how the contents of the field must relate to the contents of the Compare To box:
    - Equal To (match)
    - Not Equal To (not match)
    - Less Than
    - Greater Than
    - Less Than Or Equal
    - Greater Than Or Equal

• Is Blank (the merge field must be empty)

• Is Not Blank (the merge field must not be empty)

 TIP For these mathematically inclined comparisons, Word evaluates numbers using the conventional manner (1 is less than 11 and so on) and text using the American National Standards Institute (ANSI) sort order: *ax* comes before *blade* alphabetically, so *ax* is "less than" *blade*. You could also use State Is Greater Than Or Equal To V to filter records for Vermont, Virginia, Washington, and Wyoming. For fields that mix text and numbers, Word treats the numbers as text characters, which means that 11 will be sorted between 1 and 2 (and so on).

---

5. In the second and subsequent rows, choose And or Or in the unnamed first column before the Field column to add a finer filter to the filter in the previous row or to apply another filter. For example, you could choose And LastName Is Equal To Green to restrict your merge to Greens in Vermont. Click the Clear All button if you need to reset all the filtering fields.

6. Click the OK button when you've finished defining your filtering criteria. Word will return to the Mail Merge Helper dialog box (unless you got to the Query Options dialog box by clicking the Query Options button in the Merge dialog box, in which case Word will take you there).

Sorting the Records to Be Merged

You can use sorting to restrict mail merges too. By default, Word creates or prints the merge documents in the same order as the records are listed in the data source. (If you haven't sorted your data source, this will be the order in which you entered the records into the data source.) Often, you'll want to sort your records before merging the documents—for example, you might want to sort the records by state and then by city to keep the mail clerk in a reasonable temper.

To sort your records, follow these steps:

1. Choose Tools ➤ Mail Merge ➤ Filter And Sort to open the Query Options dialog box.

2. Click the Sort Records tab to bring the Sort Records page to the front if it isn't already there. Figure 10.7 shows the Sort Records page of the Query Options dialog box.

3. In the Sort By box, choose the first field you want to sort by from the drop-down list and then choose an Ascending or Descending sort order.

4. To sort more precisely, choose the second field in the first Then By box. (For example, to sort by city within state, choose State in the Sort By box and City in the first Then By box.) Again, choose Ascending or Descending order.

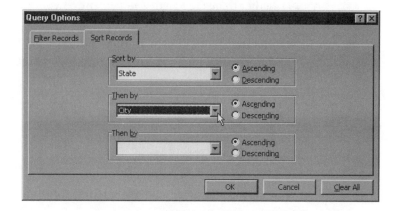

5. Specify another sort field in the second Then By box if necessary, and choose the order.

6. Click the OK button to close the Query Options dialog box.

• If you want to filter your sorted data, click the Filter Records tab instead to display the Filter Records page and skip to step 3 in the next section.

• If you choose the wrong sort fields, click the Clear All button to reset the drop-down lists to no field.

Merging Your Data

Now you're all set to merge your data source with your main document. Click the Start Mail Merge button on the Mail Merge toolbar (the button with "Merge..." on it). Word will display the Merge dialog box (see Figure 10.8). If you've set filtering or sorting for the merge, the bottom line of text in the dialog box will read "Query options have been set," as in the figure. If you haven't set filtering or sorting, this text will read "No query options have been set."

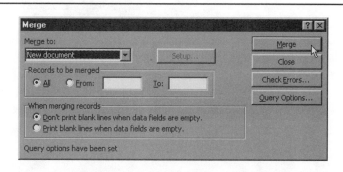

To merge your data:

1. Choose whether to merge to a new document, to your printer, or to e-mail:

- If you merge to a new document, Word will divide the resulting documents as it thinks best. For example, it will put page breaks between form letters or envelopes so that they're ready for printing, whereas mailing labels will share a page with each other.

 TIP By merging to a new document, you give yourself a chance to check the merged documents for errors—and, if you want, to add to particular documents a personalized note that you didn't want to put into your data source.

- If you merge to your printer, Word prints all the documents and doesn't produce an on-screen copy.

- If you want to merge to e-mail, click the Setup button to display the strangely named Merge To Setup dialog box (see Figure 10.9). Specify the field that contains the e-mail address in the Data Field With Mail/Fax Address drop-down box, add a subject line for the message in the Mail Message Subject Line text box, and select the Send Document As An Attachment check box if the document contains formatting that will not survive transmission as an e-mail message. (This depends on the sophistication of your e-mail package and of the service provider you're using: With basic, text-only e-mail, not even bold or italic will make it through unscathed.) Then click the OK button to close the Merge To Setup dialog box and return to the Merge dialog box.

FIGURE 10.9

In the Merge To Setup dialog box, specify the merge field that contains the e-mail address and add a subject line for the message.

2. If need be, choose which records to merge in the Records To Be Merged group box. Either accept the default setting of All, or enter record numbers in the From and To boxes.

- • If you're using sorting or filtering, the records will be in a different order from that in which they were entered in the data source.

- • To merge from a specific record to the end of the record set, enter the starting number in the From box and leave the To box blank.

3. In the When Merging Records group box, select the Print Blank Lines When Data Fields Are Empty option button if you need to track gaps in your data. Usually, though, you'll want to leave the Don't Print Blank Lines When Data Fields Are Empty option button selected to produce a better-looking result.

4. Click the Check Errors button and verify which option button has been selected in the Checking And Reporting Errors dialog box (shown in Figure 10.10). The default choice is Complete The Merge, Pausing To Report Each Error As It Occurs; you can also choose Simulate The Merge And Report Errors In A New Document if you consider the merge potentially problematic, or you can choose Complete The Merge Without Pausing. Report Errors In A New Document. Click the OK button when you've made your choice.

FIGURE 10.10
In the Checking And Reporting Errors dialog box, choose how to handle any errors that occur during the merge.

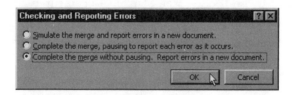

5. Click the Merge button to run the mail merge.

- • If you're merging to a new document, Word will display it on screen. You can then check the merged document for errors before printing, and you can save it if you want to keep it for future use.

- • If you're merging to a printer, Word will display the Print dialog box. Choose the page range and number of copies, if necessary, and then click the OK button to print the documents. When Word has finished printing, it will return you to your main document. Word doesn't create the merged document on disk, so you can't save it.

• If you're merging to e-mail, Word will check your MAPI profile settings, and then mail the messages and documents (if you're currently online or connected to the network that handles your e-mail) or place them in your Outbox (if you're not currently online or connected to the network).

Merging Labels and Envelopes

If you create form letters, you'll probably want to merge envelopes or labels in which to send the letters. In this section, I'll discuss how to merge labels and envelopes.

 WARNING Before you start learning about merging labels and envelopes, one word of warning: If you get tangled up in the merge process (and it's easy enough to get tangled up) and need to start over, close down all documents *and exit Word and restart it* before trying to perform the merge over. Why exit Word? Because Word can hold a data source document open in the background, where you can't see it and won't close it. So when you try to use the document again (without shutting down Word and restarting it), Word will tell you that the document is "in use by another program" and won't let you use it.

To merge labels or envelopes, follow these steps:

1. Choose Tools ➤ Mail Merge ➤ Document Type to display the Document Type dialog box.

2. Select Mailing Labels or Envelopes as appropriate in the list box and click the OK button. Word will display the first Open Data Source dialog box.

3. Select your data source as usual. If you choose to use the Address Book, Word will display the Microsoft Word In Works message box shown in Figure 10.11, telling you that Word needs to set up your merge document.

4. Click the OK button. (As you can see in the figure, you don't have much choice.) Word will then display the Mail Merge Helper dialog box (see Figure 10.12).

5. Click the Setup button to display the Label Options dialog box (shown in Figure 10.13) or the Envelope Options dialog box (not shown, but similar).

FIGURE 10.12

Click the Setup button in the Mail Merge Helper dialog box to proceed with the merge.

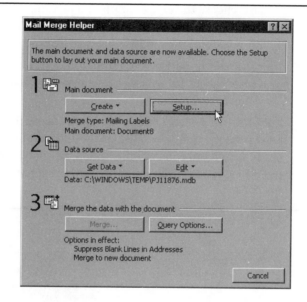

6. Choose the type of labels or envelopes you want to create:

FIGURE 10.13

In the Label Options dialog box, pick the type of label you want to use.

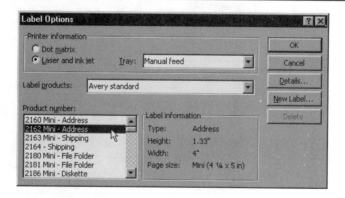

- If you're creating envelopes, use the Envelope Size drop-down list on the Envelope Options page of the Envelope Options dialog box to choose the size of envelope you're using. (Check the envelope's packaging for the size before you get out your ruler to measure an envelope.)

- If you're creating labels, choose the type of printer you'll be using: Dot Matrix or Laser And Ink Jet. Then choose the printer tray that you'll put the label sheets in by using the Tray drop-down list. Choose the category of label by using the Label Products drop-down list. In the Product Number list box, choose the type of labels you're using. (You should be able to find this number on the box of labels.) The Label Information group box will show the details for the type of labels you selected in the Product Number list box.

• Click the OK button in the Label Options dialog box. Word will display the Create Labels dialog box or the Envelope Address dialog box so that you can set up a label format.

7. Click the Insert Merge Field button and choose the fields for the labels or envelopes from the drop-down list, as shown in Figure 10.14. Word will insert them in the Sample Label box or the Sample Envelope Address box. Include punctuation and spaces, and start new lines as appropriate.

FIGURE 10.14

In the Create Labels dialog box (shown here) or the Envelope Address dialog box, set up your labels or envelopes for merge printing.

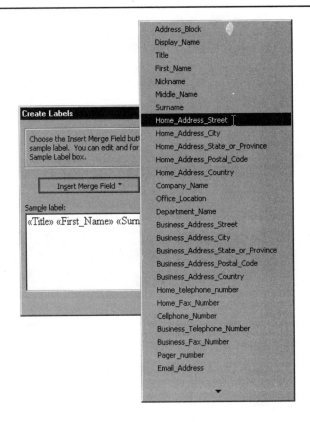

TIP You can apply formatting to the merge field codes by selecting them and either using keyboard shortcuts (such as Ctrl+B for boldface and Ctrl+I for italic) or right-clicking and choosing Font from the context menu to display the Font dialog box. You can adjust the paragraph layout by right-clicking and choosing Paragraph from the context menu.

8. If you want to include a postal bar code for the address, click the Insert Postal Bar Code button to display the Insert Postal Bar Code dialog box (see Figure 10.15). Select the fields from the Merge Field With ZIP Code and Merge Field With Street Address drop-down lists.

FIGURE 10.15
Use the Insert Postal Bar Code dialog box to insert a postal bar code on your labels or envelopes.

9. Click the OK button to close the Insert Postal Bar Code dialog box. Word will insert a boldfaced line saying **Delivery point bar code will print here!** at the top of the Sample Label box in the Create Labels dialog box or the Sample Envelope Address box in the Envelope Address dialog box.

10. Click the OK button to close the Create Labels dialog box or the Envelope Address dialog box.

Word will create the main document for the labels or envelopes from the contents of the Sample Label box or the Sample Envelope Address box and will return you to the Mail Merge Helper dialog box. From there, click the Merge button to display the Merge dialog box, and follow the instructions in the section titled "Merging Your Data" to complete the merge.

Using a Word Document as a Data Source

In this section, I'll show you how to use a Word document as a data source for a mail merge. First, I'll show you how to create a data source in Word. Second, I'll demonstrate how to hook up a Word document as a data source for a merge. Doing so with the Works add-in for Word is a little trickier than it should be, but you'll get the hang of it quickly enough.

Creating a Data Source in a Word Document

Word's regular mail-merge feature provides a handy way of creating a data source in a Word document. Creating a data source in Word is useful for projects for which you don't have a Works database or an Access database (or don't want to create one) and for which your Address Book is not adequate for whatever reason. Unfortunately, the Works add-in for Word disables some of Word's regular merge apparatus, so you have to take some extra steps when working from a copy of Word installed as part of Works rather than as part of Office.

Start by creating a main document as described earlier in this chapter, or opening an existing document that you want to use as the main document.

To create a new data source, choose Tools ➤ Mail Merge ➤ Options to display the Mail Merge Helper dialog box (see Figure 10.16).

FIGURE 10.16
To create a data source in a Word document, you need to use the Mail Merge Helper dialog box rather than the Works add-in for Word.

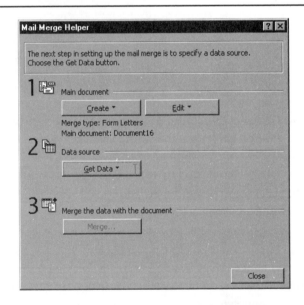

Click the Get Data button and choose Create Data Source from the drop-down list. Word will display the Create Data Source dialog box (see Figure 10.17).

FIGURE 10.17
Create a new data source in the Create Data Source dialog box.

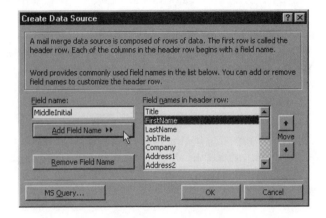

First, you create the *header row* for the data source—the field names that will head the columns of data and that you will enter in your main document to tell Word where to put the variable information.

Word provides a list of commonly used field names for you to customize: Title, FirstName, LastName, JobTitle, and so on. You'll find these more suitable for some projects than others—for example, for a parts catalog, you'll probably want to customize the list extensively, whereas the list is pretty much on target for a business mailing.

- To add a field name to the list, type it in the Field Name box, then click the Add Field Name button. (The highest number of fields you can have is 31, at which point Word will stop you from adding more.)

 TIP Field names can be up to 40 characters long, but you'll usually do better to keep them as short as possible while making them descriptive—ultra-cryptic names can cause confusion later in the merge process. Names can use both letters and numbers, but each name must start with a letter. You can't include spaces in the names, but you can add underscores instead (to create field names such as Career_Prospects)—which helps make them readable.

- To remove a field name from the list, select it in the Field Names In Header Row list box and click the Remove Field Name button.

- To rearrange the field names in the list, click a field name and then click the Move buttons to move it up or down the list.

 TIP The list of field names in the Field Names In Header Row list box forms a loop, so you can move the bottom-most field to the top of the list by clicking the down button.

When you have the list of field names to your liking, click the OK button to close the Create Data Source dialog box and save the data source you're creating.

WARNING Clicking the MS Query button in the Create Data Source dialog box takes you off into the world of Structured Query Language (SQL, pronounced *sequel* by aficionados, in case you're wondering). Don't click it unless you're experienced in SQL queries and are happy playing with databases.

Word will now display the Save As dialog box for you to save the data source. Save your document in the usual way. Word will then display the data source document, which will be set up as a Word table (see Figure 10.18) that uses your fields as column headings.

FIGURE 10.18
Word displays the data source document, which is set up as a Word table with column headings that consist of the fields you entered.

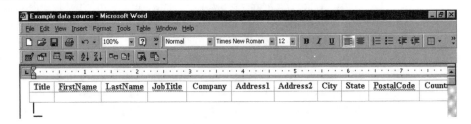

As you can see in the figure, Word has also displayed the Database toolbar, which contains buttons for issuing the commands associated with manipulating databases in Word. Figure 10.19 identifies the buttons on the Database toolbar.

FIGURE 10.19
The Database toolbar provides quick access to the commands for manipulating databases.

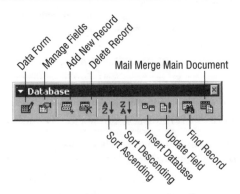

You can enter information directly in the table if you like, but for most data entry it's easier to use the Data Form dialog box, which is built for the purpose. Click the

Data Form button on the Database toolbar to display the Data Form dialog box. As you can see in Figure 10.20, the Data Form dialog box is a custom dialog box built from the field names you entered in the Create Data Source dialog box.

FIGURE 10.20
In the Data Form dialog box, enter records for the data source you just created.

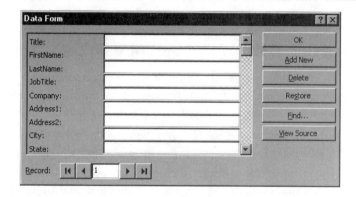

Now add data to your data source as follows:

- Type information in the fields in the dialog box, pressing Enter or Tab to move from one field to the next.
- Click the Add New button to begin a new record after entering the first one.
- Click the Delete button to delete the current record. This gets rid of the record completely, and you cannot recover it from the Data Form dialog box. (If you have previously saved the document, you may be able to recover it by closing the Data Form dialog box and closing the document without saving changes, but you will then lose any other changes you have made to the document.) Once you've deleted a record, Word displays the next record if there is one; if you delete the last record in the list, Word displays the previous record.
- Click the Restore button to restore the record to its previous condition (the information it contained before any changes you just made on screen). The Restore button will not restore a record you have deleted, because the record is no longer there to be restored.
- Click the View Source button to close the Data Form dialog box, update the data source document with the information you've entered so far via the Data Form dialog box, and return to the data source document. (Click the Data Form button again if you want to return to the Data Form dialog box.)
- Click the Record buttons at the bottom of the Data Form dialog box to see your records: The four buttons call up the first record, previous record, next record, and last record, respectively, and the Record box lets you type in the record number that you want to move to.

Click the OK button when you've finished adding records to your data source. Word will close the Data Form dialog box and return you to your data source. Click the Mail Merge Main Document button on the Database toolbar to return to your main document with the Mail Merge toolbar displayed. You can now add merge fields to the main document as discussed in the section titled "Adding Merge Fields to the Main Document," earlier in this chapter.

Specifying a Word Document as a Data Source for a Merge

If you've already created a Word document data source (for example, for a previous merge), you can specify it easily as a data source for the current merge by taking the following steps once you've started creating a main document:

1. Choose Tools ➤ Mail Merge ➤ Options to display the Mail Merge Helper dialog box.

2. Click the Get Data button to display its pop-up menu, then choose the Open Data Source item to display the Open Data Source dialog box. This version of the Open Data Source dialog box will include the item All Word Documents in the Files Of Type drop-down list. This item should be selected by default; if it's not, select it.

3. Navigate to your data source document and select it.

4. Click the Open button. Word will attach the specified data source document to the main document but will not display the data source document.

You can now add merge fields to the main document as discussed in the section titled "Adding Merge Fields to the Main Document," earlier in this chapter.

Restoring a Main Document to a Regular Document

If you know you won't need to use your main document again for a mail merge, be reassured that it isn't merged forever—you can easily restore it to a regular Word document.

To restore a main document to a regular document:

1. Open the main document.

2. Choose Tools ➤ Mail Merge ➤ Options to display the Mail Merge Helper dialog box.

3. Click the Create button and choose Restore To Normal Word Document from the drop-down list. Word will break the main document's attachment to its data file and restore it to normal document status.

4. Click the Close button to dismiss the Mail Merge Helper dialog box.

5. Choose File ➤ Save to save the document.

CHAPTER 11

Using the Works Word Processor

In addition to Word, the 800-lb. gorilla of the word-processor world, Works Suite ships with its own word processor, called (as you might guess) the Works Word Processor. The Works Word Processor is included in the Typical installation of Works, while in the Custom installation, you can choose to include it if you want. But in either installation, the Works Word Processor is hidden from view like an embarrassing cousin, and the Task Launcher gives you no way to run it directly—even refusing to store the Works Word Processor documents in its History list.

In this chapter, I'll show you how to unearth the Works Word Processor and how to use it. Because many of the features of the Works Word Processor are similar to, or are stripped-down versions of, features in Word, I'll refer you to the relevant parts of the previous eight chapters rather than reinventing the wheel at excruciating length.

What Is the Works Word Processor?

The Works Word Processor is a modest word processor—essentially, one built for people who can't afford Word or can't handle Word's complexity. Because Works Suite 2000 includes Word (in order to increase its usefulness and its appeal, not necessarily in that order), the Works Word Processor has been (shall we say) de-emphasized.

Figure 11.1 shows the Works Word Processor open with a simple document in progress.

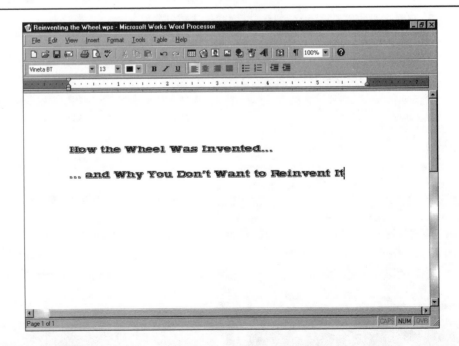

FIGURE 11.1
The Works Word Processor is a modest word processor that creates simple documents effectively.

If you're familiar with Word, or if you've even glanced through the preceding eight chapters, you'll find that the Works Word Processor's interface bears a strong similarity to Word's interface—so you'll be able to intuit what most of the toolbar buttons and commands do, and which items you'll find on each menu. (That said, if you're familiar with Word and comfortable using it, you'll probably have no reason to use the Works Word Processor beyond incurable curiosity.)

Why Use the Works Word Processor?

Compared to Word, the Works Word Processor is small, simple, and limited. Its simplicity and limitations provide both the advantages and the disadvantages to using it.

There are two key advantages to using the Works Word Processor:

- It's very easy to use compared to Word. You can get started in next to no time, and you can avoid Word's plethora of potentially confusing options and commands.

- It runs quickly and well on an underpowered computer. (That said, if your computer's not up to running Word effectively, you may have trouble with other Works Suite programs as well.)

There are three key disadvantages to using the Works Word Processor:

- First, it's limited in its features. (If you need a fuller-featured word processor, use Word instead of the Works Word Processor.) For example, a Works Word Processor document can have only one section (whereas a Word document can have dozens, hundreds, or thousands of sections) and so can have only one header and footer for the document (whereas a Word document can have a different header and footer for each section).

- Second, the Works Word Processor comes with no templates, so it's suitable only for creating documents from scratch. (You can create your own templates, but the features are much inferior to Word's.)

- Third, the Works Word Processor is no longer integrated into the Works Suite 2000 package, so you cannot launch it from the Task Launcher. Nor can you access your files from the History page of the Task Launcher, because the Task Launcher essentially ignores what you do with the Works Word Processor. To add insult to injury, you will also see the occasional irritating error message when using the Works Word Processor—even if you haven't done anything wrong.

If you still want to use the Works Word Processor, read on. If not, skip the rest of this chapter. (The next chapter discusses how to get started with the Works Spreadsheet application, which you may find a more stimulating topic.)

Creating a Way to Run the Works Word Processor

If you intend to run the Works Word Processor frequently, create a shortcut for it on the Windows Desktop or on your Quick Launch toolbar (if you use one) so that you can launch it with a click or two of the mouse. To create a shortcut, follow these steps:

1. Right-click the Desktop and choose New ➤ Shortcut from the context menu. Windows will display the Create Shortcut dialog box.

2. Click the Browse button to display the Browse dialog box.

3. Navigate to the \Program Files\Microsoft Works\ folder.

4. Click to select the WksWP executable file (WksWP.exe).

5. Click the Open button to place the file's name and path in the Command Line text box in the Create Shortcut dialog box.

6. Click the Next button to display the Select A Title For The Program dialog box.

7. Windows will suggest WksWP as the name of the shortcut. Change this to something more readable, such as **Works Word Processor**, then click the Finish button. Windows will create the shortcut on your desktop.

8. If you want the shortcut on your Quick Launch toolbar rather than on the Desktop, right-click the shortcut's icon, keep the right mouse button held down, and drag it to the Quick Launch toolbar. When the I-beam appears where you want the shortcut to be, release the mouse button and choose Move Here from the context menu. (If you want to copy the shortcut rather than move it, choose Copy Here from the context menu instead.)

You'll now be able to launch the Works Word Processor by clicking the shortcut on your Quick Launch toolbar or double-clicking the shortcut on the Desktop.

 TIP If you just want to run the Works Word Processor once to see what it looks like, choose Start ➤ Run to display the Run dialog box, then click the Browse button to display the Browse dialog box. Navigate to the WksWP executable file (WksWP.exe) in the \Program Files\Microsoft Works\ folder, click to select it, and click the Open button. Doing so will place the file's name and path in the Open text box in the Run dialog box. Then click the OK button in the Run dialog box to run the Works Word Processor.

Setting Up the Works Word Processor Window

The Works Word Processor interface is simple in the extreme. Figure 11.2 shows the Works Word Processor interface with labels. As you can see, the Works Word Processor displays two toolbars by default—the Standard toolbar and the Formatting toolbar—with other toolbars, such as the Header And Footer toolbar and the Print Preview toolbar, appearing when required by the features with which they're associated. If you've just launched the Works Word Processor, you may be seeing the Works Help pane as well; in the figure, I've dismissed it already.

FIGURE 11.2
The Works Word Processor bears a strong family resemblance to Word.

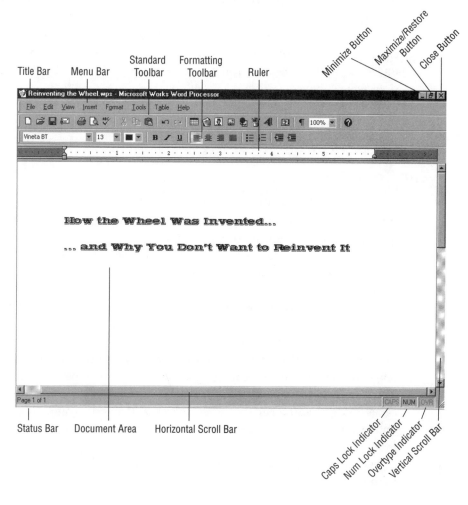

The Ruler and the Status Bar

The Works Word Processor has a ruler and a status bar. Both are displayed by default, but you can toggle them on and off by choosing View ➤ Ruler and View ➤ Status Bar, respectively. As you can see in Figure 11.2, the Works Word Processor status bar bears much less information than Word's status bar does—just the page number and total number of pages, a Caps Lock indicator, a Num Lock indicator, and an Overtype mode indicator.

The Menus

The Works Word Processor's menu bar contains eight menus: File, Edit, View, Insert, Format, Tools, Table, and Help. Unusually for a Windows application, the Works Word Processor does not have a Window menu, because, although you can have multiple Works Word Processor documents open at the same time, each runs in a different Works Word Processor session. So instead of using the Window menu to navigate from one document to another, you need to use the Windows Taskbar, and when you choose File ➤ Exit from the Works Word Processor, it exits only the active session of the Works Word Processor. (You'll need to exit any other Works Word Processor sessions separately.)

You can use the Tile Windows Vertically and Tile Windows Horizontally items on the Taskbar's context menu to arrange Works Word Processor windows the way you would any other application windows.

The Toolbars

The Works Word Processor has a Standard toolbar and a Formatting toolbar. Both these toolbars are displayed by default. You can toggle them on and off by choosing View ➤ Toolbars ➤ Standard or View ➤ Toolbars ➤ Formatting, as appropriate. You can choose View ➤ Toolbars ➤ Large Icons to toggle the toolbar icons between their regular size and a larger size that can be useful to people with poor vision or poor mouse control.

You can customize the placement of the toolbars and the menu a little, though you can't undock them, and you can't dock them to a side of the application window other than the top. Simply click the movement handle (the little bump at the left-hand end) on a toolbar or the menu bar, and drag the toolbar or menu bar up or down to rearrange the order in which the toolbars and the menu bar appear. For example, you might drag the menu bar down so that it appeared below the Formatting toolbar. (You can also drag the Standard toolbar down so that it and the Formatting toolbar appear on the same line, but doing so isn't especially useful unless you're using a high screen resolution, as part of one toolbar will usually be hidden.)

Many of the commands on the Standard toolbar and Formatting toolbar are similar to those in Word, as you can see in Figure 11.3.

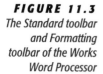

FIGURE 11.3
*The Standard toolbar
and Formatting
toolbar of the Works
Word Processor*

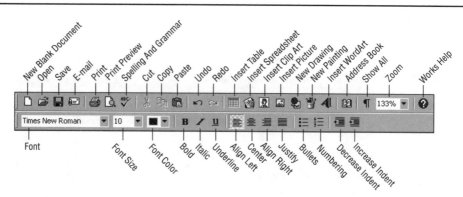

The Scroll Bars

The Works Word Processor has a horizontal scroll bar and a vertical scroll bar. You can't hide these scroll bars, as you can in Word.

Normal View and Print Preview

Compared to Word, the Works Word Processor is very limited in the views that it offers, providing only the default view and Print Preview.

To display a document in Print Preview, click the Print Preview button on the Standard toolbar or choose File ➤ Print Preview. Figure 11.4 shows a document in Print Preview, with labels indicating the buttons on the Print Preview toolbar.

The buttons on the Print Preview toolbar are easy to use:

- Use the Next button and the Previous button to navigate from one page (or set of pages) to the next or previous page (or set).

- Use the Magnifier to zoom in and out on the document (once you've clicked this button, one click makes the document larger, and one click makes it smaller).

- Use the Zoom drop-down list to zoom in and out more precisely than with the Magnifier.

- Use the One Page button and the Multiple Pages button to change the number of pages displayed.

- Click the Page Setup button to display the Page Setup dialog box.

- Click the Print button to start printing the document.

- Click the Close Preview button (or press Esc, or choose File ➤ Close Print Preview) to exit Print Preview.

- Click the Works Help button to display Works Help.

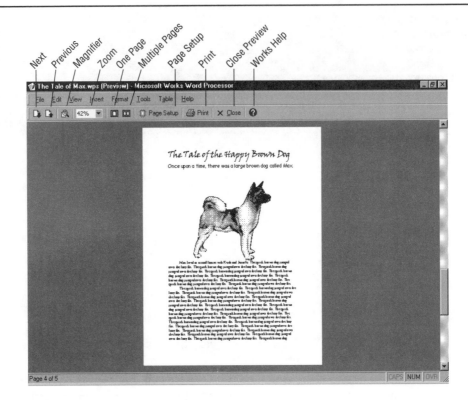

FIGURE 11.4
Use Print Preview to get a clear idea of how your documents will look when printed.

Zooming the View

You can zoom the view in (to magnify what's displayed on screen) or out (to reduce it) by using the Zoom drop-down list on the Standard toolbar or by choosing View ➤ Zoom to display the Zoom dialog box (see Figure 11.5), choosing the zoom setting you want, and clicking the OK button. For many purposes, you'll find Margin Width the best setting, as it maximizes the amount of text that you can see on screen at one time.

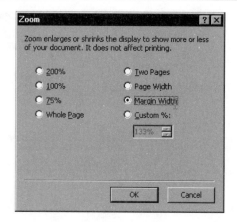

FIGURE 11.5
Use the Zoom dialog box to zoom the view in and out so that you can comfortably see what's displayed on screen.

Creating, Saving, and Opening Files

You create, save, and reopen files in the Works Word Processor in much the same way as in Word.

- To create a new document, click the New Blank Document button on the Standard toolbar.

WARNING Don't choose File ➤ New to create a new document from the Works Word Processor. Because the Works Word Processor isn't integrated with the Works Task Launcher in Works Suite 2000, this command doesn't work the way it should. Instead of getting a helpful dialog box, you'll see a Microsoft Works message box complaining that the Task Launcher "does not have information about the program you were using" and suggesting you try reinstalling the program. Click the OK button, return to the Works Word Processor (Works will have activated the Task Launcher), and click the New Blank Document button instead.

- To save a document, click the Save button on the Standard toolbar or choose File ➤ Save. The Works Word Processor will display the Save As dialog box (see Figure 11.6). Navigate to the folder in which you want to save the document, enter the name for the document in the File Name text box, and click the Save button.

TIP If you want to exchange documents created in the Works Word Processor with people who use different word processors, choose a different file format from the Save As Type drop-down list in the Save As dialog box before you save the document. Word 6.0/95 (*.doc) and Rich Text Format (*.rtf) are both widespread formats that you might try using.

FIGURE 11.6
Use the Save As dialog
box to save your
documents.

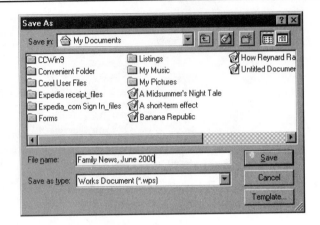

- To save a document under a different name, choose File ➤ Save As to display the Save As dialog box. Assign the new name (and location, if necessary) for the document and click the Save button.

- To close a document, choose File ➤ Close or click the close button in the upper-right corner of the document's window.

- To open a document, click the Open button on the Standard toolbar or choose File ➤ Open to display the Open dialog box (see Figure 11.7). Navigate to the folder containing the document, select the document, and click the Open button.

FIGURE 11.7
Use the Open dialog
box to open an existing
document.

Entering Text and Pictures in Your Documents

Entering text in the Works Word Processor is straightforward, so I'll cover it only briefly here:

- Use the keyboard and the mouse to position the insertion point where you want your text to appear, then start typing. Like Word, the Works Word Processor will automatically wrap the text as it reaches the end of a line, so you need to press the Enter key only at the end of a paragraph or to deliberately break a line.

- As you reach the end of a page, the Works Word Processor will automatically break text onto the next page. You can start a new page at any point by pressing Ctrl+Enter to insert a page break.

- Like Word, the Works Word Processor lets you insert text in both Insert mode and Overtype mode. To toggle between the modes, double-click the OVR indicator on the status bar. When the OVR indicator is darkened, Overtype mode is active; when the indicator is grayed out, Insert mode is on, as it is by default.

- Use the Word keyboard shortcuts listed in Chapter 4 (except Ctrl+PageUp and Ctrl+PageDown) to move the insertion point.

- Use the Cut, Copy, and Paste commands as you learned for Word. The only difference is that the Works Word Processor uses the Windows Clipboard rather than the Office Clipboard, so you can cut or copy only one item at a time. (If you cut or copy a second item, it overwrites the current item on the Clipboard.)

- Use the Undo and Redo buttons on the Standard toolbar, or the Edit ➤ Undo and Edit ➤ Redo menu items, to undo and redo actions one at a time. The Undo and Redo buttons do not have a drop-down list of actions the way Word's Undo and Redo buttons do, but they display a ScreenTip showing the type of action to be undone or redone (for example, "Undo Paste" or "Redo Typing").

- Choose Insert ➤ Date And Time and use the Insert Date And Time dialog box (see Figure 11.8) to insert a date or a time. This dialog box works in the same way as Word's Date And Time dialog box, which you learned about in Chapter 4.

FIGURE 11.8
*Use the Insert Date And
Time dialog box to
insert a date and time
in your documents.*

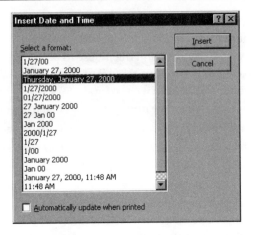

- Choose Insert ➤ Special Character and use the Insert Special Character dialog box (see Figure 11.9) to insert symbols and special characters in your documents. This dialog box is very similar to Word's Symbol dialog box (discussed in Chapter 4): The Symbol page contains a wide range of symbols for the font currently selected in the Font drop-down list, and the Special Character page contains frequently used symbols for quick access.

FIGURE 11.9
*Use the Insert Special
Character dialog box to
insert symbols and
special characters
(such as ®, dashes,
and fractions).*

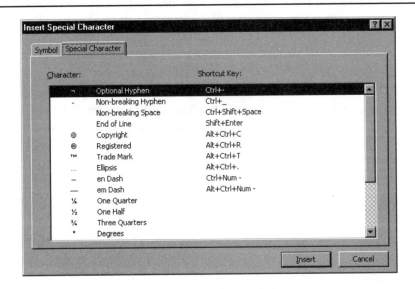

- To insert a picture in a document, click the Insert Picture button on the Standard toolbar, or choose Insert ➤ Picture ➤ From File, to display the Insert Picture dialog box (see Figure 11.10). Navigate to and select the picture file, then click the Open button to insert it into the document. You can then resize the picture by dragging its sizing handles.

FIGURE 11.10
Use the Insert Picture dialog box to insert pictures into a document.

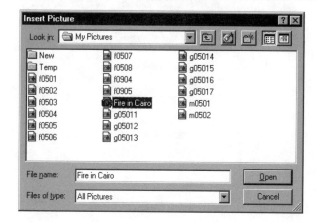

- To insert a text box, choose Insert ➤ Text Box. Works will enter a default-sized text box anchored near the position of the insertion point. You can then drag the text box to where you want it to appear; resize it by dragging its sizing handles; and enter text and graphics in it.

- To toggle the display of the tabs, spaces, and paragraph marks in your document, click the Show All button on the Standard toolbar or choose View ➤ All Characters.

- To insert page numbers in a document, position the insertion point in the header or footer and choose Insert ➤ Page Numbers. (You can use this command to insert the current page number at the position of the insertion point anywhere in the document, but to get page numbers on each page, you need to use the header or footer.)

Formatting Your Documents

You can format your Works Word Processor documents quickly by using some of the same techniques discussed for Word in Chapter 5:

- Use the Font, Font Size, and Font Color drop-down lists to apply the font you want, set its size, and choose an appropriate color. Use the Bold, Italic, and Underline buttons to apply boldface, italic, and underlining. Alternatively, choose Format ➤ Font to display the Font dialog box (see Figure 11.11), make your choices, and click the OK button to apply them.

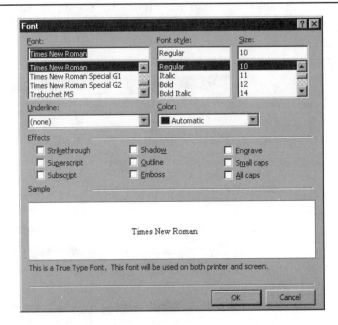

- Use the four alignment buttons and the two indentation buttons on the Formatting toolbar to set alignment and indentation. Alternatively, choose Format ➢ Paragraph to display the Format Paragraph dialog box (see Figure 11.12), make sure the Indents And Alignment page is displayed, set indentation and alignment, and click the OK button. Note that the Works Word Processor won't let you set negative indents (indents beyond the margins).

FIGURE 11.12
Use the Indents And
Alignment page of the
Format Paragraph
dialog box to set
indentation and
alignment.

- Choose Format ➤ Paragraph to display the Format Paragraph dialog box, click the Spacing tab to display the Spacing page (see Figure 11.13), select the spacing you want, and click the OK button.

FIGURE 11.13
Use the Spacing page of the Format Paragraph dialog box to set line spacing.

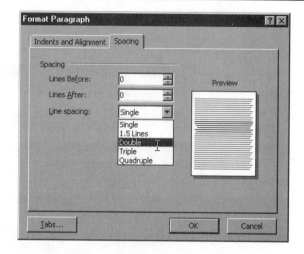

- Click in the ruler to set a left tab. Alternatively, double-click in the lower half of the ruler (or choose Format ➤ Tabs) to display the Tabs dialog box (see Figure 11.14), then set tabs as discussed in Chapter 5.

FIGURE 11.14
Use the Tabs dialog box to set tabs.

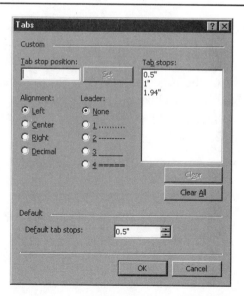

- Use the Bullets button and the Numbering button on the Formatting toolbar to apply regular bulleting and numbering to paragraphs of text. To apply other bulleting or numbering, choose Format ➢ Bullets And Numbering to display the Bullets And Numbering dialog box (see Figure 11.15), choose bullet options on the Bulleted page or numbering on the Numbered page, and click the OK button to apply them.

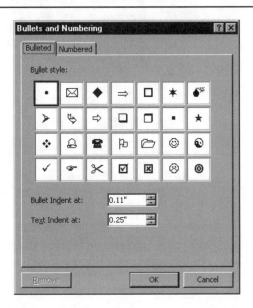

FIGURE 11.15
Use the Bullets And Numbering dialog box to apply alternative bullets or numbering to paragraphs.

- Use the ruler to set left and right margins, or choose File ➢ Page Setup to display the Page Setup dialog box. On the Margins page (see Figure 11.16), set the margin placement and the distance of the header and footer from the top and bottom of the page (respectively). On the Source, Size & Orientation page (see Figure 11.17), choose portrait or landscape orientation and set the source and size of the paper you'll be using.

FIGURE 11.16
Use the Margins page of the Page Setup dialog box to set margins and the distance of the header and footer from the top and bottom of the page.

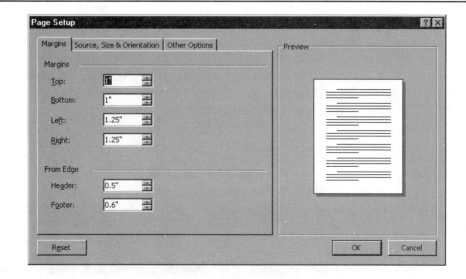

FIGURE 11.17
Use the Source, Size & Orientation page of the Page Setup dialog box to set portrait or landscape orientation and the details of the paper you want to use.

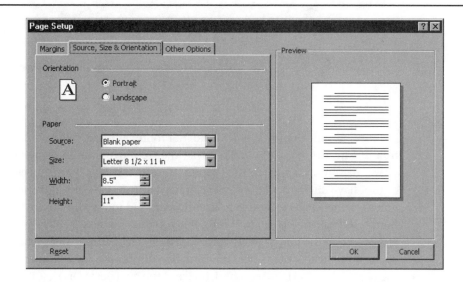

Creating Headers and Footers

Works Word Processor lets you create simple headers and footers in your documents, so you can repeat information on each page of the document if you need to.

To create a header or footer, choose View ➤ Header And Footer to display the Header area for the document. The Works Word Processor will automatically display the Header And Footer toolbar. Figure 11.18 shows the header area of a document and the Header And Footer toolbar.

FIGURE 11.18
The Header And Footer toolbar contains buttons to help you create the headers and footers you need.

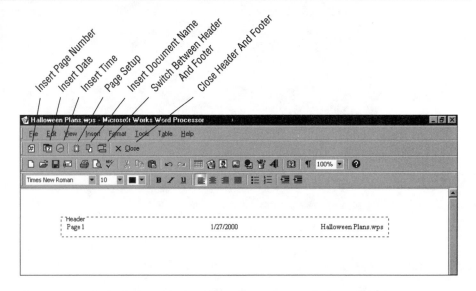

Enter text and graphics in the header or footer as usual. Press the ↓ key to move from the header to the footer. Press the ↑ key to move from the footer to the header.

As I mentioned earlier in the chapter, because a Works Word Processor document cannot have different sections, you can have only one header and one footer in a document (rather than being able to vary headers and footers from page to page, and section to section, as you can in Word). But you can suppress the display of the header and footer on the first page by choosing File ➤ Page Setup to display the Page Setup dialog box, clicking the Other Options tab to display the Other Options page, selecting the No Header On First Page check box and the No Footer On First Page check box as appropriate, and clicking the OK button to close the Page Setup dialog box.

To enter page numbers in a header, position the insertion point where you want the page numbers to appear, then choose Insert ➤ Page Numbers. The Works Word Processor offers no options on page numbers, so this command inserts them immediately, without displaying a dialog box.

When you've finished creating the header or footer, click the Close Header And Footer button on the Header And Footer toolbar to return to your document.

CHAPTER 12

Creating Worksheets and Entering Data

Works provides a full-featured spreadsheet program that you can use to enter, manipulate, and crunch data. The data can be pretty much anything—deposits in your daughter's bank account and putative interest accrued by the year 2015, employee hiring and firing information for your home business, or detailed data on the mating habits of frogs in Borneo.

In this chapter, you'll start by learning about the spreadsheet features that Works provides and what you can do with them. After that, I'll show you how to create a spreadsheet, enter data, change it, and format it as appropriate.

What Is a Spreadsheet?

Works Spreadsheet is a spreadsheet program—a program designed to work with numbers (as opposed to a word processor, such as Word, which is designed to work with words). You enter your data in *cells* arrayed into horizontal rows and vertical columns on a *worksheet*, an arrangement somewhat reminiscent of an accountant's ledger but far more flexible.

In Works, each spreadsheet file contains one spreadsheet. (More powerful spreadsheet programs such as Excel can have multiple spreadsheets in one file.) Each spreadsheet file has 16,384 rows (numbered from 1 to 16384) and 256 columns (numbered from A to IV—the first 26 columns are numbered A to Z, the next 26 AA to AZ, the next 26 BA to BZ, and so on through IV.

Starting Works Spreadsheet

You can start Works Spreadsheet in any of several ways:

- Choose Start ➤ Programs ➤ Microsoft Works ➤ Microsoft Works Spreadsheet. (That's the Microsoft Works submenu—the item with the arrow to its right—rather than the Microsoft Works item, which launches the Task Launcher.) Doing so launches Works and creates a new blank spreadsheet.

- On the Tasks page in the Task Launcher, select a task that creates a Works Spreadsheet spreadsheet, and then click the Start button.

- On the Programs page in the Task Launcher, select Works Spreadsheet in the list of programs, and then click the Start A Blank Spreadsheet link.

- On the Programs page in the Task Launcher, select Works Spreadsheet in the list of programs, select a task, and then click the Start button.

- On the History page in the Task Launcher, click a link associated with Works Spreadsheet.

Components of the Works Spreadsheet Screen

Figure 12.1 shows the component parts of the Works Spreadsheet window with a spreadsheet open. You'll see that I've closed the obligatory Works Help pane that appears when you first start Works Spreadsheet; you'll probably want to close it too, to maximize your screen real estate.

FIGURE 12.1

The Works Spreadsheet window (shown here with a sample spreadsheet) has a straightforward interface.

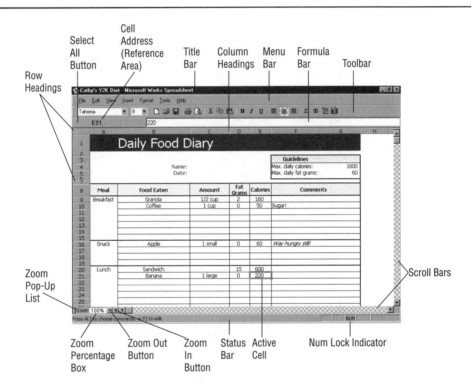

As you can see in Figure 12.1, the Works Spreadsheet screen has standard Windows application items: a title bar, a menu bar, a status bar, a toolbar, scroll bars, and more. To these items, Works Spreadsheet adds the following:

- The *cell address* (also known as the *reference area*) displays the location of the active cell.

- The *Formula bar* is where you enter and edit data and formulas.

- *Cells* are the spreadsheet units in which you enter dates and formulas.

- *Row headings* and *column headings* let you quickly select a row or a column.

- The zoom features—the Zoom pop-up list, the Zoom Percentage box, the Zoom Out button, and the Zoom In button—let you quickly adjust the degree to which the spreadsheet is zoomed so that you can see more of it at a smaller size or less of it at a larger size.

WARNING Unlike many Windows applications, which can reverse several actions (or any number of actions), Works Spreadsheet can undo only one action.

Using the Toolbar

As you can see in Figure 12.1, Works Spreadsheet has only one main toolbar. This toolbar is displayed by default; you can toggle it on and off by choosing View ≻ Toolbar.

Figure 12.2 shows the Works Spreadsheet toolbar with labels. Here's what the buttons do:

- The Font and Font Size drop-down lists let you quickly set the font and font size of the active cell or selected cell.

- The New button creates a new blank spreadsheet.

- The Open button displays the Open dialog box.

- The Save button saves the spreadsheet. If the spreadsheet has never been saved, clicking the Save button displays the Save As dialog box.

- The Print button displays the Print dialog box.

- The Print Preview button displays the spreadsheet in Print Preview, so that you can see how it will look when it is printed.

- The Cut, Copy, and Paste buttons work as usual in Windows applications.

- The Bold button toggles boldface on and off for the active cell or the current selection.

- The Italic button toggles italics on and off for the active cell or the current selection.

- The Underline button toggles underlining on and off for the active cell or the current selection.

- The Left Align, Center Align, and Right Align buttons apply their alignment to the active cell or the current selection.

- The AutoSum button automatically creates a sum formula in the active cell.

- The Currency button toggles currency formatting on and off for the active cell or the current selection.

- The Easy Calc button displays the Easy Calc dialog box for creating formulas. I'll show you how to use this feature in the next chapter.

- The New Chart button starts the wizard for creating a new chart. I'll show you how to create charts later in this chapter.

FIGURE 12.2

The Works Spreadsheet toolbar contains buttons for common operations in spreadsheets.

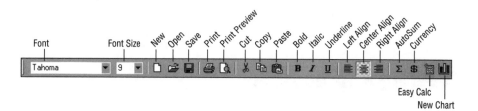

Easy Calc
New Chart

 TIP If you're familiar with Excel, you should find Works Spreadsheet easy to use. The main difference is that Works Spreadsheet has only one worksheet in each spreadsheet.

Navigating in a Spreadsheet

You can move from cell to cell by using the mouse or the arrow keys (←, →, ↑, and ↓). To move with the mouse, click the cell you want to make active. If the cell you want to activate isn't currently visible, use the scroll bars to bring it into view.

Here's how you move by using the navigation keys:

- The arrow keys (←, →, ↑, and ↓) move the active cell one cell in their direction.

- The Tab key moves the active cell one cell to the right.

- The Home key moves the active cell to column A in the current row.

- The End key moves the active cell to the last occupied cell in the current row.

- Ctrl+Home moves the active cell to cell A1.

- Ctrl plus an arrow key moves the active cell to the next cell in the specified direction that is not blank. If there is no cell in that direction with contents, these key combinations move the active cell to the end of the spreadsheet in that direction: Ctrl+↓ moves the active cell to the last row, Ctrl+↑ moves the active cell to the first row, Ctrl+← moves the active cell to the first column, and Ctrl+→ moves the active cell to the last column.

- PageUp and PageDown move the active cell up and down one screen's worth of rows.

To select a *range* of cells (a rectangular block of contiguous cells), click and drag from one end of the range of cells to the other, or position the active cell at one corner of the range, hold down the Shift key, and use the arrow keys to extend the selection in one or both directions until you reach the other corner. You can select the range in any direction—from upper-left to lower-right (or vice versa) or from upper-right to lower-left (or vice versa). You can also select a range with the mouse, then hold down the Shift key and use the arrow keys to reduce the selected range or extend it further.

To select a row or column, click its heading or position the active cell in it and choose Edit ➤ Select Row or Edit ➤ Select Column, as appropriate.

To select the whole spreadsheet, click the Select All button (the cell in which the row headings and column headings meet) or choose Edit ➤ Select All.

Creating a Spreadsheet

In this section, I'll show you an example of creating a spreadsheet and entering data in it. Along the way, you'll learn the different types of data that Works Spreadsheet recognizes, because the data type affects the appearance as well as the format of the data you enter in the cells of any spreadsheet.

Starting a New Spreadsheet

You can start a new spreadsheet by starting Works Spreadsheet from the Start menu or the Task Launcher (as described earlier in this chapter), by starting a new spreadsheet-related task from the Task Launcher, or by clicking the New button on the toolbar. If Works Spreadsheet displays a First-Time Help dialog box, select the Don't Display This Message In The Future check box, then dismiss the dialog box.

Works Spreadsheet comes with a good selection of templates for creating different kinds of documents—anything from a fitness-tracking spreadsheet to a car-loan worksheet. The techniques I'll show you in this chapter for working with spreadsheets apply to these types of spreadsheet just as they do to any spreadsheet.

To work through this section, create a new blank workbook by clicking the New button on the toolbar.

Types of Data in Works Spreadsheet

Before you enter data in a spreadsheet, you need to know a little about how Works Spreadsheet handles data. Works Spreadsheet is designed to make creating spreadsheets and entering data as simple as possible, but if you don't know what you're doing, you can get results that are completely wrong.

Works Spreadsheet recognizes five types of data: numbers, dates, times, formulas, and text. The following sections tell you what you need to know about each of these.

Numbers

Numbers are values that can be calculated. Numbers can consist of the numerals 0 through 9, with a decimal point (a period) as a separator for decimal places and with commas as separators for thousands.

Numbers can start with a dollar sign ($) or other currency symbol, or with a + or − sign. They can end with a % sign. They can also be enclosed in parentheses (as an alternative to the − sign, for indicating negative numbers).

You control the display of numbers by formatting the cells that contain them. For example, you can format a cell to display currency amounts with two decimal places for conventional use. I'll discuss how to format cells later in this chapter.

 NOTE If a number, date, or time is too wide to be displayed in a cell, the cell will display pound marks (######) instead of the portion of the entry that will fit. Simply widen the column to display the number.

Dates

Works Spreadsheet handles dates as *serial numbers*, numbers that represent the number of days elapsed since 1/1/1900, which is serial number 1. For example, January 31, 1900, is serial number 31, because it's 31 days after 1/1/1900. With serial numbers, Works Spreadsheet can perform calculations easily—to sort 2/1/2000, 1/15/2000, and 5/27/2000 into reverse order, Works Spreadsheet works with the dates 36557, 36540, and 36673 (respectively).

The good news comes in two parts: First, Works Spreadsheet handles the serial numbers in the background, so you don't need to worry about them (and you don't typically even see them), and second, if you enter a date in a date format such as **12/25/01** or **1/2002**, Works Spreadsheet will automatically identify it as a date, store it as a serial number, and represent it to you as a date formatted in the way you choose.

 WARNING Unlike some other spreadsheets, Works Spreadsheet does not recognize dates entered with hyphens instead of slashes. For example, **12/25/01** will be recognized as a date, but **12-25-01** will be stored as text.

Times

Works Spreadsheet uses serial numbers for times as well as dates, representing the 24 hours of the day as values between 0 and 1. For example, 6AM is 0.25, noon is 0.5, 6PM is 0.75, and so on. You can enter times in the formats listed below; specify AM or PM if you don't want Works Spreadsheet to use the 24-hour format. You can enter times with or without a space before the AM or PM designation.

Time Format	Example
HH:MM	10:15
HH:MM:SS	22:15:17
HH:MM AM/PM	10:15 PM
HH:MM:SS AM/PM	10:15:17 PM

Formulas

Formulas are mathematical formulas telling Works Spreadsheet to perform calculations on data in cells. For example, to add the data in the cells A1, B2, and C3 and display the result in cell D4, you would enter the formula **+A1+B2+C3** in cell D4. I'll show you how to create and use formulas in the next chapter.

Text

Works Spreadsheet considers any data that it does not recognize as a number, date, time, or formula to be text. This means that most data containing letters (other than cell addresses, AM or PM, and so on) will be treated as text. For example, if you enter a list of employees' names, positions, and work histories, Works Spreadsheet will treat them as text.

Works Spreadsheet will also treat as text any numeric entries that are formatted outside its accepted number, date, and time formats. For example, if you type an entry such as **10%8**, Works Spreadsheet will treat the entry as text because it's not correctly formatted as a percentage, a number, or a time.

Text too long for the cell it's in will be displayed over the cell or cells to the right if they're empty. Otherwise, only the part that fits in the cell will be displayed, though all the text is stored. (To see the whole contents of a cell, make it active by clicking it, and Works Spreadsheet will display the contents in the Formula bar.)

Entering Data

To enter data in the active cell, type it in. Alternatively, cut or copy the information from elsewhere, and then paste it into the active cell. As you type the first character, it will appear both in the cell and in the Formula bar, which will display a Cancel button (the × button), an Enter button (the ✓ button), and a Help button (the ? button), as shown in Figure 12.3.

FIGURE 12.3
As you enter data in the active cell, it appears in both the cell and the Formula bar, and Works Spreadsheet displays Cancel, Enter, and Help buttons.

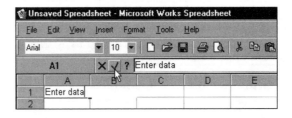

After you finish typing the entry, you can take any of the following actions to enter the entry in the cell:

• press the Enter key

• press one of the arrow keys (←, →, ↑, or ↓)

- press the Tab key or the Shift+Tab key combination
- click the Enter button
- click in another cell with the mouse

Works Spreadsheet will enter the data and will hide the buttons that had appeared in the reference area. (If you've gotten the entry wrong, you can click the Cancel button or press the Cancel key to cancel the entry.)

If you pressed one of the arrow keys to enter the information, Works Spreadsheet will move the active cell to the cell in the direction of the arrow key. If you pressed the Enter key, Works Spreadsheet will move the active cell down by one cell. If you pressed the Tab key, Works Spreadsheet will move the active cell one cell to the right. If you pressed the Shift+Tab key combination, Works Spreadsheet will move the active cell one cell to the left.

 TIP Sometimes you may need to persuade Works Spreadsheet to treat a number as text. For example, you may need a zip code to retain a leading zero rather than being truncated to its "true" value. You can force Works Spreadsheet to treat a number as text by entering the label prefix for text—an apostrophe (')—in front of the number.

You can enter the same text quickly in multiple cells by selecting the cells, typing the text in the active cell, and pressing Ctrl+Enter.

Using the Fill Feature

The Fill feature lets you quickly enter recognizable series of data, such as dates, text, or numbers, in your spreadsheets. After you've entered just enough information to let Works Spreadsheet know what you're trying to enter in the cells, you drag the Fill handle to tell Works Spreadsheet which cells you want to affect.

To see the Fill feature in action, follow these steps:

1. Start the series in the first cell of the range that will contain the information:

   - For a series of numbers that increase by a given amount, enter the first two numbers in the first two cells. For example, you might enter a progression of numbers such as **100** in cell A5 and **200** in cell A6, or dates such as **2000** in cell B5 and **2001** in cell B6.

   - For a known text series such as the months of the year, enter the first text label. For example, you might enter **January** in cell A1. That's enough to start the series; you don't need to enter **February** in cell B1 as well, though you could enter **January** in cell A1 and **April** in cell B1 if you wanted to fill a series with every third month.

2. Select the cell or cells containing the information.

3. Move the mouse pointer over the lower-right corner of the rightmost or bottom-most cell in the range so that the Fill handle appears, as shown in the top part of Figure 12.4.

4. Click the Fill handle and drag the resulting border across or down through the cells that will contain the rest of the information, as shown in the middle part of Figure 12.4.

5. Release the Fill handle. The Fill feature will fill in the information from the series in the remaining cells, as shown in the lower part of Figure 12.4.

FIGURE 12.4
Use the Fill feature to quickly fill in a series of information in a range of cells.

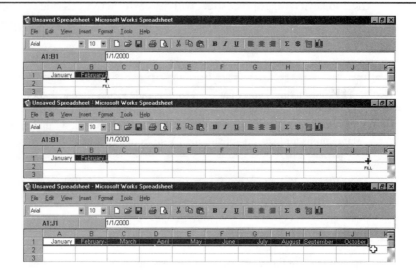

Formatting Cells

Once you've entered information in your spreadsheet, you'll probably want to format at least some of it so that it has the impact you want. Spreadsheet formatting includes everything from font formatting on a cell, to adjusting the height of a row or the width of a column, to setting up the page and adding headers and footers.

Cell Formatting Is Independent of Cell Contents

The formatting on a cell is independent of the cell's contents. Once you've applied formatting to a cell, that formatting sticks with the cell, no matter how often you enter new data in a cell or delete its contents.

It's easy to spot formatting such as borders and shading, because it will be staring you in the face. Font formatting and alignment manifest themselves only when the cell has contents and usually are easy to recognize and fix. One thing to watch out for in colorful spreadsheets is cell text formatted the same color as the background. If in doubt about a cell's contents, select the cell and check the readout in the Formula bar.

Number formatting also manifests itself only when the cell has contents and can be disconcerting because it can appear to give you completely the wrong result in a cell. So if you find yourself getting an unexpected result in a cell, check the formatting and change it as necessary. For example, if you enter **150** in a cell but see it display May 1900, you'll know the cell has date formatting that needs to be changed.

Formatting a Cell

To format a cell or a range of cells, you can use either the buttons on the toolbar or the options in the Format Cells dialog box. The toolbar provides quick access to common formatting, while the Format Cells dialog box provides a fuller range of choices.

In either case, start by selecting the cell or the range of cells that you want to affect. Then click one of the toolbar buttons to apply boldface, italics, underline, or alignment (left, right, or centered). Alternatively, you can choose one of the first five commands on the Format menu (Number, Alignment, Font And Style, Border, or Shading) to display the Format Cells dialog box with the relevant page displayed. (You can also access each page by clicking its tab once you've displayed the Format Cells dialog box.)

The Number page (see Figure 12.5) contains options for number formatting—telling Works Spreadsheet what sort of number it should treat the information in the cell as. These are the formats you'll likely use most frequently:

- The General format is good for text and for numbers that don't need to be in a specific format such as currency or percentage.

- The Currency format lets you specify the number of decimal places required (two for most conventional purposes), whether to display negative numbers in red, and whether to use the euro symbol.

- The Date format offers a selection of date options (for example, 9/30/00 or September 30, 2000).

FIGURE 12.5
Use the Number page of the Format Cells dialog box to apply number formatting to a cell.

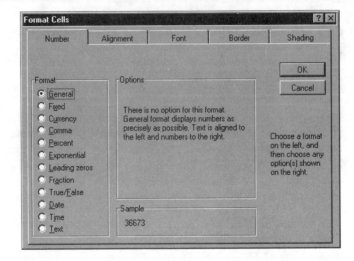

• The Time format offers a variety of time options, both 24-hour and AM/PM.

• The Text format lets you treat numeric entries as text rather than as numbers.

The Alignment page of the Format Cells dialog box (see Figure 12.6) provides option buttons for both horizontal and vertical alignment. Select the Wrap Text check box if you want to wrap text to a second line within the cell rather than having it extrude across the next column.

FIGURE 12.6
Set horizontal and vertical alignment on the Alignment page of the Format Cells dialog box.

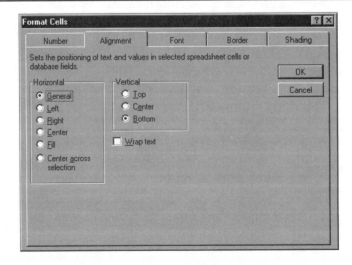

The Font page of the Format Cells dialog box (see Figure 12.7) provides many of the font formatting options common to Windows applications.

FIGURE 12.7
Apply font formatting from the Font page of the Format Cells dialog box.

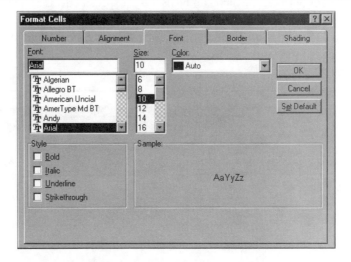

 TIP To set default font formatting for each cell in each spreadsheet and database you create, choose the font formatting on the Font page of the Format Cells dialog box. Then click the Default button and click the Yes button in the confirmation message box that appears.

The Border page of the Format Cells dialog box (see Figure 12.8) provides a good range of border-formatting options. Start by specifying the type of border in the Border group box, then select the color in the Color list box and the line style in the Line Style group box.

FIGURE 12.8
Specify border formatting on the Border page of the Format Cells dialog box.

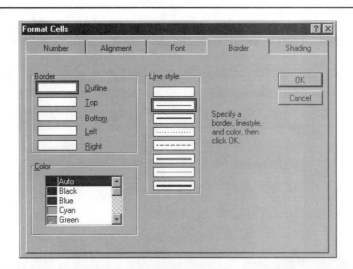

The Shading page of the Format Cells dialog box (see Figure 12.9) lets you apply shading to cells, which can be useful for special effects and layouts but may obscure the meaning of data-intense spreadsheets. Choose options in the Pattern list box and colors in the Foreground and Background list boxes. Watch the Sample area to get an idea of the resulting effect.

FIGURE 12.9
Choose a shading type and foreground and background colors on the Shading page of the Format Cells dialog box.

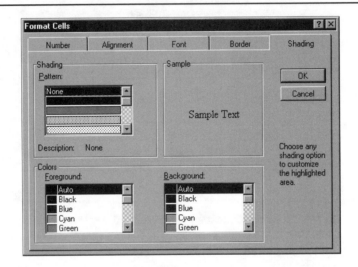

Adjusting Row Height and Column Width

Works Spreadsheet automatically increases the height of each row to accommodate its tallest entry. For example, if you have a row containing entries in 10-point font and you increase the point size of one cell to 20 points, Works Spreadsheet will increase the row height to show the 20-point entry. However, if you then make that 20-point entry smaller (or delete it), Works Spreadsheet will leave the row height set at the larger height.

You can adjust row height manually in two ways:

• Move the mouse pointer over the lower border of the row's heading so that the mouse pointer displays ADJUST, then drag the border up or down to change the row's height (see Figure 12.10).

FIGURE 12.10
*You can adjust row
height by dragging the
row heading's lower
border up or down.*

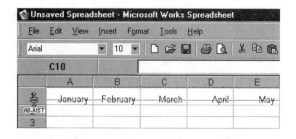

- Select the row or rows whose height you want to change, then choose Format ➤ Row Height to display the Format Row Height dialog box (see Figure 12.11). Click the Standard button to reapply the standard row height; click the Best Fit button to have Works Spreadsheet adjust the row's height to fit its contents; or enter a height in points manually in the Row Height text box. Click the OK button.

FIGURE 12.11
*You can also use the
Format Row Height
dialog box to change
row height.*

Works Spreadsheet doesn't adjust column width automatically. Here's how to adjust column width manually:

- Move the mouse pointer over the right-hand border of the column's heading so that the mouse pointer displays ADJUST, then drag the column border to the right or left to increase or decrease the column's width (see Figure 12.12).

FIGURE 12.12
*You can adjust column
width by dragging the
column heading's right-
hand border.*

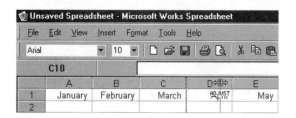

- Select the column or column whose width you want to change, then choose For-mat ➤ Column Width to display the Column Width dialog box (see Figure 12.13). Click the Standard button to reapply the standard column width; click the Best Fit button to have Works Spreadsheet adjust the column's width to fit its contents; or enter a width in characters manually in the Column Width text box. Click the OK button.

FIGURE 12.13
You can also use the
Column Width dialog
box to set column width.

Inserting and Deleting Rows and Columns

Often, when designing a spreadsheet, you'll need to insert and delete rows and columns to give yourself a suitable layout. Here's what to do:

- To insert a column to the left of the active cell, choose Insert ➤ Column. Alternatively, right-click a column heading and choose Insert Column from the context menu.

- To insert a row above the active cell, choose Insert ➤ Row. Alternatively, right-click a row heading and choose Insert ➤ Row from the context menu.

- To delete a column, right-click its heading and choose Delete Column from the context menu.

- To delete a row, right-click its heading and choose Delete Row from the context menu.

Page Setup

Works Spreadsheet comes with its page setup preset to workable default settings such as portrait-orientation letter-size paper with 1-inch margins top and bottom and $1\frac{1}{4}$-inch margins left and right. But sooner or later you'll want to change the page setup—for example, to print on a different size of paper, or to use the paper in landscape (wide) orientation rather than portrait (tall).

Here's how to change the page setup:

1. Choose File ➤ Page Setup to display the Page Setup dialog box. Initially, you should see the Margins page on the multi-page object in the lower half of the dialog box (see Figure 12.14).

FIGURE 12.14
Set margins and header and footer placement on the Margins page of the Page Setup dialog box.

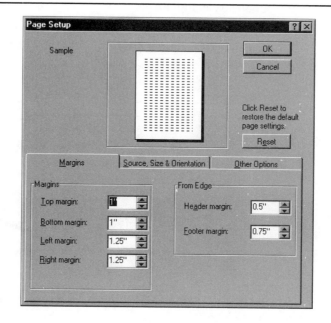

2. In the Margins group box, adjust the Top Margin, Bottom Margin, Left Margin, and Right Margin measurements as necessary.

3. In the From Edge group box, change the Header Margin and Footer Margin measurements if you want to alter the distance the header and footer appear from the edges of the page. (I'll show you how to create headers and footers in the next section.)

4. Click the Source, Size & Orientation tab to display the Source, Size & Orientation page (see Figure 12.15).

FIGURE 12.15
Use the Source, Size & Orientation page of the Page Setup dialog box to specify a different type or layout of paper for your printouts.

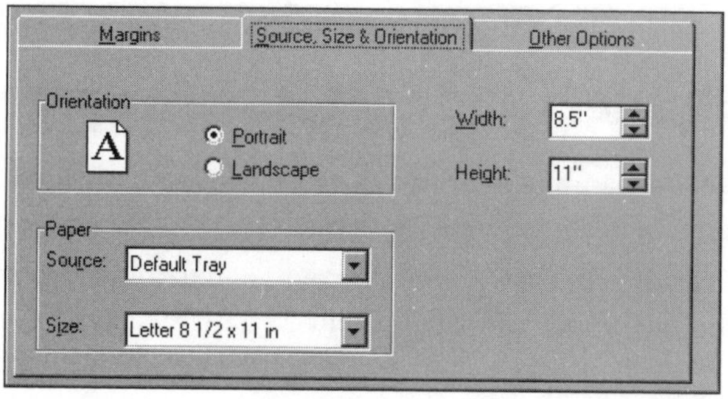

5. Select the Portrait option button or the Landscape option button in the Orientation group box as appropriate.

6. Change the paper source and size as necessary by using the Source drop-down list and either the Size drop-down list or the Width and Height text boxes.

7. Click the Other Options tab to display the Other Options page (see Figure 12.16).

FIGURE 12.16
On the Other Options page of the Page Setup dialog box, you can set a starting page number and specify whether to print gridlines and row and column headings.

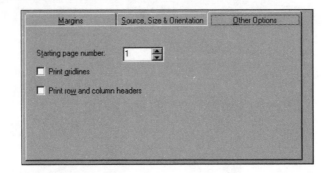

8. To change the starting page number, enter the number in the Starting Page Number text box.

9. To print the gridlines or the row and column headings, select the Print Gridlines check box or the Print Row And Column Headers check box. Gridlines are useful for keeping information visually separate on dense spreadsheets. Row and column headings are primarily useful if you're reviewing a printout of the spreadsheet with someone and need to refer to cells by their column and row position.

10. Click the OK button to close the Page Setup dialog box and apply your choices.

 TIP To reset all the settings in the Page Setup dialog box to their defaults, click the Reset button.

Adding Headers and Footers to a Spreadsheet

If you're planning to print a spreadsheet, you'll probably want to add a header or a footer (or both) to it. Follow these steps:

1. Choose View ➢ Headers And Footers to display the View Headers And Footers dialog box (shown in Figure 12.17 with a header and footer entered).

FIGURE 12.17
Use the Headers And Footers dialog box to create headers and footers for your spreadsheets.

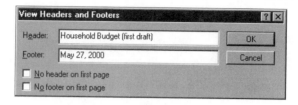

2. Enter the text for the header in the Header text box.

3. Enter the text for the footer in the Footer text box.

4. If you need to prevent the header or footer from appearing on the first page of the printout, select the No Header On First Page check box or the No Footer On First Page check box as appropriate.

5. Click the OK button to apply the header or footer to your spreadsheet.

Splitting and Freezing a Spreadsheet

You can split the Works Spreadsheet window so that you can see nonadjacent parts of a spreadsheet at the same time. Doing so makes it easier to compare data spread out over a number of rows or columns.

To split the window, choose View ➤ Split. Works Spreadsheet will display an ADJUST pointer and split bars, as shown in Figure 12.18. Drag the split to where you want it to be, and then click to place it.

FIGURE 12.18
Drag the split bars with the ADJUST pointer to where you want the split to appear, then click to place it.

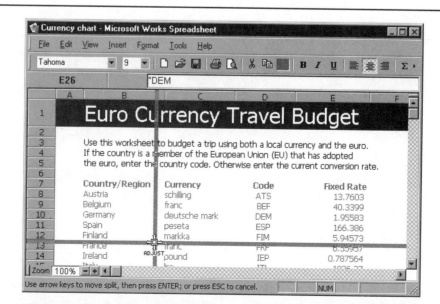

To adjust the split, choose View ➤ Split again, and move the mouse pointer to reposition the split.

To remove the split, drag the split to the upper-left corner of the Works Spreadsheet window.

Once you've split the window, you may also want to freeze the titles at the top of the screen and the columns on the left of the screen so that they do not move when you scroll. By doing this, you can keep row and column headings visible while you scroll to far-flung regions of your worksheets.

To freeze the tiles, make active the cell to the left of which and above which you want the columns and rows to be frozen, and then choose Format ➤ Freeze Titles. Works Spreadsheet will display lines indicating the division. For example, if you freeze the panes with cell C5 active, Works Spreadsheet will freeze the rows above row 5 and to the left of column C.

To unfreeze the titles, choose Format ➤ Freeze Titles again.

Sorting a Spreadsheet

To get your data into the shape you need, you'll often have to sort it. Here's how to do that:

1. To sort just some of the data in a spreadsheet, select the data; to sort the whole spreadsheet, click the Select All button (at the intersection of the row and column headings).

2. Choose Tools ➤ Sort. If you selected a range of cells, Works Spreadsheet will display the Sort dialog box shown in Figure 12.19 to make sure you want to sort only the range you've selected.

FIGURE 12.19
Works Spreadsheet displays this Sort dialog box when you issue the Sort command with some cells selected. Click the OK button.

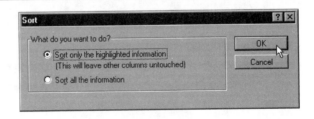

3. Click the OK button to confirm this choice. Works Spreadsheet will then display the Sort dialog box shown in Figure 12.20.

FIGURE 12.20
The main Sort dialog box offers simple sorting.

4. In the Sort By group box, specify the column by which to sort. If your data has a row of headers, each column will be identified by its heading. If your data has no headers, the columns will be identified by their letter, as in the figure.

5. Choose the Ascending option button to sort in ascending order (A to Z, 1 to 9) or the Descending option button to sort in descending order (Z to A, 9 to 1).

6. In the My List Has area, make sure that the Header Row option button is selected if your data has a header row and that the No Header Row option button is selected if it doesn't. (If you have the No Header Row option button selected but do have a header row, your header row will be sorted along with the rest of the data.)

7. If you need to perform more complex sorting, click the Advanced button to display an extra section of the Sort dialog box. Choose further sorting criteria from the first Then By and second Then By group boxes as necessary.

8. Click the OK button to perform the sort.

Working with Charts

There's no simpler way to enliven tedious figures or to illustrate a trend in data than to use a chart. Works Spreadsheet provides strong charting features, with enough options that you can create effective and convincing charts. You can attach multiple charts to a spreadsheet and display them individually. Each chart appears on a separate page (unlike, say, Excel, in which you can create a chart embedded in a worksheet).

In this section, I'll show you how to create and format charts in Works Spreadsheet to present your data to maximum advantage.

Chart Terms and Basics

The first thing you need to learn about charts is the different parts that make up a chart. A typical chart, such as the one shown in Figure 12.21, includes the following elements:

Element	Description
Axes	Two-dimensional charts have an X-axis (the horizontal axis) and a Y-axis (the vertical axis). Three-dimensional charts also have a Z-axis (the depth axis).
Titles	A chart will typically have a chart title and a title for each axis.
Legend	The *legend* identifies each data series (for example, by color or by pattern).
Data series	A *data series* is one of the sets of data from which the chart is drawn. A pie chart has only one data series, but most types of charts can have two or more data series.
Gridlines	*Gridlines* are the lines drawn across the chart from the axes for visual reference.
Categories	*Categories* are the items by which a data series is separated. For example, if a chart showed a company's gross sales for the years 2000–2009, each year would be a category.

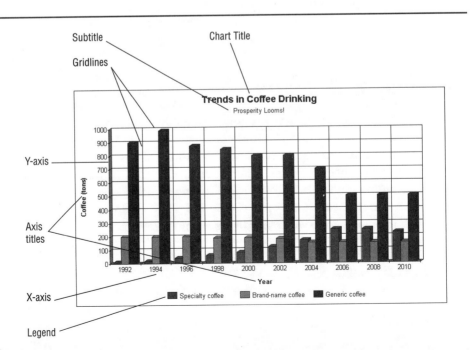

FIGURE 12.21
The elements of a typical chart

Choosing the Right Type of Chart

Works Spreadsheet offers a good selection of different types of charts, and choosing the right chart for the data you need to present can be a tough call. In this section, you'll learn the basic chart types and what they're most useful for. The good news is that once you've created a chart, you can quickly modify it (by adding legends, titles, and so on) or even switch it to a different and more suitable chart type without losing any data.

Works Spreadsheet offers the following types of charts:

- *Area charts* are good for showing how much different data series contribute to a whole. These charts use connected points to map each series, and the space between the series is filled in with a color or pattern.

- *Bar charts* are the type of chart typically used for showing performance against benchmarks. Each data point is marked by a horizontal bar that extends to the left or right of the baseline.

- *Column charts*, which are similar to bar charts but use vertical bars instead of horizontal bars, are typically used for showing sales figures, rainfall, and the like.

- *Line charts* are good for showing changes in data series over time. A typical use of a line chart would be for charting temperature or changes in price. The data points in each data series are connected by a line.

- *Pie charts* are notorious enough from math class and sales presentations to need no introduction: A single data series is divided up into pie slices showing the relative contribution of the various data points. Pie charts are great for showing market share, survey results, and the like.

- *Radar charts* represent data points as symbols around a central point (the supposed radar scanner), with the value of each data point represented by its symbol's distance from the scanner. Radar charts can be confusing when misused, so use them with care (unless you want to be confusing).

- *Stacked line charts* are line charts in which each line is presented separately in a vertical stack, so that no line crosses over any other line. Stacked line charts are most useful when it's hard to make out the individual lines on a line chart (for example, because they're too close together, or they cross too frequently, or you're stuck with using black and white rather than color) and you want to compare the shape of each data series.

- *X-Y charts* or *scatter charts*, typically used for charting the results of surveys or experiments, plot a series of data pairs against XY coordinates. The result often resembles a line chart that's lost its lines. (That said, some scatter chart formats do use lines.)

- *Combination charts* add a line chart to a column chart or bar chart, plotting one or more data series as lines and the others as bars or columns. You can use combination charts to demonstrate two trends at once. You can also use them to obscure the meaning of your data when even visually confusing charts such as radar charts are too clear for your liking.

- *3-D charts* include 3-D area charts, 3-D column charts, 3-D line charts, and 3-D pie charts. Use 3-D charts when the complexity of your data requires more than two dimensions.

Creating a Chart

In this section, you'll learn how to create a chart in Works Spreadsheet. Follow these steps:

1. Open (or create) the spreadsheet that contains the data you want to use for the chart, then select the range of data from which you want to create the chart. I'll use the spreadsheet shown in Figure 12.22.

FIGURE 12.22
The spreadsheet from which I'll create a chart

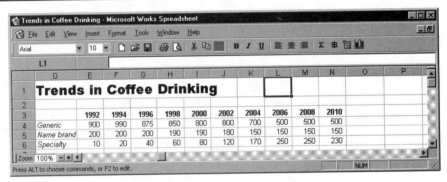

2. Click the New Chart button on the toolbar, or choose Tools ➢ Create New Chart, to display the New Chart dialog box.

3. On the Basic Options page of the New Chart dialog box (see Figure 12.23), choose basic options for your chart as follows:

    - In the What Type Of Chart Do You Want? group box, select the type of chart you want to create. Use the Your Chart preview on the right of the dialog box to make sure you've chosen something appropriate.

    - In the Finishing Touches group box, enter the title for the chart in the Title text box. Select the Border check box if you want to have Works Spreadsheet add a border around your chart, and select the Gridlines check box if you want the chart to display gridlines. (Gridlines are useful for comparing data points closely.)

FIGURE 12.23

Choose basic options for the chart on the Basic Options page of the New Chart dialog box.

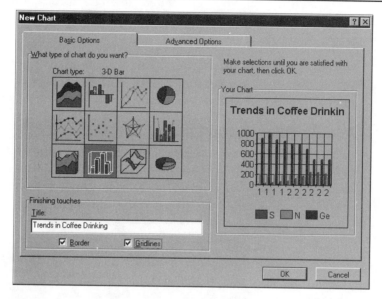

4. If your data doesn't appear to be organized correctly in the chart, click the Advanced Options tab to display the Advanced Options page of the New Chart dialog box (see Figure 12.24). Then change the settings for the option buttons in the How Is Your Spreadsheet Data Organized? group box until you achieve the look you need.

FIGURE 12.24

Use the Advanced Options page of the New Chart dialog box to reorganize the data series and legend in your chart.

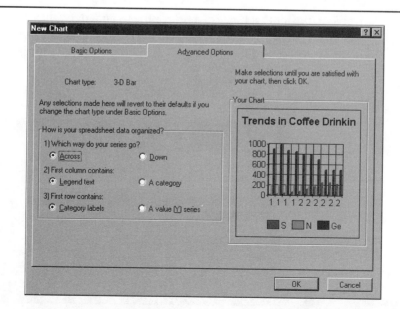

5. Click the OK button to dismiss the New Chart dialog box. Works Spreadsheet will create the chart from your data and insert it into the spreadsheet as a new page.

Editing a Chart

You probably noticed that the New Chart dialog box didn't give you a whole lot of options for customizing and formatting a chart. No problem—you just have to edit it afterwards, as described in this section.

Adding Titles to the Chart

To add titles to your chart, choose Edit ➤ Titles to display the Edit Titles dialog box (see Figure 12.25). Change the chart title, and add a subtitle and axis titles as necessary. Then click the OK button to close the dialog box and apply your changes.

FIGURE 12.25
You can add a subtitle and axis titles by using the Edit Titles dialog box.

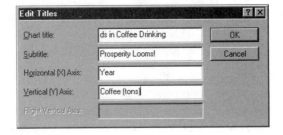

Changing the Font and Style of a Title or the Legend

To change the font and style of a title or the legend, right-click it and choose Font And Style from the context menu to display the Format Font And Styles dialog box (see Figure 12.26). Select font formatting, color, and style, and change the orientation if appropriate. Then click the OK button to close the dialog box and apply your choices.

FIGURE 12.26
Use the Format Font And Styles dialog box to apply font and style formatting to a title or to the legend.

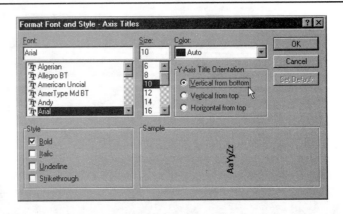

Changing the Legend

To change the legend, right-click it and choose Legend/Series Labels from the context menu to display the Edit Legend/Series Labels dialog box (see Figure 12.27). In the Series Labels list box, enter for each series either the text to assign or the address of the cell that contains the text. Click the OK button to close the dialog box and apply your legend. (Alternatively, you can select the Auto Series Labels check box to have Works Spreadsheet apply generic labels, such as Series 1 and Series 2, to your series, but there's usually little point in doing so.)

FIGURE 12.27
*Use the Edit Legend/
Series Labels dialog
box to change the
legend.*

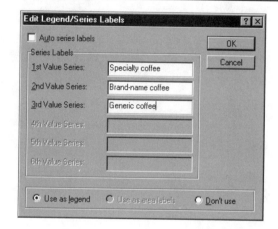

Changing the Chart Type

If you decide your chart doesn't look good, you can try changing it to a different type. Choose Format ➢ Chart Type to display the Chart Type dialog box (see Figure 12.28). On the Basic Types page, select the basic type of chart. Then click the Variations tab to display the Variations page, and see if one of the variations looks better.

FIGURE 12.28
*Use the Chart Type
dialog box to change
the type of a chart.*

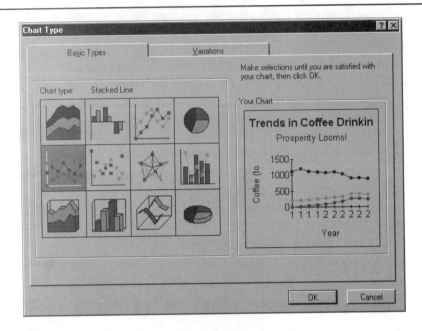

When you've decided which type of chart to use, click the OK button to apply it.

Renaming a Chart

Works Spreadsheet assigns to each chart in a spreadsheet a default name: Chart1, Chart2, and so on. To assign a more descriptive name so that you can identify your charts more easily, choose Tools ➢ Rename Chart to display the Rename Chart dialog box (see Figure 12.29). Select the chart in the Select A Chart list box, type a name in the Type A Name Below text box, and click the Rename button. Then click the OK button to close the Rename Chart dialog box.

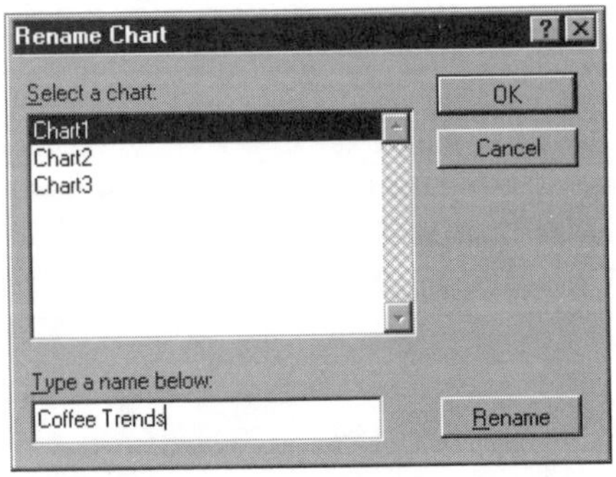

FIGURE 12.29
*Use the Rename Chart
dialog box to assign a
descriptive name to
a chart.*

Duplicating a Chart

By duplicating a chart, you can quickly make a new chart that you can then alter to present different information or to present information differently.

To duplicate a chart, choose Tools ➤ Duplicate Chart. In the Duplicate Chart dialog box (see Figure 12.30), select the chart to duplicate in the Select A Chart list box, enter the name for the duplicate in the Type A Name Below text box, and click the Duplicate button. Click the OK button to close the Duplicate Chart dialog box.

FIGURE 12.30
Use the Duplicate Chart dialog box to duplicate a chart.

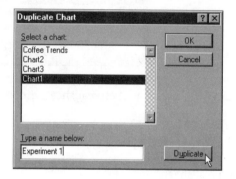

Deleting a Chart

To delete a chart, choose Tools ➤ Delete Chart. In the Delete Chart dialog box (see Figure 12.31), select the chart to delete in the Select A Chart list box, and click the Delete button. Click the OK button to close the dialog box. Be warned that deleting a chart is not an undoable action.

FIGURE 12.31
Use the Delete Chart dialog box to delete a chart.

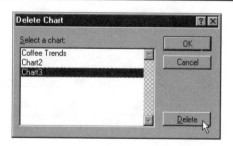

Displaying a Chart

To display a chart, choose View ➤ Chart. Works will display the View Chart dialog box (see Figure 12.32). Choose the appropriate chart, then click the OK button.

FIGURE 12.32
*Use the View Chart
dialog box to navigate
to a chart.*

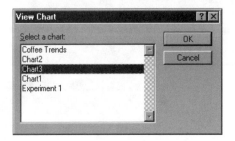

To return from a chart to its spreadsheet, choose View ➤ Spreadsheet.

Saving a Spreadsheet

To save a spreadsheet:

1. Click the Save button on the toolbar, or choose File ➤ Save, to display the Save As dialog box (see Figure 12.33).

FIGURE 12.33
*To save a spreadsheet,
specify a filename and
folder in the Save As
dialog box, and choose
whether to save a
backup copy of the file.*

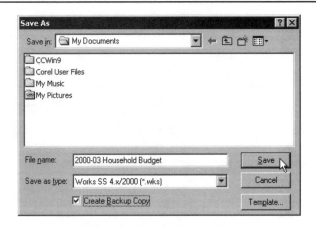

2. Choose a suitable folder for the spreadsheet in the Save In drop-down list or list box.

3. Enter the name for the spreadsheet in the File Name text box.

4. If you want to save the spreadsheet in a format other than Works Spreadsheet, choose the format in the Save As Type drop-down list. For example, if you planned to share the spreadsheet with someone who used Excel, you might choose Excel 97–2000.

5. If you want to create a backup copy of the spreadsheet, select the Create Backup Copy check box. (This is a good idea for important files.)

6. Click the Save button to save the spreadsheet.

Printing a Spreadsheet

This section shows you how to print a spreadsheet.

Your first step should be to make sure that Works Spreadsheet will print the area of the spreadsheet that you want to print. By default, Works Spreadsheet guesses the appropriate area of the spreadsheet by examining blocks of cells that have contents and ignoring stragglers. For example, if you have a block of information in cells A1 to D5, and a single cell with stray information in cell K25, Works will print the cells A1 to D5 and ignore cell K25.

To set the print area manually, select the area you want to print, then choose Format ➤ Set Print Area. Works Spreadsheet will display the Microsoft Works dialog box shown in Figure 12.34 asking you to confirm your choice. Click the OK button.

FIGURE 12.34
Works Spreadsheet checks that you know what you're doing when you set the print area manually.

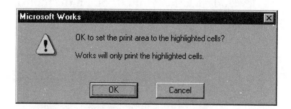

Then choose File ➤ Print Preview, or click the Print Preview button on the toolbar, to display the spreadsheet in Print Preview. Print Preview displays the information that will print, together with any header and footer you've set, so you can see how the spreadsheet will look. Use the Previous and Next buttons to navigate from page to page, and the Zoom In and Zoom Out buttons to zoom in and out on the spreadsheet.

Figure 12.35 shows a spreadsheet in Print Preview.

FIGURE 12.35
Use Print Preview to make sure that your spreadsheet is set up suitably for printing.

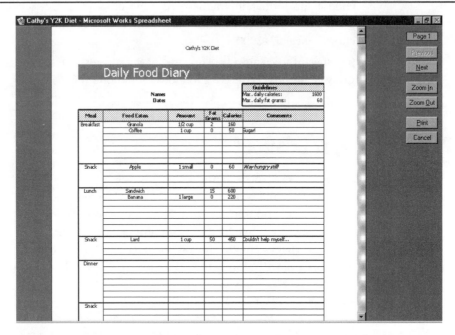

If everything looks okay in Print Preview, click the Print button to display the Print dialog box (see Figure 12.36). Alternatively, you can click the Cancel button to exit Print Preview and click the Print button on the toolbar, or choose File ➤ Print, to display the dialog box.

FIGURE 12.36
Use the Print dialog box to specify which pages of your spreadsheet to print.

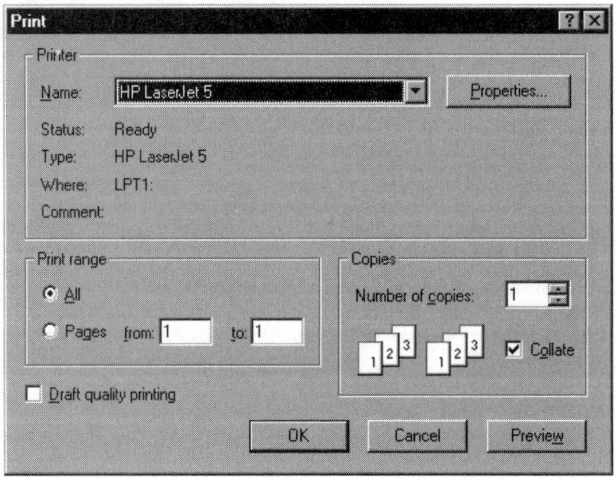

Choose options for printing as follows:

- Make sure the right printer appears in the Name box. If not, change the printer by selecting it from the Name drop-down list.

- In the Print Range group box, choose whether to print all the pages of the spreadsheet or a range of pages.

- Select the Draft Quality Printing check box if you want to print at draft quality. (Using draft quality usually makes your spreadsheet print more quickly and use less ink, but the printout doesn't look professional.)

- To print more than one copy of the spreadsheet, change the number in the Number Of Copies text box. To print each copy of the first sheet, then each copy of the second, and so on, clear the Collate check box.

Click the OK button to print the spreadsheet.

Closing a Spreadsheet

To close a spreadsheet, click the Close button (the ∞ button) at the upper-right corner of the spreadsheet window, or choose File ➤ Close.

If the spreadsheet contains unsaved changes, you'll see the Microsoft Works dialog box shown in Figure 12.37 prompting you to save them. Click the Yes button to save the file before closing it, the No button to close the file without saving changes, or the Cancel button to return to the spreadsheet (without closing it).

FIGURE 12.37
If you go to close a spreadsheet that contains unsaved changes, Works Spreadsheet will prompt you to save them.

Opening a Spreadsheet

To open a spreadsheet:

1. Click the Open button on the toolbar, or choose File ➤ Open, to display the Open dialog box (see Figure 12.38).

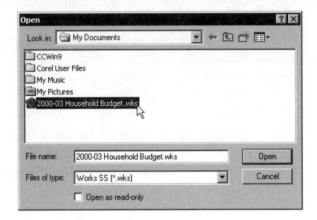

2. Navigate to and select the spreadsheet you want to open.

   • To open a spreadsheet of a type other than Works Spreadsheet, select the appropriate type from the Files Of Type drop-down list. For example, to open an Excel spreadsheet, select Excel SS.

   • To open the spreadsheet as a read-only file, select the Open As Read-Only check box. When you open a document as read-only, you will not be able to save any changes to it under its original name, though you will be able to save the document under a different name or in a different location.

3. Click the Open button to open the spreadsheet.

CHAPTER **13**

Using Formulas and Functions

Every spreadsheet program needs a full set of formulas and functions in order to be properly useful, and Works Spreadsheet is no exception: Its list of formulas and functions is enough to terrify large mammals and deflect swarms of angry bees. The good news is that Works Spreadsheet makes the most important formulas and functions very easy to use, and if you want to create a simple formula that, say, adds the contents of the cells in a column or divides the contents of one cell by the contents of another, it will take you no more than a few clicks of the mouse. Works Spreadsheet's Easy Calc feature also makes creating more complex formulas relatively straightforward (though of course it helps for you to know what you're doing).

In this chapter, I'll stick to the practical at the expense of the esoteric. You'll learn what formulas and functions actually are (and what the difference between the two is), what they consist of, and how you can enter them in your spreadsheets quickly and easily. At the end of the chapter, you'll learn how to create named ranges for quick reference and quick access to your data.

What Are Formulas and Functions?

A *formula*, as you'll remember from those blissful days in math class, is a recipe for performing calculations on numerical data. A formula can be anything from simple addition, such as the hours on an invoice, to complex calculations on the distance of Santa Fe from Tierra del Fuego in miles, inches, or multiples of the length of the average earthworm.

A *function* is a predefined formula built into Works Spreadsheet. Works Spreadsheet ships with enough functions to satisfy most computing needs—everything from a straightforward SUM formula (for adding two or more values) to an ugly STD for calculating standard deviation (if you don't know what that is, don't ask) of a population based on samples. But for specialized projects, or if you can't be bothered to dredge through Works Spreadsheet's functions for an unknown function that will meet your needs, you can create your own powerful formulas swiftly and safely.

The Parts of a Formula

To create a formula, you need to specify the data to be used in the computation and the operation or operations to be performed. Data can consist of constants (numbers) and references to cells, as you'll see in the next section. Operations use four categories of operators: arithmetic, logical, text, and reference.

Constants

A *constant* is a number entered directly into a formula—it uses a constant value in every calculation (unless you change the formula). For example, you could enter the following formula in a cell to subtract 31 from 33:

```
=33-31
```

When you press Enter, the cell will display **2**. The initial = sign tells Works Spreadsheet that you're entering a formula in the cell; **33** and **31** are constants, and the minus sign is the operator for subtraction.

The example probably seems pointless: You would do better to enter **2** in the cell and forget about using the formula. And as you can imagine, using constants for all the values in a calculation in a spreadsheet is about as slow (and accurate) as punching them into a calculator. Usually, you will want to use references in your formulas instead of constants.

References

A *reference* indicates to Works Spreadsheet the location of the information you want to use in a formula. By using references instead of constants, you can build formulas that you don't need to change when the data in your worksheet changes. For example, to perform the calculation 33-31, you could enter **33** in cell B4 and **31** in cell B5 and then enter this formula in cell B6:

```
=B4-B5
```

This formula tells Works Spreadsheet to subtract the contents of cell B5 from the contents of cell B4. Now you can change the data in cells B4 and B5, and Works Spreadsheet will automatically recalculate the values and display the result in cell B6.

One of the easiest ways to enter the references to a formula is to use range names, which I'll show you how to do at the end of this chapter. For example, if you've assigned the name **TotalIncome** to one cell and the name **TotalOutgoings** to another, you could use this formula to calculate the net income:

```
=TotalIncome-TotalOutgoings
```

By using range names, you avoid having to specify which cell or range of cells the information is currently residing on. This can save you a great deal of time and effort.

Operators

The *operator* is the way in which you tell Works Spreadsheet which operation to perform with the data you've supplied by using constants and references. Works Spreadsheet uses four types of operators: arithmetic, logical, text, and reference.

Arithmetic Operators

The six *arithmetic operators* are the old standbys from math adapted slightly for the keyboard:

Operator	Action	Example
+	Addition	=D4+E4
/	Division	=20/E4
^	Exponentiation	5^2
*	Multiplication	=E5*24
%	Percent	20%
–	Subtraction	=D4-E4

As you no doubt remember from that math class, exponentiation raises the specified number to the given power (for example, 2^2 is 2 to the power of 2—2∞2, or 2 squared). The percent operator divides the number preceding it by 100 to produce a percentage, so 20% is expressed as 0.2.

Logical Operators

Straight math is all very well, but you also need to be able to compare values. To do so, you need to use *logical operators*, which are also known as *comparison operators*. The following list shows the logical operators.

Operator	Meaning	Example
=	Equal to	=D5=6
>	Greater than	=D5>6
<	Less than	=6<5
>=	Greater than or equal to	=A33>=350
<=	Less than or equal to	=99>=100000
<>	Not equal to	=A5<>"Penguin"

As you can see from these examples, these operators compare one value or text string (such as *Penguin* in the sixth example) to another. They return a result of TRUE if the condition is true (if it is met) and a result of FALSE if the condition is false (if it is not met). TRUE is represented as a mathematical 1 and FALSE as a mathematical 0 (zero). This means that, while a cell will display TRUE or FALSE if you've used True/False number formatting on it, if you use the result of the cell in a formula, it will be treated as a 1 or a 0.

Text Operator

The third type of operator is the *text operator*, of which there's only one: the ampersand (&), which is used for joining two labels together. For example, if cell C47 contains the label *2001* and cell D47 contains the label *Projections* (with a space before it that you can't see in this book), you could use the formula **=C47&D47** to produce the result *2001 Projections* in another cell. Note that the 2001 in cell C47 has to be a label (formatted as text) rather than a number; if it's a number, the formula will return ERR, the error value.

Reference Operators

The fourth type of operator is the *reference operator*, of which Works Spreadsheet uses two:

Operator	Meaning	Example
:	Range—refers to the cells between (and including) the two reference cells	A1:A3
,	Union—for combining two or more references into one	SUM(A1:A3,A5:A7)

How Operators Work

So far the examples you've seen have been agreeably simple, using only one operator apiece. But when any formula contains more than one operator, the order in which the operators are evaluated becomes important. For example, the formula **=50*100-40** could mean that either you multiply 50 by 100 and then subtract 40 from the result (giving you 4960) or you subtract 40 from 100 and then multiply 50 by the result (60), to get 3000. As you can see, these figures are distinct enough to make an appreciable difference to the bottom line or to drive your accountant to distraction.

Works Spreadsheet evaluates operators in the order of precedence shown in the following list. When two operators have the same precedence, Works Spreadsheet evaluates them from left to right (because that's the direction you read in).

Operator	Action
−	Negation (negative numbers)
%	Percent
^	Exponentiation
* and /	Multiplication and division
+ and −	Addition and subtraction
=, >, <, <=, >=, <>	Comparison

You'll see from this list that in the example above (**=50*100-40**), Works Spreadsheet will evaluate the multiplication operator before the subtraction operator, giving you a result of 4960.

If you want to perform the calculation the other way, read the next section for instructions on how to use parentheses to change the order in which Works Spreadsheet evaluates operators.

Changing Operator Precedence in a Formula

Memorizing the operator precedence list and applying it effectively can be tricky. To alleviate this difficulty, Works Spreadsheet lets you use parentheses to change the order in which it evaluates the operators in a formula. Works Spreadsheet evaluates the contents of parentheses in a formula first, ignoring its otherwise slavish devotion to operator precedence. For example, you could change the example formula **=50*100-40** to **=50*(100-40)** to force Works Spreadsheet to evaluate the contents of the parentheses before the multiplication (and thus produce the result 3000).

When you use parentheses in a formula, you have to use them in pairs, so that each left (opening) parenthesis is matched by a right (closing) parenthesis. If you try to enter a formula that's missing a parenthesis, Works Spreadsheet will usually display a message box suggesting a way to fix the problem by adding a missing parenthesis or by removing an extra one. Figure 13.1 shows an example of this help.

FIGURE 13.1
If you miss a parenthesis in a formula, Works Spreadsheet will try to fix the formula for you.

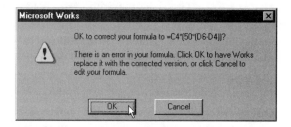

You can click the OK button to accept the automatic fix, or click the Cancel button to get a message box telling you that the formula contains an error and suggesting possible recourses (see Figure 13.2).

FIGURE 13.2
If you reject Works Spreadsheet's help in fixing a formula, you'll see a message box such as this identifying the problem.

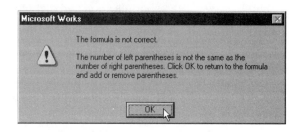

Pairing parentheses becomes even more important when you *nest* parentheses, putting one pair of parentheses inside another. As you'd guess if you're heavily into math, Works Spreadsheet will evaluate the nested parentheses first. For example, in the formula **=400-(44/A2)+(3*(C3+1))**, Works Spreadsheet will evaluate C3+1 first.

If you find it difficult to figure out what's going to be evaluated first in your formulas, you can use parentheses even when they are not strictly necessary in order to tell Works Spreadsheet how you want a formula to be calculated.

Using the Easy Calc Feature to Create Formulas

Works Spreadsheet provides a powerful feature called Easy Calc to help you put together the formulas you need for your spreadsheets. Easy Calc is essentially a wizard, though it's not described as one: It's a series of dialog boxes that walks you through the steps in creating a formula. Because different formulas need different information, the number of dialog boxes that Easy Calc displays differs from one formula to another.

In this section, you'll learn how to use Easy Calc to create custom formulas of your own. I'll show you an example of creating a formula with Easy Calc, so that you can see how Easy Calc works. After that, I'll show you some examples of editing formulas and creating formulas manually.

Starting Easy Calc

To start Easy Calc, click the Easy Calc button on the toolbar or choose Tools ➤ Easy Calc. Works Spreadsheet will display the opening Easy Calc dialog box (see Figure 13.3). As you can see, this dialog box provides buttons for five different types of common calculations—sum, multiply, subtract, divide, and average—together with an Other button for accessing the complete list of functions that Works Spreadsheet supports.

FIGURE 13.3
The opening Easy Calc dialog box provides access to five different types of common functions and to the full list of functions that Works Spreadsheet supports.

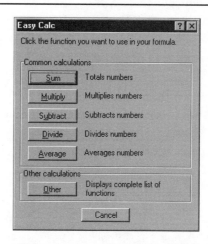

Creating a SUM Formula

Follow these steps to create a SUM formula with Easy Calc:

1. Click the Easy Calc button on the toolbar, or choose Tools ➤ Easy Calc, to display the opening Easy Calc dialog box.

2. Click the Sum button. Easy Calc will display the Easy Calc dialog box shown in Figure 13.4, with information about the SUM formula and instructions for how to proceed.

FIGURE 13.4

The first dialog box for creating a SUM formula with Easy Calc

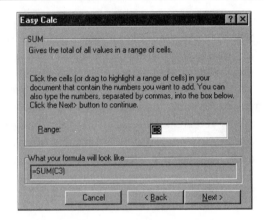

3. In the Range text box, Easy Calc will have entered the address of the active cell (in this example, cell C3), or the selected block of cells, or a range above or to the right of the active cell, that seems to be a good candidate for summing. Change this by clicking each cell you want to add, or by dragging to select a block of cells, as shown in Figure 13.5. Easy Calc will update the Range text box to match your choices, and the What Your Formula Will Look Like box at the bottom of the Easy Calc dialog box will display the formula.

4. Click the Next button to continue. Easy Calc will display the final Easy Calc dialog box for the calculation.

5. Click in the spreadsheet to designate the cell in which to enter the formula (see Figure 13.6). Easy Calc will enter the cell address in the Result At text box. (You can type the cell address in the Result At text box if you find that easier.)

FIGURE 13.5
Click or drag in the spreadsheet to specify the cells to add.

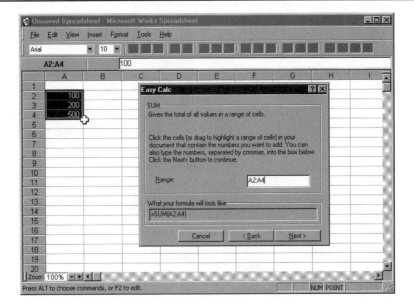

FIGURE 13.6
Specify the cell in which to enter the formula.

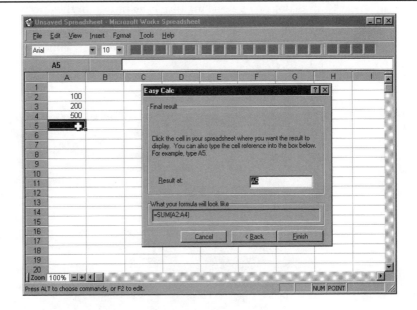

6. Click the Finish button to close the Easy Calc dialog box and enter the formula in the spreadsheet. As you can see in Figure 13.7, the result of the formula appears in the cell you specified, and the formula itself appears in the Formula bar when the cell is active.

FIGURE 13.7
The formula result appears in the cell, and the formula appears in the Formula bar when the cell is active.

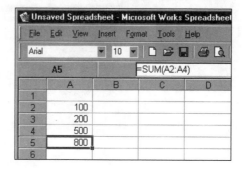

Entering a Function

For times when sum, multiply, subtract, divide, and average calculations aren't enough, you'll need to enter functions from the Insert Function dialog box. You can display this dialog box by clicking the Other button in the opening Easy Calc dialog box, but that just adds an unnecessary step. Instead, follow these steps:

1. Choose Insert ➤ Function to display the Insert Function dialog box (see Figure 13.8).

FIGURE 13.8
Use the Insert Function dialog box to insert functions beyond those handled by the Easy Calc feature.

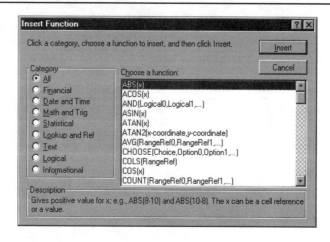

2. In the Category list box, select the category of function you're looking for. The Choose A Function list box will display the list of functions in that category. Figure 13.9 shows the functions in the Math And Trig category.

FIGURE 13.9

Select the appropriate category of functions. The Choose A Function list box will display the available functions.

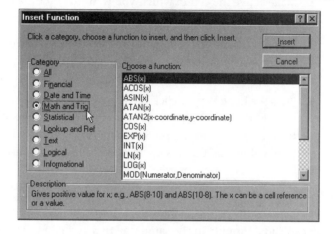

3. In the Choose A Function list box, select the function you want to use. In this example, I'll choose the SIN function, which calculates the sine of an angle. You'll notice that the function is listed as **SIN(x)**, the *x* being a variable representing the angle whose sine is to be calculated.

4. Click the Insert button to insert the function in the spreadsheet in the active cell. Works Spreadsheet will select the part or parts of the function that require further input (see Figure 13.10).

FIGURE 13.10

Works Spreadsheet inserts the function and selects the part of it that requires more input.

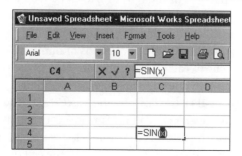

5. Click in the spreadsheet to enter the cell reference, or type it (or a value) directly in the cell.

6. Add further information as necessary. (In the case of the SIN function, only one piece of information is required.)

7. Press the Enter key to enter the formula in the cell.

Creating a Formula Manually

Once you know what a particular formula looks like, you may want to enter it manually rather than meandering through the various stages of the Easy Calc feature. To do so:

1. Make active the cell in which you want to enter the formula.

2. Type = and the start of the formula: **=SUM(**

3. You can either type cell addresses directly into the Formula bar or click (or drag, if appropriate) to enter them. (You can type directly into the cell as well as the Formula bar, but usually the Formula bar is easier to use.)

4. Press the Enter key, or click the Enter button on the Formula bar, to enter the formula in the cell. (Make sure you don't press or click Enter until you've completed the formula, or else Works Spreadsheet will display one of a variety of error messages telling you that it's incomplete and what you need to do to fix it.)

Editing a Formula

You can edit a formula in the same way that you edit the contents of any other cell: Click the cell to select it, so that its formula appears in the Formula bar. Then adjust the formula as necessary. Press the Enter key or click the Enter button on the Formula bar to enter the edited formula in the cell.

Copying a Formula

You can copy and paste a formula in much the same way that you can copy and paste the contents of any other cell—but there is one key difference: You have to make sure that the references in the resulting formula refer to the cells you want them to.

Here's how it works. By default, Works Spreadsheet uses *relative references* in your spreadsheets. Relative references work relative to the cell containing the formula. For example, say you have three columns of numbers—A, B, and C—and you want to subtract the value in each B cell from the value in the corresponding A cell and then multiply the result by the value in the corresponding C cell. You could enter in cell D1 the formula **=(A1-B1)*C1**, copy it, and paste it into the remaining cells in column D. With relative references, Works Spreadsheet will adjust the formula it enters in each cell so that each performs the same relative operation: Subtract the value in the cell three columns to the left by the value in the cell two columns to the left, and multiply the result by the value in the cell one column to the left. So cell D2 will contain the formula **=(A2-B2)*C2**, cell D4 will contain **=(A4-B4)*C4**, and so on.

Relative references are useful in creating spreadsheets quickly, but sometimes you'll want to use absolute references instead. An *absolute reference* refers to the same place in a workbook no matter where you copy and paste it to. For example, suppose you wanted to add your beloved state sales tax to the calculation in the previous example, and cell E10 held the current tax rate. If you used the relative reference **E10** in the first formula, (**=(A1-B1)*C1*E10**), Works Spreadsheet would change E10 to E11, E12, and so on when you pasted the formula into other cells. But when you use an absolute reference, Works Spreadsheet will not change the reference: Cells D2, D3, and so on will still use E10 as the reference.

Works Spreadsheet uses the dollar sign ($) to denote absolute references, so the absolute reference for cell E10 would be E10. As you can see, both the column and the row need the dollar sign for the reference to be absolute. This is because you can also create *mixed references*—references either with the column absolute and the row relative (**$E10**) or with the column relative and the row absolute (**E$10**).

To quickly create an absolute reference or a mixed reference while creating a formula manually, select the reference by clicking in its cell, and then press the F4 key once, twice, or thrice:

- Once produces an absolute reference.
- Twice produces a mixed reference relative in the column and absolute in the row.
- Thrice produces a mixed reference absolute in the column and relative in the row.

Pressing the F4 key a fourth time returns you to a relative reference.

NOTE Two quick notes here: First, when you use Cut and Paste to move a formula (rather than Copy and Paste to copy it), Works Spreadsheet does not change its references. Second, when you move all or part of a range of data referenced in a formula, Works Spreadsheet modifies the reference in the formula (whether absolute, mixed, or relative) to reflect the new location. If you move just part of a range, you may get severely unexpected results.

Creating and Using Named Ranges

A relatively advanced technique that you need to learn in order to use formulas most effectively is that of creating named ranges.

A *named range* is a range that has a name by which you can identify it. For example, instead of referring to the range A1:A10 by their addresses, you could create a named range called `Titles` and use it to refer to and access that range. And if you'd entered your consulting rate in cell Z44, you could create a named range called `Consulting-Rate` and use that in your formulas instead of the cell address.

WARNING Make sure you use a unique name for each new range you create—if you reuse a name, Works Spreadsheet will overwrite the existing range name by assigning the name to the new range.

Creating a Named Range

To name a range:

1. Select the range.

2. Choose Insert ➤ Range Name to display the Range Name dialog box (see Figure 13.11).

FIGURE 13.11
Use the Range Name dialog box to create and manage named ranges.

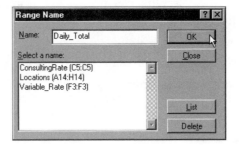

3. Enter the name for the range in the Name text box. Range names can be up to 15 characters long. They can include alphanumerics, spaces, and underscores.

4. Click the OK button to apply the range name to the range and close the Range Name dialog box.

Going to a Named Range

Once you've created a named range, you can access it quickly by using the Go To dialog box. Choose Edit ➤ Go To to display the Go To dialog box (see Figure 13.12). Select the range in the Select A Range Name list box, then click the OK button to close the Go To dialog box and make Works Spreadsheet select the range.

FIGURE 13.12
Use the Go To dialog box to go to a named range.

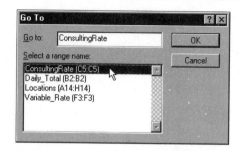

Using a Named Range in a Formula

You can use your named ranges in formulas by specifying the range name instead of the relevant cell address or range address. For example, the following formula subtracts the contents of the named range Outgoings from the named range Income:

```
=Income-Outgoings
```

Deleting a Named Range

To delete a range name, choose Insert ➤ Range Name to display the Range Name dialog box, select the range in the Select A Name list box, and click the Delete button. Click the OK button to close the Range Name dialog box.

CHAPTER 14

Creating and Using Databases

As you'll remember from Chapter 1, Works includes database functionality in the shape of the Works Database application.

Technically, Works Database is quite limited in what it can do. If you're used to a powerful database such as Microsoft Access or Corel Paradox from your workplace, you may find Works' database frustratingly limited. But for straightforward databases, such as home inventories and recipe books, it can be an effective solution.

Database concepts tend to be harder to grasp than word processing concepts or spreadsheet concepts, so in this chapter, you'll stick with the concrete. I'll start by teaching you the database essentials that you need to know before you start messing with databases. Then I'll show you how to use Works Database's Inventory Wizard to create a home inventory of videos. After the wizard has done the grunt work, you'll enter information in the database. You'll then adapt the database to learn some additional skills that will come in handy both for creating databases of your own from scratch and when modifying databases created by Works Database wizards. Finally, I'll show you how to create a database from scratch and add forms to it.

Database Essentials

Before you start messing with databases, you need to understand the key terms they use. I'll keep this section as brief as possible.

To put it crudely, a database is a bunch of organized data. A database typically consists of *records* that are built from a number of *fields*. For example, your Address Book is a database of sorts, containing a number of records, each of which holds information on one contact. The information on each contact is broken up into fields—one field for the first name, one for the middle initial, one for the last name, several for the address, and so on. Likewise, your bank and video store undoubtedly maintain databases of information on their customers, with you appearing as one record—and by recent accounts, the information on your dubious rental habits is much more secure than your spending habits. But that's another story...

There are two main types of database: flat-file and relational. A *flat-file database* is one that contains all its records in one table, so everything can be considered to be in two dimensions (hence, *flat*). A *relational database* consists of a number of two-dimensional tables that are related to each other, typically by a shared field. You can build relationships between tables that contain different fields to pull together reports that draw on data from a number of tables, and thus display only the information you need to see.

The databases that Works Database creates are flat-file, whereas more complex database programs such as Access are relational. But while Works Database's databases are relatively simple, they're plenty powerful enough for most home and home-business purposes.

Once you've organized your data in a database, you can create reports from the data. In any report, you can include information from different fields, and you can lay out and format the fields as you see fit.

If, after reading this section, you're thinking that a Works Database database sounds like a mutant spreadsheet on steroids with some additional tools bolted onto the sides, you're essentially right. But don't let that stop you from making the most of its capabilities, because even a simple customer database can supercharge your business.

Starting Works Database

You can start Works Database in any of the following ways:

- Choose Start ➤ Programs ➤ Microsoft Works ➤ Microsoft Works Database. (That's the Microsoft Works submenu—the item with the arrow to its right— rather than the Microsoft Works item, which launches the Task Launcher.) Doing so launches Works and displays the Microsoft Works Database dialog box, which lets you open an existing database or create a new database.

- On the Tasks page in the Task Launcher, select a task that creates a Works Database database, and then click the Start button.

- On the Programs page in the Task Launcher, select Works Database in the list of programs, and then click the Start A Blank Database link.

- On the Tasks page in the Task Launcher, select Works Database in the list of programs, select a task, and then click the Start button.

- On the History page in the Task Launcher, click a link associated with Works Database.

Creating a Database Using a Wizard

Start by creating a database to catalog your video collection:

1. On the Programs page of the Task Launcher, click the Works Database item to display the list of tasks associated with Works Database.

2. Click the Home Inventory Worksheets item.

3. Click the Start button to start the Works Home Inventory Wizard (see Figure 14.1).

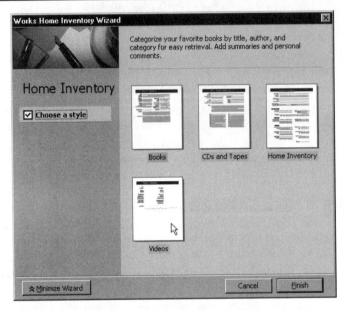

4. Click the Videos item. You'll see the Works Database window behind the Works Home Inventory Wizard dialog box change to show what the inventory will look like. If you want to see more of this preview, click the Minimize Wizard button to minimize the wizard. (Click the Maximize Wizard button to restore it when you're done looking.)

5. Click the Finish button to close the Works Home Inventory Wizard and create the database.

6. Choose File ➢ Save to display the Save As dialog box (see Figure 14.2).

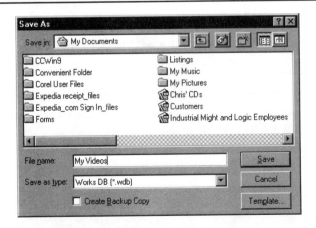

7. Enter the name for the database in the File Name text box.

8. If you want to keep a backup copy of the database, select the Create Backup Copy check box.

9. Click the Save button to save the database.

The Works Database Interface

Figure 14.3 shows the database created in the previous steps, with labels showing parts of the Works Database interface.

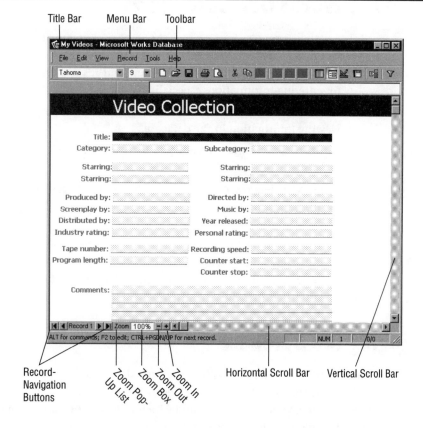

FIGURE 14.3
The database created by the Works Home Inventory Wizard

The toolbar provides both regular Windows commands and database-specific commands. Figure 14.4 shows the toolbar with labels.

FIGURE 14.4
The Works Database toolbar

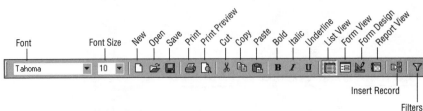

Using the Works Database Views

Works Database provides four views for viewing and organizing your data:

- List view is the basic view that you use for creating or modifying a database. You can also enter information in List view, but it's usually easier to use Form view for entering information, especially if your database is large or complex.

- Form view shows you one record at a time. You use Form view for entering and viewing information in the database.

- Form Design view is the view you use for laying out the forms you use in Form view.

- Report view lets you create and modify reports from your database.

The video collection database in Figure 14.3 is in Form view. You'll see the other views in action a little later in this chapter.

To change view, click the appropriate button on the toolbar or choose View ➤ List, View ➤ Form, View ➤ Form Design, or View ➤ Report, as appropriate. You can also press the F9 key to switch to Form view, Shift+F9 to switch to List view, or Ctrl+F9 to switch to Form Design view.

Changing the Database

The first thing you should do after creating a database with a Works Database wizard is think about changing the database. Look carefully at each of its fields and decide which to keep, which to change, and which to junk. Then add, change, format, and delete fields as described in the following sections.

Adding a Field

To add a field to a database:

1. Select the field before or after which you want to add the new field.

2. Choose Record ➤ Insert Field ➤ Before or Record ➤ Insert Field ➤ After to display the Insert Field dialog box (see Figure 14.5). As you see in the figure, Works Database will display a thick black vertical line showing where the new field will fall.

FIGURE 14.5
Use the Insert Field dialog box to insert a new field before or after the selected field.

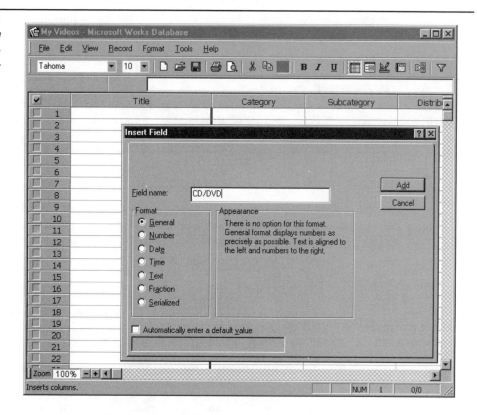

3. Enter the name for the new field in the Field Name text box. Field names can be up to 15 characters long.

4. In the Format group box, select the format for the field. For example, if you're creating a field that will always contain numeric data, click the Number option button.

5. In the Appearance group box, select any formatting options for the format you've chosen. Formats such as General and Text have no options, whereas the Number, Date, Time, Fraction, and Serialized formats have a number of options, from the number of decimal places (in the Number format) to assorted date and time formats.

6. If you want Works Database to automatically enter a default value in the field, select the Automatically Enter A Default Value check box and type the text of the

default entry in the text box. (This text box becomes available when you select the check box.) If the field will contain the same information for more than about half of its entries, having the default value entered will save you time.

7. Click the Add button to add the field.

8. Add further fields appropriate by repeating steps 3 through 7.

9. When you've finished adding fields, click the Done button to close the Insert Field dialog box.

WARNING Remember than when you add a field to a database, you'll need to enter information for that field in each existing record (or leave them blank). With large databases, adding fields becomes a logistical nightmare—and underscores why designing your databases suitably in the first place is such a good idea.

Deleting a Field

To delete a surplus field from the database, right-click its column heading and choose Delete Field from the context menu. Works Database will display the Microsoft Works dialog box shown in Figure 14.6 to make sure you know what you're doing, because deleting the field will delete all its contents as well. If you're sure you want to delete the field, click the OK button.

FIGURE 14.6
Works Database checks to make sure you really want to delete the field.

Changing a Field's Name or Format

To change the name or format of a field, choose Format ➤ Field to display the Field page of the Format dialog box (see Figure 14.7). Change the field name, the format, the formatting options, or the default value as appropriate, and then click the OK button.

FIGURE 14.7
Use the Field page of the Format dialog box to change the name or format of a field.

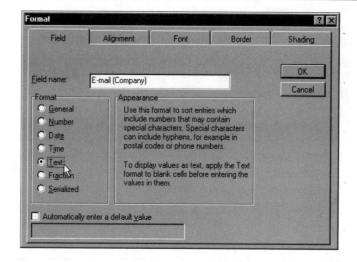

Formatting a Field

As you'll have noticed from the video-inventory database you created earlier in this chapter, you can apply a wide variety of formatting to a field. For example, the video-inventory database uses assorted shading and quite a bit of font formatting.

To format a field, choose Format ➢ Alignment, Format ➢ Font And Style, Format ➢ Border, or Format ➢ Shading as appropriate. Works Database will display the Format dialog box with the corresponding page displayed. Choose the formatting options you want, and click the OK button to apply them.

The formatting options are the same options as those for formatting a Works Spreadsheet spreadsheet, so refer back to the "Formatting Cells" section of Chapter 12 as necessary.

Changing the Field Width or Row Height

As with the columns and rows in a spreadsheet, you can adjust field width and row height as necessary:

- To widen or narrow a field, drag the right-hand border of its column heading to the right or to the left. Alternatively, choose Format ➢ Field Width and set the width in the Column Width text box in the Field Width dialog box.

- To increase or decrease the height of a row, drag the lower bound of its row heading down or up. Alternatively, choose Format ➢ Record Height and set the height in the Format Record Height dialog box.

Entering Data in Your Database

Once you've made sure that you have the appropriate fields in your database, and have them formatted to your liking, you're ready to enter information in them.

As I mentioned earlier, you can enter information in your database in either List view or Form view. List view works fine for small databases or small amounts of data, but Form view is preferable for larger databases and serious data entry.

Entering Information in List View

Entering information in List view is much like using a spreadsheet: You click in the first unused cell in the first column and type in the information, then press Tab to move to the next column (the next field in the same record) or Enter to move down to the next row (the same field for the next record). Figure 14.8 illustrates entering information in the video-collection database in List view.

FIGURE 14.8
Entering information in the video-collection database in List view

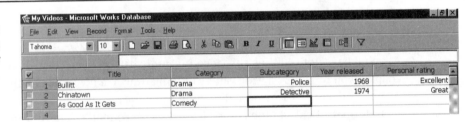

You can see the main problems: Because only five columns of information fit in the Works Database window here at this screen resolution, you can't get an overview of any given record. Also, the fields may not be in the same order as in the entry form, so you need to enter information out of order. The advantage is that you can compare fields in one entry with fields in another entry much more readily than you can in Form view.

Entering Information in Form View

Entering information in Form view is much easier. To move from one cell to the next, press the Tab key. (To move to the previous cell, press Shift+Tab.) Alternatively, click with the mouse in the cell you want to change. Figure 14.9 illustrates entering information in Form view.

FIGURE 14.9

Entering information in the video-collection database in Form view

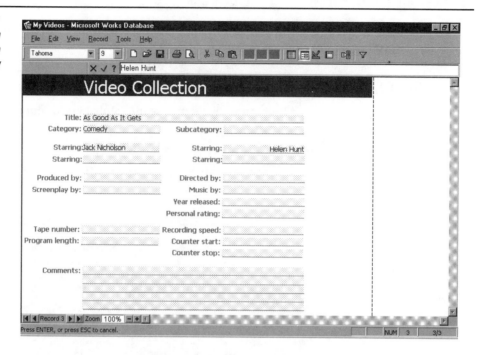

To add a new record, choose Record ➤ Insert Record; to delete the current record, choose Record ➤ Delete Record.

To move from one record to another, use the record-navigation buttons to the left of the horizontal scroll bar. Figure 14.10 shows the buttons with labels.

FIGURE 14.10

Navigate from record to record with the navigation buttons in the lower-left corner of the Works Database window.

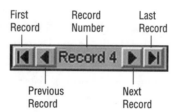

You can also navigate with the keyboard: Press Ctrl+Page Down to move to the next record, or Ctrl+Page Up to move to the previous record.

Sorting and Filtering Records

In this section, I'll show you how to sort and filter records so that you can work with the set of records you're interested in.

Sorting Records

You can quickly sort the records in a database into alphabetic or numeric order as follows:

1. Switch to List view (or Form view).

2. Choose Record ➢ Sort Records to display the Sort Records dialog box (see Figure 14.11).

FIGURE 14.11
Use the Sort Records dialog box to sort the records in your database.

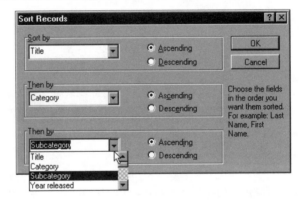

3. From the Sort By drop-down list, choose the first field by which you want to sort.

4. In the Sort By group box, select the Ascending option button to sort in ascending order (the default) or the Descending option button to sort in descending order.

5. To refine your sort, choose a second field to sort by from the first Then By drop-down list, and choose the Ascending or Descending option button as appropriate.

6. To refine your sort even further, choose a third field to sort by from the second Then By drop-down list. Again, choose the Ascending or Descending option button.

7. Click the OK button to perform the sort.

Filtering Records

By applying filters, you can restrict the display of filters to only those you want to see. Here's how to do so:

1. Click the Filters button on the toolbar, or choose Tools ➤ Filters. Works Database will display the Filter dialog box and, on top of it, the Filter Name dialog box (shown in Figure 14.12).

FIGURE 14.12
Enter the name for the filter in the Filter Name dialog box.

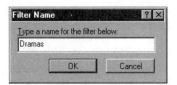

2. Enter the name for the filter in the text box and click the OK button. Works Database will close the Filter Name text box, leaving the Filter dialog box displayed (see Figure 14.13).

FIGURE 14.13
Create your filter in the Filter dialog box.

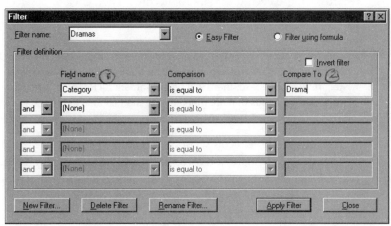

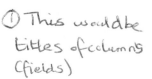
① This would be titles of columns (fields)

② This would be info reg within that column.

3. At the top of the text box, make sure that the Easy Filter option button is selected. (The alternative is to select the Filter Using Formula check box and create a formula for the filter. This alternative is more complicated, and I won't discuss it in this book.)

4. Select the field name in the first Field Name drop-down list.

5. Select the type of comparison in the first Comparison drop-down list.

6. Enter the comparison value in the first Compare To text box.

7. Specify further criteria as necessary in the next four rows of the dialog box. You can set each row either to And (to increase the scope of the filter) or to Or (to further restrict the filter defined by the first criterion).

8. Click the Apply Filter to apply the filter. Works Database will restrict the display to only the records that match the criteria in the filter.

9. To display all records again, choose View ➤ Show ➤ All Records.

To apply a filter, choose Record ➤ Apply Filter and choose the filter's name from the submenu.

Marking Records

Sometimes you'll need to filter records without an easy way of distinguishing the set you want. You could create a new custom field and set it to an appropriate value for each record, but there's an easier way—to *mark* the records temporarily. Once you've marked the records, you can filter them and then remove the marking.

The easiest way to mark records is to switch to List view, then click to select the check boxes to the left of the row headers for the records.

If you need to mark most of the records in a database, omitting only a few, you'll find it quicker to mark all the records and then unmark the exceptions. To mark all the records, choose Record ➤ Mark All Records. Then click to deselect the check boxes for the records that you don't want to have marked.

 NOTE If any records are marked, the Mark All Records command will not appear on the Record menu; instead, there will be an Unmark All Records item. Issue this command first to unmark the records that are marked, and then choose Record ➤ Mark All Records.

To unmark all the records, choose Record ➤ Unmark All Records.

To display only marked records or unmarked records, choose Record ➤ Show ➤ Marked Records or Record ➤ Show ➤ Unmarked Records, as appropriate. To display all records again, choose Record ➤ Show ➤ All Records.

Working with Reports

A *report* is a tool for summarizing information for printing. A report can include any (or all) of the fields in the database, filtered, arranged, and formatted to your liking to present the appropriate set of information effectively.

When you create a database using a wizard, the wizard automatically creates some reports for you. You can use these reports as is, or you can modify them to suit your purposes. Works Database also has a tool called ReportCreator that guides you through the process of creating a report.

A Works Database database can contain up to eight different reports, which gives you plenty of flexibility.

Creating a Report with ReportCreator

To create a report with ReportCreator:

1. Choose Tools ➢ ReportCreator. ReportCreator will display the Report Name dialog box (see Figure 14.14).

FIGURE 14.14
The first step in creating a report is to name it.

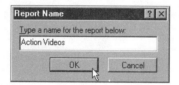

2. Enter the name for the report in the text box and click the OK button. ReportCreator will display the ReportCreator dialog box with the Title page displayed (see Figure 14.15).

FIGURE 14.15
The Title page of the ReportCreator dialog box

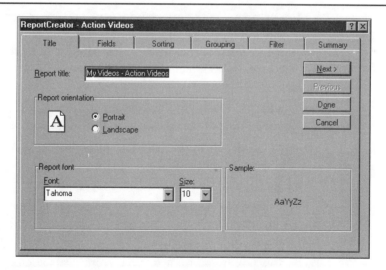

3. In the Report Title text box, ReportCreator will have entered a title derived from the name of the database and the name you entered in the Report Name dialog box. Change this name as necessary.

4. In the Report Orientation group box, choose portrait or landscape orientation as appropriate.

5. In the Report Font group box, select an appropriate font and size for the report. Watch the Sample box to see an approximation of how the currently selected font and size will look.

6. Click the Next button to display the Fields page of ReportCreator (see Figure 14.16).

FIGURE 14.16
On the Fields page of the ReportCreator dialog box, select the fields to include in the report.

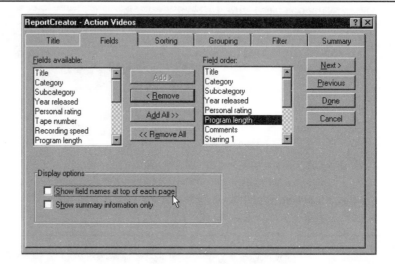

7. You can add either all the fields in the database at once, or add them one by one. Likewise, you can remove all the fields at once, or remove them one by one:

- To add all the fields in the database to the report, click the Add All button. ReportCreator will add the fields to the Field Order list box.

- To add fields one by one, select a field and click the Add button, then repeat until done. ReportCreator will add the field to the Field Order list box.

- To remove all fields from the Field Order list box, click the Remove All button.

- To remove one field from the Field Order list box, select the field and click the Remove button.

8. In the Display Options group box, select the Show Field Names At Top Of Each Page check box if you want to have Works Database print the field names as titles across the top of the pages in the report. Select the Show Summary Information Only check box if you want to reduce the report to a summary rather than having the details shown.

9. Click the Next button to display the Sorting page of ReportCreator (see Figure 14.17).

FIGURE 14.17
On the Sorting page, specify how ReportCreator should sort the items in the report.

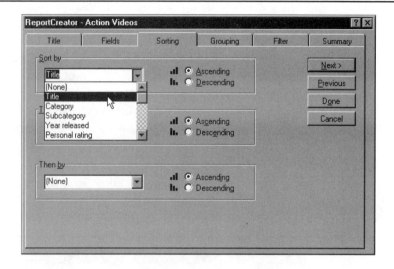

10. Use the Sort By and (if needed) the two Then By group boxes to specify sorting for the report, much as you learned in the "Sorting Records" section earlier in this chapter.

11. Click the Next button to display the Grouping page of ReportCreator (see Figure 14.18).

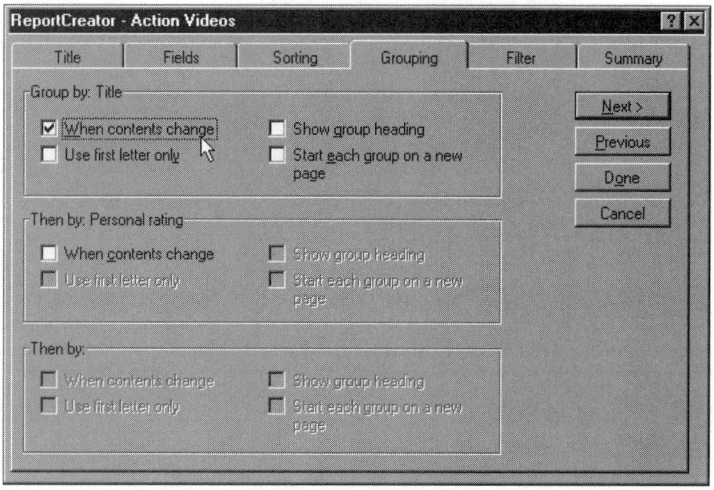

FIGURE 14.18
On the Grouping page, specify how ReportCreator should group the items in the report.

12. Specify grouping as appropriate in the Group By and two Then By group boxes. As you'd guess from their titles, these are linked to the fields you chose for sorting in the step before last. Select the When Contents Change check box to enable grouping for a field. You can then select the Use First Letter Only check box to reduce the grouping to the first letter in the field; the Show Group Heading check box to have Works Database add group headings; and the Start Each Group On A New Page check box if you want each group to start on a new page. For example, selecting the Use First Letter Only and Show Group Heading check boxes for the Action Videos report would create a group for each letter of the alphabet (at least, each letter that included videos) and would add group headings for those letters.

13. Click the Next button to display the Filter page of ReportCreator (see Figure 14.19).

FIGURE 14.19
On the Filter page of ReportCreator, select an existing filter or create a new filter.

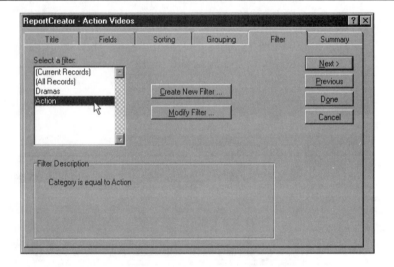

14. Select an existing filter in the Select A Filter list box or click the Create New Filter button to create a new filter as described in the "Filtering Records" section earlier in this chapter. Alternatively, select (Current Records) or (All Records) to use all current records or all records, respectively.

15. Click the Next button to display the Summary page of ReportCreator (see Figure 14.20).

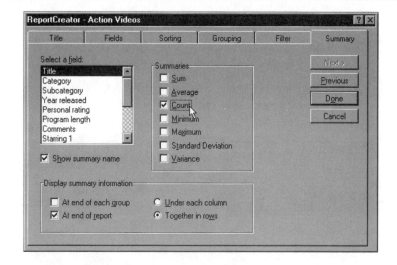

16. If you want to create a statistical summary for the report, make your selections on the Summary page:

    • Select the field, then choose the appropriate type of summary in the Summaries group box. (For example, I could select the Title field and the Count check box to create a summary that tallies the number of action movies listed in the report.)

    • Leave the Show Summary Name check box selected if you want the field name to appear with the summary. (If not, clear this check box.)

    • In the Display Summary Information group box, choose the placement of the summary information.

17. Click the Done button to close the ReportCreator dialog box. ReportCreator will display the ReportCreator dialog box shown in Figure 14.21, asking if you want to preview or modify the report definition.

18. Click the Preview button to preview your report.

19. When you've finished previewing the report, you can click the Print button to print it or the Cancel button to return to Report view in the database.

Renaming a Report

To rename a report:

1. Choose Tools ➤ Rename Report to display the Rename Report dialog box (see Figure 14.22).

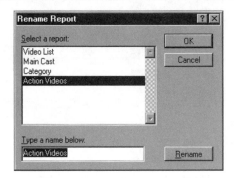

2. In the Select A Report list box, select the report.

3. Type the new name for it in the Type A Name Below text box.

4. Click the Rename button to rename the report.

5. Click the OK button to close the Rename Report dialog box.

Adding Headers and Footers to a Report

To add headers and footers to a report:

1. Choose View ➤ Headers And Footers to display the View Headers And Footers dialog box (see Figure 14.23).

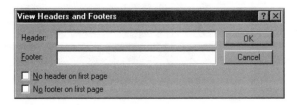

2. Enter the text for the header in the Header text box.

3. Enter the text for the footer in the Footer text box.

4. If you need to prevent the header or footer from appearing on the first page of the printout, select the No Header On First Page check box or the No Footer On First Page check box as appropriate.

5. Click the OK button to apply the header or footer to your reports.

Changing Page Setup for a Report

You can change page setup for a report as discussed in the section titled "Page Setup" in Chapter 12.

Viewing and Printing a Report

To view a report, choose View ➤ Report. In the View Report dialog box that appears (see Figure 14.24), select the report and click the Preview button to preview it.

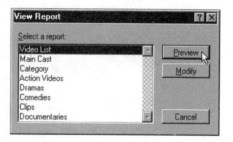

FIGURE 14.24
Use the View Report dialog box to open a report for viewing and printing.

Once you've opened the report, you can print it as usual.

Deleting a Report

Each Works Database file can contain a maximum of eight reports, so if you create a lot of reports, you may need to delete older reports in order to create new ones.

To delete a report, choose Tools ➤ Delete Report. In the Delete Report dialog box (see Figure 14.25), select the report to delete and then click the Delete button. Click the OK button to close the Delete Report dialog box.

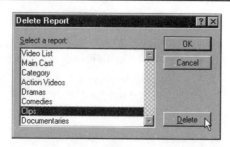

FIGURE 14.25
Each Works Database database can contain a maximum of eight reports. When you run up against this limitation, use the Delete Report dialog box to delete one or more reports.

Creating a Database from Scratch

The Works Database wizards are effective for the types of databases they offer, but their repertory is limited. Sooner or later, chances are you'll need to create a database from scratch. Here's how to proceed:

1. Plan your database (on paper or in your favorite word processor if you like). Make a list of the information the database will contain, and how you will want to have that information organized. (You can adapt the database as you go along, but you'll save a lot of time if you can plan it enough to get it right in the first place.)

2. On the Programs page of the Task Launcher, click the Works Database entry.

3. Click the Start A Blank Database link. Works Database will create a new blank database in List view and display the Create Database dialog box shown in Figure 14.26 for you to start adding fields to the database.

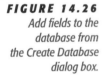

FIGURE 14.26
Add fields to the database from the Create Database dialog box.

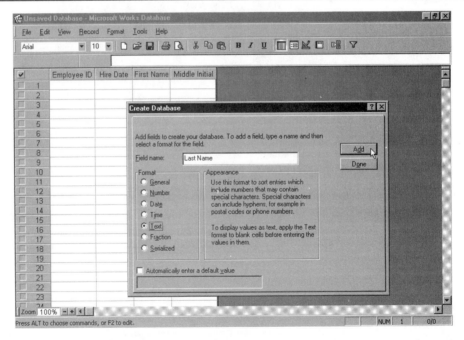

4. Add to the database the fields you've planned for it. For each field, specify the field name (up to 15 characters), a format, and formatting options as appropriate (for example, the number of decimal places to use on a Number-formatted

field). If you want Works Database to assign the field a default value automatically (to save you time), select the Automatically Enter A Default Value check box and type the value in the text box below it. Click the Add button to add each field.

5. Click the Done button when you've finished adding fields to the database.

Works Database initially displays the new database in List view, the best view for creating the fields that will contain the information.

Create the fields. Divide the information up into the smallest units you're likely to need. For example, if your database will contain people's names, divide them up into their component parts: title, first name, middle initial, last name, nickname, and suffix, at a minimum. Likewise, divide up addresses with a field for each piece of information, so that you can sort your records by street, city, state, or zip code.

 TIP The Works Address Book divides names up quite effectively. (After all, it's a database.) If you're planning a database that will include name and address information, take a glance at the Address Book to refresh your memory about which fields to include.

You can now enter information in the database as described earlier in this chapter.

Adapting a Form

When you create a database, either manually or by using one of the wizards, Works Database automatically builds a form that contains all the fields in the database. You can use this form for entering data in the database, for changing the data currently in the database, or for looking up information.

As you saw earlier in the chapter when you created the video-inventory database, the forms that the Works Database wizards create are fully formatted. By contrast, the forms that Works Database puts together for databases you create manually are plain in the extreme. Figure 14.27 shows an example of a form.

This form is fully functional, but it's not much to look at. It could benefit from a different layout, some descriptive text, and perhaps some formatting. As you might guess, you can adapt the form by working in Form Design view.

To switch to Form Design view, click the Form Design button on the toolbar or choose View ➤ Form Design. Figure 14.28 shows the previous form in Form Design view. As you can see, a shaded outline appears around each field.

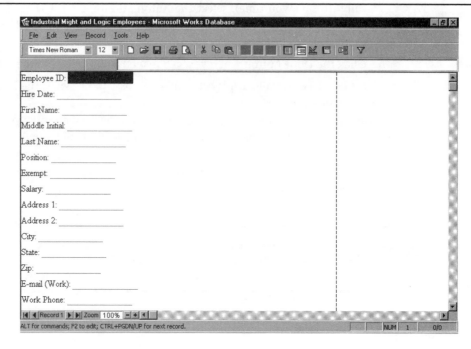

FIGURE 14.27
When you create a
database manually,
Works Database
creates a simple form
containing all the fields
in the database.

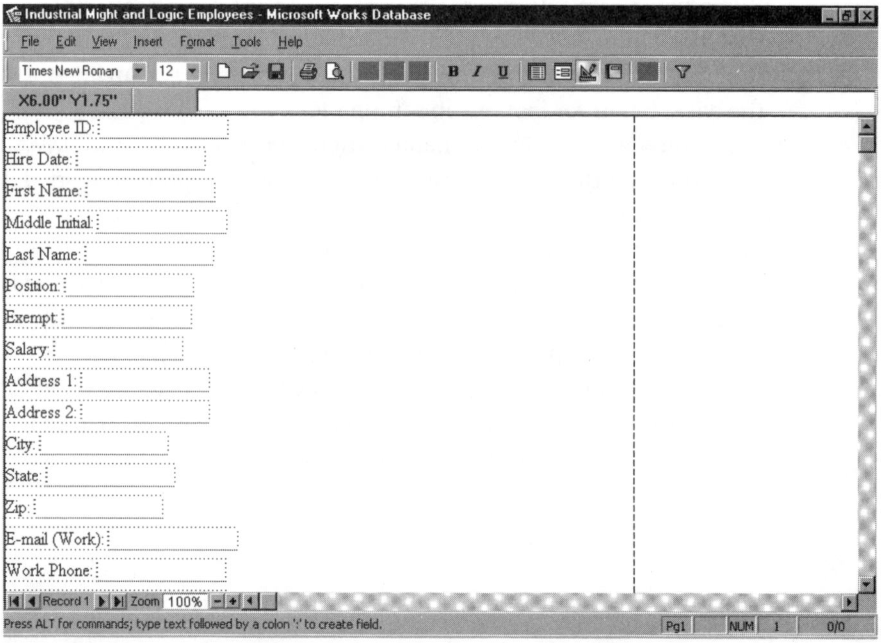

FIGURE 14.28
The previous form in
Form Design view

Moving, Resizing, and Formatting Fields

You can move, resize, and format fields as follows:

- To move a field, click it and drag it to where you want it to appear.

- To resize a field, click it to select it. Then move the mouse pointer over one of the sizing handles so that a RESIZE pointer appears, then click and drag the handle to change the field's size.

- To format a field, select it and apply alignment, font, border, or shading options as discussed in the section "Formatting a Field," earlier in this chapter.

 TIP You can switch back to Form view at any time by clicking the Form View button on the toolbar (or choosing View ➤ Form) to see how the form looks. Then switch back to Form Design view and make improvements.

Adding Labels to the Form

To make the form easier to understand or more readable, you can add labels to it. To add a label, click in the form where you want the label to appear. Works Database will place the insertion point there. Type in the text of the label.

Once you've placed a label, you can format it by using the regular formatting commands. You can also move it to a different location by dragging it, or edit it by selecting it and working in the Formula bar.

Figure 14.29 shows the form with its fields rearranged and some labels added.

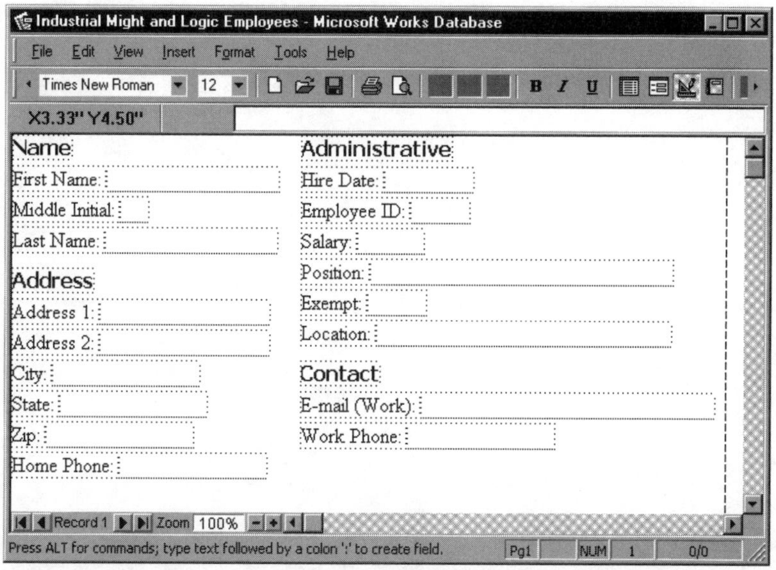

FIGURE 14.29
The form with fields rearranged and labels added

![Screenshot of Industrial Might and Logic Employees - Microsoft Works Database form showing fields organized under Name, Address, Administrative, and Contact sections]

Changing the Tab Order

The last step in adapting the form is to change its tab order. The *tab order* is the order in which you move through the fields (so called because you press the Tab key to move from field to field when entering data). You'll want to arrange the fields so that when you leave one field, Works Database moves the focus to the next field that you'll need to work with.

To change the tab order of the fields:

1. Choose Format ➢ Tab Order to display the Format Tab Order dialog box (see Figure 14.30).

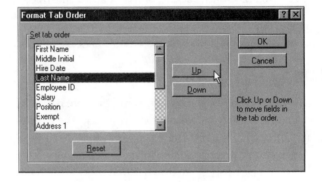

FIGURE 14.30
*Use the Format Tab
Order dialog box to
optimize the tab order
of the fields.*

2. Use the Set Tab Order list box and the Up and Down buttons to optimize the tab order: Select a field in the Set Tab Order list box and click the Up button or Down button to move it to where it belongs.

3. When you've finished changing the tab order, click the OK button to apply the new tab order to the form.

4. When you've finished making changes to your database, save it.

CHAPTER **15**

Using Works Calendar and the Address Book

Creating events and appointments

Adding holidays, birthdays, and anniversaries

Adding, deleting, and renaming categories

Finding an appointment

Printing out a calendar

Adding and deleting contacts

Importing and exporting information

Creating and using groups

Finding a forgotten contact

Works Calendar and the Address Book form the key to managing your home life or home-business life with Works Suite. By using them assiduously, you can organize your schedule and contacts with a precision that fits the twenty-first century and make sure you never miss an appointment or forget a contact's details.

As you'd guess, Works Calendar lets you work with a day, a week, or a month at a time. You can schedule appointments and events, and create reminders for them. One of the most important benefits is that you can print out the relevant parts of your calendar so that you have up-to-date information instantly accessible.

The Address Book is a friendly database that can hold the details of all your contacts—everything from their names and phone numbers (business, fax, mobile, home, pager, and more) to how many children they have and when their anniversary is. As well as storing all this information in the Address Book, you can create an e-mail message directly from a contact's name in the Address Book. You can also use the data stored in the Address Book in your mail merges.

In this chapter, I'll show you how to use Works Calendar first, then the Address Book.

Using Works Calendar

In this section, you'll learn how to use Works Calendar to schedule and manage appointments, events, and reminders. An *appointment* is an engagement that has defined starting and ending times, such as those interminable business meetings you so love and the episodes in the dentist's chair that you hate even more. An *event* is an engagement that takes place on a specific day but not at a specific time. A *reminder* is an alarm you set to remind yourself of an upcoming appointment or event.

Starting Works Calendar

You can start Works Calendar in a couple of ways:

- From the Start menu: Choose Start ➤ Programs ➤ Microsoft Works ➤ Microsoft Works Calendar.

- If you have the Task Launcher displayed: Click the Works Calendar item in the Programs list on the Programs page, and then click the Start The Calendar link.

 NOTE The first time you start Works Calendar, it will display a dialog box saying that Works Calendar is not your default calendar and asking if you want to make it your default calendar. Click the Yes button (unless you have a different calendar you prefer to use—in which case you probably shouldn't be using Works Calendar). You'll then see a Hint message box; click the OK button to dismiss it, and you'll be ready to get to work.

Figure 15.1 shows Works Calendar's interface in Day view, with one day displayed. As you can see, the interface is straightforward, with just four menus and one toolbar.

FIGURE 15.1
Works Calendar

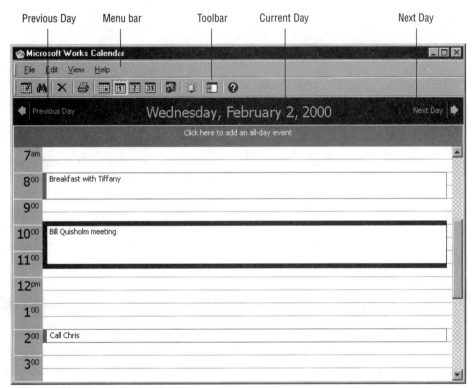

Figure 15.2 shows the buttons on the toolbar with labels.

FIGURE 15.2
Works Calendar's toolbar

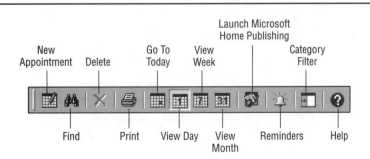

Navigating in Works Calendar

Navigating in Works Calendar is easy:

- You can view one day, one week, or one month at a time. To change the view, click the View Day, View Week, or View Month button, as appropriate. (Alternatively, choose View ➤ Day, View ➤ Week, or View ➤ Month.)

- Use the Previous link or Next link to move to the previous or next unit of time displayed (day, week, or month). If Works Calendar is displaying days, the links will be called Previous Day and Next Day; for weeks, they'll be Previous Week and Next Week; and for months, they'll be Previous Month and Next Month.

- You can restrict the view to a category of information (such as Business, Recreation, Holiday, or Sports) so that Works Calendar displays only that category. For example, you might want to see nothing but your upcoming Sports commitments. To do so, click the Category Filter button on the toolbar, or choose View ➤ Show Category Filter, to display the Category Filter pane. Select the categories you want to view, and Works Calendar will display only those appointments and events. In Figure 15.3, Works Calendar is displaying only Recreation and Sports appointments.

FIGURE 15.3

Display the Category Filter pane to filter your appointments by category. Here, the Recreation and Sports appointments are displayed; all the other appointments are hidden.

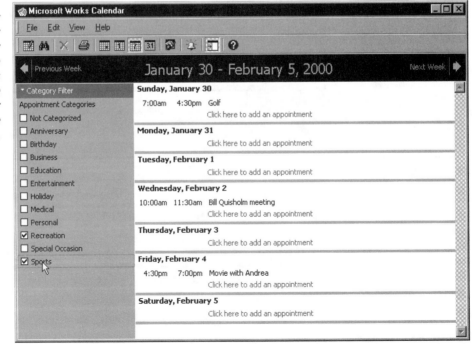

- To navigate to a specific day, week, or month, click the date display in the black bar at the top of Works Calendar. From Day view or Week view, Works Calendar will display a pop-up calendar showing a month (see Figure 15.4); from Month view, Works Calendar will display a scrolling list of months. Click the day, week, or month you want to display.

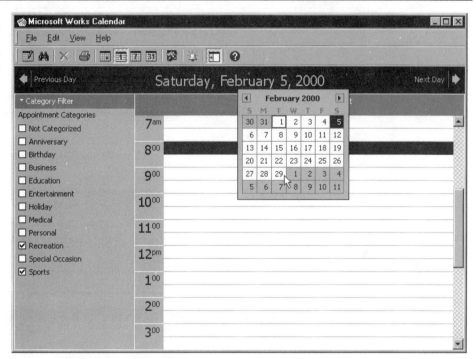

FIGURE 15.4
Click the date display at the top of Works Calendar to display a pop-up calendar for navigating to a different date.

Creating an Event

To create an event, display Works Calendar in Day view and navigate to the appropriate day. Then click the Click Here To Add An All-Day Event link below the date display. Works Calendar will display a text box for you to enter the name of the event.

Creating a Simple Appointment

To create a simple appointment—one with only a name—you can type straight into Works Calendar instead of using the New Appointment dialog box. Here's what to do:

1. Display Works Calendar in Day view.
2. Click in the appropriate time slot to select that time period.
3. Type in the text for the appointment (see Figure 15.5), then press the Enter key.

FIGURE 15.5
To create a simple
appointment, type
directly into Works
Calendar.

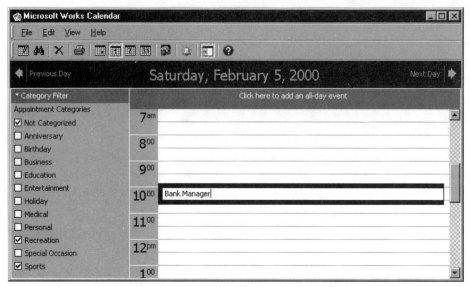

4. To change the start time or end time of the appointment, move the mouse pointer over the top or bottom border of the selected appointment, then drag it up or down as appropriate (see Figure 15.6).

FIGURE 15.6
You can change the
start time or end time of
the appointment by
dragging its top or
bottom border.

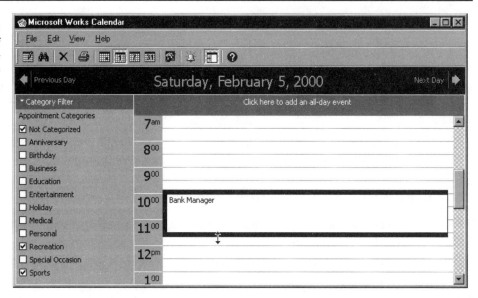

5. To assign one or more categories to the appointment, right-click it and choose Categories from the context menu to display the Choose Categories dialog box (see Figure 15.7).

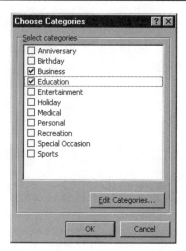

6. Choose the category or categories for the appointment, then click the OK button.

 TIP To add more detail to the appointment, you can right-click it and choose Open from the context menu to display the Edit Appointment dialog box.

Creating a More Detailed Appointment

To create a more detailed appointment, use the New Appointment dialog box as follows:

1. Right-click in the appropriate time slot and choose New Appointment from the context menu, or click the New Appointment button on the toolbar, to display the New Appointment dialog box (see Figure 15.8).

 TIP You can also display the New Appointment dialog box by selecting Works Calendar in the Programs list on the Programs page of the Task Launcher, choosing the Calendar, Set Appointment task, and clicking the Start link.

FIGURE 15.8

*Use the New
Appointment dialog
box to create detailed
appointments.*

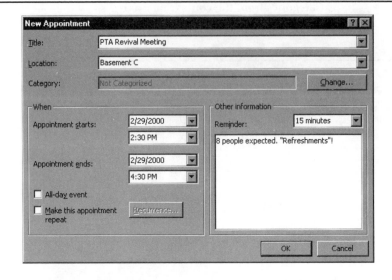

2. Enter the title for the appointment in the Title text box. The drop-down list stores each entry you make, so once you've entered some appointments, you can use the drop-down list to enter new instances of them.

3. Enter the location for the appointment in the Location text box. Again, you can use the drop-down list to reuse an earlier entry.

4. To assign a category to the appointment, click the Change button. Calendar will display the Choose Categories dialog box (shown in Figure 15.7 earlier). Select the category or categories, and then click the OK button.

5. In the When group box, change the date and time for the appointment as necessary:

   • To create an all-day event (rather than an appointment), select the All-Day Event check box.

   • To create a recurring appointment, select the Make This Appointment Repeat check box, then click the Recurrence option button to display the Recurrence Options dialog box (see Figure 15.9). Specify the recurrence in the Recurring group box and the timeframe in the Range Of Recurrence group box. In the Appointment Time group box, make sure the appointment start and end are suitable. Then click the OK button.

FIGURE 15.9
Use the Recurrence Options dialog box to create a recurring appointment.

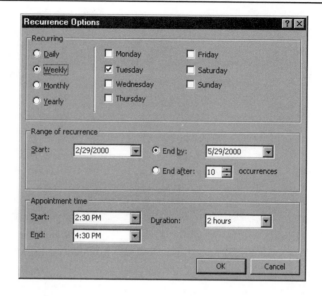

6. In the Other Information group box, select a reminder time period (None, 15 minutes, 30 minutes, 1 hour, 0.5 day, 1 day, or 1 week) from the Reminder drop-down list if you want to be reminded of the appointment. Then enter any notes related to the appointment in the text box.

7. Click the OK button to close the New Appointment dialog box. Calendar will add your new appointment to the calendar.

Adding Holidays to Your Calendar

To help you plan your work and home life better, Works Calendar lets you add holidays for a number of different countries to your calendar as follows:

1. Choose Edit ➤ Add Holidays to display the Add Holidays To Calendar dialog box (see Figure 15.10).

2. In the list box, select the check boxes for the countries whose holidays you want to add.

3. Click the OK button. Works Calendar will add the holidays and will display a confirmation dialog box to let you know all went well.

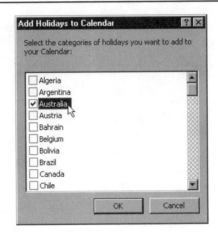

Works Calendar adds the holidays to the list of categories, so you can view the holidays by using the Category Filter pane.

Adding Birthdays and Anniversaries from the Address Book

To help you stay on good terms with your contacts, you can also add birthdays and anniversaries from the Address Book to your calendar. To do so, choose Edit ➤ Birthdays. Works Calendar will add any birthdays and anniversaries, and will display the Works Calendar dialog box shown in Figure 15.11 to tell you the results. Make sure the check box is selected if you want Works Calendar to add new birthdays and anniversaries to the calendar every time you open it. Click the OK button to close the dialog box.

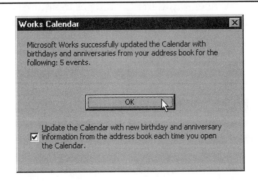

If you chose automatic updates, you'll see a dialog box like the one shown in Figure 15.12 when Works Calendar discovers a new or changed birthday or anniversary in your Address Book. Click the Yes, Update Now button to update the information. (If you don't want to be warned again about changes, select the Don't Show This Message Again check box first.)

FIGURE 15.12

If you choose automatic updates, Works Calendar will notify you of changes that need updating.

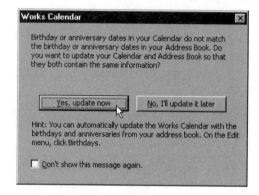

If the update is a change to a contact's birthday or anniversary date, Works Calendar will ask you to confirm the change (see Figure 15.13). Choose the appropriate option button and click the Update Now button (or click the Skip This Contact button if you need to double-check the change).

FIGURE 15.13

Works Calendar will ask you to confirm changes to existing birthdays and anniversaries.

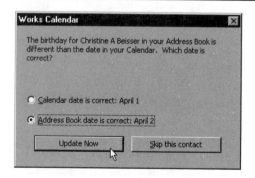

TIP Use the Anniversary and Birthday categories in the Category Filter to view anniversaries and birthdays.

Adding, Deleting, and Renaming Categories

Works Calendar comes with a number of predefined categories, but you can delete them if you want. You can also create categories of your own. To do so:

1. Choose Edit ➢ Categories to display the Edit Categories dialog box (see Figure 15.14).

FIGURE 15.14

Use the Edit Categories dialog box to add, rename, and delete categories.

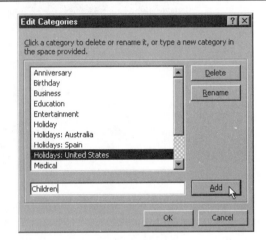

2. Add, rename, and delete categories as follows:

   • To add a category, type its name in the text box and click the Add button.

   • To rename a category, select it in the list box, type the new name in the text box, and click the Rename button.

   • To delete a category, select it in the list box and click the Delete button.

3. Click the OK button to close the Edit Categories dialog box.

If you've deleted a category that has appointments assigned to it, Works Calendar will warn you that deleting the category will remove the category from the appointments (see Figure 15.15). Click the Yes button if you want to delete the category anyway, or click the No button to keep it.

FIGURE 15.15

Works Calendar warns you when you're about to delete a category that has appointments assigned to it.

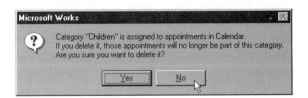

Finding an Appointment

If you lose track of an appointment, you can search for it by taking the following steps:

1. Click the Find button on the toolbar, or choose Edit ➤ Find, to display the Find dialog box (see Figure 15.16).

FIGURE 15.16
Use the Find dialog box
to find an appointment
that you've lost track of.

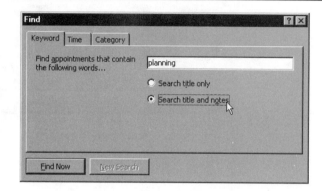

2. Specify the criteria by which you want to search:

- On the Keyword page, enter one or more keywords in the text box and choose the Search Title Only option button or the Search Title And Notes option button as appropriate.

- On the Time page, specify a time period if appropriate.

- On the Category page, you can restrict the search to the categories you select, or leave all the categories selected to search all categories.

3. Click the Find Now button to start the search. If the search is successful, the Find dialog box will expand to display a new lower half (see Figure 15.17), listing the appointments.

4. To open an appointment for editing in the Edit Appointment dialog box, select it and click the Open Item button. To delete an item, click the Delete Item button.

5. Click the Close button (the ∞ button at its upper-right corner) to close the Find dialog box.

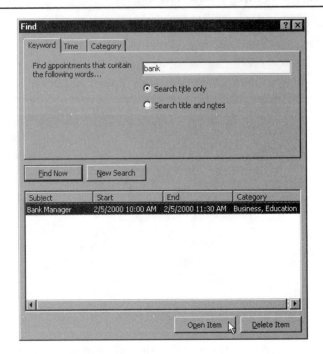

FIGURE 15.17
The Find dialog box expands to show you the results of the search.

Printing Out Your Calendar

You don't stay glued to your computer all the time (I hope)—so sooner or later, you'll need to print out your calendar to take it with you someplace your computer isn't. Here's how to proceed:

1. Click the Print button on the toolbar, or choose File ➤ Print, to display the Print dialog box (see Figure 15.18).

2. In the Style box, select the type of calendar to print: Day By Appointments, Day By Hours, Day List, Day List By Sections, Week, Month – Portrait (tall orientation), or Month – Landscape (wide orientation).

3. In the Range group box, make sure that Works Calendar has chosen the right Start Date and End Date and (for the Day By Appointments and Day By Hours styles) Start Time and End Time.

4. In the Include group box, choose the Appointments Currently Selected In The Category Filter option button if you want to restrict the printout to the current categories you have displayed. Choose the All Appointments option button if you want the printout to include all your appointments. For the Day List and Day List By Sections styles, you can also choose to include or exclude details by

selecting or clearing the Appointment Details check box. (This check box is unavailable for the other styles of printout.)

5. Click the OK button to print the calendar.

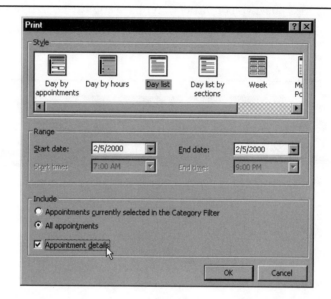

Using the Address Book

Depending on what kind of business you're in, you may find the Address Book's contact-management features even more compelling than Works Calendar's scheduling capabilities. In this section, I'll show you how to do everything from adding contacts to your Address Book to exporting all your contacts.

Works' Address Book is integrated with Outlook Express, so you can quickly create e-mail messages from the contacts in your Address Book. Address Book also uses Outlook Express' identities feature, which means that several people can treat the Address Book as their own without being burdened by each other's contacts. (I'll discuss identities in Chapter 22.)

Starting the Address Book

You can start the Address Book in various ways:

- Choose Start ➤ Programs ➤ Microsoft Works ➤ Address Book.

- On the Programs page of the Task Launcher, select Address Book in the Programs list, then click the Start The Address Book link.

- If you're working in Outlook Express, click the Addresses button on the toolbar.

The Address Book will open, showing your main identity. When you first open the Address Book, you probably won't have any entries in it (unless you've entered them from Outlook Express). Figure 15.19 shows the Address Book with a number of entries already entered in it.

FIGURE 15.19
The Address Book with a number of contacts entered

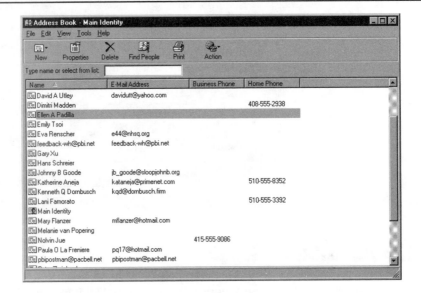

Adding a Contact to Your Address Book

To add a contact to your Address Book, follow these steps:

1. Click the New button on the toolbar to display the New drop-down list, then choose New Contact. (Alternatively, choose File ➢ New Contact or press Ctrl+N.) The Address Book will display the Properties dialog box for a new contact, with the Name page foremost (see Figure 15.20).

2. Enter the contact's name in the First, Middle, and Last text boxes, a title (if appropriate) in the Title text box, and the contact's nickname (if applicable) in the Nickname text box.

3. Once you've entered the contact's first, middle, and last names, the Address Book will automatically build entries for the Display drop-down list. Its default format is First Middle Last—for example, Randall A Chaucer—but you can choose a different format (Chaucer Randall A or Chaucer, Randall A) in the Display drop-down list if you prefer.

FIGURE 15.20
Use the Properties dialog box to create a new contact.

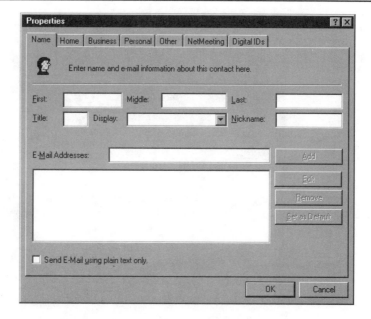

4. If you have an e-mail address for the contact, enter it in the E-Mail Addresses text box and click the Add button. Works will add the e-mail address to the list box of e-mail addresses. You can then add further e-mail addresses if the contact has them. By default, the first e-mail address you enter is set as the default address. If you add multiple e-mail addresses and want to use one other than the first as the default, select the address to use as the default and click the Set As Default button. Works will add an envelope icon to the left of the listing and the text **(Default E-Mail)** to its left (see Figure 15.21).

5. If you need to send plain-text e-mail (rather than formatted or HTML e-mail) to the contact, select the Send E-Mail Using Plain Text Only check box. (If you're not sure whether a contact can receive formatted e-mail, select this check box. That way, the contact will be able to read your message.)

6. If you have home-related information for the contact—a home address, phone numbers, or a Web page—click the Home tab to display the Home page of the Properties dialog box (see Figure 15.22) and enter the information. If this is the default address to use for the contact, select the Default check box.

FIGURE 15.21
*If you enter multiple
e-mail addresses for a
contact, be sure to
designate the right one
as the default.*

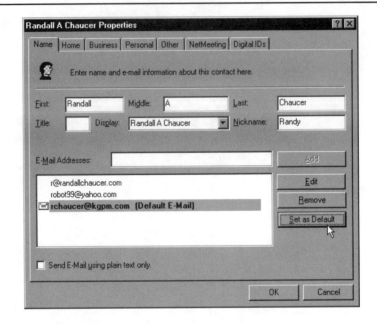

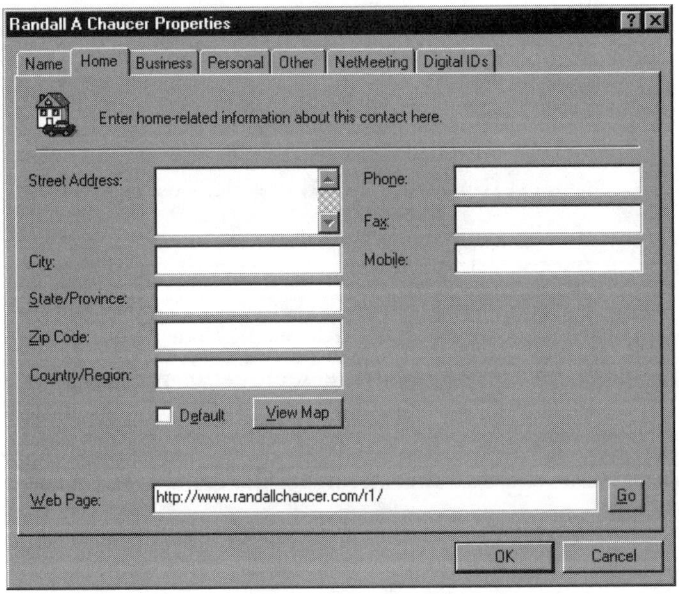

FIGURE 15.22
*Enter any home-related
information for the
contact on the Home
page of the Properties
dialog box.*

7. If you have business-related information for the contact—a company name, address, phone numbers, and so on—click the Business tab to display the Business page of the Properties dialog box (see Figure 15.23) and enter the information. Again, if this is the default address to use for the contact, select the Default check box.

FIGURE 15.23

Enter any business-related information for the contact on the Business page of the Properties dialog box.

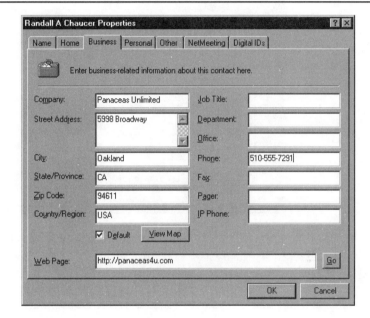

8. Click the Personal tab to display the Personal page of the Properties dialog box (see Figure 15.24) and enter personal information on the contact:

- Even if you don't know their spouse's name, their children, their birthday, or their anniversary, you should be able to change Unspecified in the Gender drop-down box to Female or Male!

- To add a child, click the Add button. The Address Book will add an entry named New Child and select the name. Type in the appropriate name and press the Enter key. (If you need to change the child's name, select the child and click the Edit button.)

FIGURE 15.24
*Enter personal
information for the
contact on the Personal
page of the Properties
dialog box.*

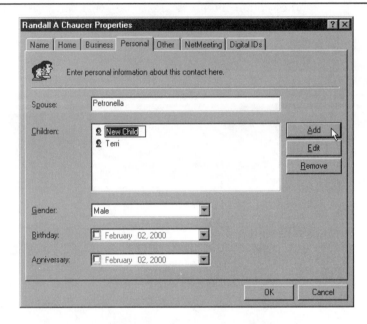

9. If you have other information about the contact, click the Other tab to display the Other page of the Properties dialog box (see Figure 15.25) and enter the information in the Notes text box.

FIGURE 15.25
*The Other page of the
Properties dialog box
provides storage for
extra information.*

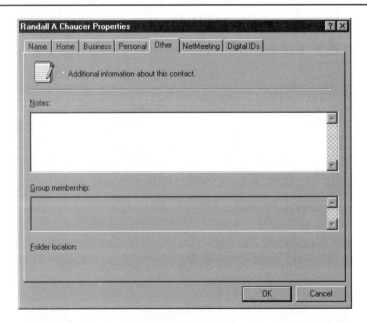

10. If you have videoconferencing information or digital ID information for the contact, enter it on the NetMeeting page or the Digital IDs page of the Properties dialog box.

11. Click the OK button to close the Properties dialog box. Your contact will appear in the Address Book.

 TIP When you're reading e-mail in Outlook Express, you can add a sender to your Address Book by right-clicking the message in the Inbox and choosing Add Sender To Address Book from the context menu. (Alternatively, select the message and choose Tools ➢ Add Sender To Address Book.) When you do this, it's usually a good idea to display the Address Book and immediately add all the information you know about the contact—before you forget.

Deleting a Contact

To delete a contact, right-click it and choose Delete from the context menu. The Address Book will display a dialog box like the one shown in Figure 15.26 asking you to confirm the deletion. Click the Yes button.

FIGURE 15.26
The Address Book
checks to make sure
you want to delete a
contact.

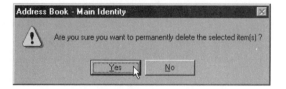

Importing Information into Your Address Book

If you already have information in a data source (for example, in an organizer or in a database), you can import it into the Address Book. The Address Book can handle formats that include the address books in Works, Exchange, Microsoft Internet Mail for Windows 3.1, Eudora (Pro and Light), Netscape and Netscape Communicator, and the LDAP Data Interchange Format. If your data is in a different format (for example, a spreadsheet or an organizer), the best way of exporting and importing the information is to use a *comma-separated value* file (CSV file for short)—a file in which the fields are separated by commas.

WARNING With some data sources, the Address Book may fail to preserve divisions between address books—for example, it may lump entries from multiple separate address books in a program such as Eudora into the same category in the Address Book. Make sure you keep your data source until you've checked your imported data carefully in case the Address Book messes things up and you need to import it all again.

In this example, I'll assume you're using a CSV file. The process for importing information from one of the address books mentioned above is similar but a little different. Follow these steps:

1. Choose File ≻ Import ≻ Other Address Book to display the Address Book Import Tool dialog box (see Figure 15.27).

FIGURE 15.27
In the Address Book Import Tool dialog box, select the type of information you want to import and then click the Import button.

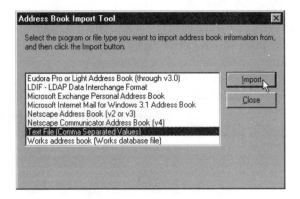

2. In the list box, choose the address book format—in this case, Text File (Comma Separated Values).

3. Click the Import button. Works will display the first CSV Import dialog box (see Figure 15.28).

4. You can either type the name in (including a path if necessary) or click the Browse button to display the Open dialog box, specify the location and name as usual, and click the Open button.

5. Click the Next button to display the second CSV Import dialog box (see Figure 15.29).

FIGURE 15.28
In the first CSV Import dialog box, specify the file you want to import and then click the Next button.

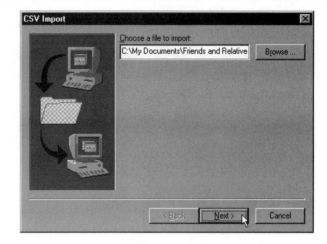

FIGURE 15.29
In the second CSV Import dialog box, check and change the field mapping, and then click the Finish button.

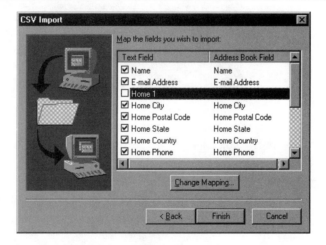

6. Check that each field in the data source (the first column) is *mapped* (matched) to an appropriate field in the Address Book (the second column) and that each text field that you want to import has its check box selected. To change the mapping of a field, select it and click the Change Mapping button to display the Change Mapping dialog box (see Figure 15.30). In the drop-down list, select the target Address Book field, select the Import This Field check box, and click the OK button.

FIGURE 15.30
Change the mapping of a field as necessary in the Change Mapping dialog box.

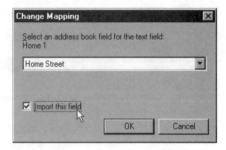

7. Click the Finish button to perform the import. If any of the entries in the file you're importing has the same name as an entry in the Address Book, the Address Book will display the Confirm Replace dialog box (see Figure 15.31) so that you can choose whether to overwrite the existing entry.

FIGURE 15.31
The Confirm Replace dialog box appears if an entry in the data source you're importing will overwrite an existing entry in the Address Book. Choose wisely.

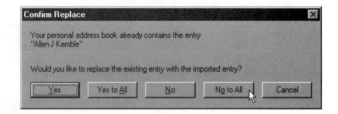

8. When the Address Book has finished importing the data, it will display the Address Book dialog box shown in Figure 15.32.

FIGURE 15.32
You'll see this dialog box when the Address Book has finished importing your data.

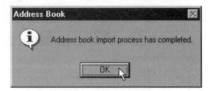

9. Click the OK button to close the Address Book dialog box, then click the Close button to close the Address Book Import Tool dialog box.

10. Double-check the resulting Address Book entries for duplicates and errors.

Exporting Information from Your Address Book

What goes in must be able to go out as well... just as you can import information into your Address Book, you can also export it so that you can import it into an organizer, database, or spreadsheet. As with importing information, you'll probably want to use a CSV file.

Follow these steps to export information from your Address Book:

1. Choose File ➢ Export ➢ Other Address Book to display the Address Book Export Tool (see Figure 15.33).

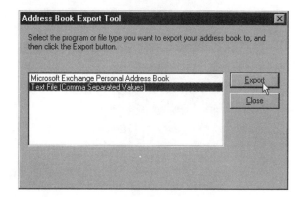

FIGURE 15.33
Use the Address Book Export Tool to export your Address Book so that you can import it into an organizer, database, or spreadsheet.

2. In the list box, select the Text File (Comma Separated Values) entry.
3. Click the Export button. The Address Book will display the first CSV Export dialog box (see Figure 15.34).

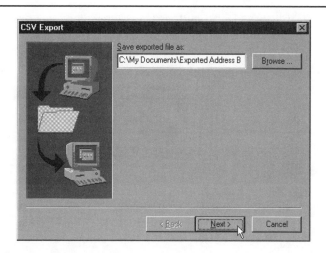

FIGURE 15.34
In the first CSV Export dialog box, specify the name under which to save the exported file.

4. In the Save Exported File As text box, enter the name under which to save the exported file. You can either type the name in (including a path if necessary) or click the Browse button to display the Save As dialog box, specify the location and name in the usual manner, and click the Save button.

5. Click the Next button to display the second CSV Export dialog box (see Figure 15.35).

FIGURE 15.35
In the second CSV
Export dialog box,
select the fields you
want to export and then
click the Finish button.

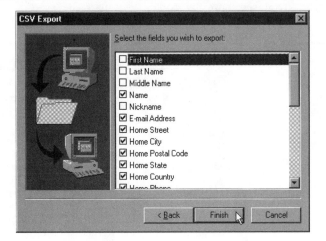

6. Select the fields you want to export. You'll notice that by default the CSV Export dialog box does not select the check boxes for the First Name, Last Name, and Middle Name fields, because it lumps the names together into a single field (called Name), which it selects. But if you need to have the individual fields as well, select their check boxes too.

7. Click the Finish button. The Address Book will display the Address Book dialog box shown in Figure 15.36 to tell you that it has completed the export procedure.

FIGURE 15.36
You'll see this dialog
box when the Address
Book has finished
exporting the data.

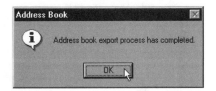

8. Click the OK button to dismiss the Address Book dialog box, then click the Close button to close the Address Book Export Tool dialog box.

You can now import the CSV file into your organizer, database, or spreadsheet.

Creating a Group

To organize your contacts, you can create groups and assign contacts to them. For example, you might create a group called Family and assign all members of your family to it. Then you might create assorted groups for your business so that you could split up your business contacts by characteristics they share.

To create a group:

1. Click the New button on the toolbar and choose Group from the drop-down list to display the Properties dialog box for the group with the Group page displayed (see Figure 15.37).

FIGURE 15.37
Use the Properties dialog box for a group to define the group and add contacts to it.

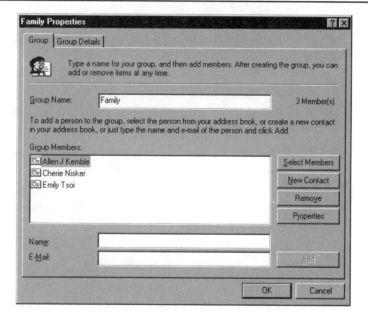

2. Enter the name for the group in the Group Name text box.

3. Click the Select Members button to display the Select Group Members dialog box (see Figure 15.38).

FIGURE 15.38
In the Select Group Members dialog box, select the contacts whom you want to make members of the group.

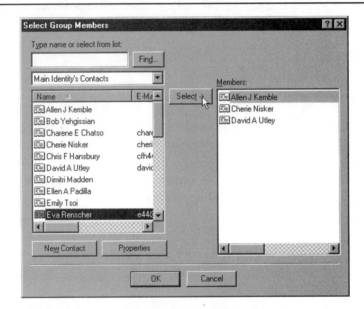

4. In the left-hand list box, select the contacts to add to the group and then click the Select button to transfer them to the group:

   • Shift+click to select a block of contacts. Ctrl+click to select multiple separate contacts or to add another contact to the currently selected block.

   • To remove a contact from the right-hand list box, right-click the contact and choose Remove from the context menu.

5. Click the OK button to close the Select Group Members dialog box. In the Properties dialog box for the group, the Group Members list box will show the members you added.

6. If you have details to add for the group (such as an address, phone number, or notes), click the Group Details tab to display the Group Details page, then enter the information there.

7. Click the OK button to close the Properties dialog box for the group.

NOTE You can check which groups a contact belongs to on the Other page of the contact's Properties dialog box.

Viewing Your Groups

To view your groups, choose View ➢ Folders And Groups to display the Folders And Groups pane in the Address Book. You can then select a group to work with the contacts in it, as shown in Figure 15.39.

FIGURE 15.39
Use the Folders And Groups pane (on the left) to view your groups.

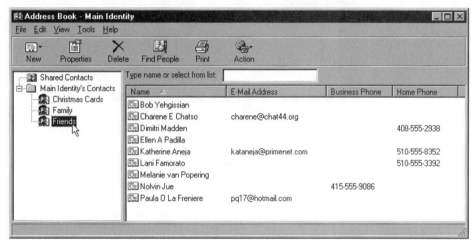

Deleting a Group

To delete a group, select it in the Folders And Groups pane and click the Delete button. The Address Book will display the confirmation message box shown in Figure 15.40, reminding you that getting rid of the group does not delete its members. Click the Yes button if you want to proceed.

FIGURE 15.40
The Address Book double-checks to make sure you want to delete a group.

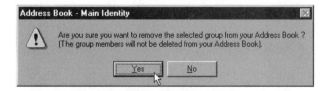

Changing the Fields Displayed

By default, the Address Book displays the Name, E-Mail Address, Business Phone, and Home Phone columns. You can change any of these fields except the Name field by right-clicking its column heading and choosing a different field from the context menu of fields that appears (see Figure 15.41).

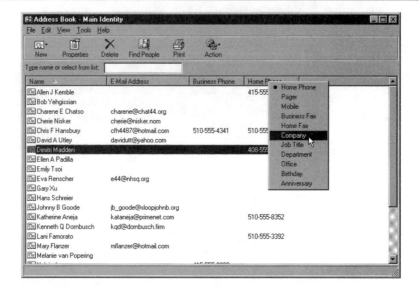

Using Views

Address Book offers four views for scrutinizing your contacts: Details view (the default view), Large Icon view, Small Icon view, and List view. You'll recognize these views from the views in Windows Explorer—they're essentially the same. Details view tends to be the most useful, because it puts the most information on screen at the same time, but you may want to use Small Icon view or List view occasionally so that you can see a larger number of contacts at once.

To change view, choose View ➤ Large Icon, View ➤ Small Icon, View ➤ List, or View ➤ Details as appropriate.

Sorting Your Contacts

By default, the Address Book sorts your contacts alphabetically by first name. If you're on a first-name basis with them, or have relatively few contacts, this works fine. If not, you'll probably need to sort your contacts into a different order sooner or later.

To sort the contacts by one of the columns displayed, click the column heading once for an ascending sort (alphabetical order) or twice for a descending sort (reverse alphabetical order).

To sort by last name, choose View ➢ Sort By ➢ Last Name. To restore the default first-name sorting, choose View ➢ Sort By ➢ First Name.

Sending Mail to a Contact

To send e-mail to a contact, right-click the contact's name and choose Action ➢ Send Mail from the context menu. The Address Book will activate Outlook Express and will start a new message to the contact you chose.

If the contact has no e-mail address, the Address Book will display an exclamation message box alerting you to the problem (see Figure 15.42) and will not activate Outlook Express.

FIGURE 15.42
Here's what happens when you try to e-mail a contact who doesn't have an e-mail address in the Address Book.

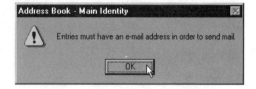

Finding a Forgotten Contact

If you use the Address Book effectively, you'll soon build up an impressive number of contacts in it—more, perhaps, than you can comfortably keep straight in your mind at all times. To help you find a contact from some remembered piece or pieces of information, the Address Book has a powerful Find feature.

Here's how to use it:

1. Click the Find People button on the toolbar, or choose Edit ➢ Find, to display the Find People dialog box (see Figure 15.43).

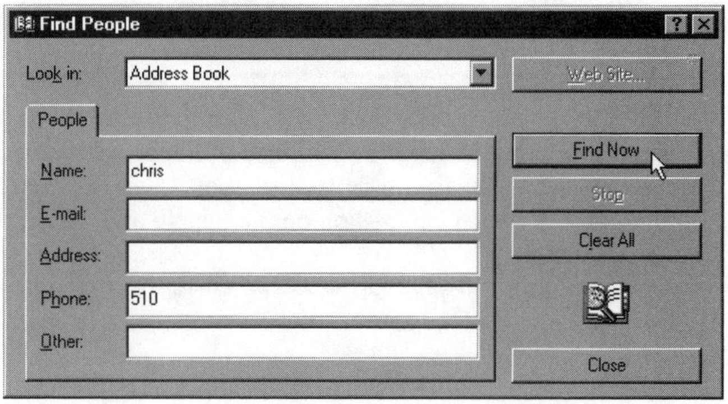

FIGURE 15.43
Use the Find People dialog box to find a contact whose full name you can't remember.

2. In the Name, E-mail, Address, Phone, and Other text boxes, enter such information as you can remember about the person. Each piece of information doesn't have to be complete: For example, you might enter only a first name in the Name text box and only an area code in the Phone text box.

3. Click the Find Now button to perform the search. If it finds matches, the Find People dialog box will display a lower section containing them (see Figure 15.44). If not, it will display a message box saying that it found no matches.

FIGURE 15.44
If it finds matches, the Find People dialog box will display them. You can work directly from the results.

4. Take such action as you need with the results (or perform a different search). Then click the Close button to close the Find People dialog box.

TIP You can also use the Find People dialog box to search for people in Internet directories such as Yahoo! People Search, Bigfoot Internet Directory Service, and the WhoWhere Internet Directory Service. To do so, click the appropriate item in the Look In drop-down list and enter your search information on the People and Advanced pages that the Find People dialog box displays.

Microsoft Encarta

Encarta combines the best qualities of a print encyclopedia with the capabilities of a computer. As you'll see, this results in a level of content that is simply not possible in a book or even with the Internet (after all, multimedia files are large and take a long time to load if your connection speed is slow). Telling someone who Ella Fitzgerald is has much less impact than playing her songs.

Encarta is a warm, friendly, and inviting application that offers information and assistance on a wide range of historical and empirical data. Simply insert the CD into your CD-ROM drive, run the installation routine (covered in the Appendix), and prepare to learn.

First, however, you need to be able to start Encarta. Encarta does not share the same space in the Start menu as the other Works icons. The quickest way to locate it is to select Start ➢ Programs ➢ Microsoft Encarta ➢ Microsoft Encarta 2000.

 NOTE The CD, which holds all the large multimedia files, must be in the drive in order for you to access all the Encarta features and content. The only way around this is to install the base files to your hard drive.

The Encarta Interface

Encarta follows the recent trend in Microsoft applications toward using a Web page interface. This puts primary components for navigation at the top of every page you view (see Figure 16.1) and will be familiar to you if you've ever used the Internet.

Fortunately, Encarta is one of the least complicated applications that you will ever use. When you start Encarta for the first time, you will be asked to register (see Figure 16.2).

Click Register Online Now, and your Web browser will open and take you to a Microsoft Web site to enter your registration information. If you are not connected to the Internet, it's not critical to complete this step now, but you'll miss some download updates that are available for Encarta on the site. If you want to register later, click Remind Me Later.

 NOTE If you do not register Encarta, you will be asked to do so every time you open Encarta unless you select the Don't Show Me This Again check box.

FIGURE 16.1

Encarta's opening screen, which looks quite a bit like a Web page

FIGURE 16.2

Encarta's software registration dialog box

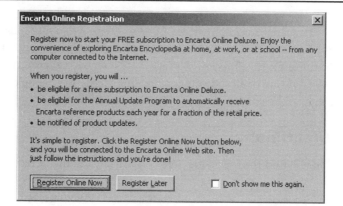

After the registration dialog box, you'll see the main Encarta home page, shown in Figure 16.3. By default, the Encarta home page appears maximized—that is, it fills the entire screen with the exception of the Taskbar—but you can change it however you like.

FIGURE 16.3
Encarta's home page

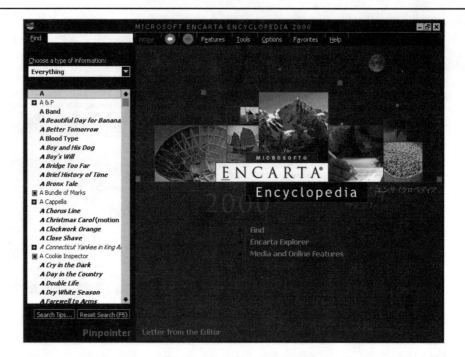

There are three main areas of this interface and a menu bar at the top. The large open area on the right contains a graphic where media and other information appear. To the left is the Pinpointer, a large black bar with a scrolling text box; this is an alphabetical listing of all subjects covered in Encarta. At the top of the window is a row that contains the command menus for the application.

The Menu Bar

You will find the following items on the Encarta menu bar, shown here:

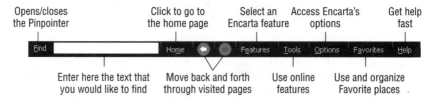

Find   Toggles the Pinpointer on and off.

Search Criterion   Lets you enter your search text. The results will be displayed in the Pinpointer.

   Home   Returns you to the Encarta home page.

Back   Returns you to the previous page that you viewed.

Forward   Takes you to the next page. Only visited pages are available.

NOTE   As you move from page to page, Encarta stores the "address" in the order that you visited the pages. If you click the Back button, Encarta returns you to the last page you visited.

Features   Lists available features, including Encarta Explorer, World Maps, Inter-Activities, Yearbook, Web Links, and MindMaze.

Tools   Lists online features, which you can access by clicking an item. The first item takes you directly to the Encarta Online Web site, or you can select Downloads to update your version of Encarta.

NOTE   When you click on a link that leads to a site outside Encarta, a dialog box will appear alerting you to this fact. If you find the dialog box bothersome, see the sidebar for a tip on how to turn off its display. Unless you've already registered and/or signed up for the Deluxe version of Encarta, you may also be pestered to register at this point.

WARNING   The version of the Encarta Online Web site accessible to Encarta 2000 Standard users contains a measly 16,000 articles, which have been abridged.

Options   Lets you work with documents or modify how Encarta works. The items on this menu are Find, Copy, Print, Closed Captions, Text Size, and Settings.

Settings Dialog Box

The items in the settings dialog box are:

Play Menu And Button Sounds   By default, Encarta is set to play sounds when you interact with its interface. Select this check box to hear the sounds.

Display Home Screen When I Start Encarta Encyclopedia   This option is enabled by default. If you turn it off, you will be returned to the last page you visited.

Ask Me For Confirmation Before Jumping To The Internet   By default, this option is enabled. By disabling this option, you turn off the reminder that you have elected to go to an Internet site.

Continued ▶

Skip Contents Page By default, this option is disabled. When you select a topic from Explorer or select an item returned by a search in the Pinpointer, the Contents page opens, displaying a listing of all the topics and subtopics available for that subject. Select the Skip Contents Page check box if you want to bypass the Contents page and go right to what you're looking for. Keep in mind, though, that the Contents page can be a helpful tool in locating what you need.

Display Tool Tips A ToolTip (a short description) appears when you point at an interface element for a few seconds. By default, this option is selected. It allows you to become comfortable with the interface.

Jump Color This option is useful for people with specific color perception problems. It allows you to select the color that you can see best against the black background.

Favorites As in Internet Explorer, you can store a list of pages you visit regularly. When you are visiting a page you want to bookmark, select Add To Favorites from the Favorites menu and click the OK button in the resulting dialog box. You may also store the Favorite in a particular folder.

Help Gives you access to help resources, troubleshooting if you have a problem with Encarta, registration information, and details on the application over the Internet or through the Help files installed with Encarta.

The Pinpointer

The Pinpointer lists all subjects that Encarta covers. The list is sorted alphabetically, so you can use the scroll bar to scan for your target topic. However, there are faster ways to find what you need.

TIP Keep in mind that the Pinpointer sorts proper names by *last* name. So, *Ella Fitzgerald* would be found under *Fitzgerald, Ella*.

WARNING When you click anywhere on the open area of the home page, the Pinpointer will disappear, making more room for the other things that will appear on screen. To restore the Pinpointer, simply click Find on the toolbar.

Encarta's primary search function is based on the Index system used in Windows Help. Start typing in letters, and the search results will narrow as you type. This search tool allows you to try many different searches without wasting time.

Until you type something in the Find text box, Encarta will display a complete listing. To demonstrate the search feature, let's perform a search for Ella Fitzgerald. Enter **ella** in the Find text box, and you will see a list of results, with Ella Fitzgerald third on the list (see Figure 16.4).

FIGURE 16.4
The search for Ella

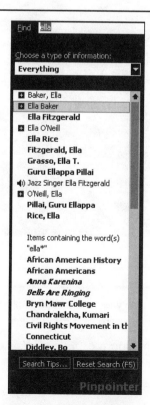

NOTE Ella also appears farther down the list, with a small speaker icon next to her name. This icon indicates that Encarta has an audio file featuring Ella Fitzgerald.

If you add a space after **ella** and begin typing **fitzgerald**, the search result list will narrow further. To see the contents of a topic, click that entry in the list. Let's follow the first audio item by clicking the entry with the small speaker in the left column. Be sure to turn up the volume on your speakers—the audio file will play as soon as the page is loaded. This audio clip offers a portion of *Satin Doll,* an Ella Fitzgerald favorite.

Encarta Explorer

Encarta Explorer is a graphical interface that allows you to navigate by selecting and moving through subjects. To access Encarta Explorer, select Features ➢ Encarta Explorer. Encarta takes you to the Explorer page, shown in Figure 16.5.

FIGURE 16.5
Encarta Explorer's main page

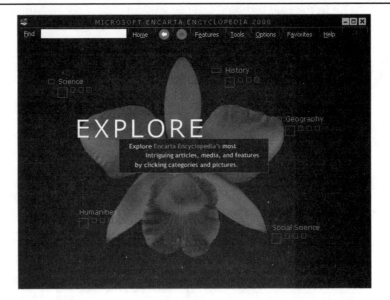

 NOTE Each time you open Encarta Explorer, it plays a different audio file.

Once the animation is complete, you can see that five major categories are available: History, Geography, Social Science, Humanities, and Science. If you point at a topic and wait—a technique called *hovering*—a list of subtopics will appear. For example, the subtopics for Social Science include Economics, Government, Anthropology, Society, and Psychology (see Figure 16.6).

FIGURE 16.6
Encarta's Explorer main page with the Social Science topic selected

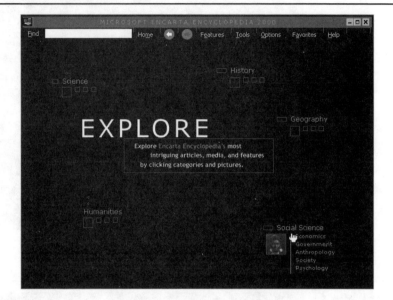

When you click Social Science, a zooming animation will appear, a sound file will play (the sound files vary by topic), and a cluster of items will be displayed in the center of the window (see Figure 16.7).

The Social Science topic hub includes a collection of pictures, topics, and a small speaker icon. If you point to the picture at the left with your mouse, the picture will spin around. Pointing to the left or right of the picture will cause it to rotate quickly, and pointing at the center will stop the picture from moving.

Clicking on the picture expands it to a much larger version. With the larger version, you can also rotate or spin the picture by using the mouse pointer.

The picture is in a special 360-Degree View format. This particular picture is of the ruins of Machu Picchu, the ancient Incan city (see Figure 16.8). Click the Back button to return to the previous page.

NOTE If you move your mouse pointer inside the picture, it becomes a four-pointed compass and allows you to move the picture by clicking and dragging.

FIGURE 16.7

A close-up of the Social Science topic hub

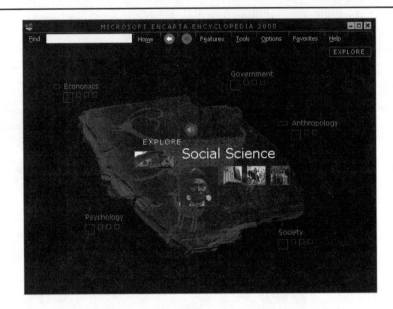

FIGURE 16.8

This window shows the ruins of Machu Picchu in the Andes Mountains of Peru.

After you've read the photo caption, click the Back button to return to the Social Science hub of Encarta Explorer. You've now successfully followed a topic thread. Let's follow this thread further by clicking the Anthropology topic.

If you select Peoples Of The World from the Anthropology topic hub, you'll see another level of subtopics. For our example, let's find out more about the Inca Empire. When you point to the photograph at the right, the caption says *Quechua* (see Figure 16.9).

FIGURE 16.9
The Peoples Of The World subtopic with the Quechua item indicated

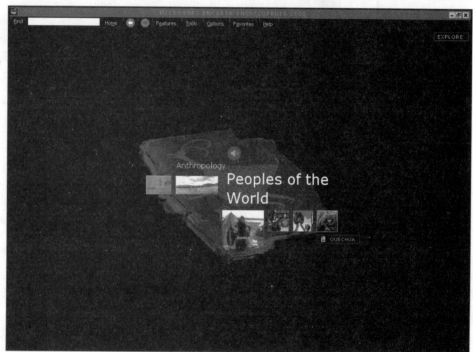

Selecting the Quechua picture takes you to another section of Encarta; this section closely resembles an encyclopedia, as shown in Figure 16.10. The left side contains explanatory text, and the right side includes links to related and Web-based information about Quechua, which we learn is the most common language in the South American Andes region and was the principal language of the Incas.

On the right side of the Quechua page is the Related Articles box. If you click the Inca Empire item, you'll see a directory of related pages (see Figure 16.11), and you can select a particular subject from the list.

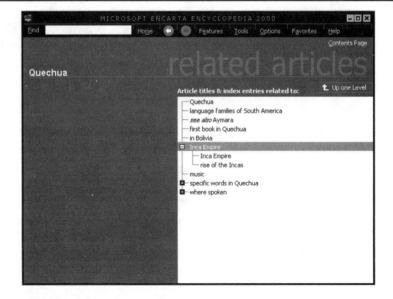

Clicking the Inca Empire takes you to the Inca Empire topic page, and a small *windoid* will appear with the contents of the previous page. You can click the links in the windoid to go to other pages. Topic pages give you access to a wide range of topics and materials (see Figure 16.12).

FIGURE 16.12
This topic page about the Inca Empire shows three sections of information.

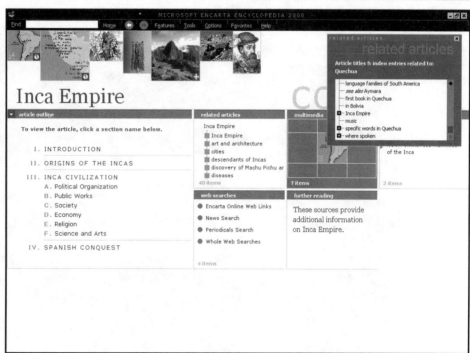

These pages are divided into sections according to the type of information available on the subject you're viewing. The three types of sections are:

- Multimedia (which includes the Multimedia section and the row of photographs along the top of the window) contains links to media materials such as audio, video, 360-Degree Views, and photographs.
- Article Outline offers you access to all main sections of a particular topic.
- Related Articles (which includes the rest of the material on the screen) contains external links and sources for additional information available from Encarta, books, or the Web.

Each sub-section has differing amounts of material, so it will look different because of that. Also, depending on the size of your monitor and what resolution it is set at, the sections may be located in different locations on your screen than what you see in Figure 16.12.

Media and Online Features

Media and Online Features extends the functionality of Encarta by giving you access and links to resources on the Internet, an updateable yearbook, and activity-based sections. You simply click the Media and Online Features link in the middle of the home page to open the page shown in Figure 16.13.

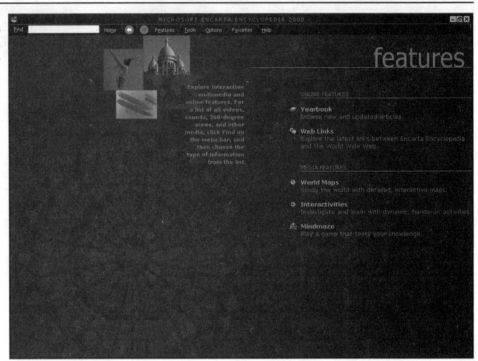

Online Features

Yearbook and Web Links offer direct access to recently updated material. You can update these features over the Internet and integrate new information into Encarta.

Yearbook

Yearbook provides up-to-date information that is not Web-based. These entries are incorporated into later editions of Encarta and are made available to you through the Downloads feature. Yearbook is organized in alphabetical order by topic. If you want to filter the subject matter, click one of the primary topic buttons on the left side of the window (see Figure 16.14). Unfortunately, you cannot search Yearbook, but you can reset your previously used filter by clicking the Start Over button on the right.

FIGURE 16.14
The Yearbook directory

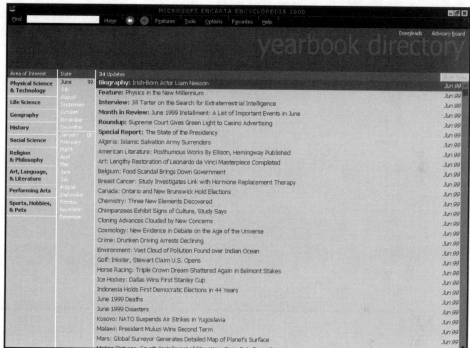

Web Links

Web Links is one of Encarta's most powerful features and allows updates with very little user interaction. When you install Encarta, it will ask if you want to update your version of Encarta. If you do—and I can't imagine why you wouldn't want to—clicking Yes will give you access to the latest updates via the Web.

NOTE Updated information downloaded from the Internet is stored on your hard drive, since your CD-ROM cannot be updated.

When the Web Links page first appears, it displays a directory of available links. If you want to filter the subject matter, click one of the primary topic buttons that run down the left side of the window (see Figure 16.15).

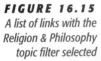

FIGURE 16.15
A list of links with the Religion & Philosophy topic filter selected

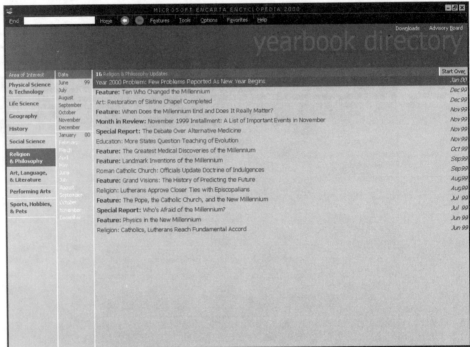

Other options include:

- View lets you select normal sort order (alphabetic) or sort topics by Most Recent Download.
- Word Search lets you look for an instance of a word. Once a search has been made, the results of that search cannot be searched again with another word to narrow the number of selections. Searching again searches the entire database.
- Start Over lets you go back to the beginning and start over again.

Media Features

World Maps, InterActivities, and MindMaze are links to some very neat and useful sections of Encarta. World Maps is a collection of, well, maps that cover the globe and allow you select subjects by location. InterActivities is a collection of multimedia activities that can teach and entertain. And then there's MindMaze. Sound intriguing? It is. I'll look at each in turn.

World Maps

This collection of detailed maps of the world (see Figure 16.16) provides yet another way to search Encarta. On the map, simply click the general location that you want to learn about. World Maps also includes links to articles related to particular locations. If a document icon appears when you point to a landmark or location, you can click that icon to open the related document.

FIGURE 16.16
The main World
Maps page

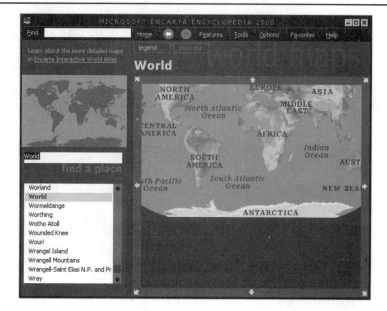

The World Maps page contains three distinct areas: an overview map in the top-left corner, a list of locations in the lower-left corner, and the main map pane on the right side. Some of the maps are larger than the available space. In such a case, you will see bars with arrows along all edges of the map. As you pass the mouse pointer over these bars, the map will begin to scroll in that direction, allowing you to see the whole map.

You first enter World Maps at an all-world view of the globe. Click any one of the primary continents to zoom to that particular area. From there you can point to a country or region, and from there you can select almost anything that interests you.

InterActivities

InterActivities—as the name implies—are interactive "lessons" that help you understand a concept or idea. They cover a range of topics—from dinosaurs to general statistics—and make the ideas more palpable. The instructions for each are clearly marked in each

InterActivity, and the tasks are simple but educational. Each link will take you to the particular activity (see Figure 16.17).

FIGURE 16.17
The InterActivities page on Encarta

MindMaze

MindMaze is a trivia game that encompasses all the information in Encarta. MindMaze takes place in a castle where each room is locked by a riddle. If you answer the riddle correctly, you can move on to the next room. As you progress from floor to floor, you earn awards, which move you closer to your goal.

MindMaze stores each player's progress through the game so you can keep track of how you're doing. Follow these directions to start a game of MindMaze:

1. Start Encarta (if necessary).

2. Select Features ➢ MindMaze. A picture of a castle will appear while the game is loading.

3. When you start the game, you will have three options (see Figure 16.18):

FIGURE 16.18
The castle gate

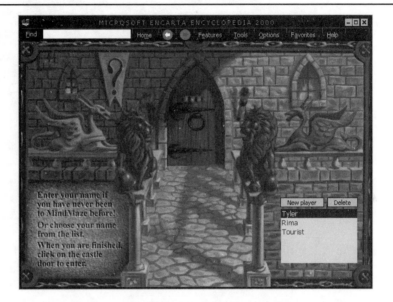

- You can enter the game as a tourist (Step 4).
- You can enter the game as yourself (Step 5).
- You can read the prelude to the game (Step 6).

4. To enter the game as a tourist, click on Tourist in the box to the right of the bridge; then, click the castle door to begin.

5. To enter the game as yourself, click the New Player button and type your name (just start typing—there's no need to do anything else). Then, click on the castle door to enter.

6. If you'd like to read the prelude (a story that explains the goal of the game) before you begin, you can click the tapestry with the large question mark located to the left of the entrance. Click the small *x* to close that windoid when you are done.

7. Just before you enter the castle, you will find yourself looking in through the door. Below the view through the bars is a control area (see Figure 16.19) that allows you to manage various aspects of the game.

FIGURE 16.19
Looking in from the
outside

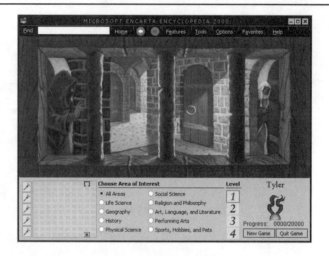

A grid at the lower left tells you where you've been and in what directions you can leave a room (rooms are indicated by a box, with gaps to indicate adjacent rooms). The map will change every time you enter the maze, but you will have a small supply of torches that can illuminate the entire map for a short time. Click the torches that appear as buttons to the left of the Map grid, and you will be able to view all rooms.

Here are a few more things to be aware of when playing MindMaze:

- You can limit the scope of questions by selecting an area of interest. All Areas offers the greatest challenge.

- There are four difficulty settings. Click on the number that corresponds to the complexity of the questions you want (1 = Easy, 4 = Difficult).

- When asked a question that you cannot answer, you can click on the small book icon to the right of each answer button, and Encarta will offer you assistance.

- By right-clicking on the game graphic, you can change the sound effects, turn the music on or off, or end or start a new game by selecting from the submenu that appears.

 TIP Turning off the sound speeds the game up considerably.

- The pictures on the walls in each room are linked to various entries in Encarta. Click one, and it will ask you if you'd like to view an article on a particular subject.

CHAPTER **17**

Expedia Streets & Trips 2000

Few things are more satisfying than leaving work, packing your bags, gathering your family, and heading off on a road trip to a popular vacation spot. On the other hand, few things are less satisfying than (and as embarrassing as) getting lost on the way to a buddy's new house or while driving a couple of towns over from your own.

If you vacation at the same place every year and do the same things every time, a map will probably not be very useful, but there are times when your path leads to unfamiliar places and a map comes in handy. Expedia Streets & Trips 2000 provides more functionality than a paper map or guide books. Read on to find out what this application is capable of doing for you.

Navigating in Streets & Trips

When you first start Streets & Trips, you'll see the Start Screen dialog box (see Figure 17.1). Several options are available, but first I'll focus on the basic operations of Streets & Trips; I'll detail the other operations later in this chapter.

First, you need to start Streets & Trips. There are two methods: You can choose Start ➤ Programs ➤ Microsoft Works ➤ Microsoft Streets & Trips 2000, or you can place Disc 7 in the drive and the program will start automatically.

 WARNING If you or someone else with access to your computer has turned off Auto Insert Detection for your CD drive, Streets & Trips will not start automatically when you close the CD drawer. If this is the case, you will have to open Streets & Trips using the Start menu.

FIGURE 17.1
The Start Screen
dialog box

Meet the Toolbar

Streets & Trips includes two toolbars: the Standard toolbar and the Mapping toolbar. The Standard toolbar is located just below the menu bar and features icons with text labels below. The Mapping toolbar is located just underneath the Standard toolbar.

 TIP If the toolbar is in your way, you can close it, move it, or float it. Close the toolbar by choosing View ➤ Toolbar ➤ Standard. To move the toolbar, click the small ridge at the far left of the toolbar and drag the toolbar to where you want it. Dragging it over the window or the desktop will make it a floater. If you want the toolbar to return to its original position, double-click its title bar.

The Standard toolbar contains the following buttons (reading left to right):

Find Enter what you're looking for here, and Streets & Trips will attempt to find it for you. Streets & Trips displays search results in a list, from most to least likely. Click an item to make it appear on the map.

Zoom Out Click this button to zoom away from the map a notch at a time.

Zoom Slider Slide the bar left or right to adjust the zoom manually.

Zoom In Click this button to zoom in on the centered area, a notch at a time.

Selection Tool Allows you to select an area for zooming or an item you want more information about.

Hand Tool Allows you to drag the map instead of using the scroller. This tool is better suited to smaller adjustments, whereas the scroller is excellent for searching and covering very large areas.

Pushpin Selector Allows you to stick "pushpins" into your map to mark points of interest.

Spot Highlighter Allows you to mark a specific point or location for reference or a future trip.

Line Highlighter Click this icon, then click your starting point, and a line will appear. Drag the line to your second mark and click again. You can set as many points as you like. Double-click or press the Esc key when you've finished.

Map Scale Toggle Turns the scale bar on or off. You can use this tool to make scale measurements.

Drawing Tools Toggle Allows you to add drawings to your maps if you find it helpful. This button turns those tools on and off.

Map Type Selector Allows you to choose which type of surface the map will display from this menu. The three types are Road, Terrain, and Political.

Finding a Place

In the Start Screen dialog box, click the Find A Place button. The Find dialog box will appear with the Place page in front, as shown in Figure 17.2.

FIGURE 17.2
When you click the Find A Place button in the Start Screen dialog box, you'll see the Find dialog box with the Place page in front.

Simply type the name of a location in the Place Name text box, click the Find button, and Streets & Trips will show you where it is. For example, if you type **White House** in the Place Name text box and click Find, Streets & Trips will generate a list of matches—the White House in Washington, D.C., is just one of many. This is an interesting way to discover new places. It's also helpful if you know only a portion of the place name. Select the home of the President (White House, Washington, D.C.), and a map of Washington, D.C. will appear beneath the interface (see Figure 17.3).

NOTE The Find utility can be surprisingly smart. It locates not only *White House,* but also any variant of it in either upper or lower case. It will even find words that *sound* like the words you're searching for.

FIGURE 17.3
*Streets & Trips will
display a map of the
location you select.*

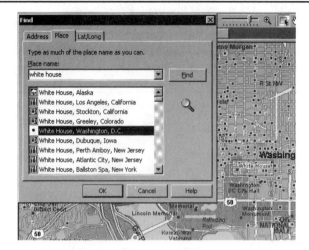

Finding an Address

In addition to searching for places, you can search for a particular address. Streets & Trips allows you to pinpoint an address and look down on it from above, as you would from an airplane flying overhead. It pinpoints locations by matching your request to its database of address points in the United States, Canada, and Mexico.

 TIP You use the Tab key or your mouse to activate text boxes when entering information.

To locate an address, select the Address tab in the Find dialog box to display the Address page (see Figure 17.4). To find your home address, enter your home data in the Street Address, City, State, and ZIP Code text boxes. Streets & Trips will search even if you don't complete all the text boxes, but the accuracy of the results will reflect the amount of information you provide. For example, 1600 Pennsylvania Ave, NE, Washington, D.C., 20500 cannot be located by entering **1600 penn dc**.

 WARNING If you're planning a trip deep into Mexico or Canada, note that Streets & Trips' route and address details are not very detailed for these areas. In fact, large areas of Mexico and especially Canada are only lightly or topologically charted.

WARNING Be careful when planning routes, as on occasion I've noticed flaws in the routes that Streets & Trips suggests. Be sure to double-check each turn in the text version with the graphical version.

FIGURE 17.4
The Address page of the
Find dialog box

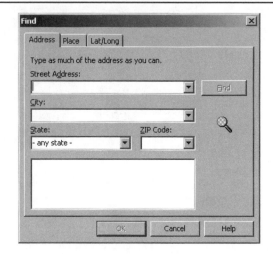

Quick Searches

Although the Find dialog box is very helpful, there is a faster way to locate a point on the map. The Streets & Trips toolbar includes a text box labeled Find.

The Find text box will accept your searches in almost any format, but following these guidelines will improve your searching success:

- Be as precise as possible. For example, entering **Hoot's** rather than **Hoot's Bar in Wheeling, West Virginia** will return a greater number of results. The less information you enter, the more results you will have to wade through.

- Maintain a standard format when searching for addresses. For example, **Fort St., Tybee Island, GA, 31328** is readable, but **fort st tybee ga** is not (at least to most people). This search resulted in Fort in Philomath, Oregon, and had no entries for the actual address.

Streets & Trips is quite intuitive at finding matches in its database, but it doesn't know everything. The more information you can provide, the better the search results will be.

TIP Separate each item in your search criteria with a comma. That way, Streets & Trips can recognize where each item begins and ends.

Moving Your Map

If your map isn't where you want it to be, you can move it a better vantage point. For example, if you feel like you're looking down on your neighborhood from an airplane, you can easily get a little more down to earth.

Rather than using scroll bars, Streets & Trips uses a scroller arrow to move the map. The scroller arrow appears as a large white arrow when you move the pointer to an edge of the map (see Figure 17.5). Just click on the arrow and drag your mouse in the direction you want while holding down the button. On faster machines (Pentium 233 MHz and above), the scrolling can move too quickly, but once you get the hang of it, it becomes very smooth.

 TIP The closer you get to the center of the map, the slower you'll scroll; the closer to the edge, the faster you'll scroll.

FIGURE 17.5
The scroller arrow appears near the edge of the map to the left of Vancouver, British Columbia.

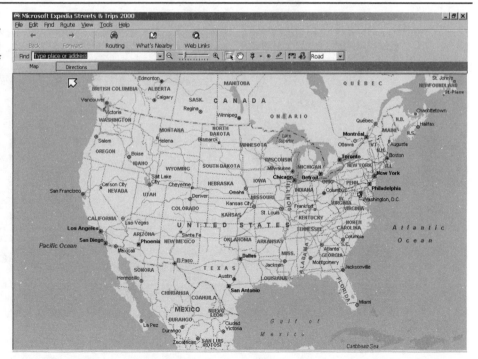

Zoom In, Zoom Out

Streets & Trips also allows you to zoom in and out from your map. The distance to the surface is measured as altitude, just as it would be from an airplane. For example, you could zoom from 31,000 miles in space (see Figure 17.6) to only one mile overhead (see Figure 17.7).

There are several ways to zoom a map to fit your needs. The easiest is to select an area and then click inside it as follows:

1. Move the pointer to a location just outside where you want to zoom in.

2. Click and drag diagonally to create a box (see Figure 17.8).

3. When the box surrounds your target, release the mouse button and the box will remain.

4. Move the pointer inside the box you created (the pointer will change into a magnifying glass with a + sign) and click once.

5. The map will zoom to fit all the area inside the box you drew.

Selecting an area of a map is the most common method of zooming, but there are several other ways available to you.

FIGURE 17.6
The view from 31,000 miles in space

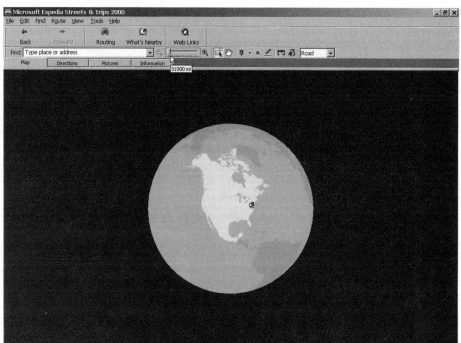

FIGURE 17.7

The view from one mile over the White House in Washington, D.C.

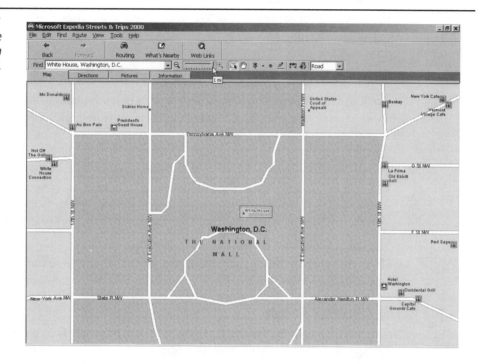

FIGURE 17.8

A selected area ready for you to zoom in

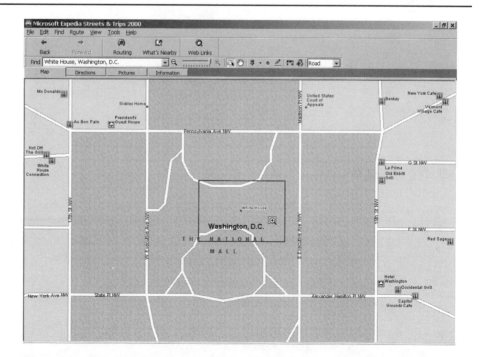

The Toolbar Zoom

In the middle of the Streets & Trips Mapping toolbar is a vertical slider with a magnifying glass at each end. The toolbar has several elements that give you a wide range of control over zooming.

You can move the slider left or right to lengthen or shorten the distance (altitude) from which you view your map. Moving the slider is the best option when you want to change the zoom level significantly.

 TIP To see at what altitude you're viewing the map, point at the slider knob for a few seconds and a ToolTip will appear with the mileage. The default altitude is 5500 Miles.

 Second, you can click on either of the magnifying glasses to zoom out (the - sign) or zoom in (the + sign). Clicking the magnifying glasses zooms in or out in small increments and is best for fine-tuning your map.

The Context Zoom

The context menu—also known as the right-click menu—will help you find locations of interest very quickly. Right-click the address and you will see the context menu, which offers you several options for how to zoom.

Going Places

Streets & Trips is perfect for preparing for long trips or finding directions. You can even tell Streets & Trips where you *don't* want to go. Streets & Trips has many features that give you a hand in creating a complete trip plan, including:

- Setting beginning and ending locations
- Setting waypoints and other layovers
- Defining your driving habits
- Accounting for current road construction hazards

Let's get started by planning a trip to Alaska.

Planning Your Trip

Streets & Trips accounts for many variables that are generally involved in taking a trip by car. When you plan a trip, Streets & Trips can help you customize your plan to your personal preferences. For example, you can specify the type of route (the options are quickest, shortest, scenic, and preferred) and how long you want to spend at any one place along the way.

You can start planning your trip in one of three ways:

- Select Plan A Route from the Route menu.
- Click the Routing button on the Standard toolbar (the little red car).
- Select Start Screen from the Help menu and click the Plan A Route button.

Any one of these methods will open the Routing pane, a pane at the left side of the application window (see Figure 17.9).

FIGURE 17.9
The Routing pane helps you start planning your route.

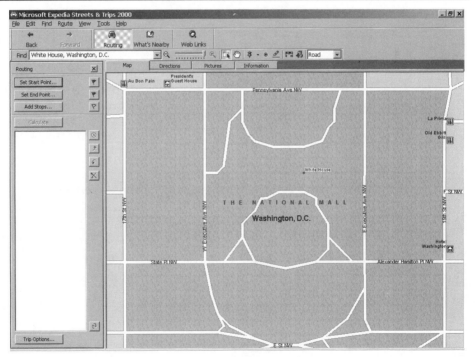

The Routing pane offers two ways to begin planning your trip:

- Click the Set Start Point button and enter a place name or an address. When Streets & Trips locates the place or address, click the OK button.

- Click the little green flag button, move the crosshair pointer to your departure location, and click OK.

Follow the same process for selecting the end point of your trip. Let's plan a trip from Macon, Georgia, to Juneau, the capital of Alaska, with stops along the way in Denver, Colorado, and Victoria on Vancouver Island, British Columbia. Follow these steps:

Set Start Point...

1. Click the Set Start Point button to open the Find A Place To Start dialog box.

2. Enter **Macon, Georgia** in the Place Name text box. Click the Find button, and the map will jump to your start point. Click the OK button to close the Find A Place To Start dialog box.

Set End Point...

3. Click the Set End Point button to open the Find A Place To End dialog box.

4. Enter **Juneau, Alaska** in the same field as Macon and click the Find button. The map will jump to your destination. Click the OK button to close the Find A Place To End dialog box.

5. Your start and end locations appear on a list in the Routing pane and are labeled 1 and 2. Select Macon and click the small clock button to the right. The Edit Time: Macon dialog box opens.

6. Select the Depart At option button and specify the time you want to start your trip from Macon. Click the OK button.

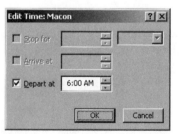

7. Select Juneau in the Routing pane list box and click the small clock button to the right. In the Edit Time: Juneau dialog box, select the Arrive At option button, specify your arrival time, and click the OK button.

8. Click the Add Stops button. In the Find A Place For A Stop dialog box, enter **Denver, Colorado** in the Place Name text box, click Find, then click the OK button to return to the Routing pane.

9. I'll show you a different way to add the second stop (Victoria, B.C.). Right-click the map, select Zoom from the context menu, and then select To North

America. This will center the United States in the Map window. In the upper-left corner, locate Vancouver.

10. Click the Selection button if it's not already selected, draw a box around Vancouver, and then click inside to zoom in (remember to wait for the little magnifying glass to appear).

11. Now that you've zoomed in the Pacific Northwest, locate Vancouver Island. Drag a zoom box from Port Alberni (top left) to Seattle (bottom right) and click inside the box. Victoria, the capital of British Columbia, should be in the middle of your screen.

12. Click the yellow flag next to the Add Stops button in the Routing pane and select Victoria. It will appear as a stop in the list.

Finding Points of Interest

America is full of points of interest, and Streets & Trips indulges the American obsession with roadside attractions—it contains a sizeable database of detailed information on a wide range of shops, restaurants, public facilities of various types, sports arenas, and many other places around the country. To start using the Points Of Interest feature, select View ➤ Show Or Hide Points Of Interest to open the Show Or Hide dialog box with the Points Of Interest page in front (see Figure 17.10). You can access and modify these features at any time.

FIGURE 17.10
The Points Of Interest page offers many categories.

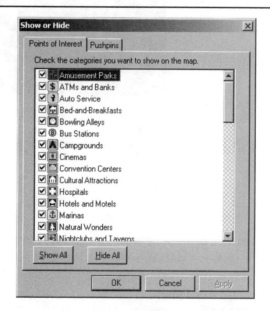

As you can see, a vast number of categories are available, falling into three general types that I call locals, visitors, and everything. Locals use Streets & Trips to get around their hometown and find new things to explore and experience. Visitors use Streets & Trips for trips away from home and into unfamiliar territory. The everything user just wants to know where *everything* is. Browse the list of categories, selecting the ones that you want, and you'll soon know which type you are.

TIP If you're an everything, simply click the Show All button at the bottom of the dialog box.

To demonstrate the Points Of Interest function, we'll see what dining options are available in Victoria. Begin by selecting Victoria from the Routing pane list box. Victoria will appear centered in the map pane. Right-click the name and select What's Nearby Victoria from the context menu. One of the first items in the resulting list is the Empress Hotel (see Figure 17.11).

FIGURE 17.11
The Empress Hotel is one the first items in the list Streets & Trips presents. Simply click the Pictures tab to see this photograph in color.

Empress Hotel

Afternoon tea, British style, is a highlight at the grand Empress Hotel in Victoria, British Columbia. This elegant hotel, situated in Victoria's Inner Harbor region, was built in 1908. Fine restaurants and luxurious lounges are a treat for guests as well as the merely curious.

F. Stuart Westmorland

The lion's share of the data in Streets & Trip is within the United States, but even what little there is about Canada is a welcome addition. To help your search for restaurants, Streets & Trips makes Zagat Survey information available to you. You can search for restaurants based on Zagat ratings. Zagat can also help you determine information such as price range, cuisine type, and/or a special attraction. On the What's Nearby pane, click the Preferences button and choose List Only Those Restaurants Rated By Zagat Survey, click Apply, and then click the OK button. This does not give additional information about restaurants but reduces the displayed restaurants to those rated by Zagat Survey.

Trip Options

You may have noticed the Calculate button in the Routing pane. After you've entered all the routing information about your trip, it's time to do some figuring. If you want to review the trip information you've entered, select Route ➤ Trip Options to open the Trip Options dialog box (see Figure 17.12).

FIGURE 17.12
Select Route ➤ Trip Options to open the Trip Options dialog box; the first page is Segments.

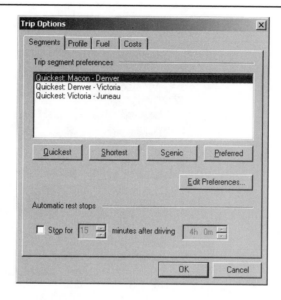

On the Segments page of the Trip Options dialog box, you'll see the three segments of the trip you've planned: Macon to Denver, Denver to Victoria, and Victoria to Juneau.

The default settings select the Quickest route for you, but you can also choose from Shortest, Scenic, and Preferred. Each leg of a trip can be calculated according to a different setting of your choice.

 NOTE Quickest is the route that takes the least amount of time. Shortest is the route that covers the least amount of distance, but it is not necessarily less time-consuming. Scenic is based on what you will see along the route. Preferred routes are based on the specific information that you set. Click the Edit Preferences button to open the Edit Preferences dialog box, and move the sliders left or right to indicate your preference for road type.

Click the Profile tab to open the Profile page, which deals with your driving time (see Figure 17.13). The more accurate and realistic the data you enter, the more accurate your results will be, particularly the driving speeds.

 TIP Streets & Trips allows you to include road construction reports in your travel plans by connecting to the Internet and downloading information.

FIGURE 17.13

The Profile page of the Trip Options dialog box

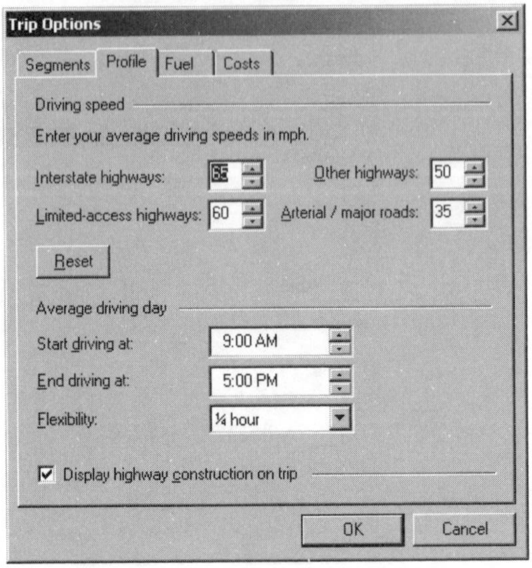

Click the Fuel tab to open the Fuel page, which helps you estimate your fuel costs for your trip (see Figure 17.14). Streets & Trips allows you to include refuel warnings in your trip planning, which can be particularly helpful when traveling in more remote areas.

FIGURE 17.14

The Fuel page of the Trip Options dialog box

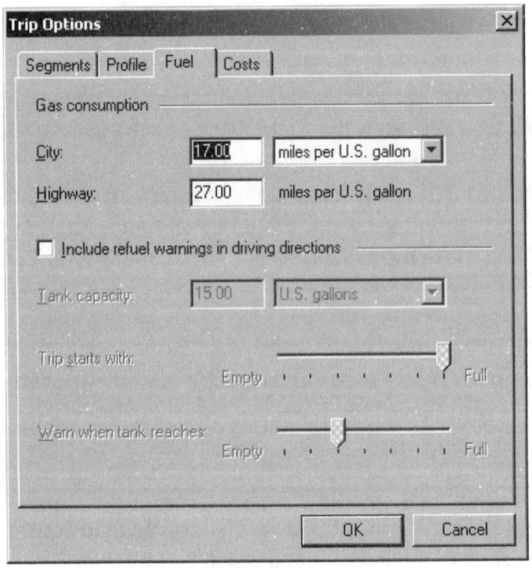

Click the Costs tab to open the Costs page, which allows you to calculate fuel costs for an entire trip.

Finishing the Route

Now that all the information for the trip has been entered, we can have Streets & Trips make all the calculations. Click the Calculate button, and a dialog box will appear showing you the variables of your trip. When it's all done, a new pane will appear above the map (see Figure 17.15).

FIGURE 17.15
Directions for our trip

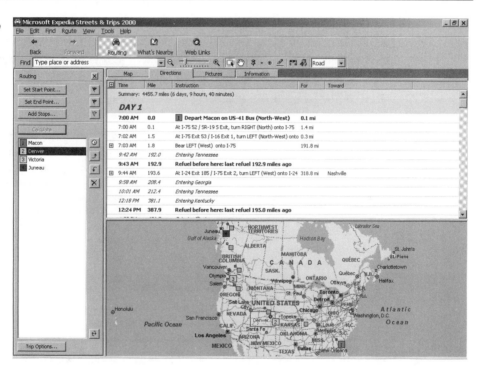

 NOTE If you have not done so ever—or at least lately—Streets & Trips will ask you if you would like to update construction information. I suggest you do so, unless you don't have an Internet connection. Major construction can have a serious impact on expectations. Let Streets & Trips plan ahead.

This represents the entire process from beginning to end, and the directions represent the *trip* from beginning to end. Each component and option is accounted for here in these directions. Now, on to a few other things we can do with our routes.

Managing Trips

Now that you've created your trip, you may want to save or print it. If you travel the same routes rather frequently, it's convenient to have all that work saved and ready to use again with a few clicks. To save a trip, do the following:

1. Make sure that all the modifications, elements, stops, and variables are already included in your trip.

2. Select File ➤ Save.

3. When the Save dialog box opens, locate the place where you would like to save your trip. The save location defaults to My Documents, but you may place the file anywhere you find convenient.

4. Enter a name for your trip file in the File Name box (if you haven't touched anything else, you can start typing immediately, as the text there is already selected and will be erased when you tap the first key).

5. Click the Save button, and your trip will be saved.

 TIP If you've saved a trip and want to make slight modifications to it while retaining the original route, follow the same steps above, but click the Save As option instead.

You'll probably want to print your directions so you can use them on the way. That's easy as well. Follow these instructions:

1. Again, double-check to make sure you've included all the necessary modifications, elements, stops, and variables.

2. Choose File ➤ Print ➤ Map Or Driving Directions. You'll see the Print dialog box (see Figure 17.16).

 TIP You can also access the Print dialog box by right-clicking the instructions and choosing Print from the content menu.

3. If you have more than one printer, select the one you would like to use from the list of printers at the top of the dialog box.

4. If you want to print only the map, click the Current Map View radio button. Otherwise, leave the default (Driving Directions).

5. Using the check boxes and drop-down menus in the Print dialog box, select and modify what portion of your trip you want to print.

6. You may enter a name for the trip in the field provided.

7. Click More Options at the bottom of the dialog box if you want to change some more esoteric options (see Figure 17.17). I imagine you'll be pleased with the default settings.

FIGURE 17.16
The Streets & Trips Print dialog box

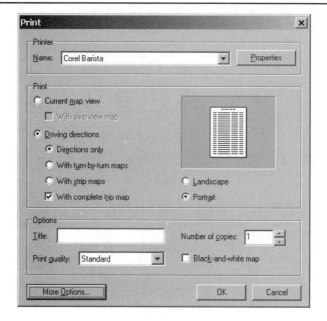

FIGURE 17.17
The More Printing Options dialog box

Using the Keyboard

Some tasks can be accomplished more quickly by using the keyboard. Table 17.1 includes a handful of Streets & Trips-specific keyboard shortcuts

TABLE 17.1: STREETS & TRIPS KEYBOARD SHORTCUTS

Keyboard Shortcut	Task
F5	Zoom the map out
F6	Zoom the map in
Ctrl-A	Find an address
Ctrl-E	Toggle the Measuring tool on and off
Ctrl-F	Find a place
Ctrl-M	Toggle the different map styles
Ctrl-N	Clear the map and create a new route
Ctrl-P	Print the map or driving directions
Ctrl-R	Create or edit a route
Ctrl-S	Save your trip to a file
Ctrl-F5	Calculate the route

Pocket Streets 3

If you have a Windows CE-based PDA (Personal Digital Assistant), Streets & Trips has a feature designed just for you. Using any handheld PC or palm-sized PC (also known as H/PC and P/PC), you can save portions of any map and view them on your PDA, rather than printing out paper maps. This requires special software, but Microsoft included this on Disc 7 (the red one).

 WARNING At the time of this writing, there were no plans for a PalmOS version of the Pocket Streets software, nor is it likely, since Microsoft is competing directly against Palm in this market.

Installing Pocket Streets 3

1. Insert Disc 7 into your CD-ROM drive. Cancel Streets & Trips if it launches automatically.

2. Open My Computer and right-click **<CD-ROM Drive Name Here> (D:)**. Select the Open from the context menu to open the CD for browsing instead of activating the AutoRun feature.

3. Open the pStreets folder and double-click SETUP.EXE. Follow the instructions to complete the installation. Note that the setup will not continue unless you have Windows CE Services or ActiveSync installed on your desktop. Also, make sure you have an active connection to your device, or it will install the software the next time your synchronize your PDA.

4. When you can only click Finish, you're done.

You don't need to have Streets & Trips installed in order to install Pocket Streets. There are a number of prepared maps included in the Maps directory in the same folder as the SETUP.EXE files for Pocket Streets. Open your PDA's Mobile Device icon in My Computer to access your PDA as if it were a folder on your computer. Drag the maps from the CD to the PDA, and you can open them in Pocket Streets.

Perhaps the most useful function of Pocket Streets is the ability to create custom maps. Creating custom maps is easy. Simply select the area that you want as a map, as if you were zooming in on it, but don't zoom. Instead, select Tools ➢ Create Map For Pocket Streets, and specify where you'd like to save the map. You cannot save maps directly to the PDA, and it's easiest to save custom maps to your Desktop until you can transfer them to your PDA. To transfer your custom map, open the Mobile Devices folder in My Computer and drag the Map and Pushpins documents you created into it.

It may take a few minutes to transfer the files to your PDA. When the Copy dialog box disappears, start your PDA and select Start ➢ Programs ➢ Pocket Streets. If you dragged only one map to your PDA, it will appear. If there is more than one map, you will need to select the one you want from a list.

Although you can create custom maps with Pocket Street, you cannot create routes. However, you can create a route in Streets & Trips, with pushpins at the key points, and then copy that route to your PDA.

NOTE Maps can be huge files. For example, a map of about 40 square miles takes up 2 MB. One way to shrink the file size for your maps is to eliminate the points of interest. To do so, select View ➢ Show Or Hide Points Of Interest (if points of interest are displayed, clicking this option deselects it).

Refer to the documentation supplied by the manufacturer for your PDA.

CHAPTER **18**

Money 2000 Standard

Money 2000 Standard is a complete money-management application for tracking all your finances and includes full Internet bank-connectivity capabilities. Every transaction you make, every check you write, every bill you pay, every check you deposit, and every money-related activity you engage in can be recorded in Money. If everything is properly categorized, Money is able to manage all your financial data for you. Microsoft also suggests that you reconcile your financial statements with the Register each month to double-check that Money is accurate.

Don't let the wide range of capabilities Money offers deter you from using this fine application; it's fully featured and has a ton of options, but that does not make it difficult to use. You can use Money as little or as much as you feel comfortable with.

Starting Money 2000 is easy. You can double-click its icon on the Desktop, or choose Start ➢ Microsoft Works 2000 ➢ Money 2000 Standard.

Setting up Money

Setting up Money and getting it running is simple, but the process can take a lot of time. If you have several accounts and credit cards, be prepared to be at your computer for some time.

 NOTE There are two ways to bypass the Setup Assistant and input your bank data into Money without going through the entire preliminary configuration. One method is to import information from a competing product like Quicken that you have already been using; the other is to go directly to online setup.

Audio assistance and clear instructions make the setup process exceedingly easy. One of the first things you'll note when you start Money is the soothing voices that clearly explain what each page is for and give you helpful examples of what to do. To help you get started, here is a list of items that will be helpful in setting up Money for daily use:

- Bank statement(s)—Although not required, bank statements do make the reconciliation process much easier.

- Checkbook(s)—Any checkbooks that you use to pay bills or to buy merchandise, and any registers that you use to record the payments.

- Credit card(s)—Any credit cards that you have and use to make purchases—even cards that you use only in case of an emergency—and their statements with credit limits and interest rates. This also should include any proprietary cards, such as department store charge cards.

- Credit card statement(s)—These make reconciling your accounts much easier, just like the bank statements.

- Loan papers—Eventually, you will pay off your loans, and Money can help you work out the best approach. In order to set up the loans in Money, you will need interest rates and terms from the original loan papers, as well as the principal balance and interest paid for your existing loans.

- Recurring bills—Billing statements for recurring expenses, such as electric, phone, gas, cellular, water, and trash. It's also a good idea to enter payee mailing information in Money if you'll be paying any of your bills electronically.

Information from these items will be required at various points during the setup. After you've gathered your paperwork, you're ready to get started. The first time you start Money, you will see a mostly blank screen with a Start Here button. Click that button to open the Money Setup Assistant, shown in Figure 18.1. We will now walk through the setup process.

FIGURE 18.1
The Money Setup Assistant shows you the sections it will cover, as well as an approximate time of completion for each section.

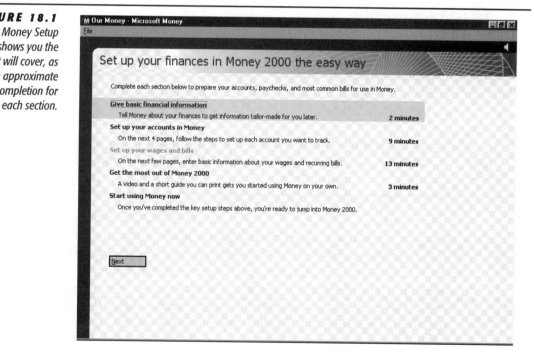

The sections you see in Figure 18.1 address several general financial areas, and the assistant will walk you through setting up accounts and learning how to use Money. The available topics are:

- Basic financial information
- Setting up accounts, wages, bills, and debt
- Getting the most out of Money

The last item, Start Using Money Now, allows you to begin using Money immediately and skip the configuration assistance. If you have never used an application like Money before, I strongly suggest you do *not* skip these steps. The Setup Assistant provides a great deal of valuable information, tips, and other guidance that can make using Money much easier.

 NOTE If you are importing information from Quicken, refer to the sidebar "Importing to Money," later in this chapter. If you're upgrading from an earlier chapter, refer to the Appendix for installation information.

Getting Started

To begin, click the Next button at the left side of the screen shown in Figure 18.1. After you click the Next button, Money will ask you to type in information about yourself and your finances. Money also provides the option of including your spouse's finances by clicking the appropriate radio button (see Figure 18.2). Click the Next button when you finish.

 NOTE Money defaults to Maximized mode and will fill your entire screen when you first start it up. You may resize it if you like.

On the next screen, What Are Your Financial Plans And Interests?, Money asks about your future financial plans. This information allows Money to offer you help in areas that interest you or when you need guidance; there are no right or wrong answers in that the information you enter reflects how you want to use Money or how much of your finances you want to manage from Money (see Figure 18.3). You also will be asked to select a currency. The list ranges from the Argentinean Peso to the Venezuelan Bolivar—the United States Dollar is the default. When you've entered the information, click the Next button.

FIGURE 18.2

Enter your name (and, if you're married, that of your spouse if you plan to include his or her finances).

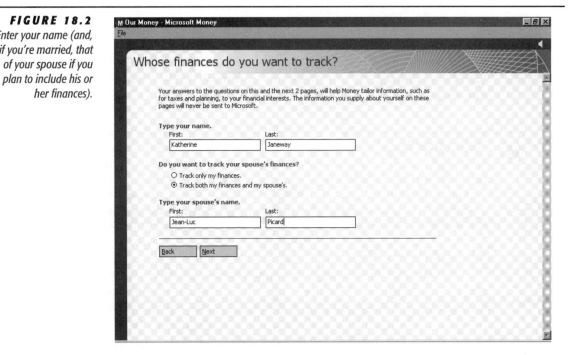

FIGURE 18.3

Select your answers to these questions so that Money can provide additional guidance.

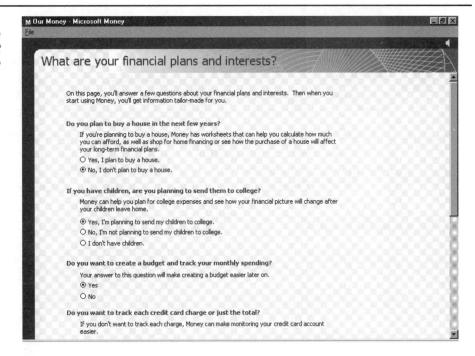

On the next screen, Describe Your Internet Connection, Money asks you about your Internet connection. If you do not have one or aren't sure, Money will help you get connected. Money also offers to connect to the Internet and retrieve the most current update of Money and the latest list of banks offering online banking. You do not have to set this up now, so feel free to wait until later to set up your Internet services. When you've finished, click the Done button, and you will be returned to the first Setup screen, where you need to click Next to continue.

 WARNING Money asks you if you would like to have access to your financial information while you are away from home. Although this option sounds tempting, keep in mind that choosing to do so places sensitive personal data onto the Internet, where unscrupulous individuals may attempt to access it illegally. Illegal access attempts may not be as common as some news outlets would lead you to believe, but this issue is of grave concern.

Entering Accounts

At this point in the Money setup process, you'll see the screen Which Accounts Do You Want To Track?. Here, you need to enter the type and number of your accounts. Select the check box beside each type of account you have or want to set up, and enter the appropriate number in the accompanying spinner box (see Figure 18.4). For instance, you may have two checking accounts, a savings account, four credit cards, dual retirement plans, three investment accounts (including online trading), and a money market account. If you forget to add an account, you can always add it later. When you've finished, click the Next button to go the next screen.

 NOTE None of the information you enter is erased if you use the Back button. Feel free to move about the pages as much as you like to make sure everything is accurate.

After you've entered the number and types of accounts, the document collection you assembled comes in handy. Get out your documentation for all the accounts you entered in the previous screen. Enter your bank accounts, credit card accounts, retirement accounts, and investment information in the spaces provided (see Figure 18.5). When you've entered the information, click the Next button.

FIGURE 18.4
Select the type and number of accounts you want to manage.

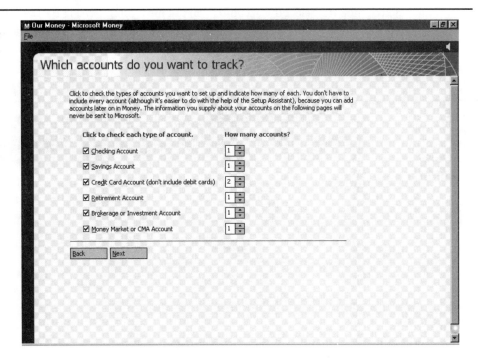

FIGURE 18.5
Enter your account information in the spaces provided.

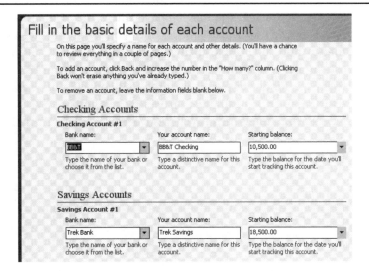

Money allows you to specify the accounts you want faster access to, based on how active they are. Select the accounts you use most often (see Figure 18.6). Even though an account may not be actively used, you may want to select those that you pay attention to daily, such as investments or money market accounts. When you've finished, click the Next button.

FIGURE 18.6

Select your most active accounts, or ones that you want to watch closely.

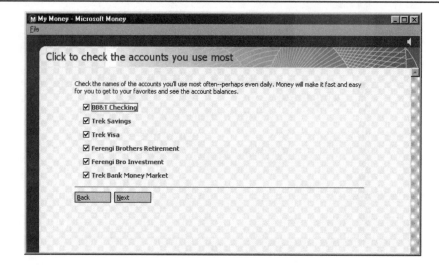

Now, on the Is Your Account Information Accurate? screen, you can check the accuracy of the information you have entered (see Figure 18.7). If anything is incorrect, simply click the Back button until you reach the screen where you entered the information you need to change. If no changes need to be made, click the Done button. Money will return you to the page shown in Figure 18.1. Before returning you to that page, Money displays a warning that you will not be able to return to the Setup Assistant once you exit. If you have finished setting up accounts, click Yes. Click Next to go to the Which Paychecks Do You Want To Track In Money? screen.

FIGURE 18.7
Double-check your information for mistakes or missing data.

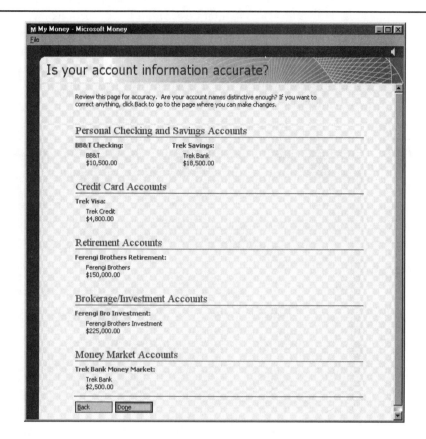

Entering Wages and Bills

Now that you've entered information about where your money *goes*, you need to tell Money where your money *comes from*. By default, Money lets you enter two income sources or paychecks (see Figure 18.8), but you can click the Add Another Paycheck button to enter additional sources.

 NOTE If you do not earn a salaried wage (i.e., you are self-employed) or are paid on an hourly basis, you will likely skip entering wage information. However, entering the information may be helpful if you do get paid approximately the same amount on a regular basis (i.e., a six-month contract as a consultant).

Simply enter who pays you, how much of that you take home (not your *gross income*, but your *net income* after taxes and other deductions), when you will next be paid, and how frequently you're paid. If you entered more than one account in the previous section, be sure you select the account where your income(s) are deposited using the Who Pays You? drop-down menu. If you're paid by direct deposit, select the Paid Via Direct Deposit check box. When you're done, click the Next button to go to the What Bills Do You Pay Regularly? screen.

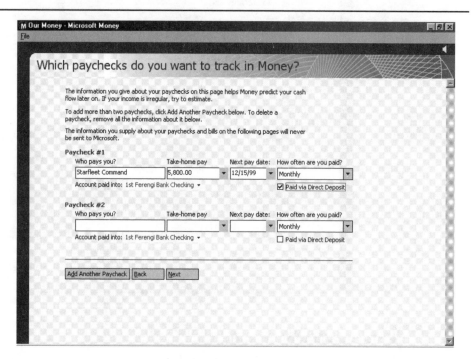

Next, you enter data about the bills that you pay regularly. The first section deals with credit card bills. By default, Money selects all those accounts, so you'll need to deselect any for which you don't want Money to track payments (see Figure 18.9).

Below that section is a list of common bill types. Select the types of bills that you pay and adjust the number of bills. For instance, you may have more than one telephone bill (local, long-distance, cellular, etc.). If there are any other bills you pay that do not have a category, you can add generic entry forms for these bill types. After you've accounted for all your bills, click the Next button to enter the specific information for each bill.

FIGURE 18.9
Money helps you track all the bills that you pay regularly and notifies you of upcoming payments.

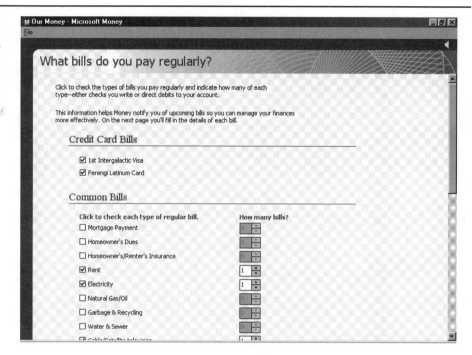

The next screen asks you to enter details about each of the bills you selected on the previous screen. The entry format is very similar to the paycheck form, but keep in mind that this money is going out, not coming in (see Figure 18.10). As with your paycheck(s), be sure you select the proper banking institution from the Whom Do You Pay The Bill To? drop-down menu and choose the account from which the bill should be paid. If your bills are not always the same amount each month, average them out using as many invoices as possible.

After you've entered the details of your bills, click the Next button, and Money will give you an opportunity to review the information for accuracy (see Figure 18.11) on the Is Your Paycheck And Bill Information Accurate? screen. If you missed something, this is the perfect time to go back and fix it. When you've reviewed the information and made any necessary changes, click the Next button. Money will display the Are You Sure? dialog box; simply click the OK button, and Money will return you to the home screen.

FIGURE 18.10

Money tracks the details of where and when your bills are paid, not the amounts.

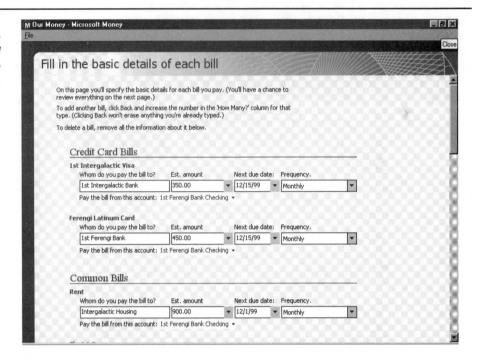

FIGURE 18.11

The bills confirmation screen

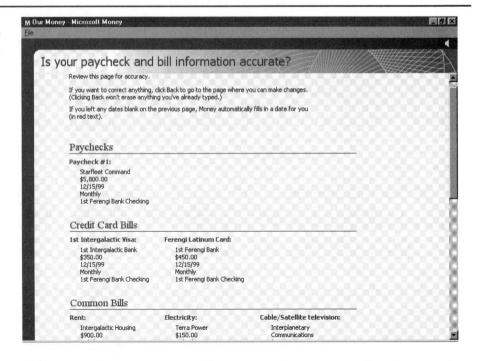

You have now entered most—if not all—of your personal financial data in Money. If you are so inclined, there's a video presentation titled "Get the most out of Money 2000" that gives you pointers and tips about using and navigating Money. Viewing this video presentation takes only a few minutes. When you've finished, click the Next button to go to Money's home page.

Importing to Money

If you've been using Quicken and want to give Money a try, Microsoft makes it easy to switch. Instead of manually inserting all your data into Money, you can easily import the information. If you have Quicken, Money will detect it and offer to import your data automatically. The process works like this:

1. Run Money.

2. Select File ➤ Convert Quicken File.

3. In the resulting dialog box, select your Quicken file.

4. Follow the instructions for conversion.

5. View the summary file. If you want, you can save a copy or print out the summary.

Note that Quicken cannot be running during the conversion because it keeps the file open. Also, Money lets you have only one active budget, whereas Quicken lets you have several.

Things to look for when you're importing Quicken files to Money include:

- Categories are shortened because Money supports only one subcategory rather than Quicken's multiple subgroups.

- Scheduled transactions assigned to transaction groups are lost, but you can add them later.

- General passwords are retained, but passwords set to transactions are lost.

- Investment accounts that are linked to checking accounts will be added to the cash of a similar account type in Money. If they're not linked, Money will create them.

Continued ▶

- If you make electronic loan payments in Quicken, there will be two entries for each electronic payment in Money. You will have to remove the duplicates by hand.

- Manually entered loan payments from Quicken are not imported.

- Money takes only the most recent interest rate from Quicken, which may affect various charts, graphs, and other rate-based schedules and tables.

Getting Around Money

Money is a very rich application, and you will most likely appreciate the elegance of many of these features. Of course, at other times you may scratch your head in wonder. First, I'll address the basics, beginning with navigation.

Navigating in Money

The main Money screen features three primary areas: Category, Function, and Navigation (see Figure 18.12). Generally, you will select a category and then perform functions in that category. First, you will need an anatomy lesson because the interface may be only partially familiar to you.

 TIP Whenever you point at a link (text or a graphic that, when clicked, leads to another page), the cursor changes to a hand, just like in a Web browser. These links are only to pages within the Money application, but when you point to an external link—on the Internet—a tiny globe appears under the hand, letting you know that an Internet connection is required.

Keep in mind that Money, like most Works 2000 applications, uses a Web page metaphor and a hierarchical interface design. This means that you have a main topic with subtopics and that each subtopic may have its own subtopics. Across the top of the window you will see the title bar, the menu bar, and the Category bar, as shown in Figure 18.12. The Category bar is a fast way of accessing the items you want.

FIGURE 18.12

The Category, Function, and Navigation areas of the home screen

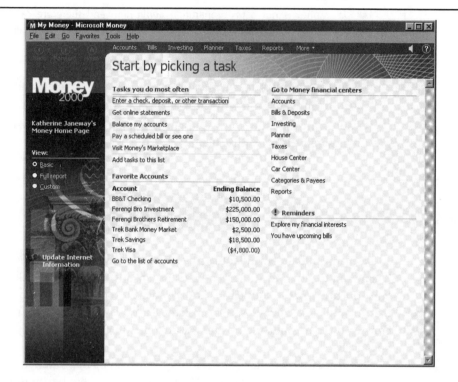

The Category Bar

The items included in the Category bar are:

- Accounts—Where Money stores all your accounts and related information
- Bills—Provides specifics on bills and other regular debits
- Investing—Offers information related to, and connections regarding, investments and stocks
- Planner—Provides details and assistance on making a financial plan and help in being prepared for nearly any contingency
- Taxes—Contains information pertaining to taxes and assistance in filling out tax forms

NOTE Money is *not* a tax-preparation application and therefore cannot prepare your taxes automatically. Money can offer assistance and links to other resources, including online tax submission.

- Reports—Provides utilities and help in creating detailed and specific charts, reports, and tables about your money
- More—Includes the House Center, Car Center, and Categories & Payees (which I'll examine later in this chapter)

Navigating Money is similar to using a Web browser in many ways (see Figure 18.13). If you want to return to Money's home screen at any time, simply click the Home button. To return to a previous page, click the Back button. If you want to return to a page

 that you just backed out of, simply click the Forward button. If you've never used a Web browser, this navigation method may seem somewhat unfamiliar, but you should pick it up quickly.

Another easy way to navigate in Money is the Go menu, which includes items for all of the major sections of Money. Now that you have your bearings, you can move on to using Money.

 TIP If you prefer to navigate using the keyboard, you'll notice that a keyboard shortcut appears to the right of each item on the Go menu.

What You Can Do with Money

When you first open Money following a complete setup or import procedure, you'll see what appears to be a Web page. Microsoft is migrating its interface designs to use Web conventions and standards, making it easier for you to move from a local application to the Internet. Most of the applications in Works Suite 2000 use this method.

The Home Screen

On the home screen, Money asks you to "Start by picking a task." You choose from a list of the tasks grouped by category. The view shown earlier in Figure 18.12 is called

Basic and contains only the essential information that you need to work with Money. Common activities such as checking your balance, inputting purchases, and balancing the Register are included, along with a list of the accounts that you selected as your favorites.

The home screen features links to Money's various financial centers that provide information to help you manage your money. Each one leads to a relative wealth of information on a given topic. Below the topics is a list of reminders that require your attention. Each of the entries on this page is actually a link, much like that of a Web browser. For instance, under the Tasks You Do Most Often header, when you click Enter A Check, Deposit, Or Other Transaction, you are taken to another page where you can select the account you want to change.

Accounts

This category will likely be your most common and direct interaction with Money. The Accounts page is where you'll manage all your accounts (see Figure 18.14). Let's start with entering transactions. Select an account by clicking on its name in the list. Now, you can either enter information from your receipts (you can download your transactions into Money via the Internet, which is covered later in the chapter).

FIGURE 18.14
The main
Accounts page

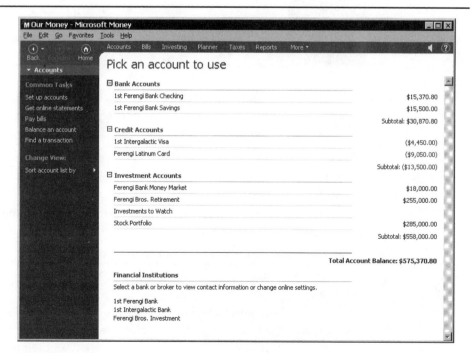

If you select the first account listed under Favorite Accounts, its register will appear, as shown in Figure 18.15. The Register should be familiar because it looks like the paper registers that you get with a box of checks.

FIGURE 18.15

A typical account register showing transaction forms at the bottom

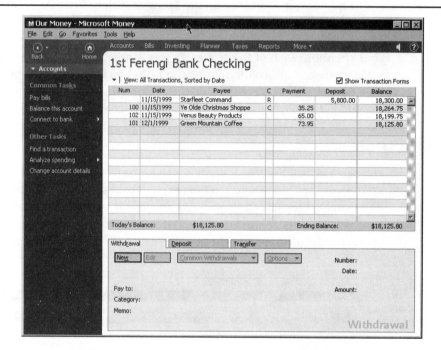

The transaction forms are designed to look like checks. Gather some receipts from your transactions or your check register you've probably collected from the last few days, and enter them in the Register as follows:

1. First click New to bring up an empty check form.

2. Click the down arrow on the Number field, and choose Next Check Number or type in the number you want on the check.

3. Check the date (Money inserts the current date from your computer system, but you can type in any date you like).

4. In the Pay To text box, enter the name of the merchant.

5. Press the Tab key to move to the Amount text box, then enter the amount of the purchase.

6. Press Tab again and select a primary category for the purchase. Primary categories are higher level with no detail—for example, food or taxes. Press Tab again to select the secondary category; Money already knows the primary category

you selected and will offer only items related to that category. If neither drop-down menu offers the primary category or secondary category you need, type one of your own in the text box. Money will save that category for future transactions.

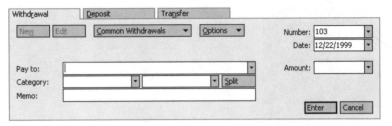

7. Press Tab again to highlight the Split button. Click Split, and enter the category and subcategory for the items that fall into different categories. Enter the separate amounts for each, with a short description.

 NOTE Splits are used to break up into their aggregate categories single payments consisting of several item categories. Confused? Here's how it works. Let's say that you go to Earl's House of Pizza and Auto Repair for lunch and an oil change. Both the lunch and oil change go on your credit card as a single transaction. This qualifies as a split purchase. In this case, you'd have an entry for Food:Dining Out and another for Automobile:Maintenance.

---

8. Press Tab to move to the Memo text box, where you can type a memo if you like.

9. Press Tab once more to move to the Enter button. Don't forget to enter a check number or date information before finalizing the entry. When you've finished, you can either click the Enter button or press the Enter key or spacebar on your keyboard.

Now that you have entered the data in the form and clicked the Enter button, the data appears in the Register (see Figure 18.16). The default view shows a single line per transaction. This line includes the check number, transaction date, payee, bank status, columns for deposits and debits, and the updated balance. At the bottom of the Balance column is the Ending Balance field.

 TIP If you prefer to enter the transaction data in the Register itself, deselect the Show Transaction Forms check box above the Deposit and Balance columns. Doing so also allows you to see more of the Register at one time.

FIGURE 18.16
The Register showing
the Withdrawal
transaction form

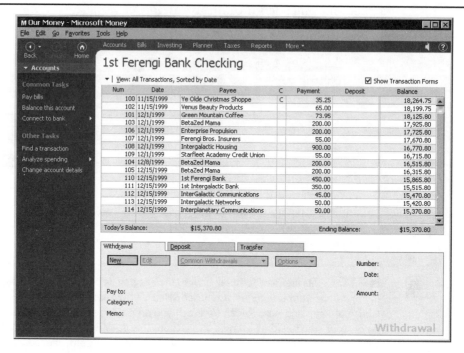

The Deposit and Transfer forms work in much the same manner. Enter your data and click Enter to add it to Money. Transfers appear in the Register as Payments and Deposits, just like all other transactions.

NOTE Each transaction form has a Common Actions menu. For example, in the Common Deposits menu you may choose from recurring deposits such as paychecks, deposits with cash back, and even deposit multiple items.

Account Functions

You may have noticed the function buttons along the left edge of your screen. The Accounts category (the green bar located beneath the Back, Forward, and Home buttons, shown in Figure 18.17) has various functions that directly relate to the operation of the category. Note that there are two sections: Common Tasks and Other Tasks. This area is called the Functions section.

FIGURE 18.17
*The functions area of
the Accounts screen*

The items included in Common Tasks are:

- Set Up Accounts—On the page that appears when you click this item, you can add new accounts, get online account access (if your bank offers it through Money), assign payees to an account, create or remove categories, and many other functions. At the bottom of the page is a list of existing accounts that you can modify.

 TIP Click the Back button at any time to return to the previous page.

- Get Online Statements—Click this item to download financial statements for your accounts. Access is provided through the Internet, so be sure you are already connected. Follow the instructions or see the section "Banking Online" for details on how to set up an online account.

- Pay Bills—Clicking this item takes you directly to the next category, Bills. Here, you can make payments and account for particular debits, among other tasks.

- Balance An Account—Click this item to go to a list of accounts. Select the account you want to balance, and Money takes you to the account's Register and opens the Balance Account dialog box. The instructions are clear, and you can always cancel the process.

- Find A Transaction—Clicking this item opens the Find And Replace dialog box shown in Figure 18.18, which allows you to enter search terms and other information. This feature can be helpful if you have more than a couple of years of transactions and you need to find one for a credit card dispute, for example.

Under the Change View heading in the Functions area is one item: Sort Account List By. Clicking the item displays a menu offering you various options for sorting and displaying your information.

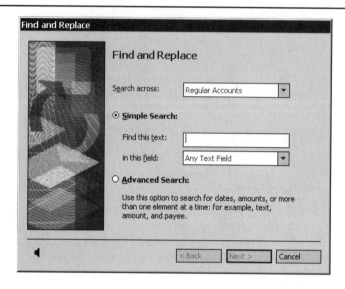

After you enter an account, items specific to that account appear in the Functions area under Common Tasks:

- Pay Bills—Clicking this item takes you to the Bills category.

- Balance This Account—Once you are in an account, you don't need to select it, but your choice is limited to balancing only the open account. To select an account from a list, return to the Accounts main screen.

- Connect To Bank—If you have already signed up for and are receiving information from your banking institution, you'll see an arrow next to this item. When you click the arrow, you'll see another menu with related items. If you haven't already signed up to receive information from your bank, clicking the Connect To Bank item displays a submenu labeled Do Other (name of bank) Tasks, which, if chosen, allows you to view your account, learn about setting up your online accounts, and view the bank's contact information.

TIP Click any item with a small arrow or ellipsis next to it to open a dialog box with more options.

Other Tasks includes these items:

- Find A Transaction—Click this item to open the Find And Replace dialog box you saw in Figure 18.18.

- Analyze Spending—This topic allows you to analyze where your money went, see who received your money, view payments to and from specific categories, view payments to and from specific payees, see how much you'll have left after you pay the bills, view recent account balances, and review all available reports on your accounts. If you select the Review All Available Reports item, you can select a category and a chart or report, then click the Go To Report/Chart button at the bottom of the page. Click the Customize button to specify payees to include and give the report or chart a date range. Modifying the date range can afford you a clear look at income and expenditures over a long or short period of time.

- Change Account Details—Clicking this item is the same as selecting an account from the main Accounts page and then selecting Set Up Accounts from the Common Tasks list. This is simply a more direct route.

Bills

Money will handle your bills quite well, but it can go only so far. It can't walk your check down to the mailbox, but there are options for electronic bill payment. Click the Bill Category to go to the main Pay Bills screen. You'll see a list of bills (see Figure 18.19) that resembles an account's Register.

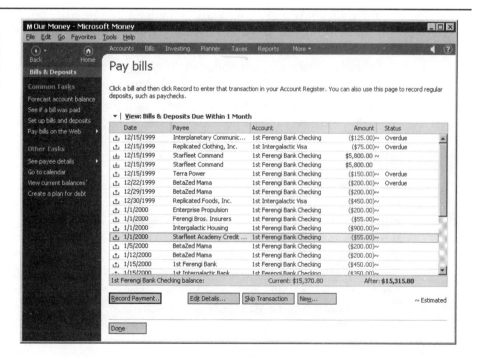

FIGURE 18.19
The Pay Bills screen displays a list of bills that resembles an account's Register.

NOTE You may note the Overdue status on some bills in our fake account. When you enter one of your bills, for example a cable television bill or rent, and the billing cycle, into Money, it will tell you if payment is overdue on that bill. Don't worry—this isn't a way for your landlord to send you a message!

Using the four buttons—Record Payment, Edit Details, Skip Transaction, and New—at the bottom of the page, there are functions you can perform from the Bills Category screen. You can also choose the period of time covered by the due bills to be displayed by selecting the time frame from the drop-down list that appears when you click the down arrow just above the top left corner of the bill list. The default is one month, but you can select up to a year.

Select an operation from the list of functions in the Bills & Deposits Function, and follow the concise instructions that walk you through the steps. You'll see these items in the Common Tasks group:

- Forecast Account Balance—Shows you up to 12 months of balance forecasting based on the information available in your accounts.

- See If A Bill Was Paid—Although helpful, this feature is not nearly as simple as it sounds. It tracks when you mark a bill paid and then tries to match that bill with updates from the bank (or reconcile by hand). If the amount paid isn't exactly what you noted, the bill will not appear as paid. If you know it was paid but can't locate it in the list, use the Find function.

- Set Up Bills And Deposits—This feature is a way of entering new bills or bills that you didn't add during the setup procedure. To add a bill, click New.

Investing

Money provides a solid collection of tools for managing your investments. When you click on the Investing category button, you'll see several key areas that let you work with your investments, money markets, stocks, funds, and 401(k) plans. Investing is also tightly integrated with the Web, so you have immediate access to the latest information possible.

There is a downside, however: Investing does not follow Money's established interface format. Instead, Microsoft chose to place all the function items in a horizontal row across the top of the Manage Your Investments And Savings screen, as shown in Figure 18.20.

FIGURE 18.20
The Investing main
screen includes tools
for managing your
investments and
savings.

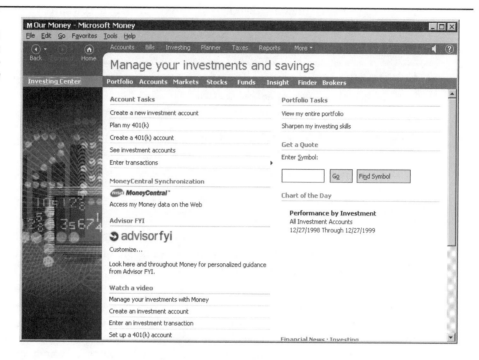

Manage your investments and savings

Manage your investments and savings

Portfolio Accounts Markets Stocks Funds Insight Finder Brokers

Items included in the Investing navigation bar are:

- Portfolio—The Portfolio contains all your investment information. Money, by default, creates an account called Investments To Watch, which points to this place. You can add any number of investments and perform a wide range of activities related to them. The investment analysis function may prove to be helpful, depending on your investment analysis needs.

NOTE The Record A Special Activity feature allows you to transfer accounts from one form to another and to record stock splits. The See A Different View feature offers you a wide range of ways to view your investment data, as well as a wide range of customization options.

- Accounts—Lists all your investments and actions related to handling your accounts.

- Markets—Clicking this item provides you with a link to the MSN MoneyCentral Web site titled Market Report: Investor, which contains information about working with investments.

NOTE The next few items are all Web sites on Microsoft's MSN network, specifically Money-Central (`http://moneycentral.msn.com`).

- Stocks—A large collection of information on all areas and disciplines of stocks investing, including the Research Wizard.
- Funds—Information about mutual funds and other funds of interest.
- Insight—An online magazine that tracks trends in the various investment markets.
- Finder—A handy set of tools that can temporarily take the place of real stock and market analysts and help you understand the market; includes simple, advanced, and custom searches.

NOTE Before viewing any analysis, you will be prompted to download ActiveX Control—if it hasn't already been installed on your computer—so that you can view the data in your browser. When the dialog box appears asking if you trust content from Microsoft, click the Yes button. The control will simply download if you have previously approved Microsoft as a trusted provider.

- Brokers—Once you've gathered your data and have an investing plan in mind, you can select an online firm or a broker to perform your transactions. Keep in mind that no matter how you trade stocks, you will be charged a fee for each sale and/or purchase.

Budget Planner

You can access the Budget Planner by clicking the Planner category button. The Budget Planner consolidates a number of different functions located in various places within Money. All these functions are related to helping you plan your financial future.

NOTE Keep in mind that the information presented in these pages is based on what you enter in Money and how you answer questions that Money asks you. The more information you can give the Budget Planner, the better.

The main Plan Your Finances screen (see Figure 18.21) includes the following items:

- Create A Budget—Click here to start the Budget Planner. In the Functions/Common Tasks panel, a list of items will appear that you will work with through the planner. Clicking the Next button on the right will move you from item to item. Read all the instructions and fill in as many details as you can to make your budget as accurate as possible.

FIGURE 18.21
The Budget Planner helps you plan your financial future.

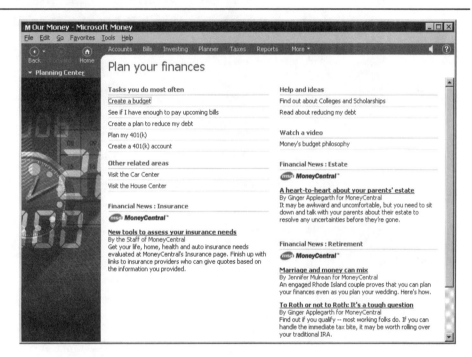

- See If I Have Enough To Pay Upcoming Bills—Clicking this item takes you to the Bills & Deposits balance forecaster page. Select the account that you want to look at—and how far ahead you want to look—and the chart will give you a clear indication of what it *thinks* your balance will be, based on your spending and income pattern so far. This feature is most accurate when you have a consistent level of inflows and outflows without any extraordinary expenses (the new car) or income (selling the motor home).

- Create A Plan To Reduce My Debt—Click this item to start the Debt Reduction Planner. Similar in function to the Budget Planner, this planner helps you arrange your existing financial structure to better meet your debt needs.

Taxes

Money can help you get your taxes in order long before April 14 rolls around. Clicking the Taxes category button takes you to a number of functions that deal specifically with tax preparation (see Figure 18.22).

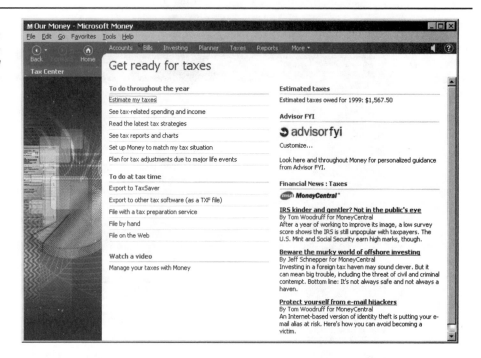

The section To Do Throughout The Year includes these functions:

- Estimate My Taxes—This provides only a rough estimate based on the figures you enter. Checking with a good tax preparation professional is highly recommended.

- See Tax-related Spending And Income—Click this item to see a list of all deductible items, sorted by form. You can access the Tax Category Manager from here to add specific items.

- Read The Latest Tax Strategies—Get the latest information and helpful tips on all things tax-related from this MSN site. You'll also find good information about Microsoft's tax package, TaxSaver (`http://taxsaver.msn.com`).

- See Tax Reports And Charts—Clicking this item takes you directly to the Reports category with the Taxes function. Choose from one of the four items available to get a closer look at your tax-related finances. Use the Date Range menu to choose the date range you want to see.

- Set Up Money To Match My Tax Situation—Money can be customized to display your financial data in direct relation to your taxes and how your taxes affect your monetary concerns for the year. The items listed on the setup screen simply point to other resources that you've already seen.

- Plan For Tax Adjustments Due To Major Life Events—Click this item to open the Money Help pane. You'll also see a link for downloading the latest tax information.

The section To Do At Tax Time includes:

- Export To TaxSaver—This function allows you to export all your tax data to TaxSaver (more on this later) for assistance during the tax preparation process.

- Export To Other Tax Software (As A TXF File)—This function will export your selected tax data to a globally accepted file format called TXF (Tax Exchange Format) and allows you to print a tax report for your records.

- File With A Tax Preparation Service—This function resembles the one above; you can also prepare your files to be printed, either for you or for your CPA.

- File By Hand—This item offers much of the same functionality as the previous item, without the TXF or CPA options, and allows you to print a report to use to prepare your taxes, as well as a tax report for your records.

- File On The Web—Microsoft Money 2000 offers you access to a new application called TaxSaver.

 WARNING At the time of writing, TaxSaver was not fully functional, but it's worth investigating for your taxes.

Reports

Nothing could be simpler than reports. Just click on the Reports category. The only problem may be in reading some of them—their complexity can increase exponentially—but Money is quite good at explaining everything on the charts and reports that it generates. Money also comes with a huge array of predefined charts and reports (see Figure 18.23).

To use Reports, select the function you want, highlight the chart or report you want to see, set the parameters at the bottom of the page, and click Go To Report/Chart to open the report or chart. Here, you can change the parameters, display a different chart or report type, and even customize how your charts and reports are displayed. In the lower-left corner are four icons; click the appropriate icon to change to Report, Bar, Line, or Pie Chart. Click the Customize button to open the Customize Report dialog box, which lets you modify the specifics of a chart or report.

FIGURE 18.23
Money comes with a
wide variety of
predefined charts
and reports.

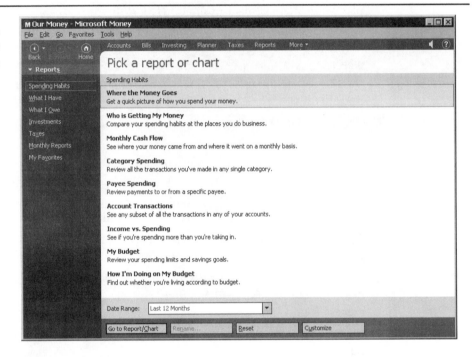

Functions in Reports

The Reports main page offers a selection of functions, and each function includes items you may choose from.

Spending Habits

The Spending Habits function includes these items:

- Where The Money Goes
- Who Is Getting My Money
- Monthly Cash Flow
- Category Spending
- Payee Spending
- Account Transactions
- Income Vs. Spending
- My Budget
- How I'm Doing On My Budget

Each item gives you a look at how your money is spent. Clicking an item will take you to the page where the chart or report was created. The Where The Money Goes page clearly shows just where it all goes (see Figure 18.24).

FIGURE 18.24
A sample Where The Money Goes pie chart indicating a category's name and value

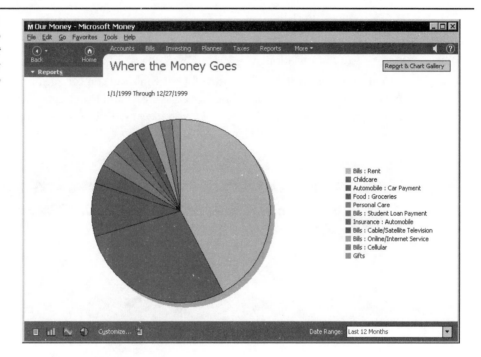

What I Have

The What I Have function includes these items:

- Net Worth
- Net Worth Over Time
- Account Balances
- Account Balance History
- Account Details

When you need to know exactly what your assets are, this is the best place to look. It's also helpful to see everything in one place so that you can get a feel for the overall scope of your finances. The Account Balance History shows you whether your overall balance has been growing or shrinking.

What I Owe

The What I Owe function includes these items:

- Upcoming Bills
- Upcoming Bills And Deposits This Month
- Credit Card Debt
- Loan Terms
- Loan Amortization

This function covers every aspect of what you owe. You can see future bills, current bills, and deposits in combination, as well as credit and loan items. The Credit Card Debt report can be an invaluable tool if you have multiple cards and juggle their credit lines on a regular basis (see Figure 18.25).

FIGURE 18.25
A sample Credit Card Debt bar chart for two accounts

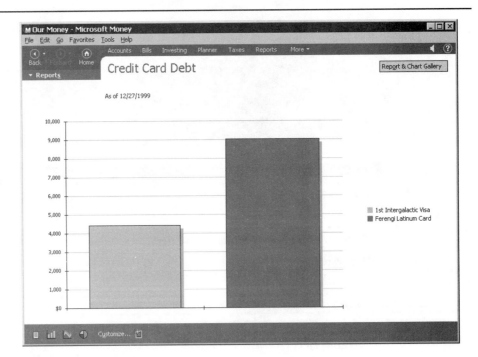

Investments

The Investments function includes the following items:

- Portfolio Value By Investment Account
- Portfolio Value By Investment Type

- Performance By Investment Account
- Performance By Investment Type
- Price History
- Investment Transactions
- Bond Summary
- Bond Performance

When you are actively tracking an investment package, these charts and reports can help immensely.

Taxes

The Taxes function includes these items:

- Tax-related Transactions
- Capital Gains
- Loan Interest
- Top Software Report

This section is definitely smaller than the others, but it includes the very important capital gains and loan interest items.

Monthly Reports

The Monthly Reports function is different from the others because it holds information that relates directly to you. Choose a monthly report from the Pick A Report Or Chart list, and all activity for that month is gathered and placed in a special report form that shows the results of a list of activities. This report form can show you how much you've saved or where potential problem areas are. The functions in a Monthly Report (see Figure 18.26) include the following:

- Spending
- Net Worth
- Advisor FYI
- Potential Problems
- Next Month
- Taxes

FIGURE 18.26
*The Monthly Reports
section showing credit
card spending in
December for two
cards.*

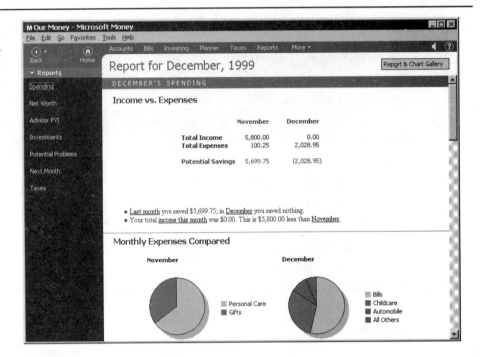

My Favorites

My Favorites in Money does not provide a great deal of functionality—at least compared with Internet Explorer or Netscape Navigator. Despite the Web page paradigm that Microsoft has imposed on the Money interface, you cannot add any page in Money as a favorite. These favorites apply only to external links or "real" Web pages.

NOTE   Money's My Favorites don't show up in Internet Explorer, but they do appear in the Financial Links menu under Favorites ➤ Internet Favorites.

House Center

Choose More ➤ House Center to open the House Center. This category has a number of functions related to locating, buying, owning, protecting, and managing your home (see Figure 18.27). For example, selecting How Much House Can I Afford? takes you to a worksheet where you can figure out just that. This is also an excellent place to start tracking your possessions and insuring yourself against theft, loss, or damage. Renters especially will find these features helpful—it's not easy to keep track of everything if you have moved often in the last several years.

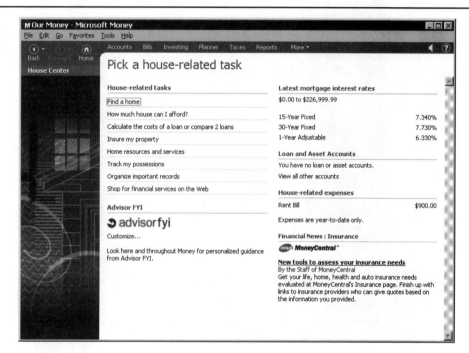

FIGURE 18.27
The House Center main screen

Car Center
Choose More ➤ Car Center to open the Car Center. Here you can obtain information about buying a new car, financing, insurance, and even a nice personal auto page from MSN's CarPoint, a motor vehicle information center where you can track details about your car, its service record, and its current market value (see Figure 18.28). Reviews of new cars and information on cars from the Kelley Blue Book are also available.

FIGURE 18.28
MSN's CarPoint page in Money

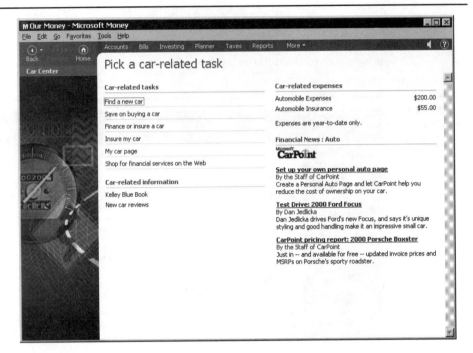

Categories

Choose More ➤ Categories & Payees to display the Categories & Payees page. Every time you enter a debit or deposit, you place it in a category for easier sorting and better income/expense tracking. All of these categories are listed here so you can remove, augment, or simply modify them to make them better fit your personal needs. You can even move categories and subcategories so they serve a more complete or accurate purpose for you. For example, you could create a Utilities category and make the Electricity, Garbage, and Recycle and Natural Gas/Oil subcategories to consolidate your utility expenses (see Figure 18.29).

FIGURE 18.29
*The Categories &
Payees main screen*

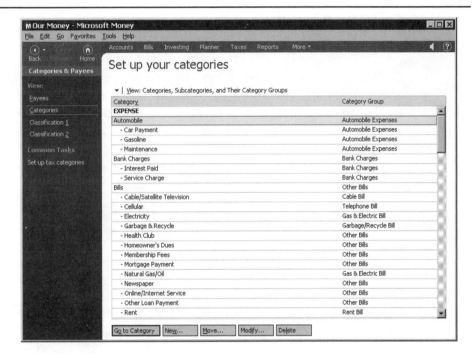

Payees

Choose Payees from the Functions panel. Payees are the persons or companies that get your money for a service they provide or an item you purchase. To safely deliver their fee to them, you need to enter their data into Money so it knows where and how to send the payment. Any payees that you enter appear here. You can add, delete, and modify payees from the Set Up Your Payees screen.

Classifications

Select Classification 1 or 2 in the Function panel. Classifications allow you to refine your custom category sets to more closely meet your personal financial needs. The default categories in the Add Classification dialog box are:

- Family Members
- Properties
- Projects

- Hobbies

- Vacations

- Job Expenses

- An open slot that you can name whatever you like

Because there are only two custom classification categories, it's best to limit your selections to things that are not easily pigeonholed. For instance, you probably don't want to use categories like projects, hobbies, or vacations because these can easily be integrated into the regular categories. Unique items, such as family members, properties, or job expenses, are good candidates.

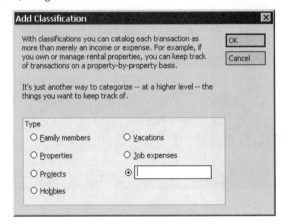

Creating your own classification is simple and allows you to tailor Money to your specific financial needs. In the Add Classification dialog box, select one of predetermined types Money supplies or create your own.

Setting Up Tax Categories

Choose Set Up Tax Categories in the Categories & Payees panel. Money can help track your tax-oriented expenses by associating certain categories with taxes. In the category and subcategory list, you can click any item, select the Include On Tax Reports check box, and enter the specifics (see Figure 18.30).

 TIP If you are a small business owner, freelancer, or consultant, setting up tax categories is often the easiest way to track expenditures without paying for a full-time tax consultant.

FIGURE 18.30
Associating categories with taxes

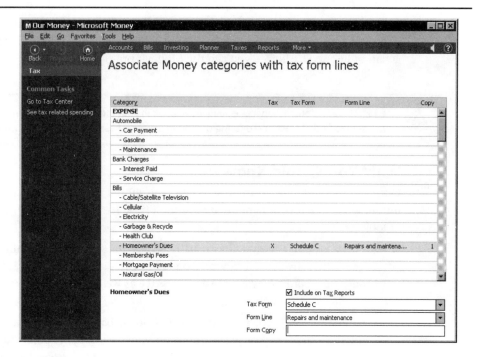

Banking Online

One primary reason to use Money is to get your financial statements online. Before you embark on setting up an online account, gather this information:

- Account number(s)
- Personal identification (drivers license, Social Security, etc.)
- Your bank's online information

It may seem paradoxical to require you to *be* online to *get* online, but if your bank offers online services, you will need to connect to the bank's Web site as securely as possible. Some banks require you to use Internet Explorer 4 or 5 or Netscape Communicator 4.*x* and up, with 128-bit encryption.

NOTE This level of security is more than sufficient to protect your sensitive data and is likely more secure than withdrawing cash from an ATM machine, because you can deal with your finances in total privacy and on your own time.

Setting Up Online Services

Using Money online is easy if you already have an Internet access account with a local or national Internet service provider. However, if you're not connected, you need to get an online service before you can use Money's online features.

 TIP Locating online services is fairly easy. Look in your local yellow pages under Internet and you should find at least one offering unlimited access, or ask a friend for a recommendation.

What You Should Know

Once you have established Internet access, you should find out all you can about the online services that your banking institution offers. Here are a few things to ask about or look for:

- Access or usage fees—Banks usually charge for services, and online banking is generally considered a service. Access fees can range from $5 to $20 per month, and some banks may charge an access fee as well as a usage fee (typically $0.25 per megabyte of data).

- Limitations on access or access caps—Some banks that offer online services impose a usage cap or place a limit on your access. Some banks impose this by technological means, and others will charge you if you exceed a certain limit.

- Compatible software—Most banks support Intuit Quicken, QuickBooks, and Microsoft Money, but some banks offer only one of these options.

- Customer and technical support—A good technical support department should be able to walk you through an installation and setup of your package.

 NOTE Some banks will require that you contact them directly to establish an account over the phone. Others will allow you to do so via a secure Internet connection through your Web browser. Either way, you will need to create a username and a password. The username identifies who you are, and the password validates that you are that person. You will also be asked for your account number and possibly other pertinent personal information for verification.

Getting Online with Your Bank

To begin, you need to select an account for which you want to set up online access. Follow these steps (I'm assuming you're starting from the home page):

1. Click the Accounts category.
2. Select the appropriate account from the list that appears.

3. Click the Connect To Bank function and select Do Other *<your bank name>* Tasks.

4. Click the Set Up Online Services function.

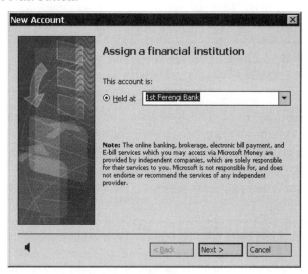

5. To the right of your chosen account, click the Set Up button to open the New Account dialog box.

6. From the Held At drop-down menu, select the bank where the account is held. Click the Next button.

7. If your bank is not listed, all is not lost. Below the list box is an option button with the name of your bank; select the radio button and then click Next.

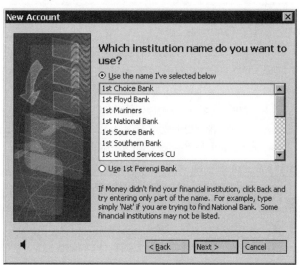

8. The next dialog box asks you to select a name for your bank. If your bank isn't on the list and Money can't find information for your bank, find out whether your bank offers Web-based downloads for Money or online services of any kind. You will need to contact your bank for information on how to access your account information via the Internet using a Web browser.

9. If your bank is on the list, select it and click the Next button. Now you're all set up. When you return to the Connect To Bank function on the Accounts page, you will have the option to download your recent activities.

 NOTE Some banks now operate entirely online and do not have any branch offices—for example, WingSpan (http://www.wingspan.com).

Click the Get Online Statements function on the Accounts page, and you will likely be taken to your bank's Web site to either set up an account or enter the details that you received from your bank when you set up your online account over the phone. If everything goes well, you'll receive your first online statement. If things do not go well, contact your bank's online services support department.

 WARNING One common online account problem is case sensitivity. Many banks will not indicate whether your username and password information is case sensitive. For example, if your username is Carlos and your password is A1b2C3d4, a case-sensitive system requires that you enter the information exactly as listed here. A non-case-sensitive system will accept the data in either uppercase or lowercase characters.

Your Bills Online

Bills can be paid online. You can also receive bills online. You may be able to receive and send all of your bills online. Setting up your bills online in Money is easy. Follow these steps:

1. Click the Bills category at the top of the window.

2. Locate the Pay Bills On The Web item and click to open its menu, which contains a single item, Set Up Online Services. Select it.

3. In the next screen, click the first Set Up button, in the Pay Bills Online section. You are now back in the Accounts category.

4. Select the account you want to use for online bill paying.

5. Click the Set Up button next to the Bill Payment item, and you'll see the Bill Payment Setup dialog box (see Figure 18.31). Follow the instructions and you'll

have the information you need to set up an online bill-paying account. The two current systems available are CheckFree and MI Data Services.

FIGURE 18.31
The Bill Payment Setup dialog box offers two providers for online bill paying.

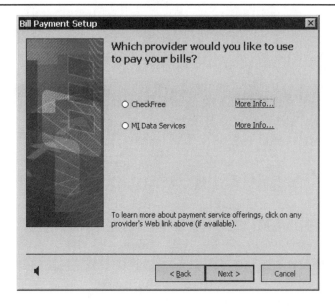

You'll need your Social Security number and some other information, such as your username and password. If you don't have this information, the wizard will help you. Simply follow the concise directions and you'll soon be paying bills the easy way.

NOTE You must have at least one account set up for online access in order to use online bill-paying services.

Security Considerations

If your Web browser is not already enabled with 128-bit encryption, you'll need to update it.

- If you use Internet Explorer, click Start ➤ Windows Update, which will take you to Microsoft's update site. Select Internet Explorer 5 128-bit Encryption; this download is about 600KB and takes only a few moments to download, even on a slow modem.

Continued ▶

- If you use Netscape's Communicator/Navigator, you'll have to download a new installation file. In other words, you need to install a new version of your browser to migrate to 128-bit encryption. Point your current Web browser to `http://www.netscape.com/download/selectplatform_1_702.html` and follow the instructions.

In general, even if your bank does not require you to upgrade to 128-bit encryption, you should do so anyway. Most systems will encrypt data at the maximum available depth so that your sensitive data will be protected. The primary benefit of banking online is that your banking can be more productive and accurate because you receive more data about your accounts.

CHAPTER **19**

Microsoft Home Publishing 2000

Microsoft Home Publishing is your personal card shop, print shop, Web design shop, and more! If you have a computer and a good printer, Home Publishing allows you to create all the printed products you need. With a connection to the Internet, you don't even have to lick the stamps. E-mail or your personal Web site can do a great job of displaying your efforts.

What Is Home Publishing?

Microsoft's Home Publishing application has its roots in the desktop publishing revolution that began in 1984 when Apple Computer introduced the Macintosh personal computer. Although desktop publishing began with the Macintosh, today's Windows operating systems are well suited to desktop publishing and host many well-known professional products, such as Adobe's FrameMaker, Corel's Ventura, and Microsoft's own Publisher. Home Publishing is Microsoft's consumer-level desktop publishing application and is designed primarily for home use.

Home Publishing allows you to choose from hundreds of formats, styles, and concepts to create simple greeting cards, special e-mail messages, banners, birthday announcement Web pages, or even multipage newsletters. Home Publishing simplifies the process of creating these items by giving you a choice of projects—sometimes referred to as templates—that contain almost everything you'll need.

Navigating Home Publishing

Home Publishing's interface is designed to work like a Web page. This means that you point and click on links that take you to other pages. The Web page metaphor is used throughout Works.

Starting Home Publishing

Starting Home Publishing is easy. Select Start ➤ Programs ➤ Home Publishing 2000 and you'll see the window shown in Figure 19.1.

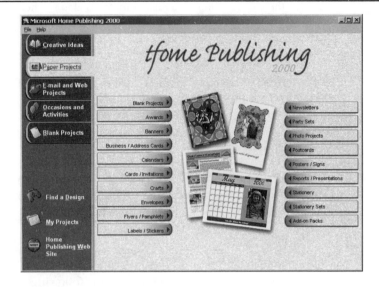

FIGURE 19.1
The Home Publishing
start page

Home Publishing Categories

The left side of the main Home Publishing window is divided into five main tabs, each representing a category:

- Creative Ideas
- Paper Projects
- E-Mail And Web Projects
- Occasions And Activities
- Blank Projects

Below the Blank Projects tab are the following three additional items:

- Find A Design
- My Projects
- Home Publishing Web Site

Click any of these tabs to go to that group of projects.

The categories at the left side of the page are your primary starting points in Home Publishing. From here you can go anywhere in the application and start any project.

By default, Home Publishing should open to the Creative Ideas page—if it does, select the Paper Projects tab. If it doesn't, then it has likely opened at Paper Projects already. However Home Publishing starts, we want to be on the Paper Projects page. This page displays two columns of buttons and a collage of various project types in the center. As you select different tabs (Creative Ideas, Paper Projects, E-Mail And Web Projects, etc.), the available items on the right (the main part of screen) change accordingly.

NOTE The collage in the center is not for looks alone, although it is attractive. Move the mouse pointer over one of the items, such as the Calendars button, and a collage of examples relevant to that topic will appear.

Each tab leads you to a large list of projects. There are far too many to detail in this chapter, but all the projects function in the same or a similar fashion; once you've learned how you operate one project, you've learned them all.

Basic Navigation

The File and Help menus are available at all times, but when you're working in a project, the project tabs will disappear. When you need to perform a basic operation, such as saving a file, the File menu is your only option.

The File Menu

The File menu includes several options that are active or inactive depending upon what you're working on. These items include the following:

- New creates new Blank Paper, Blank E-mail, or Web projects.
- Open opens saved, e-mailed, or downloaded files.
- Close And Return To Opening Screen closes the current window and returns to the opening screen.
- Close And Return To Design Selection returns you to the Main selection screen.
- Save saves the open file. If you haven't saved the file before this, you'll be prompted to name the file and select a location. If you've already saved it, Save will update the file with the latest changes.
- Save As saves the open file with another name as a separate file. This is particularly useful when you're creating your own templates.
- Publish To Web allows you to "print" your files to the Internet. I'll discuss this in more detail later in this chapter.
- Send By E-Mail lets you send your creations by e-mail to friends and family.
- Send Options lets you specify options for sending files by e-mail (more details later in this chapter).
- Preview In Web Browser enables you to review your work and see what everyone else will see. This is a great way to make sure your files look the way you want.
- Exit quits the application. If you haven't saved your document, you'll be prompted to do so.

NOTE If you've already opened files and saved them with this copy of Home Publishing, they will appear in a list above the Exit command with your most recent file first. This list helps you keep track of recent or current projects.

The Help Menu

The Help menu provides access to assistance, information, and the Home Publishing Web site. The menu contains three items:

- Help & Ideas offers a lot of helpful and creative information. Look here if you have a problem with Home Publishing or need ideas.

- About Microsoft Home Publishing 2000 provides you with access to system, licensing, registration, and warranty information. This can be a very helpful tool if you need to call technical support.

- Microsoft Home Publishing 2000 On The Web offers a link to a Web site dedicated to Home Publishing addicts. Click the link to open your default Web browser, and you can begin exploring.

WARNING The Home Publishing Web site is at http://home-publishing .com/HomePub/default.asp. Although you may view the Home Publishing Web site with Netscape's Communicator or Opera Software's Opera browser (http://www .operasoftware.com), it is best viewed with Internet Explorer. The other browsers tend to encounter errors such as pages that never appear.

When you visit the Home Publishing Web site, keep an eye on Quick Tips, Power Pointers, Add-On Packs, and Offers & Free Stuff. These areas change often and provide a great deal of help and new stuff to use with your projects.

Paper Projects

The projects in this section are—oddly enough—designed for printing on paper. With today's relatively inexpensive color ink-jet and laser printers, creating a wide range of paper projects is both fast and easy using Home Publishing. The items you can create with Paper Projects include:

- Cards/invitations
- Newsletters
- Party sets
- Posters/signs
- Stationery

Creating Cards

Clicking any of the buttons in Paper Projects will take you to a window where you can choose from a large selection of more specific types. For instance, clicking Cards/Invitations takes you to a wide array of card types (see Figure 19.2).

FIGURE 19.2
Cards/Invitations offers a wide range of card types.

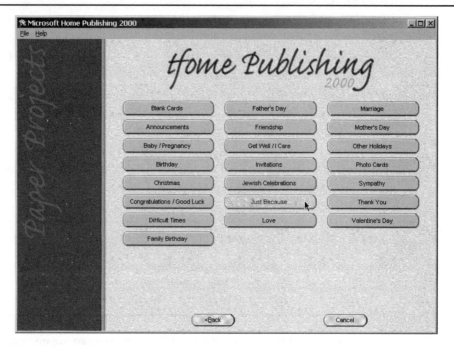

When you select a card type, you'll be asked to insert the Microsoft Works Disc 5, which contains art for Home Publishing. Once the CD loads, you'll be given a choice of designs. For example, Figure 19.3 shows the cards available in the Women's Issues theme of the Just Because series.

By default, project descriptions accompany large-size thumbnails. You can use the View Options menu to turn off the description display or specify smaller thumbnails. If you want to view a different theme, click another item in the Themes list box and choose from Men's Issues, Workplace, Technology, People You Live With, Series Cards, or Shared Experiences. You may also choose a style classification—such as All (the default), Cute, Funny, or Serious—using the Style drop-down box.

Select (that is, single-click) the thumbnail picture of the card you want, and a new field appears to the left. This field contains the default inscription that comes with the card. If you'd like to take a closer look before making your final choice, click Preview. Home Publishing opens a new window in which you can examine the item more closely. In the Preview window (see Figure 19.4), you can look at each page and cycle through the available inscriptions. To accept the selection, click the Open This Design button at the bottom of the page.

FIGURE 19.3
The selection window for Women's Issues

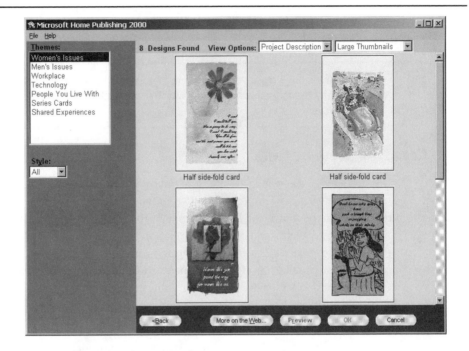

FIGURE 19.4
The Preview window lets you examine a card more closely.

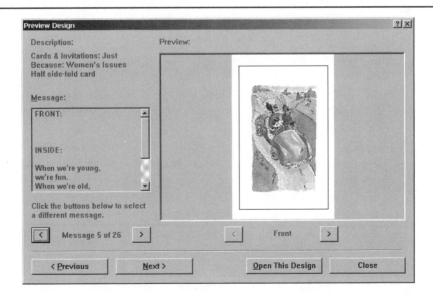

Once you have opted to work with a project, either from the Preview window or from the selection screen, the project will open in a new space, where you can edit it to suit your needs.

Creating your own inscriptions from scratch, both inside and out, lends a personal touch to your card. Home Publishing will even let you modify the logo on the back of the card for an extra personal touch.

 NOTE If for some reason you end up in a project you didn't want, go to the collection of buttons along the left-hand side of the window and click the one marked Go Back To The Selection Screen.

Creating Newsletters

A newsletter is a great way to get the word out for your group or local business, and Home Publishing offers many templates for different types of newsletters. As an example, let's create a newsletter for Delilah Handy, Handyperson, a small shop trying to drum up more business. The newsletter will include information about the business, relevant news and articles (such as "How To" articles), pricing and contact information, and graphics that entice people to take a longer look at the newsletter. Let's begin at the main Home Publishing window and select a newsletter format from the predefined templates provided on Microsoft Works Disc 6.

1. Select the Newsletters item at the top of the right column.
2. From the Themes list box, select Personal Communication.
3. In the top right-hand column is a thumbnail of a newsletter titled Mr. Handy. Select it.
4. Click the OK button to load the template.

This is quite a colorful newsletter and is bound to attract some attention and new business. The template is a great place to start, but the newsletter will be much more effective if it is tailored to Delilah Handy's business. Home Publishing's Main Options list provides you with various means to modify the newsletter template to your needs (see Figure 19.5).

The logical place to start customizing this newsletter is the headlines because these will be the most prominent features. As you can see by comparing your copy with Figure 19.6, we changed the heading for the newsletter to *Mrs. Handy* and added a headline for an article about dishwasher repair. In addition, we included a line at the top of the page that prompts newsletter readers to call for a quote. The Mrs. Handy heading stands out not only because it's at the top of the page but also because we used white text on a dark background. For the rest of the newsletter, we used a soft gray banding and underlying beige. The banding contains article headings, contact information, job information, and other tidbits of interest. The beige areas contain the article text.

FIGURE 19.5
The newsletter template

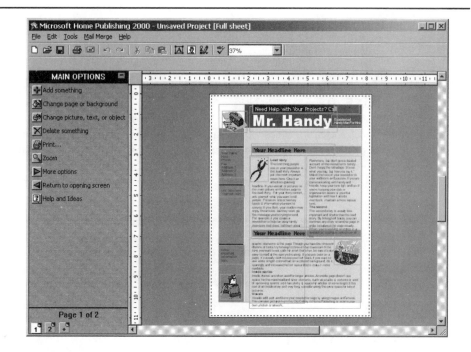

FIGURE 19.6
The updated Mrs. Handy newsletter

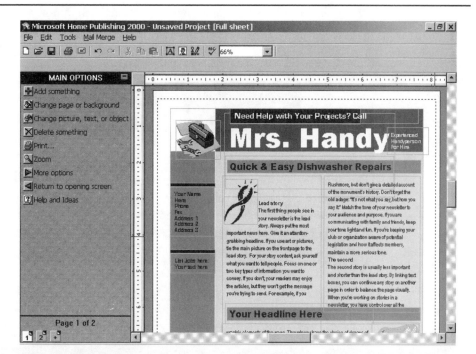

Now that you've seen the result, let's look at how we changed the headline *Mr. Handy* to *Mrs. Handy*:

1. Click the *H* in Handy, and the lightly shaded boxes around it will be selected, as shown in Figure 19.7.

 NOTE Home Publishing uses "bounding" boxes to hold objects like pictures and text. When you click on the *H* you are telling Home Publishing that you want to work with the "Mr. Handy" object. Whichever object has the box around it is the active box, and anything you do will possibly affect that object directly. Be sure you've selected the object you want to modify before doing anything.

FIGURE 19.7
When the Mr. Handy title is selected, you can edit it.

2. Click within the text and edit the title.

3. The eight blocks (called *handles*) that appear around the edges of the selection box allow you to resize the object. Click and drag one of the handles to resize the title. The pointer will indicate the directions each handle allows you to drag it (see Figure 19.8).

FIGURE 19.8
The pointer over the handle of the selected box indicates the directions the box can be resized.

If changing the size of one box obscures portions of the surrounding boxes, you can move the affected boxes. To do so, place your cursor along the edge of the bounding box you want to move. Don't point *to* a handle but *next* to one, and use the four-arrow pointer (see Figure 19.9) to drag the box to a new location.

FIGURE 19.9
*Use the four-arrow
pointer to drag the box.*

The bounding boxes in Home Publishing will adjust automatically to some text changes. For instance, in Figure 19.10 we've changed *Handy Man* to *Handyperson*. To do this, select the box, then click at the end of *Man*, delete the characters and space, and type in the new text.

FIGURE 19.10
*The bounding box will
adjust automatically to
fit the new text.*

Next, we will add *For a Quote!* to the text at the top of the page. This is designed to spur people to call and attract some new business. Point your cursor to the text until the I-beam cursor appears and then click to set the insertion bar. Move the insertion bar to the end of *Call* and add the *For a Quote!* line. Now that we've added the text, the black band behind the text is too short, so we need to adjust that. So how do we select it?

> Need Help with Your Projects? Call For A Quote!

There are two ways you can select the black band:

- You can press F3 and cycle through all the objects until the black band is selected.

Or

- You can drag-select, which is the more direct way, using the following steps:

  1. Point to a place just above and to the left of the document and click-hold.

  2. Drag your mouse diagonally down to create a box. You've now created a marquee (so named because when selected dots crawl around it like lights on a movie theater marquee).

3. Drag your mouse down until the black band is surrounded by the marquee and let go. The black band should now be selected (when the black band is selected, the bounding box is smaller than the text).

4. Using your mouse, move and resize the black band until all the text is inside the box.

After we've made all these changes to the template newsletter, it looks quite different. Figure 19.11 shows the final product, with revised text and resized and moved boxes. Next we're going to make some more modifications to the newsletter and learn more about the editor controls in the process.

FIGURE 19.11
The Mrs. Handy
newsletter in final form

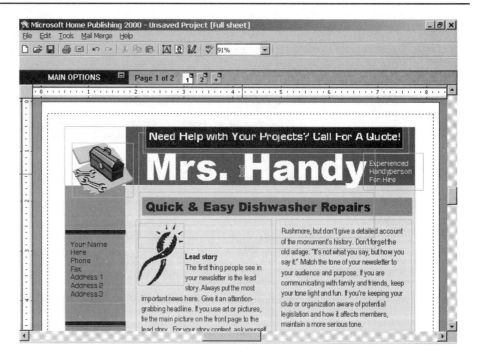

Printing Your Projects

Once you've finished creating your paper projects, you'll want to print them out. Home Publishing makes it easy to print these projects, many of which involve turning the paper over in a special way to have it printed on both sides. For example, you can fold a single 8.5-inch x 11-inch sheet of paper into a nice card that looks like it came from a card store.

 NOTE For my example, I'll use a greeting card that has a rabbit sitting in a chair. Just select Cards/Invitations ➢ Get Well/I Care ➢ For Kids.

To print a project, follow these steps:

1. Open your project and make sure all the changes you want have been made (Figure 19.12).

FIGURE 19.12
Our sample project

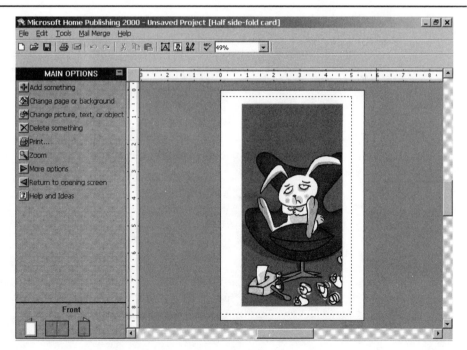

2. Choose File ➢ Print to open the Print dialog box.

3. Select the printer you want to use (see Figure 19.13). If you are using a local printer, there will be only one option, but if your computer is connected to a network, there may be several printer choices.

FIGURE 19.13
Selecting a printer

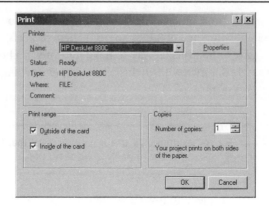

4. Home Publishing has project-specific options in this dialog box, so be sure to select or deselect the options you want for this project. For example, with a greeting card, you can choose to print both the inside and outside of the project.

5. If this is the first time you've printed anything using Home Publishing, the application will need to determine how your printer works. After clicking Print, you'll see the Printer Test dialog box (see Figure 19.14). Click the OK button. As the dialog box says, you'll only need to go through this process once—unless you add a new printer.

FIGURE 19.14
*The Printer Test
dialog box*

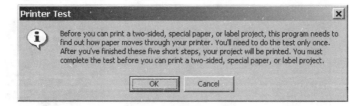

6. After you click the OK button, you'll see the Printer Test dialog box shown in Figure 19.15. Select the image of a printer in the dialog box that best matches yours. Click the Continue button when you're done.

FIGURE 19.15
*Beginning the Printer
Test process*

FIGURE 19.15
*Beginning the Printer
Test process*

7. Next, remove any special paper from the printer and insert normal, plain paper (8 $^1/_2$-inch x 11-inch) for the test. Click the OK button when you're ready.

8. A page should start printing. Wait until it has finished printing, and then follow the directions that appear on that page. A dialog box will appear after the page prints with directions that you can then follow. Click the OK button and you'll see the dialog box shown in Figure 19.16.

9. Your screen will show rotating page representations (see Figure 19.16). Examine them closely to determine the one that best matches the output of your printer. The application uses the page option you chose to tell you how to insert the paper so that both sides are printed properly. Select the radio button beneath the page representation that matches the output of your printer and click the OK button.

FIGURE 19.16
*Selecting the right
printed version of the
test page*

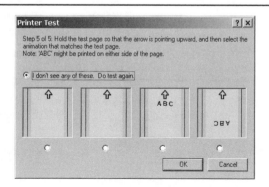

10. Now that you've entered your specifications, Home Publishing knows how the paper runs through your printer and will use an on-screen animation to remind you when you need to add paper (see Figure 19.17).

FIGURE 19.17
The printer loading animation in action

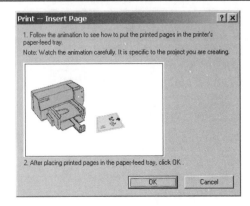

That takes care of printing your projects. You might want to have a ruler or other firm straight-edged item around for flattening the creases on your printed projects. Cards and the like can unfold if not flattened well. Enjoy!

The Editor Controls

In the Mrs. Handy newsletter project, you may have noted the blue panel on the left side of the window. This is the Options pane, and it includes a list of actions you can perform as you prepare your projects (Main Options, Text Options, Picture Options, and Drawing Options). For instance, when you select an image box, the Picture Options appear and allow you to make changes directly to pictures (see Figure 19.18). The pane changes to give you the tools you need for the job at hand.

FIGURE 19.18
The Picture Options let you make changes directly to pictures.

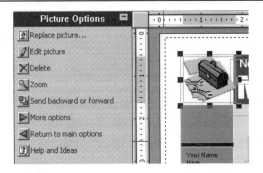

When you select a text box, the Text Options appear and enable you to modify text (see Figure 19.19).

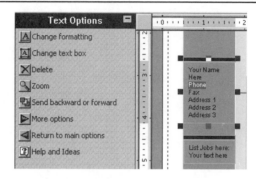

In addition to the Picture and Text Options, the Main Options give you global control over the page itself. The Main Options appear when you click the area around the page or in the white fringe (called a margin) to deselect whatever type of box may have been selected (see Figure 19.20). The last item of interest is the Drawing Options panel.

In the Main Options panel, there is an item called Add Something. When you click Add Something, a menu appears, which contains an item called Shape Or Line. Clicking this opens another menu. For our example, go ahead and select the Shape item. Yet another menu will appear, but this time it is a panel filled with predefined shapes. Select the arrow from the fourth row, second column (see Figure 19.21).

FIGURE 19.21
Selecting the
arrow shape

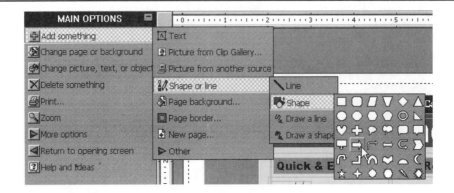

The arrow you selected will appear on the document and is active, which allows you to move it. You'll also note that a new set of tools has appeared—the Drawing Options panel (see Figure 19.22). This works just like the other panels, but the tools work with drawings and shapes.

FIGURE 19.22
The Drawing
Options panel

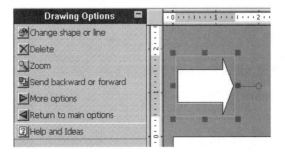

Cool Shape Tricks

There are some tricks that you can use in the Drawing mode to make your shapes and other objects work even better. Here's a rundown:

Change Shape Or Line Located at the top of the Drawing Options panel, this option lets you choose another shape for the selected object, change the fill color, change the line color, and change the thickness of a shape's border.

Continued ▶

Send Backward Or Forward If you think of objects as pieces of paper that you're laying down onto a canvas, this function is easier to visualize. The options are Bring To Front, Send To Back, Bring Forward, and Send Backward. The first two options take a selected object and either bring it on the top of the stack (so it is fully visible but can obscure other objects placed beneath it) or push it to the bottom (this places it underneath all other objects so it can be obscured or even completely hidden from view by other objects). The Bring Forward and Send Backward options move objects up and down in the stack one layer at a time.

More Options ➢ Border Allows you to use special shapes and pictures as a drawing border. Select the object you want to change the border for and click More Options ➢ Border. The Border dialog box will open, and you can select a border category, which then gives you a list of border styles in the list below. Finally, you can define how big you want the border to be by entering a numerical value in the Border Size text box at the bottom of the dialog box. If you click on a border style, a sample will appear in the preview box that consumes the right-hand side of the dialog box.

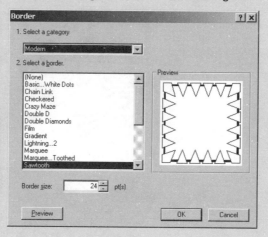

 TIP The border of a drawing is *not* the line that makes up the shape, but the area that the bounding box of the object occupies. So, if you have made a star object, when you add a border to it, that border will be a square around the star.

Now, let's say you want to delete something using the Main Options. Deselect any objects by clicking outside the document and click the Delete Something item. A small box will appear with a list of object types. Select and click the object type you want to delete—for example, the picture, text, or other object.

You'll see a small box (with rounded edges and floating in the middle of the document) prompting you to select an object. Once you've selected the object, the options pane will offer graphics, drawing, or text options, including an option for deleting the object. Another way to delete an object is to select the object and choose Option ➢ Delete.

You can also change the appearance of pictures by selecting a picture box and choosing Picture Options ➢ Edit Picture. Using the toolbox from the Mrs. Handy newsletter, select Edit Picture ➢ Antique and watch the change in the graphic.

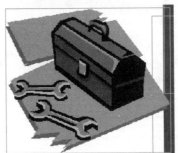

The Antique filter gives the graphic an "older" look. For a different look, select Edit Picture ➢ Painted Effect. This option adds a rough, paint-like edging, along with a slight darkening of color. You'll find more choices under the More Options item.

Other options available in the More Options menu are:

- Duplicate duplicates the selected item and places the copy below and to the right of the original and in a selected state.

- Flip allows you to flip the selected item in various directions.

- Crop allows you to crop or cut out a part of the whole image. For example, if you have a square photograph that is surrounded by an inch-wide margin of blank space, you'd cut out the photograph and discard the unneeded fringe.

- Undo Editing allows you to remove mistakes. The curved arrow icon on the toolbar also allows you to undo the last function.

- Add To Favorites In Clip Gallery saves a graphic in your personal Clip Gallery Favorites list. This option is especially helpful if you have a graphic that you want to use in all your publications or projects.

- Save Picture As lets you save a graphic in a new location and with a different name.

- Border adds a border to your project.

Main Options offers several additional functions under More Options, including the following:

- Check Spelling spell-checks your documents before you send them or make them public.

- Send By E-Mail lets you send projects you create via e-mail as opposed to "snail mail."

- Publish To Web Site provides you with step-by-step instructions for publishing your project to the Web.

NOTE You may need to get specific information from your Internet service provider to successfully publish to the Web.

Mail Merge

With Mail Merge, you can automatically address hundreds, or even thousands, of newsletters or other items to different recipients. Most commonly, addresses are printed to labels and then applied to the publication. This is a real timesaver if you have more than 20 newsletters to mail.

If you already have an extensive collection of addresses in your Windows Address Book, you can easily use those addresses by selecting Mail Merge ➤ Address Book. You can also use other sources, such as a database application or an Excel spreadsheet.

Alternatively, you can enter data directly in Home Publishing by choosing Mail Merge ➤ Create Address List. The New Address List dialog box will open, where you can enter the person's name, address, and other contact information (see Figure 19.23). When you finish entering each address, click the New Entry button to save the data and clear the form. You can scroll through your list of addresses by using the View Entry Number controls. The double arrows with bars at the tips will show you the first and last entry.

FIGURE 19.23
The New Address List
dialog box

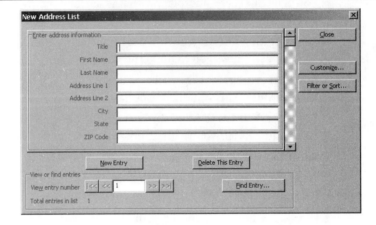

You can also modify the amount of data you enter. If all you need is a simple name and address list, you can remove the business- and detail-oriented items from the list of fields. Click the Customize button to open the dialog box shown in Figure 19.24. You can add, rename, or delete fields or reorder them by highlighting a field and clicking the Move Up or Move Down button.

FIGURE 19.24
The Customize Address
List dialog box

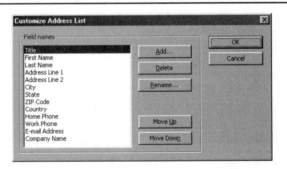

You can also sort and filter the list by clicking the Filter Or Sort button. In the resulting dialog box, you can select criteria to sort by. You can also filter out certain entries.

 TIP   If you've entered a large number of addresses in the New Address List dialog box, you can find one quickly by clicking the Find Entry button and entering identifying text in the Find This Text text box.

Creating a Project

Now that you've been introduced to the tools and options available in Home Publishing, it's time to test yourself. Let's create a set of stationery using the E-Mail And Web Projects tab, which provides the option to e-mail or publish your project to the Web.

To begin, return to the main page by selecting Close And Return To The Main Menu or by pressing Ctrl+N. Next, click the E-Mail And Web Projects tab, click the Stationery button, and then click the Special Interest button. In the Special Interest window, scroll down and select the Travel theme, then choose the project in the top-right corner with the small boat (see Figure 19.25). Click the OK button to open your project in the editor.

FIGURE 19.25
Selecting an e-mail or
Web project

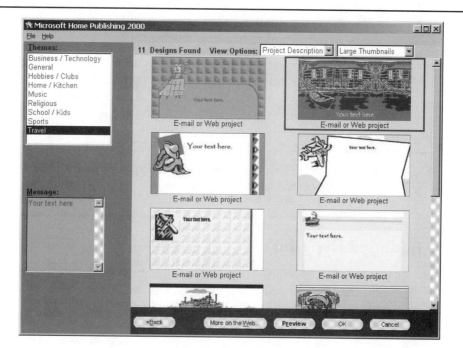

NOTE Home Publishing includes numerous animated projects. This may present a problem because not everyone uses Windows. Some of the animations are exclusive to Windows applications, such as Internet Explorer 4.*x* and Outlook Express 4.*x*. Unless you know for sure that the recipient of your project uses Windows, you may want to avoid sending animated projects via e-mail.

The project with the boat that you've selected is a rather simple page that includes animation, but you'll want to add some text as well as move and modify a graphic. First, you need to delete the default text from the project and create a new text box. Of course, you'll want to put your own name inside the brackets using the same technique as with the Mrs. Handy newsletter earlier in this chapter.

Now that you've adjusted the text, let's modify the boat graphic. Select the boat object, and the graphic editing toolbar will appear. Using the first double triangle icon, perform a horizontal flip so that the boat faces the other direction. After the boat is flipped horizontally, drag it to the other side of the screen.

 TIP The mirrored pair of triangles pointing up perform a horizontal flip and the ones pointing to the left perform a vertical flip. If you hold your mouse over the other buttons, you will be able to see what they do, too.

Now that your boat is pointed in the right direction, let's modify the new text box you created by changing the text size to 18 points and the typeface to Arial. With the text selected, click on the small *A* to the right of the list of text sizes and choose the white block, which will change the text color to white.

 TIP One of the best ways to learn new Windows software is to right-click everything. In the resulting context menu, you'll find most, if not all, of the functions and features of the program you're using.

Adding a Hyperlink

You can add a hyperlink to almost any object in an e-mail or Web project. Once you hyperlink an object, clicking it will open another page or object. This is how the Web works. Adding hyperlinks allows you to connect a number of different sources to each other. You can add hyperlinks to objects outside your projects or to projects that you create. You can use them to point to your personal Web site or so your recipient can send you an e-mail from the project.

To add a hyperlink, follow these steps:

1. Select the object, text, or graphic that you want to link. Let's create a hyperlink for the boat in your current project.

2. Select the boat object, then right-click and select More Options from the context menu. Choose Hyperlink to open a dialog box where you'll enter the address (URL) of the item you want to link to. The default is the HTTP protocol, or the language of the Web.

TIP The best way to add an address in the Hyperlink dialog box is to locate the item you want to link to on the Web, copy its address from the address bar, and then paste it into the dialog box. You can work in Internet Explorer while that dialog box remains open in Home Publishing. Keep in mind that the dialog box automatically adds http:// so you don't need to copy that part. If you do, the dialog box will not accept it as it would not be a properly formatted address. You will have to remove the extra http:// for the dialog box to accept the URL.

3. In this case, enter **http://www.boating.com** in the dialog box. This is the address for a boating Web site.

E-Mail and Publish Your Projects to the Web

In addition to printing out your projects, Home Publishing allows you to send your projects via e-mail or publish them to the Web. The process for both these options is quite similar.

E-Mail Your Projects

E-mail is a quick way to send projects you create to people. For example, let's say you just finished an e-mail greeting card project for your grandmother. Follow these steps to send it to her:

1. Save your project by selecting File ➢ Save. Name the file (for example, **Grandmother's e-mail card**).

2. Select the More Options item from the Main Options, then click the Send By E-Mail option. A dialog box will appear listing all your available e-mail clients. Select the e-mail program you use and click the OK button.

 TIP If you always use the same e-mail client, you can select the box that will make it the default e-mail client.

3. When your e-mail client starts, create a new e-mail message and then attach the card you saved in Step 1.

4. Enter the address of your grandmother and then click Send.

NOTE Many people use text-based e-mail that doesn't display pictures or animations. They won't be able to see your projects, no matter how great they look.

Publishing Your Projects to the Web

Much of the Internet's popularity stems from the fact that anyone can publish materials to the Web for very little or even no cost. Many Internet service providers (ISP) offer space for their users to post Web pages, and there are also free services such as Xoom, GeoCities, and Tripod that will give you space in exchange for placing ads on your site.

 NOTE Home Publishing uses File Transfer Protocol (FTP) to publish projects to the Web. If your ISP does not support FTP access, you will not be able to publish to the Web.

Many of the projects that Home Publishing includes in the E-Mail And Web Projects section give you the option of posting them to your Web site; you can create entire Web sites this way. If you take many, *many* pictures of your children/boat/favorite tree/ vacation and want to share them with your family, publishing them to the Web is a great way to save money on reprints and show your pictures to lots of people.

To get started, create a project that you want to publish to the Web in Home Publishing. After you've saved it, follow these steps:

1. Select File ➢ Publish To Web ➢ Publish To A Web Site.

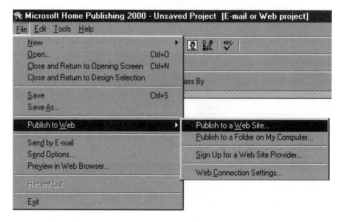

2. If you already have a Web site that Home Publishing supports automatically, select it from the Host Name list box in the Publish To Web dialog box. (In case you don't have an ISP, I'll tell you how to set up an account in a moment.)

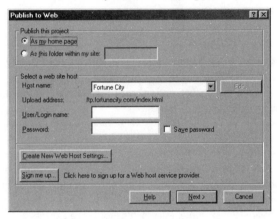

3. Enter the username and password for the service you'll use. Select Save My Password, and you won't have to enter it every time you want to add or change something.

 WARNING If you elect to save your password, this means that anyone who has access to your computer will be able to access the pages secured by the password you chose.

4. Specify whether you want to publish this project as your home page (if you don't have one already), replace your current page, or publish your project in its own folder so you can add it to an existing site.

5. Click Next, and Home Publishing will begin to convert your project into a Web page. When the conversion is finished, Home Publishing will send the page to your site. If there are any problems, it will notify you. The most common problem is an incorrect username or password. If you see this error message, double-check your login information, reopen the dialog box, reenter the login information, and then click Next again.

If everything works properly, the page or pages you published to the Web will be available to view on the Internet. Surf on over to your site and take a peek. If you published your project as a new folder, you'll need to create links on your Web site so that people can view your new Web pages.

NOTE Publishing to a folder (see Figure 19.26) simply means that instead of placing it on a Web site somewhere, you put those materials into a folder located on your computer. When you select that option, click the Browse button and select a location to store your newly created page or pages.

WARNING You cannot add links to pages that were not created in Microsoft Home Publishing. If you want to add links to a home page or pages already on the Web that you created using another program, you'll need to use that program or any other Web publishing software—for example, Microsoft's FrontPage Express.

FIGURE 19.26
The Publish As A Folder dialog box

What if you don't have an ISP that offers you space for your own Web site? Follow these instructions to create your own Web site using a free Web page hosting service:

1. Choose File ➢ Publish To Web ➢ Publish To A Web Site.

2. Click the Sign Me Up button. This will open your default browser and take you to the Home Publishing Web site. There you'll find a small updater for the services that Home Publishing understands (see Figure 19.27).

3. Scroll to the lower half of the page. There you'll see two lists: one for free sites and the other for services that charge a fee. This, however, is slightly inaccurate. The sites in the free list are service providers that do not offer Internet access. The services on the fee-based list are well-known ISPs.

4. Select a site from the "free" list (these sites aren't really free since you are required to display advertising on your site). These all provide similar services and features (free Web space, free e-mail address, page-making assistance, and similar services).

FIGURE 19.27
Signing up for a Web page hosting service

5. Follow the instructions for signing up and make sure you read the terms of service carefully—free services often have certain restrictions.

CHAPTER <u>20</u>

Picture It! Express

Picture It! Express is a graphics application that you can use for creating and editing pictures. Using Picture It! Express, you can create a variety of graphical items, including collages, cards, calendars, mats and frames, and more. You can also edit existing pictures, even using Picture It! Express to remove red eye from your digital photos.

In this chapter, I'll show you how to use the key features of Picture It! Express, leaving you to explore the more esoteric features on your own.

As you may have noticed, when Microsoft uses "Express" in an application's name, it designates a reduced or stripped-down version of the application: For example, Outlook Express is a limited version of Outlook, the "desktop information manager" application in Microsoft Office, and Picture It! Express is a stripped-down version of the Picture It! application. (Note that Microsoft has passed up a couple of opportunities for Express versions in Works: Works Spreadsheet might be called "Excel Express" if it had a few more features, and Works Database probably dreams of growing up into "Access Express" one day.) Picture It! Express's Helpful Movies offering includes one touting the benefits of Picture It!, encouraging you to upgrade; and as you work with Picture It! Express, it will periodically prompt you to learn how wonderful Picture It! is. Keep your patience about you.

Starting Picture It! Express

You can start Picture It! Express in several ways:

- From the Start menu: Choose Start ➤ Programs ➤ Picture It! Express.
- From the Programs page of the Task Launcher: Click the Picture It! Express item in the Programs list, then click the Start Picture It! Express link.
- From the Tasks page of the Task Launcher: Choose a task that uses Picture It! Express, and then click the Start link.

If you start Picture It! Express with your display settings set to too few colors for the program to display pictures effectively, it will display the Suggest Changing Monitor Settings dialog box shown in Figure 20.1. Select the Yes option button to get help changing your display settings, or select the No option button to resist the offer of help. If you don't want to see this suggestion again, select the Don't Show Me This Again check box. Then click the OK button.

If you chose to get help, Picture It! Express will display the Display Settings dialog box together with information on how to adjust your display settings by using it. Once you've done that, start Picture It! Express again, and it should come to life without protest.

When you start Picture It! Express, it will automatically display the Helpful Movies dialog box (see Figure 20.2) until you tell it not to. To watch a movie, select it in the list on the left of the dialog box, then click the Play button at the bottom of the picture frame. Use the Stop, Pause, Forward, and Back buttons to control the flow of the movie. To avoid the Helpful Movies dialog box in the future, select the Don't Show Me This Again check box. Then click the Close button to close the dialog box.

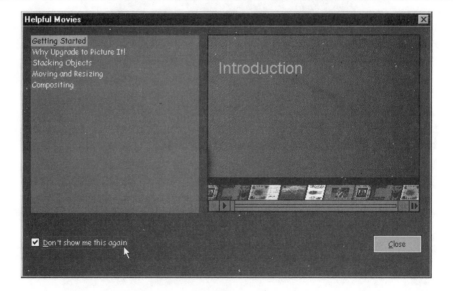

Picture It! Express will then display the Getting Started dialog box (see Figure 20.3), which displays a number of options and the last few pictures you worked on (if any). Click the Close button to start Picture It! Express. If you don't want the Getting Started dialog box to bother you again, select the Don't Show Me This Again check box before clicking the Close button.

FIGURE 20.3

The Getting Started dialog box lets you quickly start creating a new picture or open an existing picture. If you prefer not to see this dialog box, select the Don't Show Me This Again check box.

The Picture It! Express Interface

Figure 20.4 shows the Picture It! Express interface. As you can see, Picture It! Express has several unique features, including the Picture Pane, the Stack, and the Filmstrip. But perhaps the most unique is the left-hand panel, which in the figure is displaying the Workbench page. As you'll see later in the chapter, this panel morphs into a number of dialog boxes necessary to complete operations in Picture It! Express.

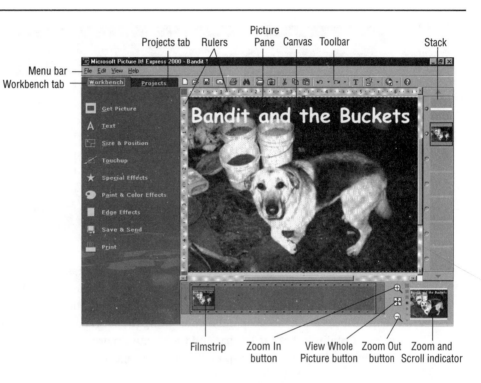

FIGURE 20.4
The Picture It! Express interface includes a number of unique items.

The Picture Pane

The Picture Pane is the main area of the Picture It! Express window, and (as you'd guess) it's where you create and edit pictures. Following the artistic metaphor, the white area in the Picture Pane is called the *canvas*.

The Workbench and Projects Pages

The Workbench page and the Projects page appear on the left-hand side of the Picture It! Express window. The Workbench page (shown in Figure 20.4 above) provides quick access to the main commands of Picture It! Express, while the Projects page (shown in Figure 20.5) presents Picture It! Express's projects broken down into five categories—Collages, Cards, Calendars, Fun Stuff, and Mats & Frames—and a Go Online option.

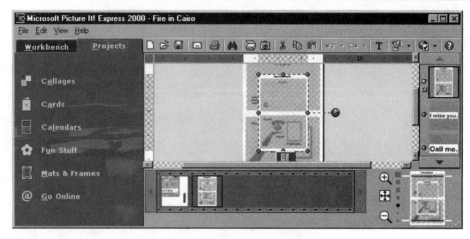

FIGURE 20.5
The Projects page lets you quickly start the different kinds of projects that Picture It! Express offers.

The Workbench page provides a way into many of the tasks that Picture It! Express can perform. For most common purposes, however, you can access the commands more quickly and easily from the toolbar and the menus. The instructions I give in this chapter focus on the toolbar and menus, using the Workbench page only when it provides capabilities that the toolbar and the menus do not.

Click the Projects tab to display the Projects page; to display the Workbench page, click the Workbench tab.

The Stack

The Stack is the vertical bar at the right-hand side of the Picture It! Express window. The Stack contains all the different objects (elements defined by a border) in a composite picture, enabling you to easily get hold of any object (even if it's buried under other objects) and to see at a glance which object you're currently working with. (If a picture has only one object, it will appear in solitary splendor at the top of the Stack.)

The Filmstrip

The Filmstrip is the horizontal strip at the bottom of the Picture It! Express window. The Filmstrip shows a miniature of each picture currently open. You use the Filmstrip as a navigational tool for selecting a picture, either to work with it or to add it to the current picture in a collage.

The Retriever

When you click a picture in the Filmstrip, Picture It! Express displays the picture in the Retriever (see Figure 20.6), a dialog box that contains a miniature of the Picture Pane and the Stack.

FIGURE 20.6
Use the Retriever to switch to another picture or to add it to a collage.

You can take the following actions from the Retriever:

- Switch to the picture shown in the Retriever by clicking the Switch To button.
- Add an object from the picture in the Retriever by dragging it from the Retriever's Stack to the Picture Pane in the main window or by selecting it in the Receiver's Stack and clicking the Add To Cutout button (the blue button with the yellow figure on it).
- Add the whole picture in the Retriever to the picture in the main window by clicking the yellow button in the lower-right corner of the Retriever.

Taking any of these actions closes the Retriever.

The Toolbar

Figure 20.7 shows the buttons on the Picture It! Express toolbar.

FIGURE 20.7
The buttons on the Picture It! Express toolbar provide access to frequently used commands.

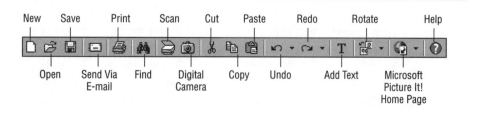

To make more space available to work in, you can hide the toolbar, the Stack, or the rulers. To do so, choose View ➤ Toolbar, View ➤ Stack, or View ➤ Rulers. (To display the items again, repeat these commands.)

Opening a Picture

To open a picture, follow these steps:

1. Click the Open button on the toolbar, or choose File ➤ Open, to display the Open Pictures dialog box panel (see Figure 20.8).

FIGURE 20.8
Use the Open Pictures dialog box panel to open one or more pictures.

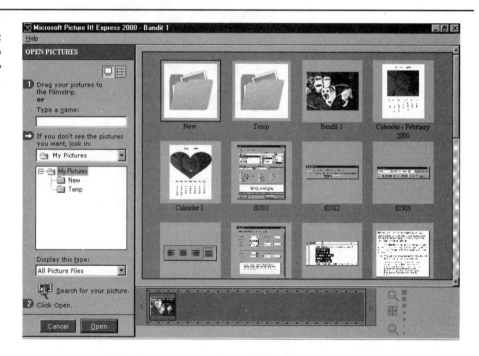

2. Navigate to the folder that contains the pictures. You'll notice that the files contained in the selected folder appear in the pictures area to the right of the dialog box panel rather than being listed in the dialog box panel itself.

3. Either drag the pictures onto the Filmstrip at the bottom of the window, or just select pictures in the main list box.

 TIP Click the Show File List button in the upper-right corner of the Open Pictures dialog box panel to display a list of files rather than the default previews. Click the Show Previews button to restore the previews.

4. Click the Open button to close the Open Pictures dialog box panel. If you dragged a picture to the Filmstrip, Picture It! Express will have displayed a Done button in place of the Cancel button. Click the Done button to close the dialog box panel.

Starting a New Project

You can create a new project in two ways:

- You can create a blank project, so that you have complete freedom in adding things to it.
- You can create a project based on one of the project templates that Picture It! Express includes. Picture It! Express's selection of templates is little more than minimal, but it's enough to get you started.

I'll show you each method in turn.

Creating a New Blank Project

To create a new blank project, follow these steps:

1. Choose File ➤ New to display the New dialog box panel. Figure 20.9 shows what you'll see if you don't have any other pictures open; if you do have pictures open, you'll see them in the Filmstrip. The title bar displays a default name for the new picture; in the figure, it reads *Picture 5* because this was the fifth new picture I created in this Picture It! Express session.

FIGURE 20.9
Use the New dialog box panel to create a new blank project.

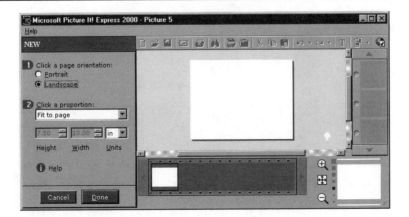

2. In the Click A Page Orientation area, select the appropriate option button: Portrait (tall) or Landscape (wide). The canvas in the Picture Pane will preview your choice.

3. In the Click A Proportion area, choose the size and proportion for the project:

- Select the Fit To Page item to maximize the use of the canvas.

- Select the Full Screen item to use the whole screen.

- Select the item for one of the predefined paper sizes: 8 × 10 inches, 5 × 7 inches, 4 × 6 inches, 3.5 × 5 inches, Postcard (Classic) (also 4 × 6 inches), Business Card (2 × 3.5 inches), CD Insert (4.8 × 4.8 inches), Square (10 × 10 inches), or Panorama (3 × 9 inches).

- Select the Custom item and specify the height and width by using the Height and Width text boxes and the Units drop-down list.

4. Click the Done button to create the project you've chosen.

You can then add items to the project and adjust them as described in the rest of this chapter.

Creating a Project from a Project Template

Follow these steps to create a project from a project template:

1. Click the Projects tab to display the Projects page.

2. Click the category of project you want to create: Collages, Cards, Calendars, Fun Stuff, or Mats & Frames. For this example, I'll create a calendar. Picture It! Express will display a pop-up panel showing the available calendar designs (in my case, only one, as you can see in Figure 20.10).

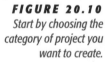

FIGURE 20.10
Start by choosing the category of project you want to create.

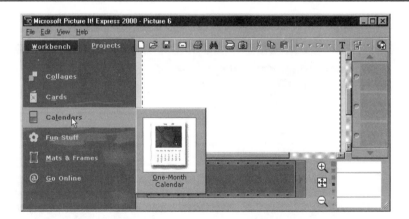

3. Select the design you want to use, then follow the steps in the template's wizard, clicking the Next button at the bottom of the Projects panel when you finish each step. For example, Figure 20.11 shows the second stage of the One-Month

Calendar template's wizard, in which you get to specify the month for the calendar and the day on which you want each week to begin. You'll notice that the wizard displays instructions for each step in the Projects panel. Some projects have just a few steps, while others have half a dozen or so.

FIGURE 20.11
Choose options that the template's wizard offers you.

4. Most project templates give you the chance to add pictures to the project. Figure 20.12 shows the One-Month Calendar project at this stage. You can add pictures as follows:

   • If you have a picture you want to add currently open on the Filmstrip, drag it from the Filmstrip to the project.

   • To open a picture, click the Open A Picture button and use the Open Pictures dialog box to open the picture.

   • To scan a picture, click the Scan A Picture button and follow the procedure described in the next section.

   • To download a picture from a digital camera, click the Download From Digital Camera button and follow the prompts.

5. At the end of the procedure, most project templates offer you the chance to print the project or save it. Click the Print It or Save It button as appropriate, then click the Done button to close the template's wizard. You can then work with the project, manipulating its objects as you wish. When you've finished, save and close the project.

FIGURE 20.12

Most project templates let you add your choice of art to the project and manipulate the objects in their Stack.

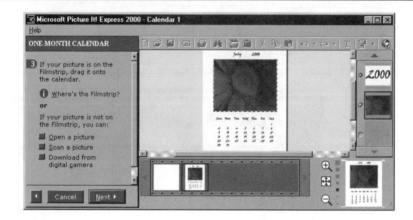

FIGURE 20.12

Most project templates let you add your choice of art to the project and manipulate the objects in their Stack.

Scanning a Picture

One of Picture It! Express's most appealing features is its ability to work with your scanner to scan in pictures and import them directly. Here are the steps to follow:

1. Click the Scan button on the toolbar, or choose File ➤ Scan, to display the Scan Picture dialog box panel. Figure 20.13 shows the Scan Picture dialog box panel you'll see if you're using a flatbed scanner; for other types of scanner, you'll see a different Scan Picture dialog box panel.

FIGURE 20.13

Use the Scan Picture dialog box panel to scan a picture using your scanner.

2. From the Click A Scanner drop-down list, choose your scanner. (Unless you have multiple scanners or similar devices, chances are that Picture It! Express will identify it the first time.)

 NOTE The first time you go to use Picture It! Express with your scanner, Picture It! Express may claim that it doesn't recognize the scanner and request that you identify it. Comply, and all should be well.

3. Put your picture in the scanner, preferably aligned with the horizontal and vertical edges, and preferably the right way up.

4. If you want to use Picture It! Express's Smart Task Scan feature, choose the Smart Task Scan option button and make sure the Correct Brightness And Contrast check box is selected. If not, choose the My Scanner Software option button and select the Help Me Fix My Picture After Scanning check box. (Depending on the type of scanner you have, this option may not be available.)

 TIP Try the Smart Task Scan feature first. If it doesn't work for your scanner, use the My Scanner Software option as a fallback.

5. Click the Scan button. You'll see the Progress Monitor dialog box (see Figure 20.14) as Picture It! Express scans the picture.

FIGURE 20.14
The Progress Monitor dialog box will show you the progress of the scan.

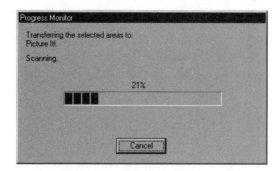

6. Picture It! Express will then display the scanned picture in the Picture Pane (see Figure 20.15).

• Your scanner may display the scanned picture in its own software. If this happens, close the scanner software. Doing so should return you to Picture It! Express.

FIGURE 20.15
Picture It! Express
automatically displays
the picture when it's
finished scanning it.

Cropping a Picture or an Object

If a picture or an object shows more than you want it to, you can crop it to show only part of it by following these steps:

1. If you want to crop an object, use the Stack to select it.

2. Choose Edit ➢ Crop to display the Crop dialog box panel (see Figure 20.16). If you chose an object in step 1, the dialog box will display its Object page, as in the figure; if you chose to work with the whole picture, it will display the Whole Picture page.

3. In the Click A Shape area, select the shape you want to use for cropping. Picture It! Express will automatically display that shape superimposed on the image so that you can see the effect you'll get.

4. Specify the size for the crop. You can either click one of the handles around the crop area and drag it to change the size, or select the Enter Exact Dimensions For check box and use the Height, Width, and Units text boxes to specify the size.

5. Click the Done button to apply the cropping to the picture or object.

FIGURE 20.16
Use the Crop dialog box panel to crop a picture or an object.

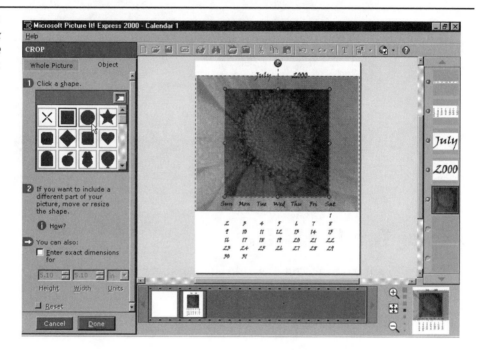

Rotating an Object

Picture It! Express makes it easy to rotate an object. You can rotate an object either in predefined steps or by a custom amount.

To rotate an object quickly, select the object, then click the Rotate button on the toolbar and choose the amount of rotation you want: Rotate Left (90 degrees widdershins), Rotate Right (90 degrees deasil), Flip Horizontally, or Flip Vertically.

To rotate an object by a custom amount, select the object and choose Edit ➤ Rotate to display the Rotate dialog box panel (see Figure 20.17). Either type into the Custom text box or use the spinner arrows to enter a custom amount of rotation. (Changing the value in the Custom text box will automatically select the Custom option button, so you don't need to click it explicitly.) Then click the Done button to apply the rotation.

FIGURE 20.17
Use the Rotate dialog box panel to rotate an object a custom amount.

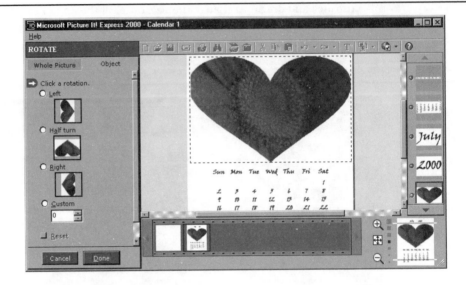

Adding Text to a Picture

To add text to a picture, click the Add Text button on the toolbar. Picture It! Express will display the Add Text dialog box panel (see Figure 20.18). Type the text in the Type Your Text box, select font formatting and color options, and then click the Done button to enter the text.

FIGURE 20.18
Use the Add Text dialog box panel to add text to a picture.

To move the text object you've entered, move the mouse pointer over it so that it displays a MOVE pointer. Then click the object and drag it to where you want it to appear.

To change the font size, drag one of the sizing handles on the text object to increase or decrease the size of the object. Picture It! Express will automatically adjust the font size accordingly.

Fixing Red Eye

As you'll know if you've ever suffered from it, flash-induced red eye can make even a friendly person look like a werewolf with a spirituous hangover. Modern cameras with sophisticated flashes that trick the victim's eye with a multistage flash progression have reduced the problem, but too late for many millions of photos already taken. For such pictures, Picture It! Express's feature for removing red eye comes in handy. It works for red eye in any color, including the light green that animal eyes often become in flash-lit pictures.

To remove red eye from a picture:

1. Open the picture that suffers from red eye.

2. On the Workbench page, click the Touchup item and choose Fix Red Eye from the menu preview panel. Picture It! Express will display the Fix Red Eye dialog box panel (shown in Figure 20.19 with a close-up of the dog Bandit doing a Hound-of-the-Baskervilles turn).

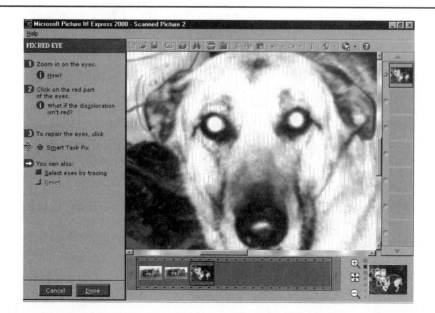

FIGURE 20.19
Use the Smart Task Fix feature to remove red eye from a scanned picture.

3. Zoom in on the eyes until they're nice and large.

4. Click the red part of the eye, then click the Smart Task Fix icon in the dialog box panel.

5. Repeat for any other affected eyes.

6. Click the Done button to close the Fix Red Eye dialog box panel.

Figure 20.20 shows Bandit restored to something approaching normality.

FIGURE 20.20
Here's the photo with red eye removed.

Saving a Picture

Once you've created a picture in Picture It! Express, you'll probably want to save it. Saving in Picture It! Express is similar to saving in other applications, but there are three wrinkles:

- First, Picture It! Express displays its Save As dialog box in its left-hand panel. This wrinkle is cosmetic.

- Second, you can save a picture in a variety of file formats, depending on what you intend to do with the picture afterwards.

- Third, you can specify a description as well as a filename and location.

Follow these steps to save a picture for the first time:

1. Click the Save button on the toolbar, or choose File ➤ Save, or click the Save & Send item on the Workbench page and choose the Save item on the menu preview. Picture It! Express will display the Save As dialog box panel (see Figure 20.21).

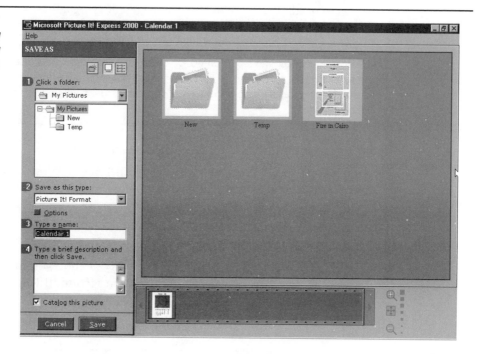

2. In the Click A Folder list box, navigate to and select the folder in which you want to store the picture.

 TIP To create a new folder, click the New Folder button at the top of the Save As dialog box panel and use the resulting Create New Folder dialog box panel to create the folder.

3. From the Save As This Type drop-down list, select the picture type to use for the picture. These are the four formats you'll usually want to use:

   • Use the Picture It! Format item to save the picture in the MIX file format that Picture It! and Picture It! Express use. When you use this file format, Picture It! Express preserves the objects in the Stack, so that you will be able to adjust them further as necessary.

- Use the Graphics Interchange Format (GIF) item for graphical images that are not photos, such as clip art.

- Use the JPEG Filter item to create compressed files of graphical images such as photos. Because JPEGs are compressed, they are useful for posting to the Web and sending via e-mail.

- Use the Windows Bitmaps format to create a Windows bitmap that you can view or edit in most Windows-based graphics programs.

 NOTE When you create a GIF, a JPEG, or a bitmap, Picture It! Express fuses all the objects in the picture into a single image. This means that you will not be able to manipulate the objects individually again—not necessarily a bad thing, just something you need to know about in advance.

4. In the Type A Name text box, enter the name for the picture.

5. In the Type A Brief Description And Then Click Save text box, enter a description for the picture. You will be able to use this description to search for the picture later if necessary.

6. If you want Picture It! Express to catalog the picture, make sure the Catalog This Picture check box is selected.

7. Click the Save button to save the picture. If you chose a format other than Picture It!, you'll see the Save In Other Than Picture It! Format dialog box shown in Figure 20.22.

FIGURE 20.22
If you choose to save a picture in a format other than Picture It!, Picture It! Express warns you about the possible consequences.

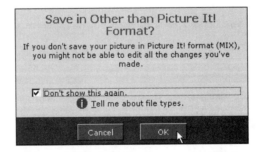

Save in Other than Picture It! Format?

If you don't save your picture in Picture It! format (MIX), you might not be able to edit all the changes you've made.

☑ Don't show this again.
ⓘ Tell me about file types.

Cancel   OK

8. Select the Don't Show Me This Again check box if you don't want to see this warning again, then click the OK button to save the picture.

Printing a Picture

To print a picture from Picture It! Express, follow these steps:

1. Click the Print button on the toolbar, or choose File ≻ Print, to display the Print This Picture dialog box panel (see Figure 20.23).

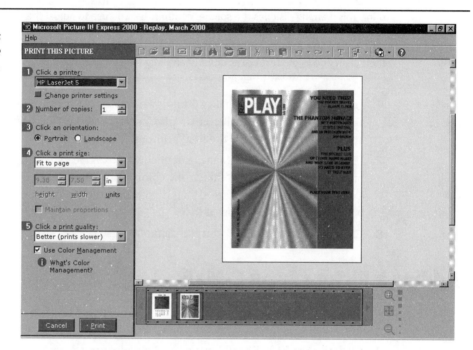

2. Make sure the right printer is selected in the Click A Printer drop-down list. (If not, change it.)

3. Set the number of copies you want in the Number Of Copies text box.

4. Choose the orientation you want—Portrait (tall) or Landscape (wide)—in the Click An Orientation area.

5. In the Click A Print Size area, specify the size of the page on which you'll be printing.

   • To maximize the use of the current paper size, select the Fit To Page item.

   • To use one of the predefined paper sizes (8 × 10 inches, 5 × 7 inches, 4 × 6 inches, or 3.5 × 5 inches), select it in the drop-down list.

   • To print the picture at its current size, select the Exact Size item.

   • To use a custom size of paper, select the Custom Size item and use the Height, Width, and Units text boxes to specify the dimensions of the paper.

Select the Maintain Proportions check box if you want to maintain the current proportions of the picture rather than stretching it differently in each dimension.

 TIP If the paper size you chose is smaller than the picture, Picture It! Express will display a warning that the picture won't fit and invite you to drag to select the part that you'd like to print. This warning disables the spinner controls that you use to adjust the Height and Width text boxes for custom paper sizes. To clear the warning, choose a larger paper size from the Click A Print Size drop-down list before switching to the Custom item. (Alternatively, type into the Height and Width text boxes rather than using their spinner controls.)

6. From the Click A Print Quality drop-down list, select the print quality you want: Good (Prints Fastest) or Better (Prints Slower). Use the Good setting for drafts and the Better setting for the final printout.

7. Make sure the Use Color Management check box is cleared. (The Color Management feature attempts to match the colors printed to those you see on screen. Color Management is worth trying if your printouts look wrong, but you'll do best to try printing without it first.)

8. Click the Print button to print the picture.

Adding a Picture to an E-Mail

If you're using Outlook Express as your e-mail client, Picture It! Express makes it easy for you to e-mail to someone a picture you've created. Follow these steps:

1. Click the Send Via E-mail button on the toolbar (or choose File ➤ Send) to display the Send Or Save For E-Mail dialog box panel (see Figure 20.24).

2. In the How Large A Picture Do You Want To Send area, select the Small, Medium, or Current option button as appropriate.

3. In the How Do You Want To Send Your Picture area, make sure the Put The Picture In An E-Mail Message option button is selected.

4. Click the Done button. Picture It! Express will automatically create a message in Outlook Express (see Figure 20.25) with the picture attached, the generic advertising subject line "Picture from Microsoft Picture It!", and some prosy instructions to recipients on how to view the picture and change their display settings.

FIGURE 20.24

Use the Send Or Save For E-mail dialog box panel to insert a picture quickly into an Outlook Express e-mail message.

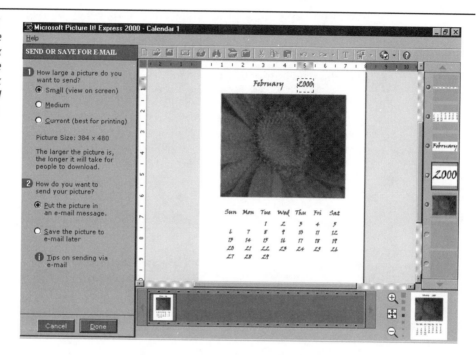

FIGURE 20.25

Picture It! Express automatically creates a message in Outlook Express with the picture attached. You'll probably want to change the default subject line and message text.

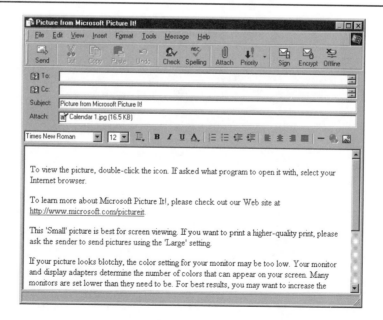

5. Specify one or more recipients for the picture in the To text box and the Cc text box. (See Chapter 22 for the details on creating e-mail messages with Outlook Express.)

6. Change the subject line and the message text as appropriate.

7. Click the Send button to send the message.

CHAPTER **21**

Surfing the Web with Internet Explorer 5

Internet Explorer, the Microsoft Web browser, is an integral part of Microsoft's computing solutions. If you bought your computer recently, chances are that Internet Explorer came pre-installed. If not, Works will install Internet Explorer for you when you install Works itself.

In this chapter, you'll learn how to browse with Internet Explorer and how to configure Internet Explorer's most important settings, including the security settings. I will assume that you already have an Internet connection configured, through a dial-up connection (via a modem), through a cable modem or digital subscriber line (DSL), or through a local area network (for example, your office's network).

Starting Internet Explorer

You can start Internet Explorer in various ways:

- On the Programs page of the Task Launcher, click the Internet Explorer program listing, then click the Start Internet Explorer link.
- On the Programs page of the Task Launcher, select one of the MSN-related tasks. (MSN is the Microsoft Network, Microsoft's Internet service provider.)
- Double-click the Internet Explorer icon on the Desktop.
- Click the Internet Explorer icon on your Quick Launch bar (if you have the Quick Launch toolbar displayed).
- Choose Start ➢ Programs ➢ Internet Explorer.

Using the Internet Explorer Interface

Figure 21.1 shows the main features of the Internet Explorer window.

The status bar shows information on the current operation (for example, *Connecting to site www.microsoft.com*) or information on any hyperlink the mouse pointer is currently pointing to (as in the figure).

As you can see in the figure, Internet Explorer provides a three-part toolbar for navigating the Web and Internet. When you start Internet Explorer, the Address bar is displayed as the lower layer of the toolbar, with the Links bar reduced to just a button at the right-hand end of the Address bar. You can customize the size and position of the three parts of the Internet Explorer toolbar by clicking and dragging the toolbar handles at the left end of each toolbar. For example, you can drag the toolbar handles of the Links bar to the left from their default position to display more of the Links bar and less of the Address bar. Alternatively, you could drag the Links bar down to display it below the Address bar.

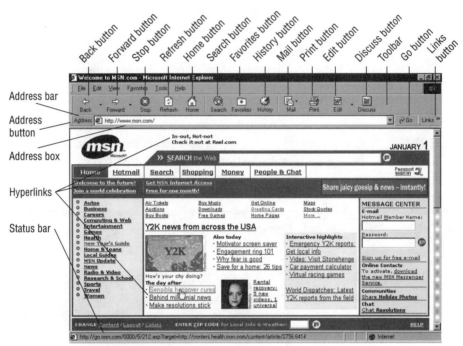

Here's how to use the buttons on the toolbar in Internet Explorer:

- Click the Back button to move to the previous page you were on. To move back more than one page, click the downward-arrow button on the Back button to display a list of pages that you can go back to.

- Click the Forward button to move forward to a page you were on before you clicked the Back button. To move forward more than one page, click the downward-arrow button on the Forward button to display a list of pages that you can go forward to.

NOTE Until there is a page to go forward or back to, the Back button and the Forward button will be dimmed and unavailable.

- Click the Stop button to stop Internet Explorer from pursuing a jump that's in progress. (For example, if the jump has stalled or if the page is loading very slowly, you might want to stop it.)

- Click the Refresh button to have Internet Explorer reload the current page. You might want to do this if part of the page fails to transfer properly, or if you think the page may have changed since you loaded this instance of it.

- Click the Home button to jump to your home page. (You'll learn about home pages in a minute or two.)

- Click the Favorites button to display the Favorites pane. (I'll discuss Favorites later in this chapter.)

- Click the History button to display the History pane (see Figure 21.2), which you can use to navigate to a site you've visited recently. Use the View drop-down list button at the top of the History panel to switch view between By Date, By Site, By Most Visited, and By Order Visited Today.

FIGURE 21.2
The History pane gives you quick access to sites you've visited.

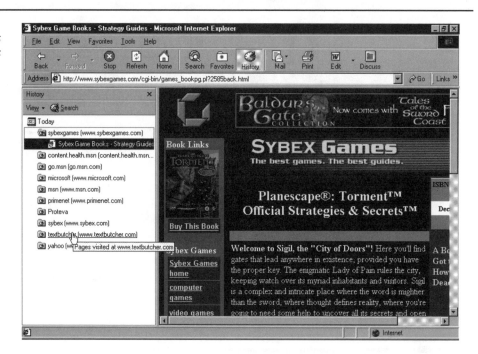

- Click the Mail drop-down list button to display a menu of the Internet Explorer components, such as the optional newsreader, you have installed on your computer. You can move to one of these components by choosing it from the menu. For example, to move to your current mail program, choose the Read Mail item. (Internet Explorer will start the mail program if it is not already running.)

- Click the Print button to display the Print dialog box, which you can use to print the current page.

- Click the Edit button to display the current page in your designated HTML-editing software (for instance, Word). Click the drop-down list button to display a list of programs that you can edit the page in (for example, Notepad and Word).

- Click the Discuss button to enter a discussion. (This is an advanced feature that I won't cover in this chapter.)

 TIP You can run two or more Internet Explorer windows at once, allowing you to download a page or a file in one window while continuing to browse in another. To open another Internet Explorer window, choose File ➢ New ➢ Window or press Ctrl+N. Be aware that all Internet Explorer windows will be sharing your connection (whether modem, cable, DSL, or network) and that they will slow each other down.

 WARNING Some Web sites will open a new browser window for you. This tends to happen when you've chosen to display a page that doesn't involve their site. Keep an eye on the number of browser windows you have open, because there may be more than you have opened yourself—and some of them may be showing items that you haven't specifically chosen to see.

Opening a Document

Each Web site or Web page is identified by an address called a *Uniform Resource Locator,* or *URL* for short. (URL is usually pronounced "earl," but it's also sometimes spelled out as "U-R-L.") For example, the URL for the Microsoft Web site is `http://www.microsoft.com`. By pointing your browser at this URL, you can access the Microsoft Web site.

To open a document on the Web or on an intranet:

1. Choose File ➢ Open to display the Open dialog box (see Figure 21.3).

FIGURE 21.3
To open a document on the Web, choose File ➢ Open, enter the address in the Open text box, and click the OK button.

2. In the Open text box, enter the address for the document or file you want to open, using any of the following three methods:

• Type the name of the document or file into the Open text box.

• To open a document or file you've accessed recently, click the down-arrow button at the right-hand end of the Open text box and select the file from the drop-down list.

• Click the Browse button to display the larger Open dialog box (see Figure 21.4), then select the file and click the Open button to place the file's name and path in the Open text box in the smaller Open dialog box.

 TIP If the address you're typing matches an address you've visited within Internet Explorer's memory, Internet Explorer will display a drop-down list of URLs. If one of them is right, use the ↓ key to select it, and then press the Enter key. If not, finish typing the new URL.

FIGURE 21.4

Click the Browse button to display the larger Open dialog box so that you can select a file to open.

 TIP You can also click in the Address box on the Address bar, type in the address of the document, and press Enter to accept it.

3. Click the OK button it the smaller Open dialog box to open the file.

You can also use Internet Explorer to open other types of documents, such as Word documents. To do so, enter the path and name of the document in the Open text box in the Open dialog box. Alternatively, click the Browse button to display the larger Open dialog box, choose All Files from the Files Of Type drop-down list, select the file you want to open, and click the Open button. Then click the OK button in the smaller Open dialog box, and Internet Explorer will open the file.

Jumping to a Hyperlink

Many Web documents contain *hyperlinks*, which are jumps to other locations. Hyperlinks are typically displayed as underlined text, graphical objects, or pictures. (For example, Figure 21.1 contains a large number of hyperlinks, several of which are labeled.)

When you move the mouse pointer over a hyperlink, the mouse pointer takes on the shape of a hand with a finger pointing upward (also shown in Figure 21.1). To jump to the hyperlinked location, click the hyperlink.

Returning to a Previous Document

Because you often will access dead ends or pages that do not offer the information you need, you will often have to return to the previous document you accessed. There are several ways to move back to a document you've visited before:

- Click the Back button on the toolbar, or use its drop-down list, as described earlier in the chapter.

- Click the down arrow at the right end of the Address box and choose the document from the drop-down list.

- Choose one of the items listed in the Go menu (for example, Go ➤ Back or Go ➤ Home Page).

- Click the History button to display the History pane (see Figure 21.5). This pane contains a complete list of the pages you've visited recently. Click the hyperlink for the item you want to return to.

FIGURE 21.5
Use the History pane to return to a previous document.

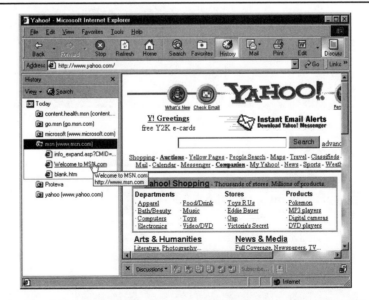

Saving a Document

Although you cannot create new documents in Internet Explorer, you can use Internet Explorer to save documents to your computer. For example, you might want to save a copy of a Web page or intranet page to your hard disk for reference.

To save the current page, choose File ➢ Save As File. Internet Explorer will display the Save As dialog box. Choose a location for the file as usual, specify a filename, and click the Save button.

Creating and Using Favorites

Internet Explorer lets you designate URLs as "Favorites," which allows you to access them quickly using the Favorites menu or the Favorites pane. (Other Web browsers such as Netscape Navigator call Favorites "bookmarks.")

To use Favorites, you create them as described in the next section, then access them from the Favorites menu or the Favorites pane (shown in Figure 21.6).

FIGURE 21.6
Internet Explorer provides the Favorites pane for accessing your Favorites quickly.

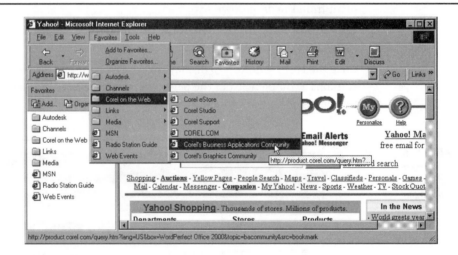

Adding a Page to Your Favorites

To add the current URL (the page that Internet Explorer is currently displaying) to your list of Favorites, follow these steps:

1. Choose Favorites ➢ Add To Favorites. Internet Explorer will display the Add Favorite dialog box (see Figure 21.7).

FIGURE 21.7

To add a URL to your list of Favorites, choose Favorites ➤ Add To Favorites to display the Add Favorite dialog box.

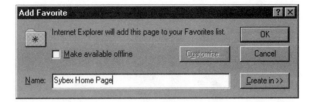

2. In the Name text box, enter the name by which to identify the Favorite. You will often need to change the default name, which will be the title of the page, to something shorter, more descriptive, or more memorable.

3. If you want to have the Favorite available offline (when your computer is not attached to the network or the Internet), select the Make Available Offline check box. Then choose a schedule and details by using the Offline Favorite Wizard as follows:

   • Click the Customize button to start the Offline Favorite Wizard. The first time you run the wizard, you'll see the introductory screen shown in Figure 21.8. Select the In The Future, Do Not Show This Introduction Screen check box and click the Next button.

FIGURE 21.8

The first time you run the Offline Favorite Wizard, you'll see this screen. Select the In The Future, Do Not Show This Introduction Screen check box and click the Next button.

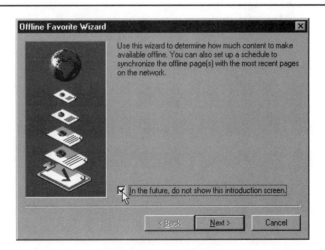

   • On the next screen of the Offline Favorite Wizard, shown in Figure 21.9, choose whether you want to download just this page or pages linked to it. To download just this page, leave the No option button selected (this is the default). To download linked pages, select the Yes option button (as shown in the figure) and specify the depth of links you want to download by entering a number in the Download Pages NN Links Deep From This Page text box. Then click the Next button.

FIGURE 21.9

On the next screen of the Offline Favorite Wizard, decide whether to download just this page or the pages linked to it as well.

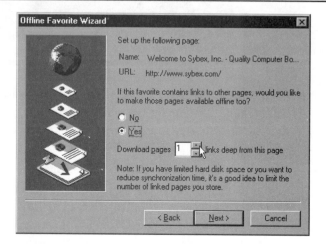

WARNING Don't set too deep a level of links to download. Setting more than one level can quickly fill up your hard drive and monopolize your Internet connection with synchronization. If you want to try this feature, experiment cautiously, setting a minimal level of links at first for any given Favorite. (Bear in mind that each Favorite is likely to need a different level of links.)

- On the next screen of the Offline Favorite Wizard, shown in Figure 21.10, decide how you want to synchronize this Favorite. You can choose among the Only When I Choose Synchronize From The Tools Menu option button, the I Would Like To Create A New Schedule option button (which lets you create a custom synchronization schedule for the Favorite), and the Using This Existing Schedule option button (which lets you use an existing schedule from the drop-down list). The Using This Existing Schedule option button will not be available until you create a schedule. Click the Next button to proceed.

- If you chose to create a custom synchronization schedule for the Favorite, you'll see the Offline Favorite Wizard screen shown in Figure 21.11. Specify the interval (in days) and the time for the update at the top of the dialog box. Enter a name in the Name text box. If you want your computer to connect to the network or Internet automatically if it is not connected when the time for the synchronization arrives, select the If My Computer Is Not

Connected When This Scheduled Synchronization Begins, Automatically
Connect For Me check box. Click the Next button.

FIGURE 21.10
*On the next screen of
the Offline Favorite
Wizard, decide
how you want to
synchronize this
Favorite.*

FIGURE 21.11
*If you chose to create a
custom synchronization
schedule for the
Favorite, specify the
details on the next
screen.*

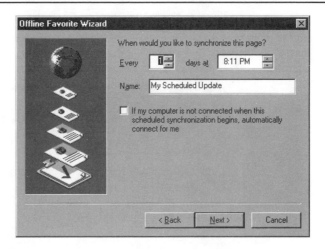

• On the final screen of the Offline Favorite Wizard (see Figure 21.12), choose
the Yes, My User Name And Password Are option button and specify your
username and password (twice) if the site requires you to enter a password
when accessing it. Click the Finish button to finish scheduling the update.

FIGURE 21.12
*On the final screen of
the Offline Favorite
Wizard, enter your
username and
password if the site
requires you to log on.*

4. Choose where you want to create the Favorite. You can create the Favorite either at the top level, so that it appears directly on the Favorites menu (and in the Favorites pane), or in a folder.

   • To create the Favorite in a different folder, click the Create In button in the Add Favorite dialog box to display an additional part of the dialog box (see Figure 21.13).

FIGURE 21.13
*Use the additional part
of the Add Favorite
dialog box to specify
where to create the
Favorite.*

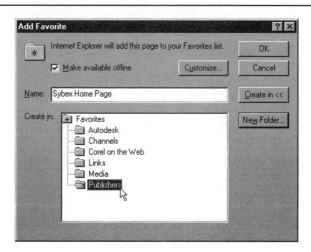

   • Select an existing folder or create a new folder. To create a new folder beneath the currently selected folder, click the New Folder button, enter the name in the Folder Name text box in the Create New Folder dialog box, and click the OK button.

5. Click the OK button to create the Favorite. If you chose to make this Favorite an offiine Favorite, you'll see the Synchronizing dialog box as Internet Explorer performs the initial synchronization.

Thereafter, Internet Explorer will synchronize the Favorite automatically if you set up a schedule. If not, or to force an immediate synchronization, choose Tools ➤ Synchronize to display the Items To Synchronize dialog box (see Figure 21.14). Select the items you want to synchronize, and then click the Synchronize button.

FIGURE 21.14

Use the Items To Synchronize dialog box to force a synchronization.

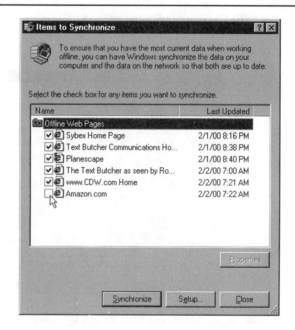

You'll see the Synchronizing dialog box (see Figure 21.15) as Internet Explorer synchronizes the pages. The dialog box will close automatically when synchronization is complete.

FIGURE 21.15

Internet Explorer displays the Synchronizing dialog box while it synchronizes your pages.

Organizing Your Favorites into Folders

Internet Explorer automatically sorts your Favorites alphabetically on the Favorites menu, which works well enough for a short list of Favorites. But if you use the Web vigorously, you'll soon build a collection of Favorites that will overrun the Favorites menu. You'll need to organize these Favorites into folders.

Take the following steps:

1. Choose Favorites ➤ Organize Favorites to display the Organize Favorites dialog box (see Figure 21.16). Alternatively, if you have the Favorites pane displayed, click the Organize button at the top of it.

FIGURE 21.16
Use the Organize Favorites dialog box to organize your Favorites into folders.

2. Organize your Favorites into folders by using the following techniques:

   • To move a Favorite to a folder, either drag it to the folder in the list box (this is difficult if your Favorites menu is long) or select the Favorite, click the Move To Folder button to display the Browse For Folder dialog box, select the folder, and click the OK button.

   • To change the order of the list, drag a Favorite or a folder up or down the list box.

   • To rename a Favorite or a folder, select it and click the Rename button. Type the new name over the existing name and press the Enter key.

- To delete a Favorite or a folder, select it and click the Delete button. Internet Explorer will display the Confirm Folder Delete dialog box; click the Yes button.

- To create a new folder, click the Create Folder button. Internet Explorer will create a new folder called New Folder at the bottom of the list box and will select its name. Type in the new name for the folder and press the Enter key.

3. Click the Close button to close the Organize Favorites dialog box.

Changing a Favorite So That It's Available Offline

Here's how to make one of your designated Favorites available even when you're not online:

1. Choose Favorites ➢ Organize Favorites to display the Organize Favorites dialog box. Alternatively, if you have the Favorites pane displayed, click the Organize button at the top of it.

2. Select the Favorite in the panel on the right-hand side of the dialog box so that its details appear in the pane on the lower left of the dialog box.

3. Select the Make Available Offline check box. When you select the check box, Internet Explorer will display a Properties button below the check box.

4. Click the Properties button to display the Properties dialog box for the Favorite (see Figure 21.17).

FIGURE 21.17
Changing a Favorite into an offline Favorite

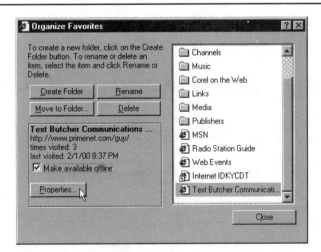

5. Click the Schedule tab to display the Schedule page of the Properties dialog box (see Figure 21.18).

FIGURE 21.18
*Designate the
synchronization
schedule on the
Schedule page of
the Properties dialog
box for the Favorite.*

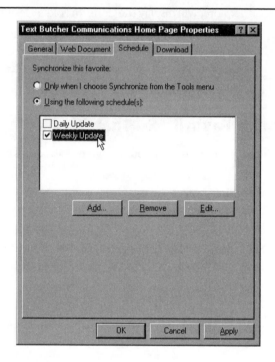

6. Select the appropriate synchronization options.

7. Click the OK button to close the Properties dialog box.

8. Click the Close button to close the Organize Favorites dialog box.

Customizing Your Start Page and Quick Links

Apart from Favorites, Internet Explorer provides several features for quickly accessing particular sites. These features include your start page, your search page, and Quick Links buttons.

Your *start page*, also called a *home page*, is the page that Internet Explorer automatically opens when you start Internet Explorer and when you click the Home button on the toolbar. You'll usually want to change your start page from the default setting to the site you want to see first in every Internet Explorer session.

Your *search page* is the page that Internet Explorer displays when you click the Search button on the toolbar. You'll usually want to set your search page to your favorite Internet or intranet directory—perhaps an Internet site, such as Yahoo! or AltaVista, or a local corporate directory page.

The Links bar provides Quick Links to regularly updated Microsoft sites, such as Best of the Web, Channel Guide, Free Hotmail, and the Microsoft site. (The names of these Quick Links vary a little in different versions of Internet Explorer.) You can access any of these sites by clicking its button on the Links bar.

To customize the Quick Links bar, navigate to a site that you like, then drag the page icon from the beginning of the Address box to the Quick Links bar, as shown in the upper part of Figure 21.19. Drop the icon in an open space on the bar. Internet Explorer will create a link for it, as shown in the lower part of the figure.

FIGURE 21.19
To add the current Web site to the Quick Links bar, drag its page icon to an open space on the bar.

To change your home page, navigate to your target page. Choose Tools ➤ Internet Options to display the Internet Options dialog box, click the Use Current button in the Home Page group box on the General page, and click the OK button.

 WARNING   Installing Microsoft applications may reset your home page to its default setting without warning you. In case this happens, create a Favorite for your start page so that you will be able to access it quickly in order to restore it as your home page.

Dealing with Common Error Messages

When you're cruising the Web, you'll often see a couple of error messages: *Server too busy*, and *The page cannot be displayed.*

The first message typically means that the Web server the browser contacted was too busy right then handling other requests to deal with your request for information. Click the Refresh button on the toolbar to try the link again. Often, you'll get straight through on the second attempt; but if the server is truly busy, you may need to retry a number of times, or wait till later.

The second message typically means either that the address you are trying to access doesn't exist or that the address is temporarily unavailable (for example, because the server that hosts the address is offline or not working). If you know that the address exists, try it later, when the server may be back online. If not, and if you typed in the URL, double-check each character to make sure you didn't miss or add anything. Then try it again.

Configuring Internet Explorer

In this section, I'll discuss the most important options that Internet Explorer offers for controlling how it runs. You can configure most aspects of its behavior—everything from the font size Internet Explorer uses to display text, to security, to improving performance over a slow Internet connection.

Internet Explorer has a plethora of options, so I won't discuss all of them. Instead, I'll concentrate on the options that will make the most difference in your daily surfing.

All these options live in the Internet Options dialog box. Start by choosing Tools ➢ Internet Options to display this dialog box.

Cleaning Up Temporary Internet Files

Every time you view a page on the Internet (or on an internal network), the information on the page is transferred to your computer. That's no surprise—that's why download times matter so much to the surfing experience. But it's not so obvious that this information is written into temporary files on your hard drive. These enable you to view the information more quickly the next time you access the page, as Internet Explorer has to download only new items if the page has changed.

The disadvantages to having the files on your hard drive are that a) they take up space, and b) you can have embarrassing or dangerous information stored on your computer without your knowledge. So it's a good idea to clear out your temporary files periodically.

Click the Settings button in the Temporary Internet Files group box on the General page of the Internet Options dialog box to display the Settings dialog box (see Figure 21.20).

FIGURE 21.20
Use the Settings dialog box to keep your temporary Internet files under control.

At the top of the dialog box, select an option button to determine how frequently Internet Explorer should check for newer versions of stored pages: Every Visit To The Page, Every Time You Start Internet Explorer, Automatically, or Never.

In the Temporary Internet Files Folder, check the amount of disk space Internet Explorer is using for temporary files. In the figure, it's 251MB—a healthy chunk of space, but relatively little for active surfing. If you have plenty of hard disk space and a slow Internet connection, you might set anywhere from 500MB to a couple of gigabytes to keep more information locally. (You can move the folder to another folder or drive if necessary by clicking the Move Folder button and using the resulting Browse For Folder dialog box to designate the folder.)

Click the OK button to close the Settings dialog box. Now click the Delete Files button in the Temporary Internet Files group box to display the Delete Files dialog box (see Figure 21.21).

FIGURE 21.21
Use the Delete Files dialog box to delete your temporary Internet files.

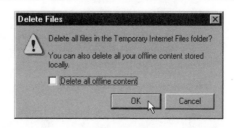

If you want to delete all your offline content, select the Delete All Offline Content check box. Usually, you'll want to keep the offline content but get rid of everything else. Click the OK button to delete your temporary files.

Rewriting Your History

As you learned earlier in the chapter, Internet Explorer's History feature tracks where you've been. History is a great feature for retracing your steps to find a site you forgot to bookmark, but it's also a threat: Those who study your History can repeat your movements step by step—which, depending on what you've been doing, could be a threat to your business's security or to your family's good name.

If you perceive a security threat, reduce the Days To Keep Pages In History text box entry in the History group box on the General page to a minimum—perhaps one day. Then click the Clear History button to clear your current history. Click the OK button in the confirmation message box that appears.

Choosing Security Options

The History feature touches on security, but Internet Explorer has a bunch of explicit security features as well. Click the Security tab to display the Security page (see Figure 21.22).

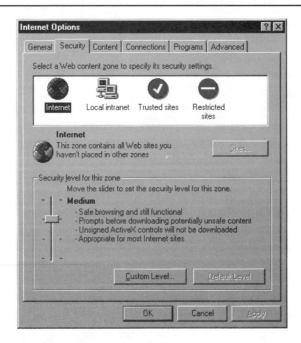

FIGURE 21.22
Choose security options on the Security page of the Internet Options dialog box.

The Select A Web Content Zone To Specify Its Security Settings box at the top of the page contains four categories of sites. The easiest way to explain them is in reverse order:

- Restricted Sites (sites you've specifically designated as potentially dangerous)
- Trusted Sites (sites you've specifically designated as trusted not to damage your computer or your data)
- Local Intranet (local sites not specifically designated as restricted or trusted)
- Internet (everything else)

You can set a different level of security for each category by selecting the category and dragging the Security Level For This Zone slider up or down. If you understand the specifics of security, you can also specify a custom level for a zone by selecting the category, clicking the Custom Level button to display the Security Settings dialog box (see Figure 21.23), selecting options, and clicking the OK button. (This is an advanced procedure that I don't have space to cover in this book.)

FIGURE 21.23
For advanced users only: Creating a custom security level in the Security Settings dialog box

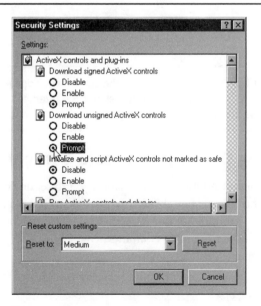

By default, the Internet category has a Medium security level designed to let you browse effectively while protecting you from harmful content. Local Intranet has a Medium-Low level; Trusted Sites has a Low level; and Restricted Sites has a High level.

To change your list of Restricted Sites or Trusted Sites, select the category and click the Sites button to display the Trusted Sites dialog box or Restricted Sites dialog box (shown in Figure 21.24). To add a site to the list, enter its URL in the Add This Web Site To The Zone text box and click the Add button; to remove a site from the list, select it in the Web Sites list box and click the Remove button. Click the OK button to close the dialog box.

FIGURE 21.24

Use the Restricted Sites dialog box (shown here) or the Trusted Sites dialog box (not shown) to adjust your list of restricted sites or trusted sites.

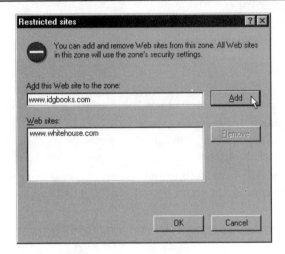

 NOTE The security zone for the current site appears in the status bar. For example, Figure 21.5 (earlier in the chapter) shows the Internet security zone, and Figure 21.31 (later) shows the Trusted Sites security zone.

Screening Out Objectionable Content

The Content Advisor feature enables you to set up content screening based on the ratings of the Recreational Software Advisory Council rating service for the Internet (RSACi). Content Advisor is very useful if children or easily offended friends or relatives may be using your computer.

To enable Content Advisor:

1. Click the Content tab to display the Content page of the Internet Options dialog box.

2. Click the Enable button in the Content Advisor group box to display the Content Advisor dialog box.

3. On the Ratings page, select the item in the Category list box and drag the Rating slider to a suitable level (see Figure 21.25). Each of the items has five levels, ranging from 0 (none of the offensive item) to 4 (lots of it). For example, the Violence levels are No Violence (0), Fighting (1), Killing (2), Killing With Blood And Gore (3), and Wanton And Gratuitous Violence (4). The Language levels are

Inoffensive Slang (0), Mild Expletives (1), Moderate Expletives (2), Obscene Gestures (3), and Explicit Or Crude Language (4).

FIGURE 21.25
Choose rating levels for Language, Nudity, Sex, and Violence on the Ratings page of the Content Advisor dialog box.

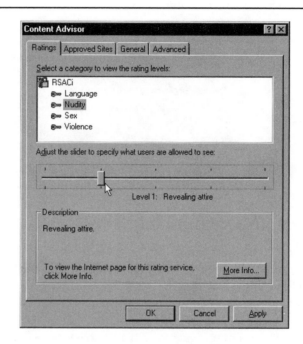

 TIP Content Advisor offers more advanced features that I won't cover here: You can maintain a list of approved and disapproved Web sites on the Approved Sites page.

4. Click the OK button to close Content Advisor. The first time you do this, Internet Explorer will display the Create Supervisor Password dialog box (see Figure 21.26).

FIGURE 21.26
Create a supervisor password in the Create Supervisor Password dialog box.

5. Enter the password in the Password and Confirm Password text boxes, then click the OK button. Internet Explorer will display a Content Advisor message box (see Figure 21.27) telling you that Content Advisor has been installed and to close Internet Explorer.

FIGURE 21.27
When Internet Explorer warns you that Content Advisor has been enabled, click the OK button and exit the application.

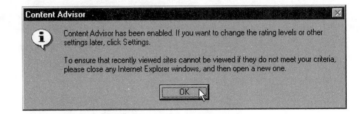

6. Click the OK button to return to the Internet Options dialog box, where the Enable Ratings button will have changed to the Disable Ratings button.

7. Click the OK button to close the Internet Options dialog box.

8. Exit all Internet Explorer windows, then reopen one.

To adjust the settings for Content Advisor, click the Settings button. Internet Explorer will display the Supervisor Password Required dialog box. Enter your password and click the OK button to display the Content Advisor dialog box, then change the settings and click the OK button.

To disable ratings again, click the Disable Ratings button. Internet Explorer will display the Supervisor Password Required dialog box. Enter your password and click the OK button. Internet Explorer will display a Content Advisor message box telling you that Content Advisor has been turned off.

When users hit a site that contains unapproved content, they'll see a Content Advisor dialog box such as the one shown in Figure 21.28. If you're the user, you can enter the supervisor password and choose the Always Allow This Web Site To Be Viewed option button (to make a lasting exception for the site), the Always Allow This Web Page To Be Viewed option button (to make a lasting exception for the page but not the site), or the Allow Viewing Only This Time option button (to make a temporary exception). Then click the OK button to access the site. (A user without the supervisor password will need to click the Cancel button and will not be able to reach the site.)

FIGURE 21.28
*Content Advisor
in action*

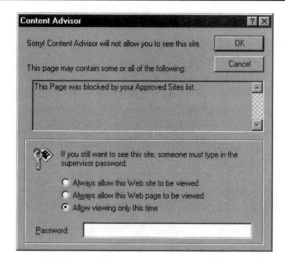

Managing Your AutoComplete Information

AutoComplete is a great feature that can save you a lot of fuss with passwords and often-repeated information. But it can also severely compromise your digital persona and your finances, so you need to understand what it does and how it works in order to use it appropriately.

Briefly put, AutoComplete automatically fills in URLs and entries on forms for you. To do so, it needs to watch as you enter URLs and information on forms, and store that information. Then, when you start typing a URL or access a form it recognizes, it can fill in the information for you. For example, the first time you access your HotMail account via Internet Explorer, AutoComplete can learn your username and password, and offer to fill them in for you in the future.

You can see the downside to this: Internet Explorer is storing sensitive or secret information, which means that other people who use your computer can more easily masquerade as you. There's also a risk that your computer could be hacked to give up this information, though this risk is less severe than the direct risk from people who can physically access your computer.

Here's how to configure AutoComplete:

1. Click the AutoComplete button in the Personal Information group box on the Content page of the Internet Options dialog box to display the AutoComplete Settings dialog box (see Figure 21.29).

2. In the Use AutoComplete For group box, specify the items for which you want to use AutoComplete:

   • The Web Addresses check box controls whether AutoComplete tracks the URLs you access and suggests matching URLs in the Open dialog box and the Address box.

   • The Forms check box controls whether AutoComplete tracks your entries in forms other than usernames and passwords.

   • The User Names And Passwords On Forms check box controls whether AutoComplete tracks the usernames and passwords you enter in forms. This is the most sensitive information, so you may want to clear this check box. If you leave it enabled (as it is by default), leave the Prompt Me To Save Passwords check box selected so that Internet Explorer gets your consent each time it's about to store a password of yours. (This way, you can use Auto-Complete for less sensitive passwords but not for high-security passwords.)

3. If you want to clear your form information or passwords stored to date, click the Clear Forms button or the Clear Passwords button in the Clear AutoComplete History group box and click the OK button in the Internet Options confirmation dialog box that appears.

4. Click the OK button to close the AutoComplete Settings dialog box.

Advanced Options

The Advanced page of the Internet Options dialog box (see Figure 21.30) contains a formidable number of options organized in a number of categories. The following sections discuss the key options.

FIGURE 21.30
Choose Advanced
options on the
Advanced page of
the Internet Options
dialog box.

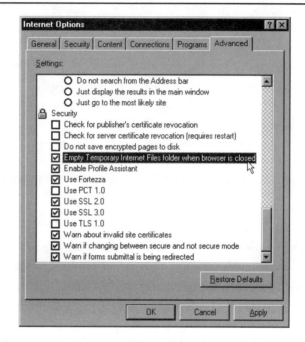

Browsing Category

These are the key options in the Browsing category:

- The Enable Offline Items To Be Synchronized On A Schedule check box lets you create offline Favorites.

- The Launch Browser Windows In A Separate Process check box controls whether Internet Explorer lets you run multiple instances of Internet Explorer or just one instance with multiple windows. The advantage to running multiple instances is that if one instance crashes, the others may not crash. If you run just one instance, all Internet Explorer windows will close if it crashes.

- The Show Internet Explorer On The Desktop check box specifies whether an Internet Explorer icon appears on your desktop. If you want to get rid of the icon, clear this check box.

- The Use Inline AutoComplete For Web Addresses and Use Inline AutoComplete In Windows Explorer check boxes control whether Internet Explorer offers

AutoComplete suggestions when you're typing an address or URL in the Address box or in Explorer.

Multimedia Category

These are the key options in the Multimedia category:

- The Play Animations check box controls whether Internet Explorer plays animations. If your computer or connection is slow, you may want to turn animations off.

- The Play Sounds check box controls whether Internet Explorer plays sounds. You may want to turn sounds off if download time is precious.

- The Play Videos check box controls whether Internet Explorer plays videos. Video hogs bandwidth, so if you have a slow connection, you may want to turn videos off.

- The Show Pictures check box controls whether Internet Explorer displays pictures. If your Internet connection is really slow (for example, if you're surfing via a cell-phone hookup), you may want to turn pictures off—but the Web is so graphical nowadays that some pages may be tough going without their pictures.

Security Category

These are the key options in the Security category:

- The Empty Temporary Internet Files Folder When Browser Is Closed check box controls whether Internet Explorer deletes all temporary files each time you close Internet Explorer. If you're concerned about security, select this check box.

- The Warn About Invalid Site Certificates check box controls whether Internet Explorer warns you if a digital certificate (information that should prove the identity of a company or a person) is invalid. Keep this check box selected.

- The Warn If Changing Between Secure And Not Secure Mode check box controls whether Internet Explorer warns you when you are switched from a secure (encrypted) connection to a server to an unsecure connection. Keep this check box selected until you've got the hang of secure connections.

- The Warn If Forms Submittal Is Being Redirected check box controls whether Internet Explorer warns you when a form you've submitted is being redirected to a different destination than its apparent destination. Because forms may contain sensitive information, it's a good idea to keep this check box selected.

Browsing Offline

Once you've set up offline Favorites as described earlier in the chapter, you're ready to browse them offline.

If your computer isn't currently connected to the network or Internet, you'll automatically be offline. If your computer is connected to the network or Internet, choose File ➤ Work Offline to start working offline. Internet Explorer will display an indicator on the status bar to show you're currently offline, as shown in Figure 21.31. (Choose File ➤ Work Offline again to switch back to online mode.)

FIGURE 21.31
When you're working offline, Internet Explorer displays this indicator in the status bar.

As long as you stay within the material you have available offline, you'll be able to surf as usual. Because the pages are stored on your hard drive, the surfing will probably be quicker than when you have to download them. When you hit a link that leads to a page that's not available, or you enter an address that's not available, Internet Explorer will display the Web Page Unavailable While Offline dialog box (see Figure 21.32). Click the Connect button to connect to the Internet or the Stay Offline button to cancel the connection request.

FIGURE 21.32
If you try to go to a URL that's not available, Internet Explorer offers you the choice of connecting to the network or staying offline.

CHAPTER **22**

E-Mail with Outlook Express

n this chapter, you'll learn how to use the e-mail features of Outlook Express, the powerful e-mail and newsreader application that comes with Works. (In the chapter that follows, you'll learn how to use the newsreader features.)

First, you'll learn how to start Outlook Express and configure it to work with your Internet service provider (ISP). Once you're set up, I'll show you how to create and send e-mail messages; to read e-mail messages; to send and receive attachments; and to use the multiple identities (personalities or roles) that Outlook Express supports to maintain multiple e-mail accounts—for example, one for business use and one for personal use. Along the way, I'll show you how to filter your e-mail, how to block e-mail from certain people, and a couple of key things about security.

To work through this chapter, you'll need to have a modem or network connection and an account with an ISP. You'll need to know the following information: your logon name and password, your e-mail address, your incoming mail server and its type (POP or IMAP), your outgoing mail server, and whether to use Secure Password Authentication (SPA). For the next chapter, you'll also need to know the name for your ISP's news server, whether you need to log on to it, and (if you do log on) whether you need to use Secure Password Authentication—so if you're asking your ISP, pop those questions too.

Starting Outlook Express

You can start Outlook Express in any of several ways:

- If you have the Quick Launch toolbar displayed, click the Outlook Express icon that appears on it by default.
- If you have the Desktop visible, double-click the Outlook Express icon that appears on it by default.
- Alternatively, choose Start ➤ Programs ➤ Outlook Express to start Outlook Express from the Start menu.
- If you have the Task Launcher displayed, click the Outlook Express item in the Programs list on the Programs page, then click the Start Outlook Express link that appears.

I'll show you the Outlook Express screen in a moment. First, you need to know what happens when you set up Outlook Express for the first time.

Setting up E-Mail with Outlook Express

The first time you start Outlook Express, you'll need to set it up to work with your Internet connection and ISP. Follow these steps:

1. Start Outlook Express in one of the ways described in the previous section. Outlook Express will display the Outlook Express dialog box shown in Figure 22.1, telling you that Outlook Express is not your default mail client and inviting you to make it so.

FIGURE 22.1

The first time you start Outlook Express, you'll see this dialog box.

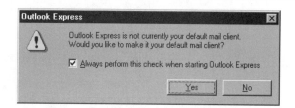

2. Click the Yes button. Outlook Express will display the Your Name page of the Internet Connection Wizard dialog box.

3. Enter the name you want to use for e-mail in the Display Name text box.

4. Click the Next button. Outlook Express will display the Internet E-mail Address page of the Internet Connection Wizard (shown in Figure 22.2 with some information entered).

   • If you have another e-mail application installed on your computer before you set up Outlook Express, you'll see the Setting Up Internet Mail page before the Internet E-mail Address page of the Internet Connection Wizard.

   • If launching Outlook Express does not start the Internet Connection Wizard, you can start it manually by double-clicking the Connect To The Internet shortcut that should be on your Desktop.

NOTE If you don't have an existing e-mail address, select the I'd Like To Sign Up For A New Account From option button and choose an Internet service provider or e-mail provider from the drop-down list. (At this writing, the only option was Hotmail, a Microsoft service.) Click the Next button to display the last page of the Internet Connection Wizard, click the Finish button, and then follow the automated procedure that you're led into.

FIGURE 22.2

FIGURE 22.2

On the Internet E-mail Address page of the Internet Connection Wizard, specify an existing e-mail address.

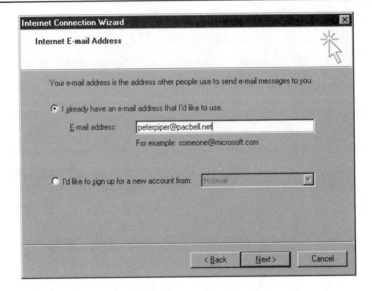

5. Select the I Already Have An E-Mail Address That I'd Like To Use option button and enter the address in the E-mail Address text box.

6. Click the Next button. Outlook Express will display the E-mail Server Names page of the Internet Connection Wizard (shown in Figure 22.3 with information entered).

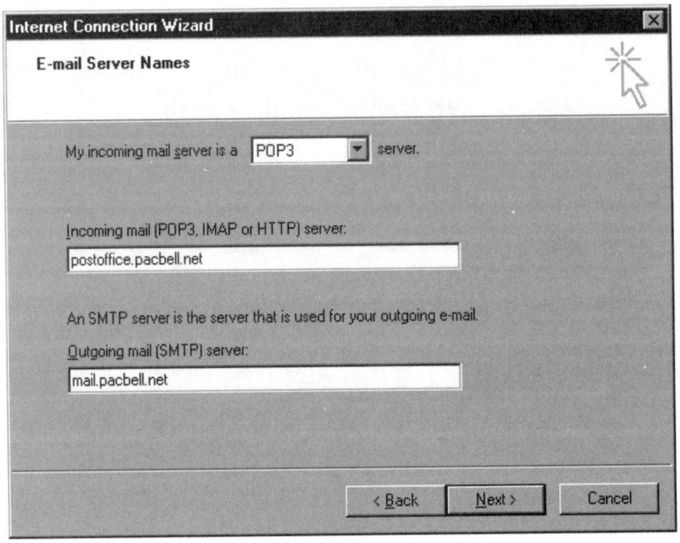

FIGURE 22.3

On the E-mail Server Names page of the Internet Connection Wizard, specify the e-mail servers you'll use.

7. From the My Incoming Mail Server Is A XXX Server drop-down list, choose POP3, IMAP, or HTTP, as appropriate for your ISP.

8. In the Incoming Mail (POP3, IMAP Or HTTP) Server text box, enter the name of your ISP's incoming mail server.

9. In the Outgoing Mail (SMTP) Server text box, enter the name of your ISP's outgoing mail server.

10. Click the Next button to display the Internet Mail Logon page of the Internet Connection Wizard dialog box (shown in Figure 22.4 with information entered).

FIGURE 22.4
On the Internet Mail Logon page of the Internet Connection Wizard dialog box, specify your account name and password.

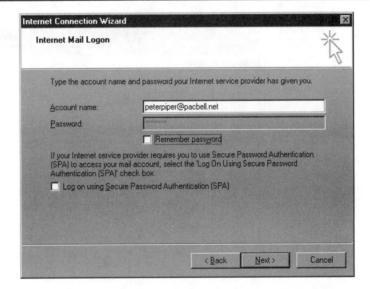

11. Enter your account name in the Account Name text box and your password in the Password text box.

12. Select the Remember Password check box if you think it's wise. (I don't—it saves you time typing your password when you retrieve your mail, but it means that anyone who can access your computer can check your mail, too.)

13. Select the Log On Using Secure Password Authentication (SPA) check box if you need to use SPA. Then click the Next button to display the Congratulations page of the Internet Connection Wizard.

14. Click the Finish button. Outlook Express will launch.

The Outlook Express Screen

Once you've configured Outlook Express, and thereafter when you start it, it displays your Start Page, as shown in Figure 22.5.

FIGURE 22.5

The Start Page provides links to the main features of Outlook Express.

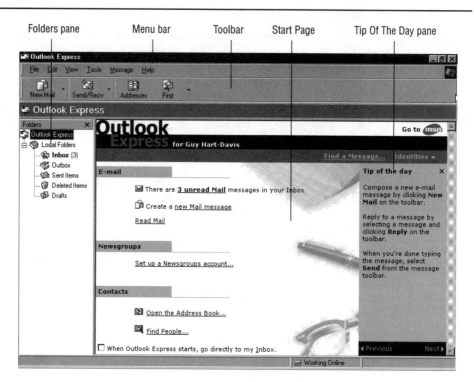

If you have a small monitor, you may want to get rid of the Tip Of The Day pane by clicking the close button in its upper-right corner to give yourself more room.

 TIP If you have a small monitor, you may want to get rid of the Tip Of The Day pane by clicking the close button in its upper-right corner to give yourself more room.

If you prefer to start your Outlook Express day in the Inbox rather than on the Start Page, select the When Outlook Express Starts, Go Directly To My Inbox check box at the bottom of the Start Page. Thereafter, when you start Outlook Express, it will display the Inbox first.

Reading E-Mail Messages

To read e-mail, click the Read Mail link to display your Inbox. Figure 22.6 shows a sparsely populated Inbox.

FIGURE 22.6
The Inbox

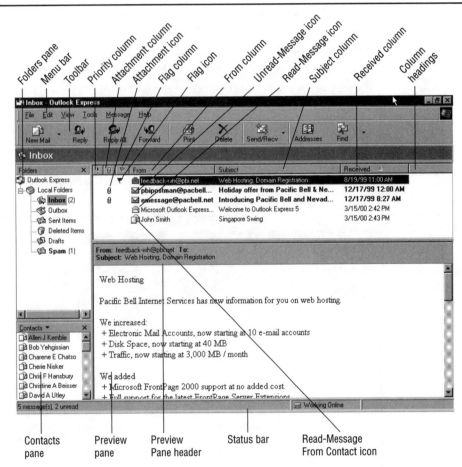

As you can see in the figure, Outlook Express displays icons to indicate information about the message headers:

- The Attachment icon means that the message has one or more files attached to it. (I'll show you how to work with attachments later in this chapter.)
- The Unread-Message icon indicates that a message has not been read.

TIP You can mark a message as unread or read by right-clicking its header and choosing Mark As Unread or Mark As Read, as appropriate, from the context menu.

- The Read-Message icon indicates that a message has been read.

- The Contact icon shows that a message is from one of your contacts. (In the figure, the message from John Smith is marked as a read message from a contact.)

- A flag is a mark you can set on a message to indicate that you need to deal with it. To set or remove a flag, click in the Flag column beside the message's header.

- If a message is marked as high priority, it will display a red exclamation point in the Priority column.

To read a message in the Preview pane, click it in the message headers listing to display it in the Preview pane.

To read a message in a separate window, double-click its message header listing. Outlook Express will display the message in a separate window, as shown in Figure 22.7.

FIGURE 22.7

Instead of reading a message in the Preview pane, you can display it in a separate window if you prefer.

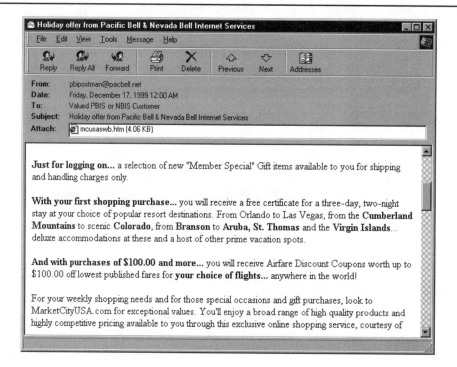

To sort your messages by one of the column headings, click the heading once for an ascending sort (alphabetical order) or twice for a descending sort (reverse-alphabetical order).

To view a subset of your messages, choose View ➤ Current View ➤ Hide Read Messages or View ➤ Current View ➤ Hide Read Or Ignored Messages. To restore the view to all messages, choose View ➤ Current View ➤ Show All Messages.

If you have multiple messages from the same conversation (on the same topic, with the same subject), choose View ➤ Current View ➤ Group Messages By Conversation to group the messages. Issue the command again to ungroup the messages.

To ignore a conversation that's going on, select one of the messages and choose Message ➤ Ignore Conversation.

Sending E-Mail

You can generate e-mail in Outlook Express by creating new messages, replying to messages you've received, or forwarding either messages you've received or messages you've created and sent before.

Composing a New Message

To create a new message:

1. Click the New Mail button on the toolbar to create a new message. Outlook Express will open a message window containing a new message. Figure 22.8 shows a message with recipients, a subject, and text entered.

   - To create a message using Outlook Express's stationery, click the New Mail button's drop-down list button and choose the type of stationery from the drop-down menu.

   - To create a message to a contact, double-click the contact in the Contacts pane, or right-click the contact in the Contacts pane and choose Send E-Mail from the context menu.

2. Enter the e-mail address of the recipient or recipients in the To text box and the names of cc recipients in the Cc text box. Separate multiple addresses with semi-colons. You can either type each address in or choose it from your address book:

   - Click the To button to display the Select Recipients dialog box (see Figure 22.9).

   - In the Type Name Or Select From List list box, select the name and click the To button, the Cc button, or the Bcc button to add the selected name to the appropriate box of message recipients.

   - Add further names to the To, Cc, and Bcc lists as applicable, and then click the OK button to close the Select Recipients dialog box.

FIGURE 22.8

Create your message in the message window.

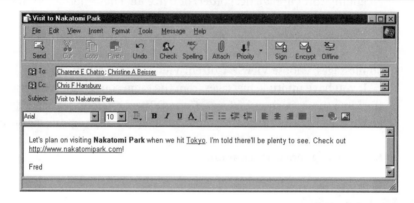

FIGURE 22.9

Use the Select Recipients dialog box to designate the recipients for the message.

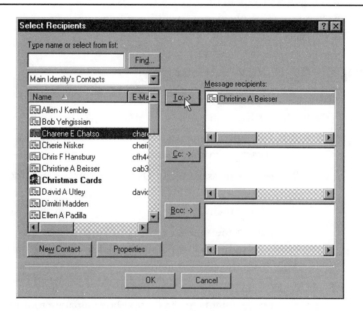

3. Click in the Subject text box and enter the subject line for the message. The more descriptive, informative, and concise the subject line is, the more useful it will be to the recipients of the message—and the more likely they will be to read the message.

4. In the message box, enter the text of the message:

   • You can enter and edit the text using the standard Works features that you've learned in this book (such as cut and paste, and drag and drop) and format the text (if you're sending a formatted message) by using the buttons on the formatting toolbar (see Figure 22.10).

FIGURE 22.10

Use the formatting toolbar to format your messages if necessary.

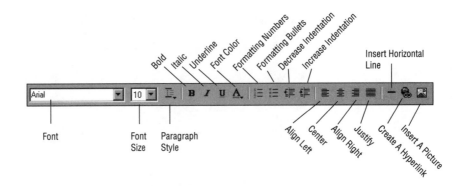

- To insert a horizontal line, click the Insert Horizontal Line button on the toolbar.

- If you type a recognizable hyperlink, Outlook Express will automatically convert it to a hyperlink. To insert a hyperlink manually, select the text to include in the hyperlink and click the Create A Hyperlink button on the toolbar to display the Hyperlink dialog box (shown in Figure 22.11 with a URL entered). Choose the type of hyperlink from the Type drop-down list (for example, http for a regular connection, https for a secure connection), enter the URL in the URL text box, and click the OK button to insert it.

FIGURE 22.11

You can use the Hyperlink dialog box to insert a hyperlink manually.

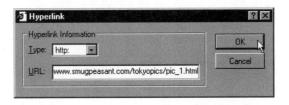

- To insert a picture, click the Insert A Picture button to display the Picture dialog box (shown in Figure 22.12 with a picture chosen and text entered). Enter the path and filename for the picture in the Picture Source text box (use the Browse button and the resulting Picture dialog box if necessary to select the picture). In the Alternate Text text box, enter text to be displayed in case the recipient cannot view the picture. Choose alignment and border thickness options in the Layout group box and horizontal and vertical spacing options in the Spacing group box, then click the OK button to insert the picture in the message.

FIGURE 22.12
Use the Picture dialog box to insert a picture. Be sure to specify alternate text in case the recipient cannot view the picture.

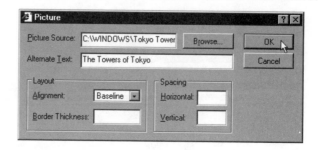

5. You're now ready to send the message. Read through the message quickly to make sure it conveys what you want it to and that you haven't written anything rash or ambiguous. Spell-check the message if necessary. Then click the Send button or choose File ➢ Send to send the message on its way.

Replying to an E-Mail Message

To reply to a message from the Inbox, click the Reply button on the toolbar, or right-click in the message header and choose Reply To Sender from the context menu.

To reply to a message from a message window, click the Reply button on the toolbar in the message window.

If you were not the only recipient of a message, you can use the Reply To All feature to reply quickly to all the recipients of that message (and to cc everyone on the Cc list, if the message has one). From the Inbox, click the Reply All button on the toolbar, or right-click and choose Reply To All from the context menu. From a message window, click the Reply All button on the message window's toolbar.

When you reply to a message, Outlook Express adds RE: to the subject line so that the recipient can easily see that the message is a reply.

Forwarding a Message

You can easily forward a message to someone who did not receive it. To forward a message from the Inbox, click the Forward button on the toolbar or right-click the message header and choose Forward from the context menu.

To forward a message from a message window, click the Forward button on the toolbar in the message window.

When you forward a message, Outlook Express adds FW: to the Subject line so that the recipient can easily see that the message was forwarded.

Sending and Receiving Attachments

In addition to sending and receiving e-mail messages, you can send and receive files as attachments to messages. Attachments are a great way of sharing files and getting information from point A to point B.

Sending Attachments

To send a file as an attachment, start a message as usual (or reply to a message, or forward a message), then click the Attach button on the toolbar to display the Insert Attachment dialog box (see Figure 22.13).

FIGURE 22.13
Use the Insert Attachment dialog box to attach a file to an e-mail message.

Select the file or files to attach, and click the Attach button. Outlook Express will close the Insert Attachment dialog box and display the Attach box on the message (see Figure 22.14) with details of the attachment. You can then complete and send the message as usual.

FIGURE 22.14
*When you've attached
one or more files to a
message, the message
displays the Attach box.*

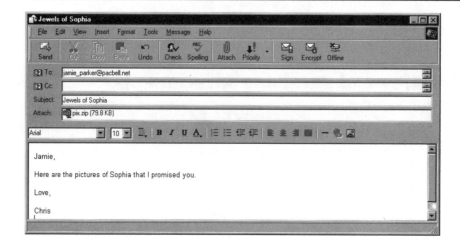

Receiving Attachments

When someone sends you a file with an attachment, the message header in your Inbox
will display an Attachment icon, as you saw earlier in this chapter. If you open the
message in a message window, it will display an attachments box.

To save an attachment:

1. Select the message header.

2. Choose File ➢ Save Attachments to display the Save Attachments dialog box (see
   Figure 22.15).

FIGURE 22.15
*Use the Save
Attachments dialog
box to save the
attachments from an
e-mail message to a
folder of your choosing.*

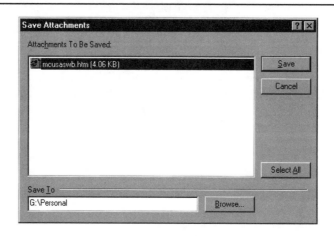

3. For each attachment, specify a destination location in the Save To text box (use the Browse button and the resulting Browse For Folder dialog box if necessary), then click the Save button.

4. Check the detached file with virus-checking software before you open it.

 WARNING *Never* open attachments from anyone you don't know without virus-checking them first. E-mail has become a prime vector of computer viruses and macro viruses, and any attachment could be infected with a virus.

 TIP For extra security, you may want to avoid using the Preview pane, because the act of displaying the message in the Preview pane can run a script that can trigger a virus. (To stop using the Preview pane, choose View ➢ Layout to display the Window Layout Properties dialog box, then clear the Show Preview Pane check box in the Preview Pane area, and click the OK button.) However, because the Preview pane helps you process your e-mail quickly, and because most viruses travel as attachments, most people choose to continue using the Preview pane.

Managing Your E-Mail Messages

To keep your Inbox in order, you'll need to manage your messages carefully, by deleting messages, moving them to folders, and being able to locate messages for reference.

Deleting a Message

To delete a message from the Inbox, select it and click the Delete button on the toolbar or press the Delete key. Doing so moves the message to the Deleted Items folder. To delete everything in the Deleted Items folder, right-click the folder, choose Empty 'Deleted Items' Folder, and click the Yes button in the confirmation message box that appears.

Moving a Message to a Folder

You can move a message to a folder in several ways:

- From the Inbox, click the message header and drag it to the appropriate folder in the Folders Pane.

- From the Inbox, right-click the message and choose Move To Folder from the context menu, or choose Edit ➤ Move To Folder, to display the Move dialog box (see Figure 22.16). Select the folder and click the OK button.

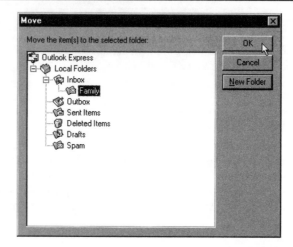

- From a message window, choose File ➤ Move To Folder to display the Move dialog box, then proceed as described in the previous paragraph.

 TIP You can also copy a message to a folder (instead of moving it) by using the Copy To Folder command instead of the Move To Folder command.

Finding a Message

To find a particular message, click the Find A Message link on the Start Page, or choose Edit ➤ Find ➤ Message, to display the Find Message window (shown in Figure 22.17 with a message found). Enter such information as you can muster about the message in the From, To, Subject, and Message text boxes; specify dates in the Received Before and Received After boxes if possible; and select the Message Has Attachment(s) or the Message Is Flagged check box if applicable to narrow the field further.

Then click the Find Now button. The Find Message dialog box will display the messages it finds in a list box at the bottom of the window, as shown in the figure. Double-click a message to open it.

FIGURE 22.17
*Use the Find Message
window to find a
particular message by
specifying information
it contains.*

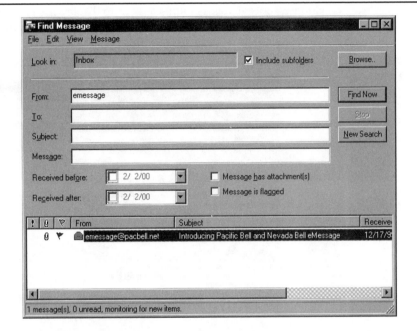

Filtering Your E-mail

Business queries, love letters, spam, messages from your family, and solicitations for mass-mailing software and pornography—these days, you never know exactly what to expect in your Inbox, though most people can count on an increasing number of messages arriving.

To help you manage the mayhem, Outlook Express lets you create rules for filtering e-mail and news. By creating a rule that defines certain conditions, you can take action when a matching message arrives. That action can be anything from moving or copying the message to a particular folder, to forwarding the message automatically to people, to deleting it unread. For example, you could create a rule that deleted any message that contained the word *marketing*.

Better yet, with Outlook Express you can block specific senders, no matter what kind of message they try to send you. Read on.

Creating Rules for Filtering E-mail

Your first priority in filtering should be to filter the e-mail you receive. By filtering e-mail, you can move messages to different folders or even delete them without your ever seeing them.

To create a rule for filtering e-mail:

1. Choose Tools ➢ Message Rules ➢ Mail to display the New Mail Rule dialog box. Figure 22.18 shows the New Mail Rule dialog box with a rule already created.

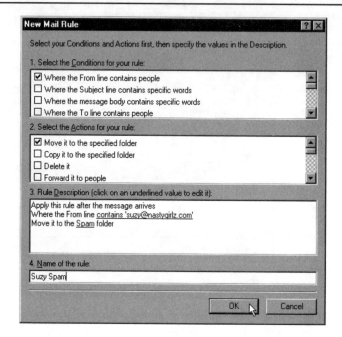

2. In the Select The Conditions For Your Rule list box, select the condition or conditions under which you want the rule to operate. For example, you might choose the Where The From Line Contains People condition in order to take action on messages from a particular e-mail account. (You get to specify which people in a moment.) You might also choose the Where The Subject Line Contains Specific Words condition to filter the subject line for particular words.

3. In the Select The Actions For Your Rule list box, select the action that you want Outlook Express to take when the condition is met. For example, you might choose the Move It To The Specified Folder action to move the message to a particular folder. (Again, you get to specify which folder in a moment.)

4. In the Rule Description list box, Outlook Express will have built the general rule. Now click one of the underlined values to edit it.

   • Continuing the example, you'd click the Contains People link to display the Select People dialog box (see Figure 22.19). Enter a name in the text box and click the Add button to add it to the list box. Or click the Address Book button to display the Rule Addresses dialog box, select the names, move them to the Rule Addresses list box, and click the OK button. The Contains condition in the Rule Description list box will be updated to reflect the names you chose.

FIGURE 22.19
Use the Select People dialog box to specify which people the rule should work on.

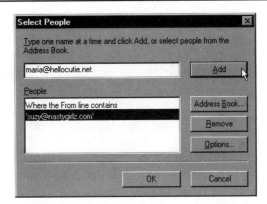

• You'd then click the And link in the Rule Description list box (this link appears when you've created two or more criteria that can be complementary) to display the And/Or dialog box (see Figure 22.20). Select the Messages Match All Of The Criteria option button if you want messages to meet each and every condition for the rule to kick in, or select the Messages Match Any One Of The Criteria option button to have one condition suffice. (In the example, I chose the Messages Match Any One Of The Criteria option button.) Click the OK button to close the And/Or dialog box.

FIGURE 22.20
In the And/Or dialog box, choose whether messages must match all the criteria (an And condition) or any one of the criteria (an Or condition).

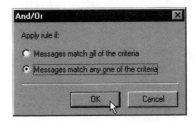

• You'd then click the Contains Specific Words link to display the Type Specific Words dialog box (see Figure 22.21). Type one word at a time into the text box, then click the Add button to add them. Click the OK button to close the Type Specific Words dialog box. The Where The Subject Line Contains condition will be updated to contain the words.

FIGURE 22.21
*In the Type Specific
Words dialog box, enter
the words for which you
want to filter.*

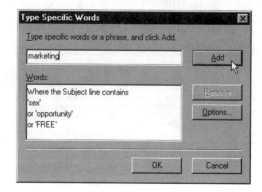

- You'd then click the Specified link to display the Move dialog box. Select the folder in the folder structure as usual (create a new folder if necessary) and click the OK button.

 TIP You can also create a rule that applies if a message does *not* contain the specified information—for example, if a message does not come from a specified sender. Click the Options button in the selection dialog box (the Select People dialog box, the Type Specific Words dialog box, or another selection dialog box) to display the Rule Condition Options dialog box. Choose options as appropriate, and then click the OK button to return to the selection dialog box.

5. In the Name Of The Rule text box, enter a memorable name for the rule.

6. Click the OK button to create the rule. Outlook Express will display the Message Rules dialog box (see Figure 22.22).

7. Click the Apply Now button to display the Apply Mail Rules Now dialog box (see Figure 22.23).

8. In the Select Rules To Apply list box, select the rules you want to apply.

9. By default, the rule will be applied to the folder you were working in when you created it. If necessary, use the Browse button and the resulting Apply To Folder dialog box to designate a different folder, and click the OK button. If the folder has subfolders to which you want to apply the rules, select the Include Subfolders check box.

FIGURE 22.22

Manage your mail rules on the Mail Rules page of the Message Rules dialog box.

FIGURE 22.23

In the Apply Mail Rules Now dialog box, choose which rules to apply to which folder.

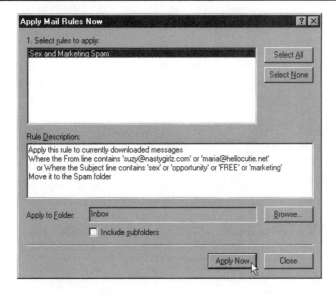

10. Click the Apply Now button to apply the rules you chose. Outlook Express will display a message box telling you that it has applied the rules to the folder.

11. Click the OK button, then click the Close button to close the Apply Mail Rules Now dialog box.

12. If you're using multiple mail rules, use the Move Up and Move Down buttons to arrange the rules in the best order.

13. Click the OK button to close the Message Rules dialog box.

Next, if possible, send yourself a message that will meet the condition. (For example, if you created the rule, you could send yourself a message with *FREE Sex* in the Subject line.) Make sure the filter catches the message. If not, adjust the filter until it works.

Blocking a Sender

To quickly block a sender from the Inbox, choose Message ➢ Block Sender to add the sender of the current message to your blocking list. Outlook Express will display the Outlook Express dialog box shown in Figure 22.24, offering to remove from the current folder all messages from that sender. Click the Yes or No button as appropriate.

FIGURE 22.24
When you block a sender, Outlook Express offers to remove from the current folder all messages sent by that sender.

To unblock a sender that you've blocked:

1. Choose Tools ➢ Message Rules ➢ Blocked Senders List to display the Blocked Senders page of the Message Rules dialog box.

2. Select the sender and click the Remove button. Outlook Express will display a confirmation message box.

3. Click the OK button to close the message box.

4. Click the OK button to close the Message Rules dialog box.

Checking Multiple E-Mail Accounts

To enable you to check multiple e-mail accounts, Outlook Express provides support for *identities*—different personalities, either for the same person or for different people. By using identities, you can maintain separate online personae for your business and personal selves, or for different members of the family. Your Outlook Express identities work for the Works Calendar and the Address Book as well.

Outlook Express starts you off with an identity called Main Identity that you get to use by default. After that, it's up to you to create and use identities as you need them.

Creating an Identity

To create an identity, follow these steps:

1. Choose File ➤ Identities ➤ Add New Identity to display the New Identity dialog box (see Figure 22.25).

FIGURE 22.25
Use the New Identity dialog box to create a new identity.

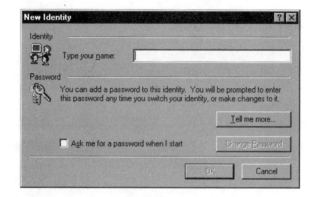

2. In the Type Your Name text box, enter the name for the identity. (This won't necessarily be your name—it might equally well be something like Business or Personal.)

3. If you want to use a password to secure the identity, select the Ask Me For A Password When I Start check box. Outlook Express will display the Enter Password dialog box (see Figure 22.26). Enter the password in both text boxes and then click the OK button.

FIGURE 22.26
Create a password for your new identity in the Enter Password dialog box.

4. Click the OK button to close the New Identity dialog box. Outlook Express will display the Identity Added dialog box (see Figure 22.27), inviting you to switch

to the new identity. Click the Yes button or the No button as appropriate. If you select Yes, you'll then need to set up Internet mail for the new identity.

FIGURE 22.27
*Outlook Express offers
to switch you to the new
identity immediately.*

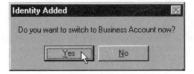

Managing Identities

Here's how to manage your identities:

1. Choose File ➢ Identities ➢ Manage Identities to display the Manage Identities dialog box (see Figure 22.28).

FIGURE 22.28
*Use the Manage
Identities dialog box to
manage your identities.*

2. In the Identity Names list box, select the identity that you want to use as your default identity.

3. Click the Make Default button.

4. In the Start Up Using drop-down list, choose the identity that you want to use by default when you start Outlook Express.

5. Click the Close button to close the Manage Identities dialog box.

TIP To delete an identity, make sure you're currently using another identity, then select the victim in the Identity Names list box and click the Remove button. Then click the Delete button in the Warning dialog box that Outlook Express displays.

Switching Identities

To switch from one identity to another:

1. Close any message windows that you've been working in.

2. Choose File ➢ Switch Identity. Outlook Express will display the Switch Identities dialog box (see Figure 22.29).

FIGURE 22.29
Use the Switch Identities dialog box to switch between your different identities.

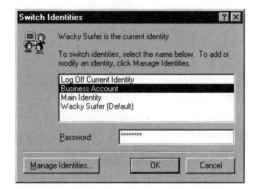

3. In the list box, select the identity you want to switch to.

4. If the identity requires a password, enter it in the Password text box.

5. Click the OK button to switch identity.

Logging an Identity Off

When you've finished working in an identity, choose File ➢ Identities ➢ Logoff *Identity Name* (for example, Logoff Main Identity). Outlook Express will log you off and will close itself.

The next time you (or someone else) go to start Outlook Express, you'll see the Identity Login dialog box (see Figure 22.30). (If you don't log off before exiting Outlook Express, you won't need to log in the next time you start it.)

FIGURE 22.30
When you log an identity off from Outlook Express, the next person to use it will need to log in before launching Outlook Express.

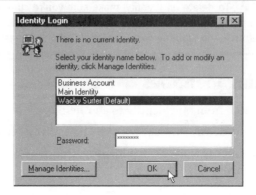

Changing the Columns Displayed in the Inbox

As you've seen earlier in this chapter, the Inbox displays six columns by default: Priority, Attachment, Flag, From, Subject, and Received. For most purposes, these are the most widely useful columns. But you can change the columns as necessary: You can remove existing columns; you can add further columns; and you can change the width of any column.

To change the columns displayed:

1. Right-click a column heading and choose Columns from the context menu, or choose View ➤ Columns, to display the Columns dialog box (see Figure 22.31).

FIGURE 22.31
Use the Columns dialog box to change the columns displayed in the Inbox.

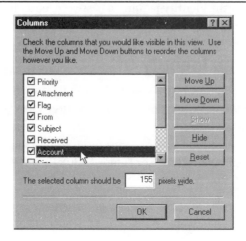

2. In the list box, clear the check box for any column that you don't want to have appear. Select the check box for any column you want to add, and specify a suitable width in the The Selected Column Should Be NNN Pixels Wide text box.

3. To rearrange the order of the columns, select a column and use the Move Up or Move Down button.

4. Click the OK button to close the Columns dialog box.

Customizing the Inbox Layout and the Toolbar

In addition to changing the columns displayed, you can customize the layout of your Inbox, displaying only the elements you want, arranging the Preview pane where you need it, and customizing the toolbar. Proceed as follows:

1. Choose View ➢ Layout to display the Layout page of the Window Layout Properties dialog box (see Figure 22.32).

FIGURE 22.32

Use the Layout page of the Window Layout Properties dialog box to display the elements you want and place the Preview pane in a suitable position.

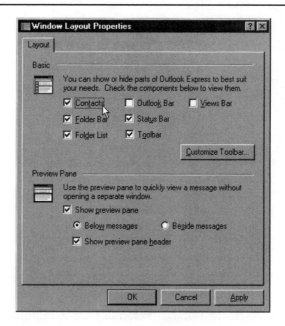

2. In the Basic area, select the check boxes for the components you want to see, and clear the check boxes for the components you want to hide. Most of the items you've seen already, but there are a couple you haven't:

   • The Outlook Bar is a vertical bar that you can display at the left-hand side of the Inbox to provide navigation between the main Outlook Express folders (the Inbox, the Outbox, the Sent Items folder, the Deleted Items folder, and the

Drafts folder). In Outlook itself, which has many more features, the Outlook Bar is a useful navigational tool, but in Outlook Express, it's seldom necessary.

• The Views Bar is a horizontal bar that appears below the toolbar and provides a drop-down list of different views: Show All Messages, Hide Read Messages, or Hide Read Or Ignored Messages. Figure 22.33 shows the Outlook Bar and the Views Bar.

FIGURE 22.33
The Inbox with the Outlook Bar and the Views Bar displayed

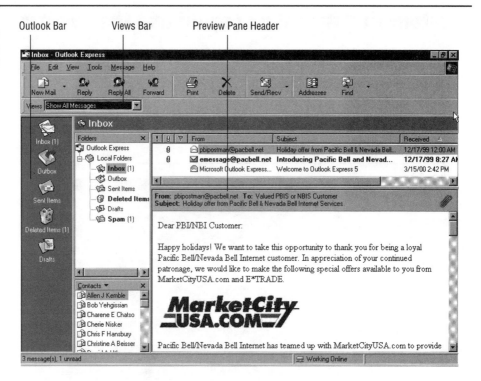

3. To customize the toolbar, click the Customize Toolbar button. In the Customize Toolbar dialog box (see Figure 22.34), customize the toolbar to your liking:

• Use the Add button to copy buttons from the Available Toolbar Buttons list box to the Current Toolbar Buttons list box.

• Use the Remove button to remove buttons from the Current Toolbar Buttons list box.

• Use the Move Up and Move Down buttons to reorder the buttons on the toolbar.

• Choose text options for the toolbar buttons from the Text Options drop-down list and icon options from the Icon Options drop-down list.

• Click the Close button to close the Customize Toolbar dialog box.

FIGURE 22.34

Use the Customize Toolbar dialog box to customize the toolbar so that it contains the buttons you need.

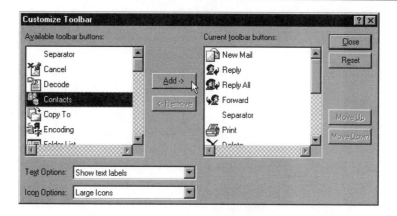

4. In the Preview Pane area, choose options for the Preview pane:

- Clear the Show Preview Pane check box if you don't want to use the Preview pane.

- If you do use the Preview pane, choose the Below Messages option button or the Beside Messages option button to determine its placement.

- Select the Show Preview Pane Header check box if you want to have the Preview Pane Header displayed. (The Preview Pane Header is the gray strip at the top of the Preview pane that shows information about the current message.)

5. Click the OK button to close the Window Layout Properties dialog box and apply your choices.

CHAPTER 23

Reading News with Outlook Express

In this chapter, I'll show you how to use the newsreader features of Outlook Express to read messages posted to Internet newsgroups and to post messages yourself.

I'll assume you've worked through the previous chapter, setting up Outlook Express and creating as many identities as you need. In this chapter, you'll need to do a little more setup, configuring Outlook Express to access the right news server.

What Is News?

News in this context refers to Internet newsgroups, a very loose agglomeration of discussion areas based on the Network News Transport Protocol (NNTP to its friends). A newsgroup consists of the messages (and sometimes attachments) that people post to the list. These messages, often referred to as *posts*, are available to anyone who chooses to take part in the group.

Internet newsgroups encompass most every topic under the sun. In the olden days of the early 1990s, newsgroups were divided up into a relatively formalized informal structure based around a dozen or so hierarchies of newsgroups with names such as alt (alternative topics), biz (business topics), comp (computer topics), and assorted others, with many groups in subgroups under each hierarchy. Nowadays, in concert with the near-anarchy of the Web, newsgroups are often named capriciously, so the best way to find a newsgroup covering topics you're interested in is to search for keywords (or get a recommendation from a friend).

The Dangers of Newsgroups

Before you get involved with Internet newsgroups, there are several things that you should keep in mind. (Forgive me if I get a little serious and moralistic here.)

First, Internet newsgroups are public. In most cases, anyone who can get online can post to them. If you dip into the right newsgroups (or maybe I should make that "the *wrong* newsgroups"), you'll sooner or later run into the full range of online humanity. Some of these are people that you wouldn't want to meet on a dark night. Actually, some of them are people that you'd probably run screaming from if you met them anywhere, even if you had your pair of trained Rottweilers and an Uzi for company and the meeting took place in broad daylight.

Some of these people post things that most people would much rather they didn't. Sooner or later (probably sooner), you're likely to run into such posts.

TIP In addition to public, free-for-all newsgroups, there are also members-only newsgroups that you may be lucky enough to be invited to join. If so, behave yourself.

Second, much of the information you find in newsgroups is incomplete, inaccurate, wrong, lies, disinformation, or even advertising. I doubt you believe everything you read on the Web; you'd be wise to apply an even greater standard of disbelief to newsgroups.

Third, newsgroups tend to get archived. (For an example of an archive, point your Web browser at Deja.com, `http://www.deja.com`, where you can search through a truly frightening number of postings recent and ancient.) This archiving means that every throwaway posting has a good chance of remaining available more or less forever—or at least long enough to severely embarrass the poster. Before you dash off an inflammatory post, remember that it may stick around to haunt you for years.

Fourth, spammers use *bots* (robot programs) to harvest e-mail addresses from newsgroups, both for direct use and for selling to other people. (Perhaps you've already received spam offering you *2 million valid e-mail addresses for only $29.99*? Right— many of those e-mail addresses will have been harvested from newsgroups.) This harvesting means that if you expose your real e-mail address, you're likely to get spam almost immediately from the current crop of spammers.

Many people who post to newsgroups change their e-mail addresses in a way that will defeat bots but enable humans to establish the real e-mail address with a minimal application of sentience. For example, if your e-mail address is `peterpiper@pacbell.net`, you might post with an address of `peterpiper@nospam.pacbell.net` and add a note saying "remove `nospam` from the address when replying." This is enough to defeat most bots, though `nospam` is getting long in the tooth at this writing—so you might want to try a custom addition to your address.

Fifth, many of the more specialized newsgroups tend to attract an expert audience that doesn't tolerate off-topic or ill-considered questions well. Before posting, be sure to read the frequently asked questions list (the FAQ) for the newsgroup, and check through its archives to make sure that the topic of your posting a) is on topic for the newsgroup, and b) hasn't been answered five times already in the last three months.

Still raring to get to those newsgroups? Okay, read on.

Setting Up Outlook Express to Read Newsgroups

To get Outlook Express set up to read newsgroups, follow these steps:

1. Click the Set Up A Newsgroups Account link from your Outlook Express Start Page. Outlook Express will display the Your Name panel of the Internet Connection Wizard. Figure 23.1 shows this panel with a name already entered.

 NOTE If Outlook Express detects an existing news account, it will display a dialog box asking whether you want to create a new Internet news account or use an existing account. The steps shown here apply to creating a new account.

FIGURE 23.1

Enter the name you'll use for newsgroups on the Your Name page of the Internet Connection Wizard.

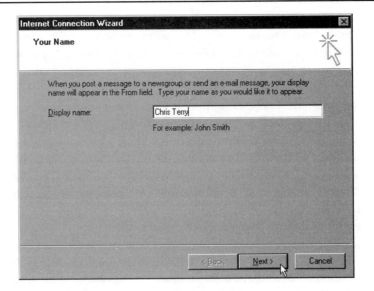

2. Enter the name you want to use for your news messages. Depending on whether you'll be posting personally or professionally, you may want to use a pseudonym, at least for some of your identities.

3. Click the Next button. Outlook Express will display the Internet News E-mail Address page of the Internet Connection Wizard.

4. Outlook Express will suggest this identity's current e-mail address in the E-mail Address text box. You may well want to use a different address to throw off spammers, as discussed in the previous section. If so, enter it now.

5. Click the Next button to display the Internet News Server Name page of the Internet Connection Wizard (shown in Figure 23.2 with information already entered).

FIGURE 23.2

Enter the name of your Internet news server on the Internet News Server Name page of the Internet Connection Wizard.

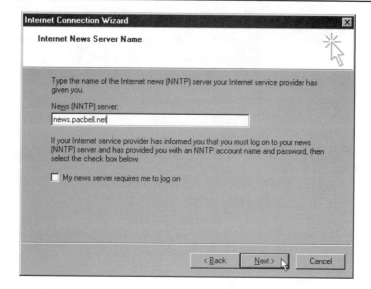

6. Enter the name of your news server in the News (NNTP) Server text box.

7. If you need to log on to the news server, select the My News Server Requires Me To Log On check box.

8. Click the Next button. If you didn't select the check box in the previous step, you'll see the Congratulations page of the Internet Connection Wizard. Click the Finish button.

9. If you did select the check box, you'll see the Internet News Server Logon page of the Internet Connection Wizard. Enter your account name and password. Select the Remember Password check box if you think it's wise. (I don't.) Select the Log On Using Secure Password Authentication (SPA) check box if you need to use SPA. Then click the Next button to display the Congratulations page of the Internet Connection Wizard, and click the Finish button.

Outlook Express will return you to your Start Page, which will now have links for Create A New News Message, Read News, and Subscribe To Newsgroups. An item for the news server you added will appear in the Folders pane (see Figure 23.3).

FIGURE 23.3
Your Start Page will now have links for news, and the Folders pane will contain an entry for the news server you added.

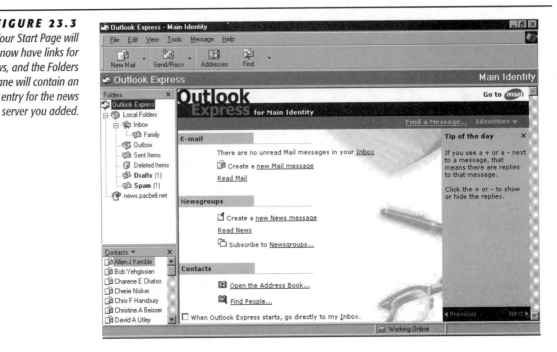

Subscribing to Newsgroups

Now subscribe to one or more newsgroups as follows:

1. Click the Subscribe To Newsgroups link on your Start Page. The first time you do this for any news server, Outlook Express will display the Downloading Newsgroups dialog box (see Figure 23.4).

FIGURE 23.4
The first time you access a news server, Outlook Express downloads the list of newsgroups the server offers.

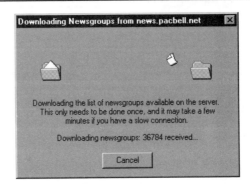

NOTE Different ISPs offer different selections of newsgroups: Some brave ISPs offer as many newsgroups as they can find (usually a figure north of 40,000), whereas others provide only the newsgroups that they think their customers want (or should want).

2. Depending on the speed of your Internet connection, it may take several minutes to download the list. Once it's finished, you'll see the Newsgroup Subscriptions dialog box (see Figure 23.5).

FIGURE 23.5
Subscribe to newsgroups in the Newsgroup Subscriptions dialog box.

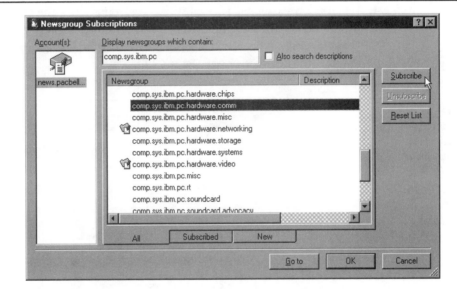

3. In the list box, select a newsgroup that you want to subscribe to, and click the Subscribe button to subscribe:

- The Newsgroup Subscriptions dialog box has three pages: All, Subscribed, and New. Typically, you'll want to start on the All page, so that you can access all the newsgroups. Once you've subscribed to the newsgroups you're interested in, use the Subscribed page to access them quickly, and use the New page to check out new newsgroups from time to time.

- To filter the thousands of newsgroups down to a manageable number, enter search text in the Display Newsgroups Which Contain text box. For example, if you're interested in PC-compatible computer systems, you could enter comp.sys.ibm.pc to display the set of newsgroups that contain that string of text, as shown in the figure.

- Select the Also Search Descriptions check box if you want to search the newsgroup descriptions for the terms in the Display Newsgroups Which

Contain text box. (Many of the newsgroups lack descriptions, however, so this step may not get you far.)

- Outlook Express places an icon to the left of newsgroups you're subscribed to, as you can see with the comp.sys.ibm.pc.hardware.networking and comp.sys.ibm.pc.hardware.video newsgroups in the figure.

- To unsubscribe from a newsgroup you're subscribed to, select the newsgroup and click the Unsubscribe button.

- To download the latest newsgroups, click the Reset List button. You'll see the Downloading Newsgroups dialog box again.

4. When you've assembled your list of newsgroups, click the OK button to close the Newsgroup Subscriptions dialog box. Outlook Express will return you to your Start Page, where the Folders pane will list the newsgroups you subscribed to under the news server (see Figure 23.6).

FIGURE 23.6
Outlook Express displays the newsgroups you've subscribed to in the Folders pane.

Reading Newsgroup Messages

To read the messages in a newsgroup you've subscribed to, double-click the newsgroup in the Folders pane to display it. Outlook Express will download the first batch of headers for the newsgroup—up to 300, at the default setting—and will display them in the header pane.

Click a message to display it in the Preview pane, or double-click a message to display it in a separate window. Figure 23.7 shows both possibilities.

FIGURE 23.7

As with e-mail, you can read newsgroups in the Preview pane or in a separate window.

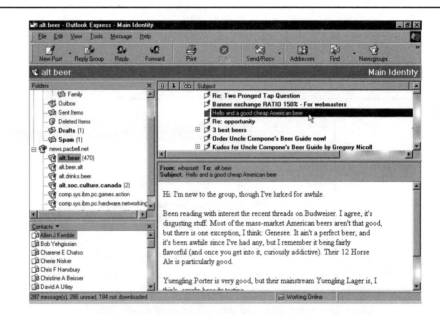

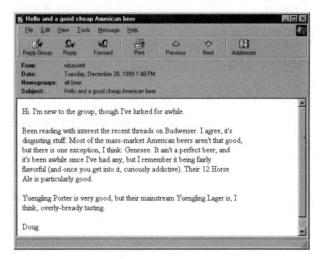

Where posters have replied to a message using the same Subject line, the messages are *threaded*—linked together in a sequence—as you see in Figure 23.8. You can expand a collapsed thread by clicking the + sign next to it, and collapse an expanded thread by clicking its – sign. Each generation of a threaded message is indented more than the previous generations.

FIGURE 23.8

Threaded messages

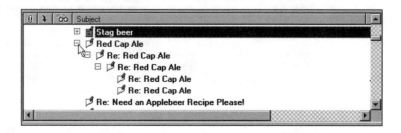

The status bar shows you the current status of your subscription to the newsgroup: how many messages there are in the newsgroup, how many you've read, and how many more you haven't downloaded yet. For example, the status bar in Figure 23.7 displays *287 message(s), 286 unread, 184 not downloaded.*

To download message headers you haven't downloaded yet, choose Tools ➢ Get Next 300 Headers.

To display another newsgroup, double-click it in the Folders pane.

Posting to a Newsgroup

You can post to a newsgroup either by creating a new post or by replying to a post:

- Click the New Post button on the toolbar to start a new post. Don't use stationery for a post to an Internet newsgroup, because chances are that many people won't be able to see it—at best, they'll have to download it as an attached graphic, which improves nobody's temper. Outlook Express will start a new post to the newsgroup, as shown in Figure 23.9.

- To reply to the newsgroup, click the Reply Group button on the toolbar. Outlook Express will create a reply message to the group, quoting the text of the original post (see Figure 23.10). Reduce this text to the minimum needed for context, because surplus quoted text is a killer in highly trafficked newsgroups.

FIGURE 23.9
Creating a new post to the alt.beer *newsgroup*

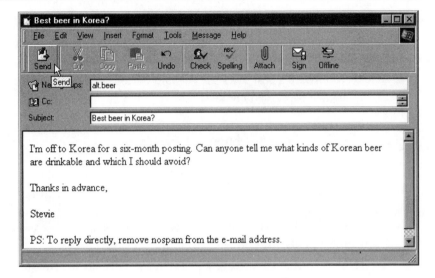

FIGURE 23.10
Creating a reply to a posting in the alt.beer *newsgroup*

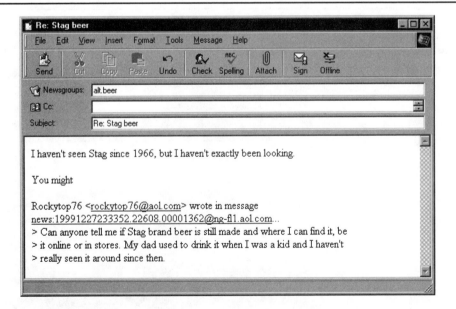

Once you've written your post, set it aside for ten minutes. Then read it carefully to make sure its meaning is clear, that there's nothing offensive in it, and that you're not about to annoy people by WRITING IN ALL CAPITALS (doing so is seen as SHOUTING). Make changes as necessary, then click the Send button to send it.

You may also want to reply only to the author of the post (particularly if you don't want to broadcast your response to the post) or to forward the post to someone else:

- To reply only to the author of the post, click the Reply button on the toolbar. Outlook will create a regular reply for you, as if you were replying to an e-mail message.

- To forward a post, click the Forward button on the toolbar. Outlook will create a regular forwarded message.

Creating Rules for Filtering News

In the previous chapter, you learned how you can filter e-mail to perform preordained maneuvers on messages that match certain criteria. As you'd guess, you can filter news messages as well.

Here's the brief version of what to do (for more specifics, look at the section titled "Creating Rules for Filtering E-mail" in the previous chapter):

1. Choose Tools ➤ Message Rules ➤ News to display the New News Rule dialog box (see Figure 23.11).

FIGURE 23.11
Use the New News Rule dialog box to create rules for handling news.

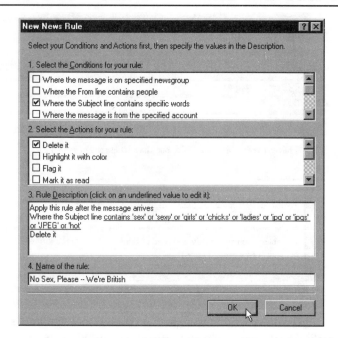

2. In the Select The Conditions For Your Rule list box, select the conditions to apply to the messages.

3. In the Select The Actions For Your Rule list box, select the actions to take when the conditions are met.

4. In the Rule Description list box, click the links to edit them as appropriate.

5. In the Name Of The Rule text box, enter a memorable name for the rule.

6. Click the OK button to close the New News Rule dialog box. Outlook Express will display the Message Rules dialog box.

7. Click the Apply Now button to display the Apply News Rules Now dialog box.

8. Select the rule in the Select Rules To Apply list box.

9. Use the Browse button and the resulting Apply To Folder dialog box to apply the rule to a different newsgroup if necessary.

10. Click the Apply Now button to apply the rule. Outlook Express will display a message box telling you when the application is complete.

11. Click the OK button to close the message box.

12. Click the Close button to close the Apply News Rules Now dialog box.

13. Click the OK button to close the Message Rules dialog box.

Creating Web Pages with Word

Over the last few years, the surge in popularity of the World Wide Web, and of internal corporate webs or *intranets*, has left many people wishing for an easy way to create Web pages from inside their word processor. Word 2000 not only provides those capabilities, and a wizard for building a complete Web site of your own, but also enables you to open Web pages (on the Web or on an intranet) in Word, alter them, and (if you have the necessary rights) save the changes to the page on the intranet site or Web site.

In this chapter, I'll show you how to use Word to create and work with Web pages. In the next chapter, I'll show you the Web-publishing features that Home Publishing offers.

At the risk of stating the obvious, to use the features described in this chapter, you need to have an Internet connection, a network connection, or both. Also, you need to have Internet Explorer installed to make the most of Office's Web features, because Word integrates with Internet Explorer for viewing Web pages.

 NOTE For you to use Word's Web features successfully on a Web server, the server in question needs to be running the Office Server Extensions. Consult your network administrator, Webmaster, or Internet service provider (as appropriate) to check that the server in question is running the extensions.

What Is a Web Page?

Essentially, a Web page is a document, stored on a Web server, that you can access using a browser such as Microsoft's Internet Explorer, Netscape's Navigator, or Opera Software's Opera. The Web server can be either on an intranet or on the World Wide Web. You can also choose to store Web pages on your local hard drive, but unless you are using a Web server tool such as Microsoft's Personal Web Server (for Windows 95, Windows 98, Windows NT Workstation, and Windows 2000 Professional) or Internet Information Server (for Windows NT Server or Windows 2000 Server), you don't gain much benefit from doing so.

Web pages are formatted using the Hypertext Markup Language, or HTML, which consists of large numbers of ugly codes within angle brackets. Previous versions of Word were able to convert Word documents to HTML-formatted Web pages, but at the cost of much of the extra information that Word stores within a document—for example, information describing styles, or bookmarks. Word 2000 improves greatly upon this by using another markup language, Extensible Markup Language (XML), to retain this information and indicate which part of a document is which. You can now save all the contents of a Word document as a Web page to a Web server. When others open that Web page in Word, they will see the document as you created it. If they want, they can save the Web page as a Word document, and it will have lost none of its information.

HTML and XML codes are complex and confusing until you've spent a considerable amount of time working with them. The best part of the Office Web features is that Word handles the translation of documents to Web pages seamlessly. If you don't want to see the HTML and XML codes, you don't need to. On the other hand, if you do want to examine or edit the HTML and XML codes, you can use the Microsoft Script Editor application that comes with Word to view the code behind the Web page and adjust it.

What Is a Web Site?

A Web site is a collection of linked Web pages stored on a Web server. (Actually, that's not exactly true: A site *can* be just one page, but there's little point in having so simple a site.)

Each Web site includes a *home page*, the page that appears when you enter the address of the site in your Web browser. For example, if you enter `http://www.sybex.com` in Internet Explorer, it will display the home page of the Sybex Web site. From the home page, links lead to other pages, from which further links lead to yet more pages.

Many sites use *frames*, separate areas of the page that can either display a separate set of information or remain more or less constant. Many sites use a frame at the top of the page or at the left side of the page to contain links, so that they're always easy to find.

Web Folders and the Web Toolbar

Most of Word's Web tools work in the background, so you see the effects of their work rather than the tools themselves. Two tools that you will see are the Web Folders feature and the Web toolbar. I'll discuss these briefly in this section. After that, you'll put the Web Folders feature into action later in the chapter, opening documents from and saving documents to Web servers. The Web toolbar you can explore for yourself.

Web Folders, as its name suggests, is a collection of the Web folders that you set up to use with the Office applications. Web Folders is the means by which Office enables you to work with files directly on a Web server: You can create a file and save it to a Web server; you can view a file on a Web server; and you can open and edit a file on a Web server. Beyond this, and more obviously, Web Folders provides an easy way to keep track of all the Web folders you work with.

Word's Web toolbar (shown undocked in Figure 24.1) provides a means for accessing Web pages from Word. For browsing Web pages, Word relies largely on Internet

Explorer, so many of the actions you take on the Web toolbar end up displaying Internet Explorer rather than opening the Web page in question in Word.

To display the Web toolbar, right-click the menu bar or any displayed toolbar and choose Web from the context menu.

FIGURE 24.1

Use the Web toolbar for browsing intranets and the Web.

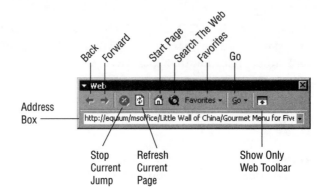

If you've used Internet Explorer (discussed in Chapter 21), you'll find that Word's Web-browsing features look very familiar indeed. Here's what the buttons on the Web toolbar do:

- Back moves to the previous page you were on.

- Forward moves forward again to the page you were on before you clicked the Back button.

- Stop Current Jump stops Word from pursuing a jump that's in progress.

- Refresh Current Page makes Word reload the current page. You may want to do this if part of the page fails to transfer properly or if you've had the page open for a while and you suspect it may have been updated in the interim.

- Start Page displays Internet Explorer, starting it if it was not already running, and jumps to your *Start Page* (the Web location your Web browser heads to when you start it; also known as your *home page*).

- Search The Web displays your chosen Web search tool in Internet Explorer.

- Favorites displays the Favorites menu. (See Chapter 21 for a full discussion of Favorites.)

- Go displays a menu of actions and jumps you can make from the current page:

  Open Displays the Open Internet Address dialog box, where you can enter a Web address to go to or click the Browse button to open a file or an address by using the Browse dialog box. Select the Open In New Window check box in the Open Internet Address dialog box if you want to open the page in a new window rather than using the same window and leaving the current page.

  Back/Forward Move you back and forward through the series of pages you've visited.

  Start Page Takes you to your Start Page in Internet Explorer.

  Search The Web Displays the MSN Search site in Internet Explorer.

  Set Start Page Offers to set your Start Page to the page currently displayed. Click the Yes button to accept the offer.

  Set Search Page Offers to set your search page to the page currently displayed. Again, click the Yes button to accept.

  The bottom of the Go menu provides a list of jumps you can take from the current page.

- Show Only Web Toolbar toggles on and off the display of all displayed toolbars other than the Web toolbar. This is good for quickly freeing up screen real estate so that you can better view Web pages—and, when you need them again, for restoring the toolbars you were using before.

- Address Box is where you can enter an address to go to in Internet Explorer or choose an address from the drop-down list of addresses you've previously visited.

Opening a Document on a Web or Intranet

To open a document on an intranet or on a Web server:

1. Click the Open button on the Standard toolbar, or choose File ➢ Open, to display the Open dialog box.

2. Navigate to the folder that contains the document:

   - For a local folder, navigate to it by using the Look In drop-down list and Look In list box as usual.

   - For an existing Web folder, click the Web Folders button in the Places panel at the left-hand side of the Open dialog box to display your list of Web folders. (Alternatively, you can choose Web Folders from the Look In drop-down list.) Double-click the folder in the Look In list box to open it.

   - To create a new Web folder and open a document from it, enter the path to the folder in the File Name text box, then click the Open button. Word will display the contents of the folder and will add the location to your Web

Folders list. Double-click the folder in the Look In list box to open it. The first time you connect to a Web server, you may need to enter your username and password in the Enter Network Password dialog box (see Figure 24.2). If you want Word to remember the password for you, select the Save This Password In Your Password List check box. Be warned that saving the password means that anybody logged on to the computer in your name will now be able to access this Web server as you.

FIGURE 24.2
In the Enter Network Password dialog box, enter your username and password. Select the Save This Password In Your Password List check box if you want Word to remember the password for you.

3. Select the document you want to open.

TIP When you're opening a document over a slow connection, such as a dial-up connection to the Web, use List view in the Open dialog box rather than Details view, Properties view, or Preview. List view needs to retrieve only the names of the documents in the folder, making it quicker than Details view, Properties view, and Preview, which all need to retrieve information about the current document selected as well. (Over a local area network, such as when you're connecting to an intranet, speed is much less of a problem.)

4. Click the Open button to open the document.

Creating a Web Site with the Web Page Wizard

If you want to create a Web site of your own, the Web Page Wizard is the place to start. The Web Page Wizard takes you through the process of creating a site, letting you specify the site and its title, which pages you want in it, how the pages should be linked to each other, and what the theme of the pages should be. Once you've made your choices and the wizard has created your site, you enter your own text and graphics in the pages. You can also add further pages and links to the site as needed.

To create a Web site with the Web Page Wizard:

1. Choose File ➢ New ➢ More Word Templates to display the New dialog box.

2. Click the Web Pages tab to display the Web Pages page at the front of the dialog box.

3. Click the Web Page Wizard icon, then click the OK button. Word will start the Web Page Wizard and display the first Web Page Wizard dialog box.

 TIP While specifying the details for your Web site in the wizard, you can move backward and forward by clicking the Back and Next buttons, or by clicking in the location squares in the location panel on the left of the wizard's dialog box. You can also click the Finish button at any time to accept the wizard's default settings for the Web site; usually, though, you'll do best to make choices for each of the options that the wizard offers.

---

4. Click the Next button to get things started. Word will display the Title And Location page of the Web Page Wizard (shown in Figure 24.3 with information entered).

FIGURE 24.3
On the Title And Location page of the Web Page Wizard, enter a title for your Web site and select a location in which to store the files.

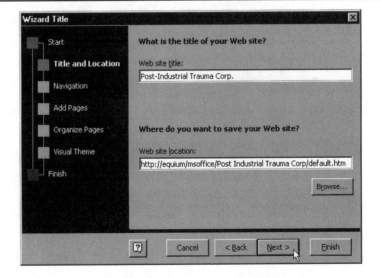

5. Enter the title for the Web site in the Web Site Title text box. The wizard will copy the title into the subfolder part of the Web Site Location text box below. For example, if you enter **Great American Industrials** in the Web Site Title text box when c:\My Documents is in the Web Site Location text box, the wizard will read c:\My Documents\Great American Industrials\Default.htm in the Web Site Location text box. If you want to save the Web site directly to a server, as in the example in the figure, you'll need to modify the location accordingly.

6. Enter the location for the Web site in the Web Site Location text box:

- You can type the location in the Web Site Location text box. This is easy if you need to make a minor adjustment to the default location that Word has suggested.

- Or you can click the Browse button to display the Save As dialog box. Select the folder as usual; for example, you might click the Web Folders button to access a Web folder. Then enter the filename in the File Name text box and click the Save button. Word will enter the location you chose in the Web Site Location text box.

7. Click the Next button to proceed to the Navigation page of the Web Page Wizard (see Figure 24.4).

FIGURE 24.4
Choose a means of navigation for your site at the Navigation page of the Web Page Wizard.

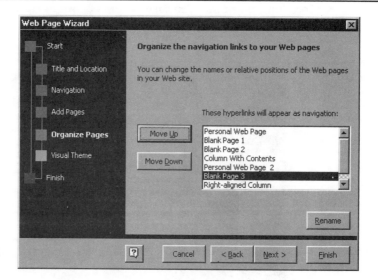

8. Select the type of navigation you want for the Web site. Your choices are:

Vertical Frame   An area at the left of the page will contain links for navigation.

Horizontal Frame   An area at the top of the page will contain links for navigation.

Separate Page   Each link will lead to a separate page that has links for navigating forward and backward. This design is good for browsers that do not support frames (separate areas of the page), but it means that the user will have to do more clicking to navigate your Web site. (Most modern browsers, such as Internet Explorer and Navigator, support frames.)

9. Click the Next button to proceed to the Add Pages page of the Web Page Wizard (see Figure 24.5).

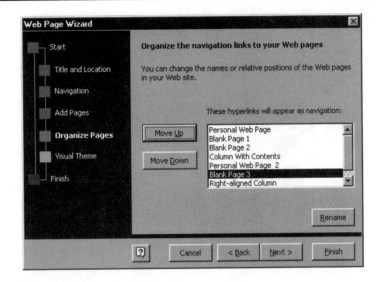

FIGURE 24.5
On the Add Pages page of the Web Page Wizard, select the pages you want to have in your Web site.

10. Choose the pages you want to have in your Web site by adding blank pages, adding pages based on Word's Web page templates, and adding existing files to the list shown in the Current Pages In Web Site list box:

- Click the Add New Blank Page button to add another blank page to the list. You get to rename these pages later.

- Click the Add Template Page button to display the Web Page Templates dialog box (see Figure 24.6). Select the type of page from the list box. Word displays the type of page you choose in the document behind the Web Page Templates dialog box, so that you can get a preview of it. Click the OK button to add a page based on the template to your Web site. The page will appear in the list under its template name; for example, if you choose Column With Contents in the Web Page Templates dialog box, the page will appear as Column With Contents in the Current Pages In Web Site list box.

- Click the Add Existing File button to display the Open dialog box. Select a file in the usual way and click the Open button to add it to the Current Pages In Web Site list box.

- To remove a page from the Web site, select it in the Current Pages In Web Site list box and click the Remove Page button.

11. Click the Next button to move to the Organize Pages page of the wizard (see Figure 24.7).

FIGURE 24.6
In the Web Page Templates dialog box, select the template on which to base the page you're adding to your Web site.

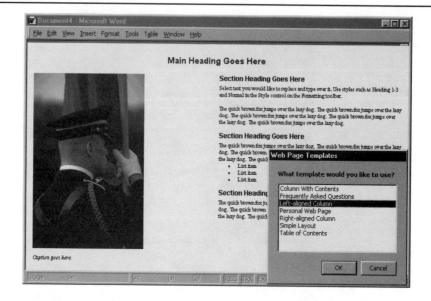

FIGURE 24.7
Use the Organize Pages page of the Web Page Wizard to get your pages into order.

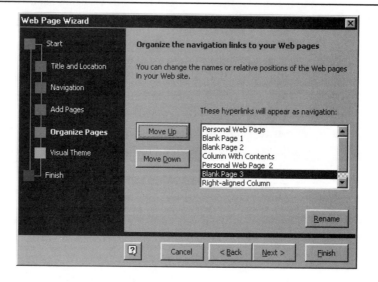

12. Change the order of the pages in the Web site by selecting a page that you want to move and then using the Move Up or Move Down button to move it to where you want it to be.

13. Assign a suitable name to each new page by selecting it in the These Hyperlinks Will Appear As Navigation list box, clicking the Rename button, entering a name in the Rename Hyperlink dialog box (see Figure 24.8), and clicking the OK button. Keep these names relatively short (say, a few words) and as descriptive as possible, because they will appear as navigation links in the Web pages. If they're too long, the navigation frames will be awkwardly big; if they're too short and cryptic, people will have a hard time navigating your site.

FIGURE 24.8

Use the Rename Hyperlink dialog box to assign names to each of the pages in your Web site.

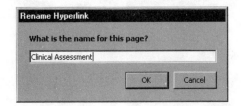

14. Click the Next button to move to the Visual Theme page of the wizard.

15. Select the visual theme you want to have for the Web site. To use a theme, select the Add A Visual Theme option button and click the Browse Themes button to display the Themes dialog box. Select the theme you want, make choices for the theme (as discussed in "Using Themes" in Chapter 6), and click the OK button. (If you don't want to use a theme, select the No Visual Theme option button.)

16. Click the Finish button to have the wizard create your site. (You can also click the Next button to display the Finish page of the wizard, and then click the Finish button from there, but there's no point.)

    The wizard will now create the site you specified. Figure 24.9 shows an example of a site created by the wizard. You'll see that the home page is saved under the name default.htm, Microsoft's name for the home page on a site.

17. Add text to the placeholders in the page by clicking each placeholder and then typing in your text. For example, to add a heading to the Personal Home Page, click in the Insert Heading placeholder and enter the text you want. Repeat for other heading placeholders in the page, such as any Subheading placeholders.

18. Replace any sample text with suitable text of your own.

19. Edit the page to suit your needs: Add, cut, and edit the text as necessary. Use the hyperlinks to move quickly to a linked part of the page.

20. Save the page when you've finished.

FIGURE 24.9
A site created by the wizard. You can now customize the contents of each page by replacing the default text and graphics with your own text and graphics.

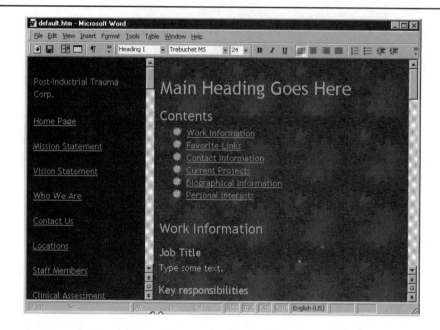

Creating Web Pages

To add to your Web site, or to add to another site, you can create pages of your own. Word provides two ways of doing so: first, by creating a new document based on one of Word's Web templates; and second, by saving an existing Word document as a Web page. In this section, I'll discuss each method in turn.

Which method you choose will typically depend on the type of Web site you work with and what your day-to-day work entails. When you create Web pages for your Web site, it will probably make most sense to start with one of the Web templates. When you are creating a paper document—a report, say, that will later be converted to a Web page and posted to a Web site, you'll do better to create it as a Word document.

Using Web Templates

To start a Web page by using a Web template, select File ➢ New and choose one of the templates on the Web Pages page of the New dialog box. Word offers such templates as Column With Contents, Frequently Asked Questions, Left-Aligned Column, Right-Aligned Column, and Personal Web Page (these are the same pages that the Web Page Wizard offers). You can download additional Web templates from the Microsoft Web site, http://www.microsoft.com.

Enter your text and pictures in the Web page, replacing the default placeholder text and graphics that the templates offer. Then save the Web page as follows:

1. Choose File ➢ Save or File ➢ Save As Web Page to display the Save As dialog box (shown in Figure 24.10 with information entered in it). You'll notice that this Save As dialog box is a little different from the regular Save As dialog box that we've been using so far in the book: There is an item named Page Title and a Change button below the main list box. You'll also notice that the Save As Type drop-down list at the bottom of the Save As dialog box shows Web Page rather than Word Document. The page title is the text that appears in the title bar of a browser that visits the page. The Web templates supply default text for the page title; you might want to change it.

FIGURE 24.10
Word uses a slightly different Save As dialog box for saving Web pages. Note the Page Title label and the Change button below the main list box.

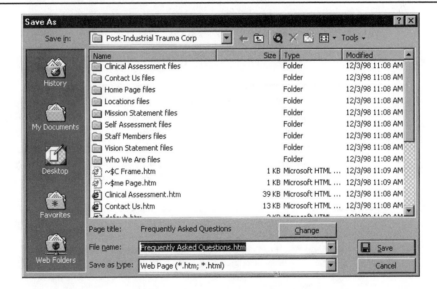

2. Navigate to the folder in which to store the Web page.

3. Enter the name for the file in the File Name text box.

4. To set a different title for the page, click the Change button to the right of the Page Title item. In the Set Page Title dialog box, enter the title you want for the page, then click the OK button.

5. Click the Save button to save the document as a Web page.

Creating a Web Page from a Word Document

Instead of using one of Word's Web templates, you can save a "regular" Word document as a Web page. This is particularly useful for documents created as paper documents that you now need to make available on your intranet or on the Web.

To save a Word document as a Web page, choose File ➤ Save As Web Page, then follow the procedure described in steps 2 through 5 of the previous section.

 NOTE If the document has previously been saved as a Word document, the title for the page will be set to the document's name; otherwise, it will be blank.

This technique works well for short documents, but longer documents inevitably produce uncomfortably long Web pages. Often, you'll want to split the document up into several (or many) Web pages, adding hyperlinks (as described in the next section) to link them.

 WARNING When saving a regular Word document as a Web page, you need to be aware that some Word elements do not translate properly to HTML format and may look different (or like the result of a bizarre formatting accident) when viewed in a Web browser. These include complex tables, bulleted and numbered lists, and graphics. If you need to include these items in a Web page, you'll probably do best to start with one of Word's Web page templates, which will help you avoid adding items that will not work effectively in a Web page.

Specifying Alternative Text for a Text Box

If you use a text box to position a graphical element in a document and then convert that document to a Web page, it's a good idea to specify alternative text to be displayed while the Web browser is loading the picture or in place of the picture if the picture is missing (or if users have turned off the display of pictures in their Web browsers).

To specify alternative text, right-click the border of the text box and choose Format Text Box from the context menu to display the Format Text Box dialog box. Click the Web tab to display the Web page, enter the text in the Alternative Text text box, and click the OK button.

Creating Hyperlinks

A *hyperlink*, often called simply a *link*, is a jump to another location. This location can be part of a Web page, part of an Office file (for example, part of a spreadsheet, or of another Word document, or even of the same Word document), an entire Office file (for example, a PowerPoint presentation), or a Web page on your computer, on a local intranet, or on the World Wide Web. You can mix and match these different types of hyperlinks to suit you.

You can create a hyperlink in any of four ways, as you'll see in the following sections.

Inserting a Hyperlink Manually

To insert a hyperlink:

1. Enter the text or insert the graphical object that you want to have displayed for the hyperlink.

2. Select that text or graphical object.

3. Click the Insert Hyperlink button on the Standard toolbar, or choose Insert ➢ Hyperlink, to display the Insert Hyperlink dialog box (shown in Figure 24.11 with a hyperlink under construction).

FIGURE 24.11
In the Insert Hyperlink dialog box, specify the details for the hyperlink.

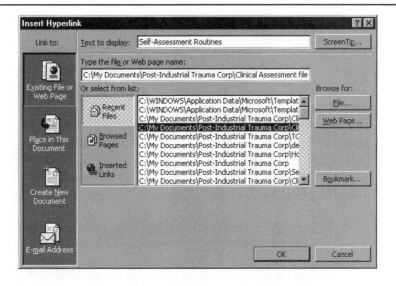

4. If you chose text, make sure that the Text To Display text box shows the correct text.

5. To have a ScreenTip appear when the user moves the mouse pointer over the hyperlink, click the ScreenTip button to display the Set Hyperlink ScreenTip dialog box. Enter the text for the ScreenTip, then click the OK button.

6. Enter the information for the hyperlink in the Type The File Or Web Page Name text box in one of the following ways:

• You can simply type in the URL or the path and the file.

• You can use the Or Select From List list box to enter the name of a file you've recently used, a page you've recently browsed, or a link you've recently inserted. Click the Recent Files, Browsed Pages, or Inserted Links button, as appropriate. Then select the entry from the resulting list in the list box.

• You can click the File button to display the Link To File dialog box and select a file from the Link To File dialog box.

• You can click the Web Page button to display Internet Explorer, navigate to the URL or page you want, and then activate the Word window again (by clicking on its Taskbar button) to enter the URL in the Type The File Or Web Page Name text box.

• You can click the Bookmark button to display the Select Place In Document dialog box, choose the bookmark you want, and then click the OK button.

• You can click the Place In This Document button in the Link To panel at the left-hand side of the Insert Hyperlink dialog box to display the Select A Place In This Document list box (see Figure 24.12). Choose the heading or bookmark you want from the list box.

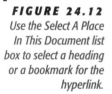

FIGURE 24.12

Use the Select A Place In This Document list box to select a heading or a bookmark for the hyperlink.

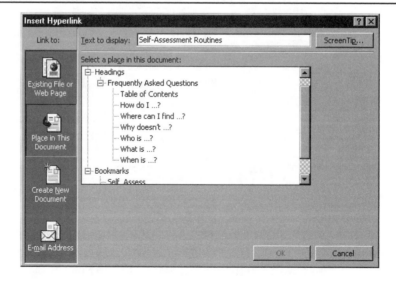

• You can click the Create New Document button in the Link To panel to display the Create New Document panel of the dialog box (see Figure 24.13). Enter the name for the new document in the Name Of New Document text box. To change the folder in which the file will be saved, click the Change button to display the Link To File list box, choose an appropriate folder, and click the OK button. In the When To Edit area, select the Edit The New Document Later option button if you don't want to work with the document now; otherwise, leave the Edit The New Document Now option button selected, and Word will open the document when you close the Insert Hyperlink dialog box.

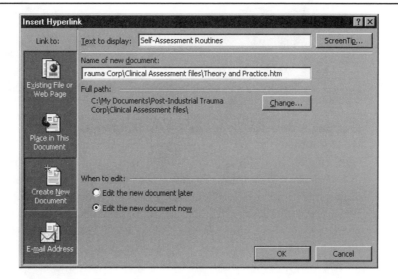

FIGURE 24.13
Use the Create New Document panel of the Insert Hyperlink dialog box to create a new document for the hyperlink.

• Finally, you can click the E-mail Address button in the Link To panel to display the E-mail Address panel (see Figure 24.14). Enter the e-mail address in the E-mail Address text box, or select the address from the Recently Used E-mail Addresses list box. Then enter a subject for the message in the Subject text box.

7. Click the OK button to insert the hyperlink in your document.

Once you've inserted a hyperlink in a document, you can click the hyperlink to jump to the document or Web page to which it is connected.

FIGURE 24.14
Use the E-mail Address panel of the Insert Hyperlink dialog box to use an e-mail address for the hyperlink.

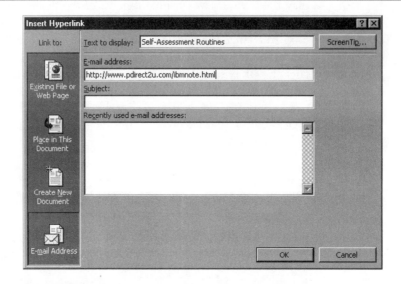

Creating Automatic Hyperlinks from Filenames

Word's AutoFormat feature can automatically create a hyperlink when you type the name of a file in a Word document. To enable this feature, choose Tools ➢ AutoCorrect to display the AutoCorrect dialog box. Click the AutoFormat As You Type tab to display the AutoFormat As You Type page, and select the Internet And Network Paths With Hyperlinks check box. Click the AutoFormat tab to display the AutoFormat page, and select the check box there too. Then click the OK button to close the AutoCorrect dialog box. Thereafter, when you type a URL or a network path and filename in a document, Word will automatically format it as a hyperlink.

NOTE To turn URLs and file paths in an existing document into hyperlinks, use the Format ➢ AutoFormat command. Make sure that the Internet And Network Paths With Hyperlinks check box on the AutoFormat page of the AutoCorrect dialog box is selected as described in the previous paragraph.

Creating a Hyperlink by Dragging

You can also create a hyperlink to an Office document by dragging the object to be linked from the application to the Word document that should receive the hyperlink. For example, you can create a hyperlink from a range of cells in Excel, a slide in Power-Point, an Access database object, or even part of another Word document.

To create a hyperlink, display Word and the other application (or two windows in Word) on screen at the same time. Then right-click and right-drag the object to where you want it to appear in the Word publication. Word will display a context menu; choose Create Hyperlink Here to create the hyperlink.

Creating a Hyperlink by Copying

To create a hyperlink by copying, select the material in its source application (or in another Word document) and copy it by right-clicking and choosing Copy, clicking the Copy button, or choosing Edit ➤ Copy. Then switch to Word (or to the Word document that will receive the hyperlink), position the insertion point where the hyperlink should go, and choose Edit ➤ Paste As Hyperlink.

Saving a Web Page as a Word Document

You can also save a Web page as a Word document. To do so, choose File ➤ Save As to display the Save As dialog box, then choose Word Document from the Save As Type drop-down list. The Save As dialog box will change from the Web variant (with the Page Title area and the Change button beneath the Save In list box) to the regular Save As dialog box. Specify a name for the document in the Save As dialog box and then click the Save button. Word will save the Web page as a regular Word document.

Viewing the HTML Source Code of a Web Page

To view the source code of a Web page, choose View ➤ HTML Source to display the HTML code for the Web page in the Microsoft Development Environment (see Figure 24.15). When you've finished, choose File ➤ Exit to close the Microsoft Development Environment and return to Word.

FIGURE 24.15
Use the Microsoft Development Environment to examine the HTML code behind a Web page.

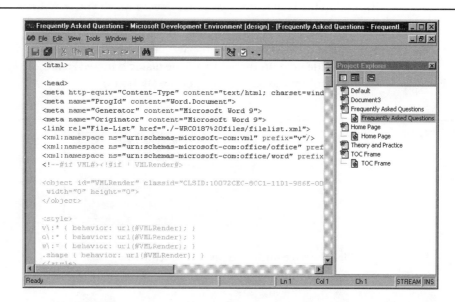

TIP I've made viewing HTML source code sound particularly unappealing—and indeed, you'll probably want to take advantage of Word's ability to create and read HTML to keep your involvement with HTML codes to a minimum. But you can use the View ➤ HTML Source feature as a way of seeing how people create particular effects in HTML. For example, if you run into a Web page that has impressive effects, you could use this feature to sneak a look at the code they're using—and perhaps even try some of the same techniques in your own files.

Saving a Word Document to a Web Site or Intranet Site

To save a Word document to a Web site or a folder on an intranet site, you use Office's Web Folders feature as follows:

1. Choose File ➤ Save As Web Page to display the Save As dialog box.

2. Navigate to the Web folder you want to use:

   • To use an existing Web folder (if you have an existing one), click the Web Folders button in the lower-left corner of the Save As dialog box to display your list of Web folders, then select an appropriate folder.

   • To add a new Web folder, click the Create New Folder button in the toolbar at the top of the Save As dialog box to display the New Folder dialog box. Enter the name of the folder in the Name text box, then click the OK button to create the folder. The Save As dialog box will display the list of folders available in that location, and Word will add the current address to the Web Folders list. To open a folder from the list shown in the Save In list box, double-click it.

3. Within the Web folder, select the folder in which you want to save the document.

4. Enter the name for the document in the File Name text box.

5. To set a different title for the page, click the Change button to the right of the Page Title item. In the Set Page Title dialog box (see Figure 24.16), enter the title you want for the page, then click the OK button.

FIGURE 24.16

In the Set Page Title dialog box, enter the title for the Web page.

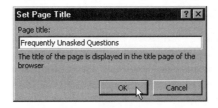

6. Click the Save button to save the document.

You'll see the Transferring File dialog box (see Figure 24.17), which shows the progress of each piece of the file as it is transferred. For example, if the Web page contains graphics, you'll see the file for each graphic being transferred in turn.

FIGURE 24.17
The Transferring File dialog box

Working with FTP Sites

In addition to working with Web pages on Web servers, Word has the capability of working with FTP servers. As you probably know from downloading material from the Internet, FTP is the abbreviation for File Transfer Protocol, the protocol (or set of communications rules) for transferring files across networks—in particular, the Internet.

In this section, you'll learn how to add FTP sites, how to open a file from an FTP site, and how to save a file to an FTP site.

Adding FTP Sites

Before you can open a file at an FTP site, you have to add that site's address to Word's list of FTP sites:

1. Choose File ➢ Open to display the Open dialog box.

2. In the Look In drop-down list, select the Add/Modify FTP Locations item to display the Add/Modify FTP Locations dialog box (shown in Figure 24.18 with information entered).

3. In the Name of FTP Site text box, enter the full address of the FTP site (e.g., ftp.sybex.com).

4. In the Log On As group box, choose how to log on to the site. If you do not have an account at the site, leave the Anonymous option button selected. If you do have an account at the site, select the User option button and enter your username in the text box.

5. Enter your password in the Password text box. For sites that you log on to as Anonymous, you'll typically use your e-mail address as your password. For sites where you're known by username, you'll need to specify your personal password.

FIGURE 24.18
Set up your FTP locations in the Add/ Modify FTP Locations dialog box.

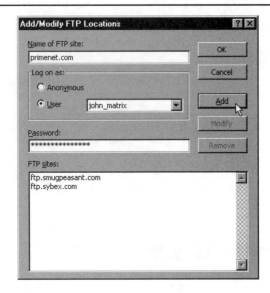

6. Click the Add button to add the site to your list of FTP sites. (Once you've created a site, you can modify it by selecting it in the FTP Sites list box, changing the information in the appropriate boxes, and clicking the Modify button; or you can remove the site from your list by clicking the Remove button.)

7. Click the OK button to close the Add/Modify FTP Locations dialog box.

Opening a File from an FTP Site

To open a file from an FTP site, use the FTP Locations feature from the Open dialog box:

1. Choose File ➢ Open to display the Open dialog box.

2. From the Look In drop-down list, choose the FTP site from the FTP Locations category. If you see no FTP sites listed, add sites as described in the previous section.

3. If you see the FTP Log On dialog box (see Figure 24.19), identify yourself as appropriate: Select your username in the Log On As group box, then enter your password in the Password text box and click the OK button. (You will not see the FTP Log On dialog box if Word is able to log you on without a password or with a password it has previously saved.)

FIGURE 24.19
*If you see the FTP Log
On dialog box, log in
and enter your
password.*

4. Navigate to the folder that contains the document you want to open (see Figure 24.20).

5. Select the document you want to open.

6. Click the Open button to open the document.

FIGURE 24.20
*Opening a folder in an
FTP location in the
Open dialog box*

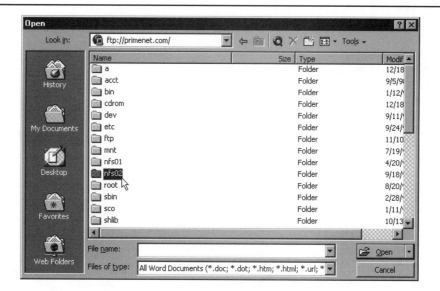

Saving a Document to an FTP Site

To save a Word document to an FTP site, choose File ➢ Save As and choose the FTP site from the FTP Locations section of the Save In drop-down list. (If you don't see any FTP sites listed there, add them as described in "Adding FTP Sites," earlier in this chapter.) Then specify the name for the document and click the Save button.

CHAPTER **25**

Publishing to the Web with Home Publishing

Publishing to a folder on your computer

Getting the latest Web-hosting information

Publishing to a folder on the Web

In this short chapter, I'll show you how to publish a Home Publishing Web project, first to a folder on your computer and then to the Web. I'll assume you've worked through Chapter 19, so that you'll be familiar with the Home Publishing interface and will have created some projects already—perhaps including a Web project that you're ready to publish to the Web. I'll also expect you to know what Web pages and Web sites are; if you don't, read through the sections titled "What Is a Web Page?" and "What Is a Web Site?" which you'll find at the beginning of Chapter 24.

Publishing a Web project to a folder on your computer is both good preparation for building a Web site and a way of creating a local Web site for your home or your company. In preparation for building a Web site, you can make sure that your projects will convert into HTML pages that are easy to view in a Web browser such as Internet Explorer, and you can iron out any flaws in the design, layout, or content before you unleash the projects on the world.

By building your Web site locally first, you can make sure that everything works effectively and troubleshoot any problems before anyone else gets to run into them. Once you've put your Web site up on an ISP-hosted server, using an ISP, everything has to be done at a couple of removes, so you typically won't have such fine or immediate control over the content of your site. For example, many Web hosts do not update your site the instant you post new pages, so visitors may receive the cached (stored) older versions of pages for a number of hours—or even days—after you post new pages.

 NOTE Home Publishing lets you publish both Web projects and non-Web projects to the Web. The main difference between the two is that the Web projects are designed for conversion to the Web, so the results tend to be more viewable than some of the non-Web projects.

Publishing to a Folder on Your Computer

Follow these steps to publish a Home Publishing Web project to a folder on your computer:

1. Open the project you want to publish.

2. Choose File ➤ Publish To Web ➤ Publish To A Folder On My Computer to display the Publish As A Folder dialog box (shown in Figure 25.1 with some choices made).

FIGURE 25.1
In the Publish As A Folder dialog box, specify the home page for the site you're creating and the folder that will contain it.

3. In the Select Or Type A Home Page For Your Web Site list box, either select default.htm or index.html from the drop-down list, or enter a custom name for the home page.

4. In the Save The Project In This Folder text box, enter the folder that you want the project to be saved in. You can either type in the folder's path and name or click the Browse button and use the resulting Select Folder dialog box (see Figure 25.2) to specify the folder. (To create a new folder, click the New Folder button in the Select Folder dialog box, enter the name for the folder in the New Folder dialog box, and click the OK button. The Select Folder dialog box will automatically select your new folder.)

NOTE Two quick things: First, the default folder for Web projects is c:\My Documents\Web\. Second, if you haven't created a Web Folder before, Home Publishing will display a message box asking if you want to create it. Click the Yes button.

FIGURE 25.2
Use the Select Folder dialog box to browse your way to a folder.

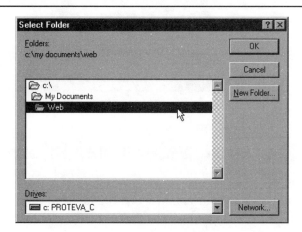

5. Click the OK button. You'll see a status report as Home Publishing publishes the project to the folder. Then Home Publishing will display the Microsoft Home Publishing 2000 message shown in Figure 25.3 to tell you that the project has been published.

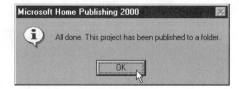

Now start Internet Explorer and navigate to the folder to which you published the project:

1. Choose File ➢ Open to display the Open dialog box.

2. Click the Browse button to display the Microsoft Internet Explorer dialog box.

3. Navigate to the folder and select the home-page file (for example, `default.htm`).

4. Click the Open button to return to the Open dialog box.

5. Click the OK button to open the page in Internet Explorer.

Test the hyperlinks to make sure they work, then return to Home Publishing, make any changes that the project requires, and publish the project to the folder again. Home Publishing will warn you that the files already exist (see Figure 25.4); click the Yes button to overwrite the existing files.

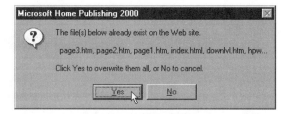

Getting the Latest Web-Hosting Information

To make it easy for you to publish projects from Home Publishing to the Web, Microsoft works with a number of ISPs and Web-hosting services and builds the details of the connection information they need into Home Publishing. It's a good idea to download the latest information on ISPs and Web-hosting services from the Web before trying to connect.

Here's how to download the information:

1. In Home Publishing, make sure you have a project open, then choose File ➤ Publish To Web ➤ Sign Up For A Web Site Provider. Home Publishing will start Internet Explorer, which will display the HomePub – Web Host Signup page (see Figure 25.5).

FIGURE 25.5
The HomePub – Web Host Signup page provides information on signing up with a Web site host.

2. Click the link to the file containing the latest Web hosting data file. (In the figure, the link is named Link To The Self-Extracting EXE Containing The Updated FTPINFO.DAT; bear in mind that the page may have changed by the time you visit it.) Internet Explorer will display the File Download dialog box.

3. Make sure the Save This Program To Disk option button is selected, then click the OK button. Internet Explorer will display the Save As dialog box.

4. Specify a location for the file and click the Save button. Internet Explorer will download the file.

5. When the download is complete, run the file by double-clicking it in Explorer. You'll see the Web Posting Update For Microsoft Greetings And Home Publishing dialog box (see Figure 25.6).

FIGURE 25.6

When you run your downloaded file, it displays the Web Posting Update For Microsoft Greetings And Home Publishing dialog box.

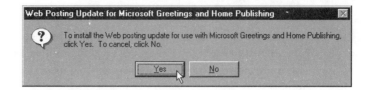

6. Click the Yes button. The program will extract the data file and display the Web Posting Update dialog box (see Figure 25.7) telling you that the installation was successful and that the new files will show up the next time you run Home Publishing.

FIGURE 25.7

When the files have been installed, you'll see this Web Posting Update dialog box.

7. Click the OK button to dismiss the dialog box, then close Internet Explorer if necessary.

You're now ready to get set up for publishing your projects to the Web.

Publishing to the Web

If you already have a working Web site and have created one or more Home Publishing projects to publish to it, you'll now be ready to start publishing to the Web.

NOTE If you don't have a Web site and need to get signed up with a Web site host, choose File ≻ Publish To Web ≻ Sign Up For A Web Site Provider. Home Publishing will activate Internet Explorer and will direct it to the HomePub – Web Host Signup Web site. From there, follow one of the links to sign up with a free Web site hosting service (such as MSN, Geocities, Tripod, or Xoom) or one of the fee-based Web site hosting services (such as America Online or EarthLink). The disadvantage to most free services is that they display ads to visitors of your Web site.

Follow these steps to publish a Home Publishing Web project to the Web:

1. Open the project you want to publish.

2. Choose File ≻ Publish To Web ≻ Publish To A Web Site to display the Publish To Web dialog box (shown in Figure 25.8 with information entered).

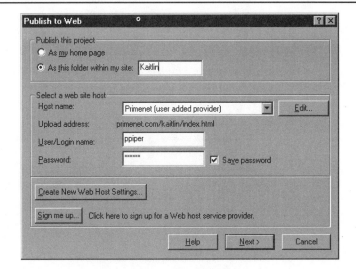

FIGURE 25.8
In the Publish To Web dialog box, specify the location and Web site host you want to use.

3. In the Publish This Project group box, select the As My Home Page option button (if you want to use this project's main page as your home page) or the As This Folder Within My Site option button (if you already have a home page and want to put the contents of this project into a separate folder).

4. If your ISP appears in the Host Name drop-down list in the Select A Web Site Host group box, select the appropriate entry from the list and go to step 6.

5. If your ISP is not listed in the Host Name drop-down list, click the Create New Web Host Settings button to display the Create New Web Host Settings dialog box (see Figure 25.9).

   • In the Friendly Name Of Your Web Site Host text box, enter an easily recognizable name for your ISP. This name is for your convenience only, so you can call it pretty much anything you want.

   • In the FTP Upload Address For Publishing To This Site text box, enter the FTP address that your ISP has given you for accessing the site. The FTP address will often start with ftp., but not always.

   • In the Web Address For Viewing Projects Posted To This Site text box, enter the address of the Web site. This address might be your own domain name (in the form http://www.yournamehere.com) or a folder under someone else's domain.

- From the Name Of Home Page File On This Site drop-down list, choose `default.htm` or `index.html`, or enter a custom name of your own.

- In the Advanced Settings group box, choose advanced settings *only if you need them* (for most Web hosts, you won't). Select the Use Passive FTP Semantics check box if you are uploading from behind a router-based firewall. (Your network administrator or ISP should be able to help you with this.) Select the This Web Site Host Requires Anonymous Login check box if your ISP requires users to log in via anonymous login.

- Click the OK button to close the Create New Web Host Settings dialog box and return to the Publish To Web dialog box, where Home Publishing will have entered the Web host you created in the Host Name text box.

FIGURE 25.9

If your ISP isn't listed in the Host Name drop-down list in the Publish To Web dialog box, use the Create New Web Host Settings dialog box to create a new Web host.

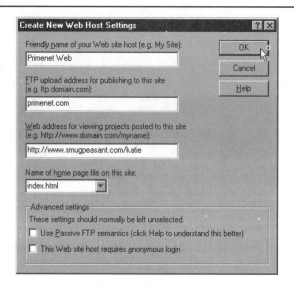

6. Enter your login name in the User/Login Name text box and your password in the Password text box. Select the Save Password check box if you want Home Publishing to store your password for future use. (Doing so is convenient but poses a security risk if other people can access your computer.)

7. Click the Next button to move on. Home Publishing will display the Microsoft Home Publishing 2000 dialog box shown in Figure 25.10 as it converts your project to HTML.

8. Next, you'll see the Publish To Web Progress dialog box (see Figure 25.11) as Home Publishing publishes your project to the Web. Depending on the complexity of the project and the speed (or otherwise) of your Internet connection, this may take several minutes.

FIGURE 25.10
You'll see the Microsoft Home Publishing 2000 dialog box as Home Publishing converts your project to HTML.

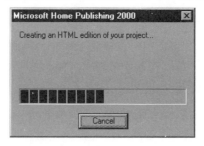

FIGURE 25.11
You'll see this Publish To Web Progress dialog box as Home Publishing publishes your project to the Web.

9. When Home Publishing has finished publishing the project, it will update the Publish To Web Progress dialog box (see Figure 25.12), providing a Visit Site Now button that you can click to fire up Internet Explorer and visit the site immediately. Do so if you wish; otherwise, click the Close button to close the Publish To Web Progress dialog box.

FIGURE 25.12
When Home Publishing has finished publishing your project to the Web, it offers you the chance to visit it immediately.

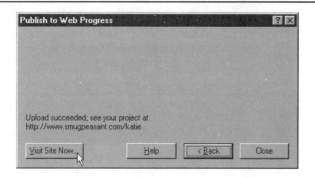

INDEX

Note to the Reader: Page numbers in **bold** indicate the principal discussion of a topic or the definition of a term. Page numbers in *italic* indicate illustrations.

X

Y

Z

Works Suite 2000 Applications

Use Encarta Encyclopedia to find the information you need (Chapter 16).

Locate places, measure distances, and plan trips with Expedia Streets & Trips (Chapter 17).

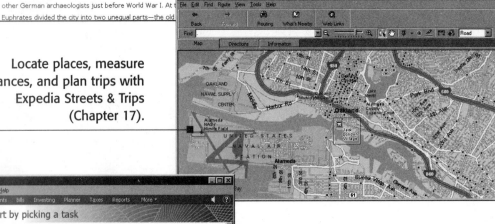

Tame your personal finances, plan your budgets, and pay your bills online with Money (Chapter 18).